LOOKING SOUTH

1825

037 Cunningham JOHn T.

NEWARK

P188

DATE DUE

REVISED & EXPANDED EDITION
NEWARK

What Price a City?
"Fifty double hands of powder,
one hundred bars of lead . . . four barrels
of beer . . . three trooper's coats . . ."
three centuries of toil . . .
And Five Nights of Fire.

REVISED & EXPANDED EDITION

NEW

THE NEW JERSEY HISTORICAL SOCIETY, NEWARK

by JOHN T. CUNNINGHAM

ARK

Designed by HOMER HILL

Books by John T. Cunningham

RAILROADING IN NEW JERSEY
THIS IS NEW JERSEY
MADE IN NEW JERSEY
GARDEN STATE
THE NEW JERSEY SHORE
THE NEW JERSEY SAMPLER
NEW JERSEY: AMERICA'S MAIN ROAD
NEWARK
CHATHAM: AT THE CROSSING OF THE FISHAWACK
CLARA MAASS: A NURSE, A HOSPITAL, A SPIRIT
UNIVERSITY IN THE FOREST (Drew University)
A CENTURY OF PROGRESS (Passaic County)
ON THE GO IN NEW JERSEY (Elementary text)
ON THE GO IN PENNSYLVANIA (Elementary text)
ON THE GO IN NEW YORK (Elementary text)
YOU, NEW JERSEY AND THE WORLD (Elementary text)
NEW JERSEY: A MIRROR ON AMERICA
THEY CALLED HIM WIZARD
NEW JERSEY'S RICH HARVEST

Library of Congress Catalog Card Number LC 88-042990
© Copyright, 1988, by John T. Cunningham
All Rights Reserved
Manufactured in the United States of America
ISBN 0-911020-18-7

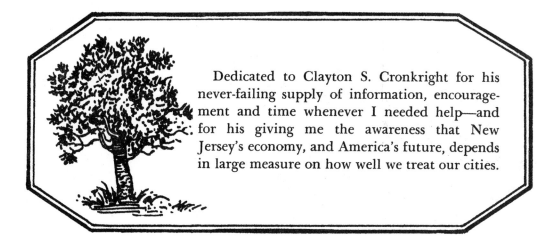

Dedicated to Clayton S. Cronkright for his never-failing supply of information, encouragement and time whenever I needed help—and for his giving me the awareness that New Jersey's economy, and America's future, depends in large measure on how well we treat our cities.

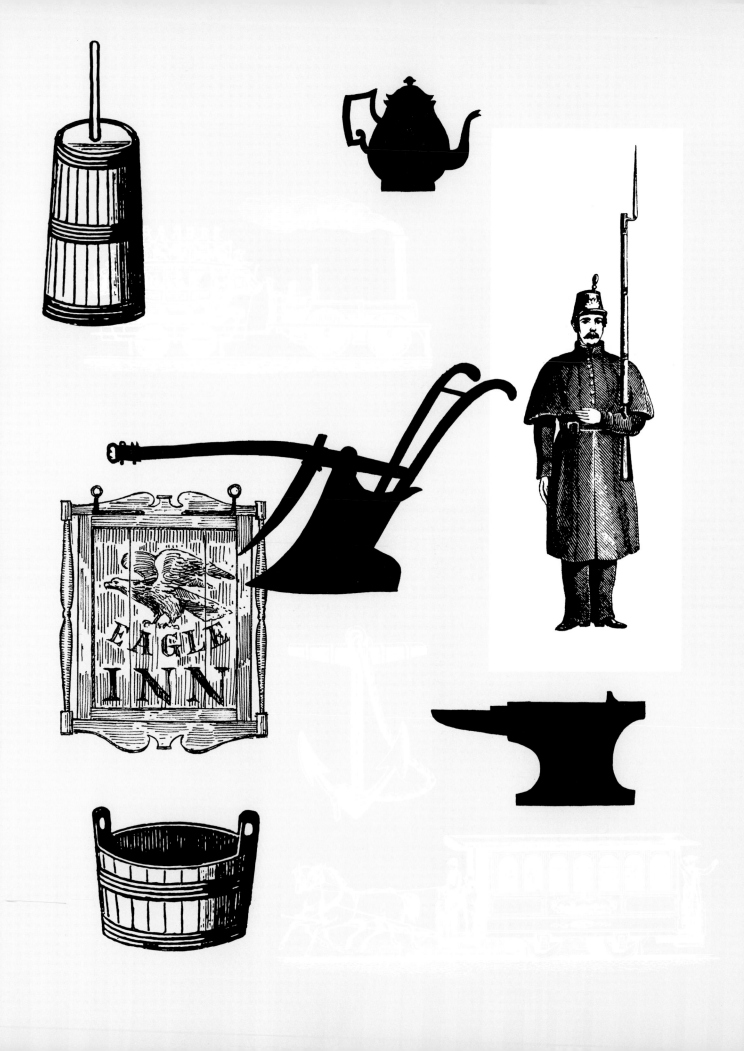

TABLE OF CONTENTS

INTRODUCTION

In 1966, when I completed the first edition of this history, Newark teetered on the brink of shattering strife. The signs were everywhere: in the ugly, blighted slums; in the segregated, uncaring police department; in callous indifference that faced minority residents wherever they turned. The inevitable explosion came. In July 1967 Newark sank into the nether world.

Now, as this revised edition heads for the presses, every sign indicates Newark's revival already has exceeded the bounds of the most optimistic of press agents. Realists know the city has a long way yet to go, but recovery seems certain if leaders can hold together the ever-fragile coalition that seeks answers to awesome problems in public housing, public health and public education.

Nevertheless, most nomadic journalists who venture into Newark on quick-in, quick-out forays prefer to ignore evidences of upward change, seeking even in 1988 to see only the sad mementoes of five days and nights of rioting in July 1967.

Admittedly there is some justification for the interest. That tumultuous uprising was equalled in the city's long history only by the balmy spring interlude in May 1666 when New England Puritans sailed into Newark Bay to found "our Town upon Passaick River in the Province of New Jersey." Old Newark was reborn in the 1967 riots, for better or for worse.

Using force to express outrage has been a recurring theme in the history of both Newark and the United States. Newark had bitter riots in the year 1700 and again in 1745, when residents took to the streets to protest what they regarded as an oppressive power structure. Revolutionists of 1776 were considered by the English to be bloody traitors. Privileged young men assaulted federal agents in Newark when the government proposed conscription in 1863.

These do not justify riots, in colonial times or in the present. Rather, they put in perspective the unceasing American quest for liberty and justice. Riots themselves are less important from the standpoint of history than how a city or a nation rebounds from them.

Another constant theme in Newark's history has been rebirth. Today's leaders talk of "renaissance," or more prosaically, a "new Newark." It is one of a long series of resurgences, each based on the failure of a previously extolled era.

The town was founded as a "new Newark," named after Newark-on-Trent in England. Robert Treat and his followers came to the banks of the Passaic from Connecticut, where they felt worldliness had trampled on their Puritan beliefs. Newark was to be a new and shining theocracy, where church and government would be one. Instead it became the last theocracy in America; town fathers compromised to admit non-believers when it became evident that "purity of religion" could not provide all the skills needed for success. Thus, almost immediately, the old gave way to the new.

Time after time a "new Newark" rose to replace an outmoded concept. Completion of two bridges in the 1790s changed Newark from an off-the-beaten-track village into a bustling center of commerce. Industrialists, inventors and railroad builders changed the city dramatically between 1810 and the Civil War. The rise of huge factories between 1870 and 1900 gave a reborn city economic diversity.

Then, in the 1920s, downtown began building upward in imitation of New York's skyline. A new airport and seaport brought links to world markets and international ideas. The

1930s and 1940s propelled Newark into prominence as a retail and cultural center. It was the latter proud "new Newark" (augmented by downtown buildings and self-congratulating boosters of the 1950s) that died in the riots of 1967.

Each revival has been a combination of imaginative entrepreneurs and newcomers encouraged to bring their needed skills or muscles to town. Thus people came—non-Puritans, immigrants from distant shores, black families from southern farms, Hispanics from Caribbean islands, Portuguese from the Iberian Peninsula. Such has been the genesis of each "new Newark." The genius has been in melding disparate people into a congenial, workable synthesis.

Newark has evolved constantly as the beneficiary of those who have come to grasp its opportunities, but there must be no glossing over the bitter fact that each group of newcomers has faced extreme prejudices. The original opposition to non-Puritans reached seething fire in hatred of early 19th-century Catholics. Nearly every immigrant from southern or eastern Europe in the late 19th century faced scathing scorn. Blacks and Hispanics, in turn, now seek a fair place in Newark's economic upsurge.

No one book can be the complete answer for Newarkers and visitors who want to know the city's entire history. No one regrets more than I the need to compress more than 320 years of history into fewer than four hundred pages. For those who note omissions, especially in modern times, I plead an obvious limitation of space. For those whose research, remembrances and interpretations of the past twenty years differ from mine, such is the difficulty of recording what is freshly remembered. My goal has been to present a balanced, fair portrait of an exciting and evolving city.

I acknowledge much assistance. The New Jersey Historical Society received limited financial aid to prepare the manuscript for printing. This came from Public Service Electric & Gas Company, Mutual Benefit Life Insurance Company, New Jersey Bell Telephone Company and First Fidelity Bancorporation.

I thank many people. Don C. Skemer, the first head of the publications department at The New Jersey Historical Society, launched the new edition, and his successor, Robert B. Burnett, saw it through to the end. Mr. Burnett, has been especially helpful in providing editorial assistance and publishing knowledge.

Most of my research was conducted at The New Jersey Historical Society and Newark Public Library. Both institutions, along with the Newark Museum, provided the bulk of the illustrations for the original book. Charles Cummings, Robert Blackwell and James Osbourn were especially helpful in gathering information and illustrations for this edition.

I received vital professional assistance from Mr. Cummings, who read all of the new material for accuracy and adequacy; Arlene Sarappo, who coordinated the work and performed a multitude of editorial requirements, and Karen Gilbert, who created the new, considerably-improved index.

Since the first twenty-six chapters originated in the first edition, I must always be mindful of people who helped in 1966: the late Miriam Studley, one of the major influences in any New Jersey project during her tenure as New Jersey librarian in the Newark Public Library; Tom Mackin, who edited the drafts of the original volume; Howard Wiseman, then head of collections at the New Jersey Historical Society; and W. Irving Tuttle, who copied nearly all of the illustrations for the first twenty-six chapters.

My quest for illustrations for the modern chapters was eased by generous, informed aid given me by New Jersey Newsphotos personnel, particularly Jean Rae Turner, Richard Koles and Don Davidson.

My final acknowledgments are to two artist friends, the late Homer Hill, who designed the original edition and whose style and flair have been continued in this edition by Marjorie Keating of Vanguard Arts.

JOHN T. CUNNINGHAM

Florham Park, New Jersey
December 1988

*Indians on shore await Newark's first settlers in May, 1666.
(From Atkinson's 1878* History of Newark*).*

The boats of Milford cruised southwestward from Connecticut in the spring of 1666, sailed through Long Island Sound and down the East River. They passed the English village of New York—whose low, jagged skyline continued to resemble a Dutch burgh—and sailed westward through the Kill von Kull that opened onto the calm waters of a great bay. Near lay the promised land.

The crude little boats, fashioned by men of agriculture, lay low in the water, for most of the thirty families aboard averaged five or six children, plus animals, household goods, weapons and a few fruit trees. If any of the immigrants wrote of the trip, their letters or journals have not been found, and history is mute as to the number of boats, the number of passengers, even the exact day of arrival. Tradition says it was May 18, 1666.

One can only imagine the poignancy and excitement of the huddled families as they neared this foreign shore. Their leader, Robert Treat, guided the fleet across the bay, northward past the swaying marsh grasses on shore and on to where the bay narrowed into a river the natives called Passaic. Near water's edge, the marsh was blue with iris; in the hills beyond, white dogwood brightened the woodland. As the course turned westward, the river bank edged sharply upward from the river, rising well above the deck line.

The ships sailed in silence on the broad river, scarcely moving as the banks lessened the wind. Nearly four miles off the bay Treat waved the boats toward shore at a spot where the bluff leveled off. No sound came from the land.

But the arrival did not go unnoticed. From the marshes near the clam beds, from the trees and the rushes, furtive Indians sullenly watched the landing. These were the Lenni Lenape on their annual spring visit from the Delaware to fish for succulent seafood. Treat knew that Indians frequented the grounds and believed that all their claims on the land had been satisfied by Governor Carteret.

The boats nudged up to a landing spot while the Indians watched in silence. First ashore, according to an abiding story, was seventeen-year-old Miss Elizabeth Swaine, aided by her attentive sweetheart and future husband, Josiah Ward. Two young lovers, then, were the first settlers to put foot on soil that would give rise to a great city.

Miss Swaine and Ward were followed ashore by the children. Released at last from the confines of the crowded craft, the youngsters scrambled from the decks and splashed into the shallow water. There were some of Treat's eight, some of Lawrence Ward's seven, the three

Dramatic moment of landing, on these pages and the next, was painted in 1906 by C. Y. Turner. Featuring Josiah Ward aiding Elizabeth Swaine ashore, the forty-foot mural is in the Essex County Court House.

young orphan brothers of Mrs. Mary Dod Blacthly, Elizabeth Swaine's seven younger brothers and sisters, Francis Linsley's two daughters and five sons.

For once, the youngsters slogging gaily through the riverbank mud were not subject to parental disapproval. The elders had something more serious on their minds: the Indians moving slowly but purposefully to the shore.

Abruptly it became clear that the natives were not a welcoming party. They used easily understood gestures to point out that neither these newcomers nor anyone else had made arrangements for this occupation of their fishing ground without payment—and they were not swayed by Treat's adamant pleas that it was an oversight. Even in rudimentary sign language the meaning of the Lenape was unmistakable: no money, no land.

Confused and angered, the New Englanders reboarded their boats and withdrew slowly down wind in the direction of Elizabethtown, many of them crossly insisting that they might better return home than bear this indignity. They dropped anchor off Elizabethtown, where Governor Carteret hastily supplied Treat an interpreter and guide to lead him and some others up the Hackensack River to the tribal headquarters of the Hackensacks.

There they met and signed a temporary agreement with Perro, an Indian acting with approval from Oraton, the aged, venerable chief of the Hackensacks. Perro agreed to come later to the new town to discuss formal terms, convinced by Treat that the newcomers wished only to live in peace. Perro and Treat acted through interpreters to hammer out terms for the would-be settlers from Milford.

Now the way was clear to grasp a dream that had been developing for thirty years and more: a peaceful sanctuary dedicated to the greater glory of God. This, in time, would be Newark.

Chapter 1

IN SEARCH OF ZION

Who were these people who sought a new life in the wilderness? Where did they come from and why were they here?

Newark did not grow from seed on the banks of the Passaic. It was transplanted, under many names, but one name was dominant: Puritan. From England to Massachusetts, to Long Island, to Connecticut and finally to New Jersey wandered these stern and unbending people in search of a Promised Land.

Rigid in their belief that all action must be related to the Bible and morally certain that they were a special object of God's care, the Puritan planters moved inexorably onward in their quest for a Kingdom of God. Newark was simply one more testing ground, and it became their last.

Most of these wanderers had been born in England or were descended from parents who had suffered by the persecution of Puritans under King Charles I. Undying were memories of their uncompromising split from both the Roman Catholic Church and the Church of England. They wanted no part of hierarchy, of dogma, of ceremony: they believed their authority stemmed not from an established church but directly from God.

Some had fled from England during the great wave of Puritan migration in the late 1630s. They tried Massachusetts briefly, knowing that their friends aboard the *Mayflower* had prospered there, then moved on to Connecticut and Long Island aware that they required isolation to keep alive their religious dream. Contact with others tended to corrupt, and so did open spaces. They needed a compact, tightly knit community, aloof from the world, if their religion was to stay unsullied.

None typified the determined searcher for religious peace more than the Rev. Abraham Pierson. A graduate of England's University of

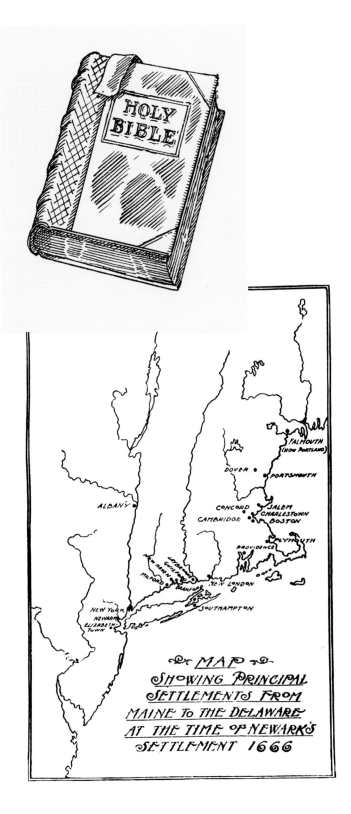

MAP SHOWING PRINCIPAL SETTLEMENTS FROM MAINE TO THE DELAWARE AT THE TIME OF NEWARK'S SETTLEMENT 1666

Robert Treat's signature, seal and his home in Milford, Connecticut.

Cambridge, Mr. Pierson emigrated to Boston in 1639, joined the congregation and found to his dismay that Puritanical beliefs already were being modified in the wilderness.

Within a year after his arrival in America he went to Lynn, Massachusetts, gathering a small band who organized their congregation by making a covenant with one another and with God. But Lynn was not to be their Zion. Following their religious will-o'-the-wisp, Mr. Pierson and his congregation wandered in the wilderness, stopping briefly in Southold, Long Island, before moving again, in 1640, to Southampton.

Southampton seemed a perfect, isolated, independent place where church and town government were one. But there was to be no peace. When Southampton was placed under the control of the Connecticut colony, Mr. Pierson led his flock out of Long Island and across the Sound to Branford, then under the jurisdiction of New Haven, a Puritan colony in its own right and not yet part of Connecticut. Immigrants from Wethersfield joined the congregation, and Branford became a center of pure thought and action, as measured by the Puritan yardstick.

Underscoring the migratory life of Mr. Pierson and his wife were the birthplaces of their eight children: one born in Lynn, three in Southampton and four in Branford.

Mr. Pierson was a man of strength and wisdom. His people followed him willingly, for he was, in effect, their church. They found him as well a bulwark in dealings with the Indians. He studied the Indian language, the better "to treat with the ignorant children of the forest concerning the things of their peace." The pastor prepared a catechism in the native language, using a translator to finish the work.

Nearby, the people of New Haven, Milford and Guilford maintained equal faith. Their towns were small, self-contained and self-sufficient, completely dedicated to the proposition that only Puritans were right. They felt that no church could save man from damnation; that must be God's decision, but if a religion could help, they had it. And they were determined that only "Godly men" must govern.

Leaders emerged. Jasper Crane, an original settler of New Haven and eventually a member of Mr. Pierson's Branford congregation, was active, energetic and restless. In his lengthening life he had helped found several New England settlements, and only what he called "the injustice and violence of the Dutch" kept him from leading a colony to Delaware Bay.

Nearby in Milford the leader was Robert Treat, one of four sons of the Richard Treat who had left England for the New World in 1638. The Treats followed the same nomadic pattern of Crane and Mr. Pierson before taking root in Wethersfield, Connecticut. The elder Treat stayed in Wethersfield, but son Robert went to Branford in 1639 at the age of sixteen, possibly to study for the ministry under the town pastor.

Although not listed among Milford's original settlers, or even as a member of the founding congregation, Treat quickly became a force through his intelligence and physical vigor. Tradition says that he helped survey and lay out the town streets, a talent that would soon be apparent in Newark.

Details of Treat's early life are sketchy, as are the early years of most Puritans. However, he did fall in love with Jane Tapp, daughter of Edmund Tapp, one of the "seven pillars" (leaders) of the Milford church. On one courting visit, Treat is said to have taken Jane upon his knee and nervously jiggled her up and down.

"Robert," said Jane, "Be still that; I had rather be *Treated* than trotted!"

That play on words, reminiscent of the traditional thinly veiled proposal of Priscilla to John Alden, apparently stirred Treat. He and Jane were married, the family genealogy says, on Christmas Eve, 1649, at a spinning bee in Edmund Tapp's spacious kitchen. The marriage was highly successful. The Treats had nine children, eight of them achieving long life. When the Treat genealogy was compiled in 1893, Robert and Jane Treat were the forebears of 3957 descendants through nine generations!

Worry constantly beset the New Englanders lest the sympathetic reign of Oliver Cromwell, Lord Protector of England, come abruptly to an end. Their worst fears were realized on May 29, 1660, when King Charles II ascended the throne. Fearful questions swept through New England. How would Charles regard the generous self-government that the Puritan colonies had enjoyed? What retribution would he demand for the beheading of his father, Charles I, in 1649?

Two of the judges who had condemned Charles I to death fled on a ship to New England in 1660. The arrival in Boston of these regicides, William Goffe and Edward Whalley, caused mixed emotions, but in New Haven a sympathetic minister took his text from the Bible: "Hide the outcasts, betray not him that wandereth." The pair went inland from hiding place to hiding place and finally found permanent lodging with Micah Tompkins in Milford on August 19, 1661.

The judges lived in utter seclusion for two years, "without so much as going into the orchard." A few townsmen, including Robert Treat, knew of their presence in Tompkins' cellar but when royal agents came seeking the pair, no Milfordite admitted anything. Tompkins must have had some difficulty within his own family, but it is related that none of his

seven children—including four curious daughters—knew that "angels were in the basement." Sometimes the innocent girls sang a popular ballad ridiculing the regicides, greatly amusing the fugitives.

Their success in hiding Goffe and Whalley only heightened the concern among Milford's Puritans. Suppose Charles decided to strike in fury at those Puritan colonies which openly hated the monarchy? Connecticut Governor John Winthrop hastened to England in 1661 to plead for terms and to seek a new charter.

As a counter-measure, Milford sent Robert Treat and three associates to New Amsterdam in November, 1661, to negotiate for land in the Dutch colony. New Amsterdam the previous spring had issued an invitation to "all Christian people of tender conscience in England or elsewhere oppressed, to erect colonies anywhere within the jurisdiction of Petrus Stuyvesant, anywhere in the West Indies, between New England and Virginia in America."

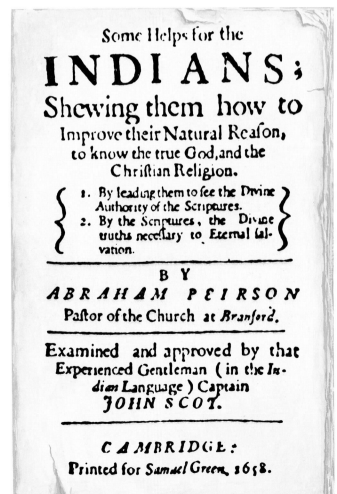

Some Helps for the

INDIANS:
Shewing them how to Improve their Natural Reason, to know the true God, and the Christian Religion.

{
1. By leading them to see the Divine Authority of the Scriptures.
2. By the Scriptures, the Divine truths necessary to Eternal Salvation.
}

BY
ABRAHAM PEIRSON
Pastor of the Church at *Branford*.

Examined and approved by that Experienced Gentleman (in the Indian Language) Captain *JOHN SCOT*.

CAMBRIDGE:
Printed for *Samuel Green*, 1658.

Title Page from Abraham Pierson's Indian catechism.

Stuyvesant demurred when the Milford applicants boldly insisted that they must have the sole right—religious and civil—to regulate their lives, without appeals to or interference from any authority, including Stuyvesant. The governor replied that he would grant full religious liberty but wanted New Amsterdam to maintain civil control, including the right of any inhabitant to appeal.

The Puritans wanted none of that. Their theology rejected government other than on a local level, administered by the church—which was logical, they felt, since only members of the church would be able to vote or hold office.

Milfordites refused to compromise, even when Winthrop brought back a charter uniting Connecticut and the New Haven communities (Milford, Branford and Guilford among them) into one colony. Winthrop's document gave Connecticut dominion over a region "eastward to the Plymouth line, northward to the limits of Massachusetts colony and westward to the Bay of Delaware, if it may be." Technically, therefore, New Amsterdam and what is now New Jersey came under Connecticut domination.

Uniting with Connecticut was bad enough. Far worse, from the standpoint of New Haven and its coastal satellites, was the charter's so-called "Half Way Covenant." This provided that all baptised persons, "not convicted of scandalous actions, are so far church members that, upon acknowledging their baptismal covenant and promising an outward conformity to it, though without any pretence to inward or spiritual religion, might present their children for baptism."

Staunch Milfordites and Branfordites seethed at the thought of "Half Way" Christians, ignoring the necessity for broadened suffrage if town and church were to be one, as in Congregational settlements. Treat joined fellow townsmen in stepping up negotiations with Stuyvesant. Not once, however, did the obdurate Puritans give an inch to stubborn Dutch insistence upon civil jurisdiction.

There matters stood in August, 1664, when invading English ships under Colonel Robert Nicolls forced Stuyvesant to haul down the Dutch flag over New Amsterdam. King Charles II reigned supreme along most of the Atlantic coast in America; Puritans felt stern controls must follow. Then came news that Charles had ceded a tract of land to Lord Berkeley and Sir George Carteret, with power to govern this region called New Jersey. Hope swelled along the Connecticut coast after Colonel Nicolls, the first English governor of New York, issued an open invitation to anyone who would settle lands west of the Hudson River.

Milford reluctantly signed the despised Connecticut charter on May 1, 1665, but Branford insisted it would have "neither part nor lot" of the document. Dissenters in Milford and non-signers in Branford knew that the time had come to move on or knuckle under, to continue as Puritans or to accept some watered-down mixture of religion and civil rule.

The way clearly led to New Jersey. Governor Nicoll's invitation already had induced a group of Long Islanders and New Englanders to found Elizabethtown in late 1664 and early 1665. Some of these Elizabethtowners were related to inhabitants of Milford and Branford and most were known by name or reputation. They began their settlement happily, only to be shocked in August, 1665, when Philip Carteret, a distant relative of George Carteret, arrived to be their governor.

New Amsterdam's Peter Stuyvesant.

16

Portion of Nicholas Visscher's 1656 map shows the Puritan world from Cape Cod to New Jersey.

If the coming of young Carteret to Elizabethtown dismayed those settlers, it provided an added gleam of hope to the Puritans fretting in Branford and Milford. Carteret brought with him the *Concessions and Agreements* of Berkeley and Carteret, proprietors of New Jersey, promising "liberty of action in all religious concernment, provided it was not used to licentiousness or civil injury to others." Puritans in the coastal towns near New Haven chose to ignore the civil injury phrase and placed their hopes in the liberty of action.

Treat and several associates sailed for Elizabethtown in the fall of 1665 to confer with Carteret. They found him cordial and cooperative. Treat first explored the Delaware River, thinking seriously about a location near what is now Burlington, before returning to seek a location closer to Connecticut.

Carteret suggested the open lands to the north, where the broad Passaic River met the still unnamed bay. There sweet green marsh grasses grew to the edge of the open waters, and to the west rose the wooded Watchung Mountains. No record exists to prove that Treat at that time

visited the future site of Newark, but it would not have been in character for him to return home without investigating. He would have liked it: well inland from the bay the land levelled off from a high river bank to the base of the mountains. Streams coursed from the mountains and in the heart of the level plain two ponds caught the gleam of the sun. Best of all here was isolation; here was land off the beaten track, a perfect place for people who sought to be alone.

It was not far different in physical appearance from the Milford location Treat had seen in its original state, a factor decidedly on the plus side. Treat had seen Milford grow into a bustling village, with a church, a Latin school, a mill and a busy shipyard. Milford-made vessels had been carrying on a sea trade with Boston since before 1640, and by 1660 ships carrying up to 150 tons of cargo used the harbor.

Treat was in the prime of life, young enough at age forty-one to continue the Puritan quest. Across New Haven Bay, the Rev. Abraham Pierson, nearing the end of his fifty-ninth year,

17

Wives gathered together precious things—a wooden bowl, an iron kettle, a spinning wheel, utensils for fireplace cooking, the family clock—for these were the things which would make the difference between comfortable living and mere existence in New Jersey.

was just as eager to start anew—for the fifth time in twenty-five years.

So it was done. The Puritans who chafed under Connecticut rule in several towns no doubt exchanged views on a new settlement— although again there is no record—and before the spring of 1666 the decision was reached to plant a new colony somewhere off the broad bay north of Elizabethtown. Treat would lead the advance guard. Others would follow when the site had been prepared.

Wives gathered together precious family belongings—some pewter, wooden dishes, a kettle, a pan or two, a clock, the family Bible, a few cherished pieces of furniture. They chose with care; their small ships must first of all carry the cattle and other animals, plus the tools, the wheel barrows and the bellows that would be far more needed than personal things. Men cleaned their guns and polished their swords; they were invading strange territory, inhabited, perhaps, by unfriendly Indians in spite of Governor Carteret's assurances that there would be no trouble.

Treat's role in the colonizing company is not clear. He was the civil leader, beyond question, but the fact that he retained his extensive real estate holdings in Connecticut indicates that he might have accompanied his neighbors largely to give them the benefit of his counsel and leadership. He also could give advice in military affairs, for he had experience in frontier tactics. He believed completely in the venture and undoubtedly took his eight children along, since they ranged in age only from three to fifteen, and could not be left behind.

Branford's spiritual leader, Mr. Pierson, was not on the first boats. He stayed behind to prepare his congregation—nearly all of Branford's population—to join him in seeking a new and better land, a Zion in the Wilderness. When he came later, he brought all church records with him, thus merely changing location of his congregation rather than establishing a new church.

The time had come to leave. Winter's icy grip had relaxed, freeing the bay in early May of 1666 as Treat led about thirty families aboard two or more boats. They said their good-byes and set sail with mingled hopes and heavy hearts.

This was not a crew of treasure-hunting adventurers. These were sound, established people, many of them well off by colonial standards. Nearly all had a reasonably good education, considering the times. Several of them were skilled—carpenters, potters, sawyers, millers—all needed in a new land. Most of them had large families, a definite asset in an agricultural economy. All were stirred by a devout faith.

They had no interest in religious toleration, in the modern sense. They never had a moment's doubt about their obligations or their rights in founding a town upon the shores of the Passaic River in 1666: They sought religious freedom—for themselves, on their own terms.

That was not unusual. Except in Rhode Island and Delaware, the concept of genuine religious freedom was non-existent in colonial times.

Indeed, had anyone asked the opinion of those aboard the Milford and Branford boats, they would have agreed completely with the early Massachusetts preacher who declared, "Tis Satan's policy to plead for an indefinite and boundless toleration." They would have understood and said "Amen" to another Puritan who denounced freedom of worship as "the first born of all abominations."

Southwestward they sailed, sure of what they were about, certain that God smiled on them all the way.

But the negative reception by the Indians in the thickets by the Passaic gave the settlers the first jolting clue that the world still intruded on their dream, even in this new-found paradise.

THE ORIGINAL PEOPLE

Newark's first inhabitants were the Lenape Indians. Their permanent homes were in simple villages in the hills and mountains near the Delaware River, but each spring they traveled across what is now New Jersey to frequent the tidal lands at the shore (including Newark Bay).

They especially cherished the banks of the Passaic River and the waters of the bay, for here the forests and marshlands abounded in anim-als and the shallow waters yielded fish, clams and oysters in abundance. They dried their game and fish for the winter and chose shells suitable for making wampum.

Early accounts describe these Indians as tall, well-built and handsome people toughened by wilderness living. They believed in a strong family relationship, educated their young to meet life in the forests and showed unfailing courtesy and kindness to strangers. Other Eastern Indians called the Lenape "The Old Women" because of their love of peace, but that characteristic made the Puritan-Indian relationship at Newark especially pleasant.

Gradually the Lenape Indians disappeared. They died from the diseases of the newcomers—particularly smallpox—and were pushed out of their fishing and hunting grounds. The last of them accepted a reservation at Indian Mills in Burlington County in 1758. The few who remained in 1802 gladly accepted an invitation to join others of their tribe then living at Lake Oneida, New York. Then New Jersey's Indian saga closed.

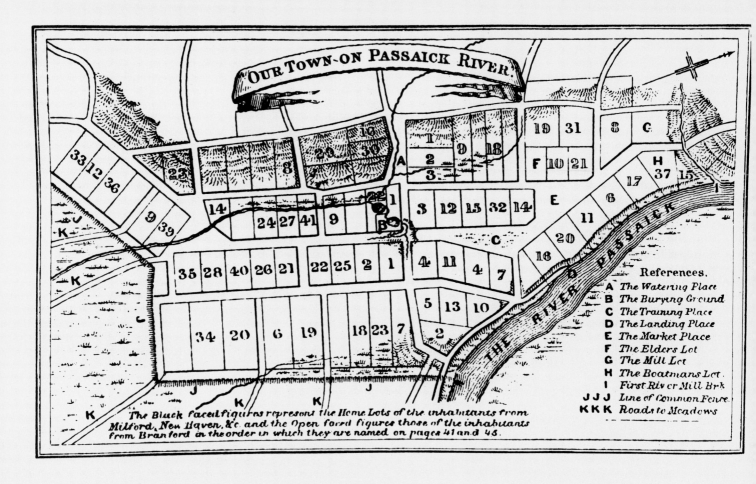

Newark in 1668, after present-day Four Corners had been laid out near two ponds at map's center. Contours show high bank on the river and mountains to the west. The numbers of lot owners are based on data in Shaw's History of Essex and Hudson Counties, *Pages 379 to 381.*

Chapter 2

TOWN ON THE PASSAIC

CONFUSION AND DISMAY, tinged with anger directed mainly at Governor Carteret for his failure to clear title with the Indians, filled the Milford boats. Some argued that such a reception could bode only evil for the future, but cooler heads persuaded the voyagers to bide their time and await the outcome of Treat's conferences with the Lenni Lenape.

The ties with Connecticut had been cut—and not without prolonged thought and prayer. Why let this irritation, this minor delay, turn them aside from their lofty purpose?

As they waited for definite word from the Indians, the colonists on the boats drew up a compact that would insure settlement by families from Branford, Guilford, Milford and New Haven. All of those present signed the covenant on May 21, requiring that Branford and Guilford emigrants must sign the document before November 1 to make it valid.

Captain Samuel Swaine carried the compact back to Connecticut, fully able to embellish it with tales of the beauties of the land in New Jersey. Here was an earthly Eden, a land of beauty and abundance.

Nearby, the Passaic River flowed wide and pure, edged by green marshlands in a manner to remind them of Connecticut. Out of the

Watchung Mountains in the west coursed several streams, one of the best of them following the base of the mountain, southward across the marshes to the lower edge of the bay near Elizabethtown. Another, much swifter in flow, bubbled eastward on the northern edge of the settlement.

Thick hardwood forests covered the Watchungs and a dense growth of cedars towered above the marshland to the east across the Passaic, but fortunately only a relatively few trees stood on the plateau where they would stake out their crossroad. Those trees on level ground were excellent sources for the tanbark needed in treating hides. Deer, elk and small game appeared in abundance on the edge of the woods, but along with those welcome supplements to the menu were natural enemies, including wolves, foxes and bears. So many wolves lurked nearby that hunters for the next two decades earned large bounties for killing them.

The first families spent the summer building crude shelters, in many cases little more than caves. Convinced that they had found their long-sought Zion, they began bringing down from Connecticut more household goods and such domestic animals as cows and sheep.

There is little question that the boats sailed often between Milford and the Passaic that summer.

Before they left to join those already in New Jersey, the heads of twenty-five Branford families carefully examined the document Swaine had brought and signed this article of faith on October 30, 1666:

"1st—That none shall be admitted freemen or free burgesses within our Town upon Passaick River, in the Province of New Jersey, but such planters as are members of some or other of the Congregational Churches, nor shall any but such be chosen to Magistracy or to carry on any part of said civil Judicature, or as deputies or assistants, to have power to vote in establishing laws, and making or repealing them, or to any Chief Military Trust or Office. Nor shall any but such Church Members have any vote in such election. Tho all others admitted to be planters have right to their proper inheri-

Puritan statue in Fairmount Cemetery memorializes Newark's founders.

No drawings or descriptions exist of the first Newark homes, but this Howard Pyle drawing of early Pennsylvania cave dwellings probably would fit this area as well.

tance, and do and shall enjoy all other civil liberties, privileges, according to all Laws, orders, grants which are or hereafter shall be made for this Town.

"2nd—We shall with care and dilligence provide for the maintenance of the purity of religion professed in the Congregational Churches, whereunto subscribed the Inhabitants of Branford."

All who signed the document, then or later, affirmed the right—indeed, the *duty*—of the church to control both spiritual and civil activities. Non-believers might come and enjoy some privileges but would have little or no say over their legal lives. They would be uncomfortable, out of place.

Jasper Crane signed the compact first for the Branford families, followed by Mr. Pierson. And then, as the signers spelled them and in order, came family names that still are notable in many parts of New Jersey and the nation:

Sam'l Swain, Laurance Ward, Thomas Blachtly, Samuel Plum, Josiah Ward, Samuel Rose, Thomas Peirson, John Warde, John Catling, Richard Harrison, Ebenezer Camfield, John Ward, Senior; Ed. Ball, John Harrison, John Crane, Thomas Huntington, Delivered Crane, Aaron Blacthly, Richard Laurance, John Johnson and Thomas L. Lyon (who inscribed an X as "his mark").

The next spring those families sailed from Branford to New Milford, as the settlement on the Passaic had been tentatively named. On June 27, 1667, the family heads already settled also signed the agreement, with Robert Treat heading the list. Others, as they signed, were:

Obadiah Bruen, Matthew Camfield, Samuel Kitchell, Jeremiah Pecke, Michael Tompkins, Stephen Freeman, Henry Lyon, John Browne, John Rogers, Stephen Davis, Edward Rigs, Robert Kitchell, J. B. Brooks, Robert V. Lymens, Francis F. Linle (Brooks, Lymens and Linle simply signed a "mark" or "X"), Daniel Tichenor, John Bauldwin, Sen.; John Bauldwin, Jr.; Jona. Tompkins, Geo. Day, Thomas Johnson, John Curtis, Ephram Burwell, Robert R. Dennison (also signed with a "mark"), Nathaniel Wheeler, Zachariah Burwell, William Campe, Joseph Walters, Robert Dalglish, Hauns Albers, Thom. Morris, Hugh Roberts, Eph'm Penning-

ton, Martin Tichenor, John Browne, Jr.; Jona. Sergeant, Azariah Crane, Samuel Lyon, Joseph Riggs, Stephen Bond.

There they were: twenty-three families from Branford, forty-one from Milford, Guilford and New Haven; sixty-four in all, totaling perhaps 350 to 375 persons. All plainly were of English stock except Robert Dalglish (probably Douglass) a Scot, and Hauns or Hans Albers.

Hans Albers always has been listed in history as Dutch or German, but it is very possible that he was a member of the large and distinguished Italian family named Albertus that had settled in New Netherlands before 1640. Originally from Venice, the Albertuses spread into Long Island and Connecticut, and Albers was perhaps a misspelling or Anglicizing of the Italian name. If this conjecture is true—and New Netherlands genealogical material offers strong support— then Newark's role as a melting pot began quickly.

(In the possible misspelling of Albertus as Albers, it should be noted that in all colonial material there is spelling inconsistency in names and places. Newark documents are no exception. The name Linle or Linsley, also was spelled Lindsey or Lindsay at various times. Treat sometimes was Treatt or Trott or Treet. Bauldwin was Baldwin. Swaine was spelled with or without the final "e". Pierson was often Peirson.)

This was an assorted group, bound together by friendship as well as religion. There were children not yet able to walk and old men who had been searching for peace for seven decades. Most were related through intermarriage in Connecticut. There were men with skills —Thomas Pierson and Benjamin Baldwin, weavers; Samuel Swaine, miller; Francis Linsley, one-time keeper of the herd in Guilford; Edward Ball, surveyor, and Albers and Hugh Roberts, tanners of leather and founders of Newark's greatest early industry.

In this new town, too, were Micah Tompkins, who had so successfully hidden the slayers of King Charles I in his Milford basement, and Lawrence Ward, one of those deputized to lead the unsuccessful Connecticut search for the fugitives. Ward's inability to find his quarry undoubtedly stemmed from a temporary ability to overlook clues. Memories of the Tompkins' hiding and the Ward search surely stirred laughter in the Puritan town.

Robert Treat was the unquestioned strong man in the new community. He conducted the continuing negotiations with the Indians, helped lay out the town, supervised buildings, was captain of the militia, served as town clerk, was elected one of Newark's first magistrates and served in the first New Jersey Assembly.

Jasper Crane led the Branford group in civil affairs. Considerably older than Treat, he was the latter's match in affairs of government and all settlers respected the wisdom of the elder Crane. The marriage of his son Azariah to Treat's daughter Mary in Milford, Connecticut, united two important families from two Puritan communities and was a foreboding of successful union in New Jersey. The marriage served as well to spread the Crane name, for Mary gave Azariah four sons in Newark—and they in turn fathered a total of 22 sons.

While Treat and Crane were the civil leaders, the Rev. Abraham Pierson was the spiritual shepherd of the flock, and there is full reason to believe that he was the dominant, if quiet, mover behind the new town. Cotton Mather, the great New England preacher, said of him, "Wherever he came he shone," and Newark was no exception. Old settlers later recalled that they changed the name of "our Town on the Passaick" from New Milford to Newark in honor of Mr. Pierson's former home in England. (Other sources indicate the name came from "New Ark" or "New Work," signifying new spiritual ventures, but the derivation from England is so simple and obvious that it seems correct. Newark in England, for that matter, was originally called New Worke, being a newly fortified town, in contrast with the old British towns walled in by the Romans.)

The settlers of Newark had much to do. First

Newark-on-Trent, England, mother city of the town on the Passaic, as painted in 1790 by Joseph Farrington.

the Indians had to be satisfied once and for all; the Puritan conscience and prudence would not have it otherwise. These red men had been here first, following the high ground above the marshlands, crossing the meadows to pluck the persimmons on the southern end of town or digging into the bay for clams and oysters. They already had raised a small monument to their activity: a shell mound near the water. Their friendship was worth cultivating, and in these early years an enduring relationship was begun.

The Newarkers signed a formal treaty with the Hackensacks on July 11, 1667, for a tract "bounded and Limited by the bay Eastward, and the great River Pasayak Northward, the great Creke or River in the meadows running to the head of the Cove, and from thence bareing a West Line for the South bounds, wh. (which) said Great Creke is Commonly Called and known by the name Weequachick, on the West Line backwards in the Country to the foot of the great Mountain called Watchung, being as is Judged about seven or eight miles from Pesayak towne . . . the bounds northerly, viz: Pesayak River reaches to the Third River above the towne, ye River is called Yauntakah, and from thence upon a northwest Line to the aforesaid mountaine. . ."

Pasayak or Passaic (a river of many spellings, even within one document), Weequachick (or Weequahic) and Yauntakah (or Yantacaw) are names still existing. The old boundaries are best located in terms of modern place names—from Clifton to Hillside, north and south; from Newark Bay to the base of First Mountain, west and east. The tract included present-day Montclair, Bloomfield, Nutley, Belleville, Glen Ridge, most of the Oranges and Irvington, parts of Maplewood and Short Hills.

For this real estate, the transplanted New Englanders gave "fifty double-hands of powder, one hundred barrs of lead, twenty Axes, twenty Coates, ten Guns, twenty pistolls, ten kettles, ten Swords, four blankets, four barrells of beere, ten paire of breeches, fifty knives, twenty howes, eight hundred and fifty fathem of wampum, two Ankors of Licquers or something Equivolent and three troopers Coates." Except for "only a small remainder engaged to them by bill," the commodities were paid on the spot.

The deed does not indicate where the ceremony took place, but eighty years later very old residents recalled that it was at the "head of the cove," now the far southern end of Weequahic Park. The pleasantness of the season, the nearness to town and the fact that Indians surely were on location for their annual summertime shellfish hunt, make it likely that a large audience looked on.

Secure in their holdings, the Puritans laid out their town on the order of New Haven, setting down street patterns that still exist. In the town center, running generally north and south along an old Indian trail, they established a magnificent street eight rods (132 feet) wide. Bisecting this, east and west, they laid out a street of equal grandeur. This intersection eventually became Broad and Market Streets, the celebrated "Four Corners." Paralleling Broad Street, two more streets were staked out, each four rods (sixty-six feet) wide and now called Washington and Mulberry Streets—but then known only as West Back Lane and East Back Lane.

The principal north-south thoroughfare (Broad Street) veered off on sharp angles at both the northern and southern ends. At these angles the town planners set aside public lands. The triangle on the northern bend was the "Training Place" (and is now Military Park). The triangle on the south end of the street is today's

Indian signatures (or "marks") on 1667 deed that conveyed Newark to the first settlers. This copy is in The State Library, Trenton.

Lincoln Park. Where West Back Lane (now Washington Street) intersected the broad street at the far north, another plot was set aside as a market place (now Washington Park.) Thus they reproduced in Newark the layout of a New England town with its orderly street patterns and town-owned greens.

West of the main intersection the town fathers established a community watering place for livestock on swampy ground near where today's Washington and Market Streets intersect. This became generally known as "The Swamp." In time, leather tanners shared the waters with the cattle—and then took over completely.

Since settlers from New Haven and Milford had mainly established temporary quarters south of modern Market Street and those from Branford were generally north of Market, they amicably agreed to keep the arrangement when land was formally assigned. Plots were allocated in a lottery, each family head drawing a number which gave him a chance to specify his choice of land. Great care was taken to see that no man suffered an injustice in receiving property.

The settlers agreed to let Robert Treat choose his lots before the drawing and gave him eight acres—two more than the six granted the others. Treat took his six acres in the town center—the southeast corner of today's Broad and Market Streets, extending east to Mulberry Street and south to beyond the location of the present First Presbyterian Church. For his "Recompense," or bonus, he chose two acres on the corner of Market Street and West Back Lane (Washington Street).

Mr. Pierson chose a lot adjacent to Treat's, south along Broad Street. Land for the meeting house and graveyard was reserved on the southwest corner of Broad and Market, across from Treat. On this lot was a glistening little pond. Settlers named it Frog Pond, undoubtedly in memory of home. Early Milford maps had a "Frog Lane."

Every settler agreed to pay taxes for the support of the "upholding of the settled ministry and the preaching of the word in our town." Highways were deemed a public necessity, and they could be built anywhere, "yea though it should fall out to be across or within any man's land."

The worth of every settler for purposes of tax-

ation was judged by a committee of seven men. Every family head was considered worth fifty pounds in his own right and every child or servant was assessed at "ten pounds by the Head." Thus a man with four children and two servants would be worth 110 pounds (his wife not counting anything of value for taxing purposes). In addition, "all other kinds of goods and estates, real and visible," were considered part of a man's worth.

Treat was the wealthiest man in town, followed closely by Mr. Pierson, Jasper Crane and Thomas Lyon. Treat was worth £660, Mr. Pierson £600 and Crane and Lyon £570 each. Lyon, interestingly, was one of the five family heads who could not sign their own names. Then came fifteen others worth at least £350, including the Kitchell brothers, who showed a joint estate of £700.

There was always the possibility that a potential trouble maker might somehow acquire land in Newark. To forestall this, the settlers voted that "in case any shall come into us or arise up amongst us that shall willingly or wilfully disturb us in our Peace and Settlements, and especially that would subvert us from the true religion and worship of God, and cannot or will not keep their opinions to themselves or be reclaimed after due time," such dissenters must "quietly depart the place seasonably." In fairness, they would be paid "valuable considerations for their lands or houses."

One nagging detail had to be ironed out with Elizabethtown before Newark could be sufficient unto itself, for a question had arisen about the dividing line between the communities. Six commissioners from Newark met with four from Elizabethtown to settle the issue.

Treat recorded details of the meeting, and in the Town Book appended this proof of witnessing: "Truly copied out of the Original agreement by Me—Robert Treatt."

The dividing line began "from the top of a little round hill, named divident hill; and from thence to run upon a North West Line, into the Country." Divident Hill is in present-day Weequahic Park. To ratify the agreement, "the said Agents of Elizabeth Town have marked an Oak Tree with an E next them." In turn, "the Said Agents of Newark Town have marked the

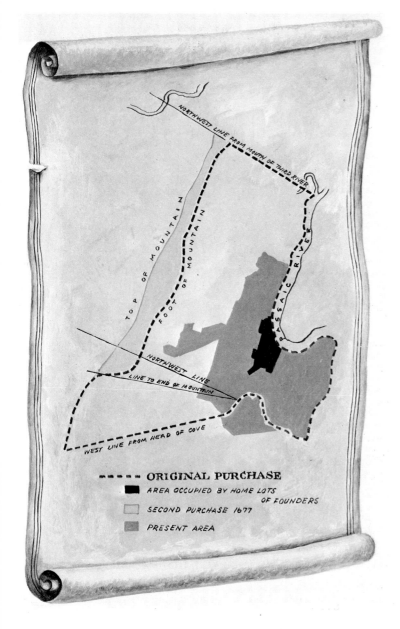

NORTH WEST LINE FROM MOUTH OF THIRD RIVER

TOP OF MOUNTAIN

FOOT OF MOUNTAIN

PASSAIC RIVER

NORTH WEST LINE

LINE TO END OF MOUNTAIN

WEST LINE FROM HEAD OF COVE

— — — — ORIGINAL PURCHASE

▪ AREA OCCUPIED BY HOME LOTS OF FOUNDERS

☐ SECOND PURCHASE 1677

▨ PRESENT AREA

The original boundary of Newark was nearly equal to modern Essex County.

Having set a boundary between Newark and Elizabeth, the town delegates asked God's blessing on their work. From Atkinson's History of Newark.

same tree with an N, on the side Next them and Their Town." Then the ten "set our hands Enterchangably" to the document which has proved more durable than the Oak tree with its carved initials.

Ogden, Watson, Bond and Joanes admired their "E", turned southward and headed into Elizabethtown. For their part, Crane, Treat, Camfield, Swain, Harrison and Johnson put finishing touches on their "N", then trooped northward down the hill to Newark Town. There was much to do; a third summer was near in the village by the Passaic River.

Chapter 3

CHANGES IN PARADISE

Until they raised their meeting house, Newark's founders felt unfulfilled. Gathered in an open air town meeting on September 10, 1668, the residents agreed to build their meeting house "as soon as may be" on a precise spot on the six-acre corner church lot to be chosen by the Rev. Abraham Pierson, Robert Treat and Deacon Ward.

All able-bodied men in town were obliged to help if given "seasonable warnings." The wealthiest were expected to contribute the most in labor, but every man was pledged to work at least two days on the meeting house.

Immediately after voting to build the church, the townspeople hired young Thomas Johnson to beat the town drum during the coming year, warning of daybreak when energetic men must be about and sounding the hour when tired men should be abed. He would summon men

to work, alert the town to danger, rout the late risers out of bed on Sunday mornings and get them headed for church. For this, young Johnson would receive eight shillings in advance, plus five shillings a month—all payable to his father.

Ward, Harrison and Rigs, carpenters, bargained with the town to build the meeting house for seventeen pounds, guaranteeing a meeting house thirty-six feet square if the town workers would "hew and bring all the rest of the timber upon the place." The town meeting accepted the offer but cannily hoped for "some abatement in the price if they can afford it."

Shortages of nails hampered the builders. Late in 1668, Henry Lyon bought seven acres of land from the town and agreed to pay half the purchase price in shingle nails. The following April, settlers agreed in open meeting "to provide nails for the closing of the Meeting House, in a voluntary way." By January of 1670, several citizens began laying a floor "of good chestnut and oak," amid assurances that the meeting house could be in use by the time the dogwood blossomed again in the Watchung hills.

Mr. Pierson watched the work with great anticipation, for this meeting house would fulfill his spiritual hopes for the town. The minister felt satisfied with his treatment—he was paid eighty pounds a year, had been reimbursed for his moving expenses, and his well dug and all his firewood brought in—but he wished that the meeting house might be built before his failing health gave way completely. The town beseeched Abraham Pierson Jr. in July, 1669, "to be helpful to his ailing father" and paid him thirty pounds "for his encouragement."

The crude frame meeting house finally was ready and it served well. Newark's Puritans approved its lack of ornamentation, the complete absence of statues or paintings. Men sat on one

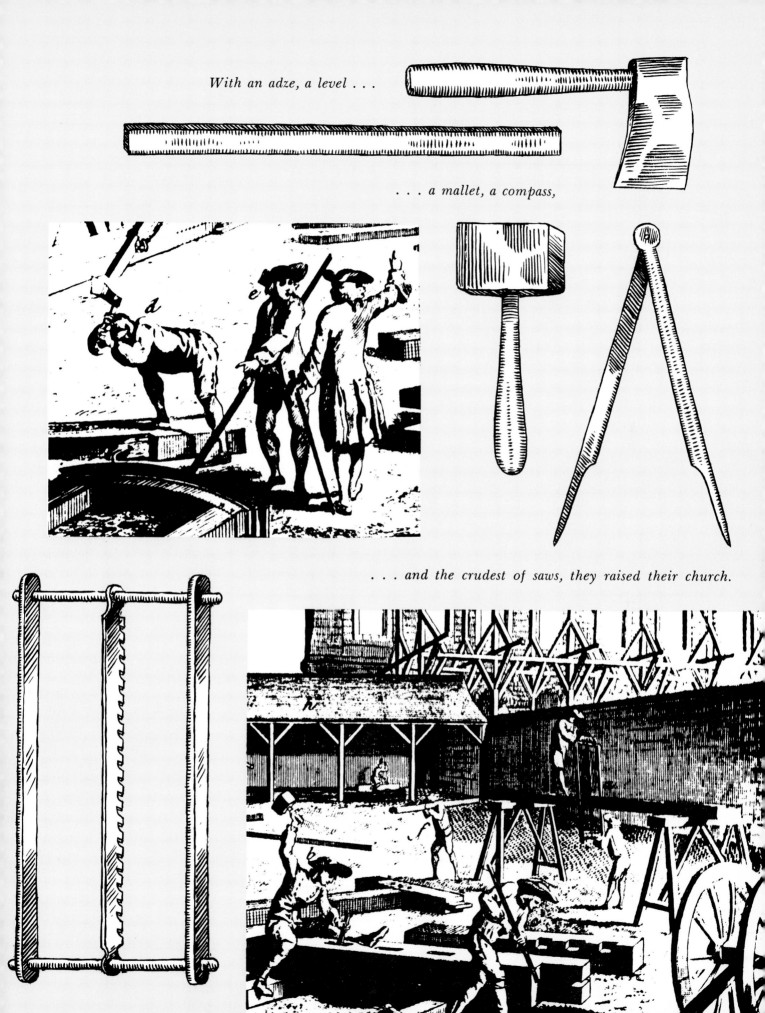

With an adze, a level . . .

. . . a mallet, a compass,

. . . and the crudest of saws, they raised their church.

side, women and children on the other, with boys and young men in the back, where they could easily be watched and punished for misbehavior.

By 1668, substantial homes also had been built, as evidenced by town orders that "every man shall provide a good ladder," indispensable in case of fire. Homes generally were a story and a half high and about thirty feet long, with sharply sloping roofs to prevent accumulations of snow or ice. Roofs were shingled and walls were covered with either shingles or rough clapboards. Between the outer covering and the framing timbers, a filling of rubble kept out the cold. Such homes were typically "New England" in the "salt box" or "cape cod" styles.

A typical house was that of William Meeker, built in 1674 near the southern end of town. It stood until 1913, and although enlarged and altered with the years, it manifested the character and shape of original Newark homesteads. On each corner of the low-slung, shingled houses stood huge barrels to catch rain water; nearby, a towering sweep dipped into the well.

Inside, a tremendous fireplace at one end of the main room provided heat, light and cooking facilities. This differed from the New England practice of a central fireplace. Logs as much as eight feet in length were dragged to the front door by oxen and then laboriously tugged across the floor to the hearth. Each evening a new log was placed on the fire, banked with burning embers and left to smoulder through the long winter nights.

In this large room that served as kitchen, living room and work room, housewives spun wool and flax for clothing and household linens, made candles and prepared meals. They wove cloth on family looms, cut it generously to fit growing bodies and sewed together homespun garments more notable for fending off the cold than for style.

Meeker homestead, built in 1674 in southern part of town, stood until 1913.

Worshippers carried guns to Sunday meetings in colonial days, lest a surprise foe—Indian or otherwise —strike from the hills. From Urquhart's A Short History of Newark.

Once housed, clothed and lifted in soul and spirit by the church, the Puritans turned to other fundamental concerns: the meadows, wandering livestock, roads and the need to attract badly needed skills.

The tide-washed meadows presented both problems and challenges, as they would throughout Newark's history, even if the problems and challenges differed in changing eras. Each spring the crisp grass had to be burned over to prepare for another crop of salt hay, and men were drummed out for that chore. Constant effort was expanded to make the great morass accessible and useful. Out there grew the lush grasses needed as bedding for Newark's cattle and horses.

The town meeting of March, 1669, appointed a committee to determine what drains were required in the meadowlands. Three months later men labored on both a drainage ditch and a new road across the meadows, contributing toil according to their assets: a day of work for each £100 of net worth on the road and a day for each £200 of worth on the ditch. A day's work was considered a ditch two rods long (thirty-three feet), two feet wide and two feet deep. Each property owner dug his share, then warned his next neighbor to take it from there. If a slacker "refused to work when warned," the

town could hire substitutes, "though it be for double or treeble wages," paid by the laggard.

As each man finished his share of the ditch or road he hammered in a stake, painted his initials on it to proclaim to his neighbors that he had dug his way.

Newark had little patience with drones or non-participants, yet reading between the lines of Treat's entries in the town Minute Book one learns there were both. Those who "refused to go when warned" of work were proof that to be a Puritan was not necessarily to be enthusiastic about either work or town affairs.

Lack of interest in community affairs began early. Henry Lyon, Sergeant John Ward and John Brown were appointed in September, 1668, to "hear every man's reason of his or their absence, late coming or disorderly departing or withdrawing, from any of our town meetings." By May, 1671, it was agreed that "any twenty of the freeholders" could carry on "any business belonging to the whole town," provided notice of meeting had been given the town. The following year the town fathers agreed to fine any man who "doth not come timely" to town meetings after receiving twenty-four hours notice.

Government business went on despite the recalcitrants. Leaders turned to such concerns as wandering livestock, further divisions of land

and the need for military preparedness.

Stephen Bond was commissioned "common brander" of horses in January, 1668, with instructions to burn all horses with differing brands to indicate ownership. Later the branding was extended to other livestock; "ear marks" became an important means of determining ownership of stray cattle, sheep and hogs.

The town fathers also grew weary of cows sloshing at will through the muddy streets. They employed Henry Lyon to build a municipal enclosure near the town center for stray cattle. It was to be of "six good rails, six foot high," twenty feet wide and thirty feet long. They named Robert Denision pound keeper, "to have a penny a head for turning the key or reception of any cattle trespassing."

Owners of "unruly" cattle, horses, oxen or cows found in the "common field" in the meadowlands faced fines of five shillings per beast, "besides all damages that they shall do to any man, his cow, grass or hay or otherwise." For cattle judged not "unruly"—a matter of some discernment—the fine was set at four shillings per beast.

Hogs presented a greater problem. Wandering down streets, they found contentment for a time by wallowing in the muck by the river. Seeking greater fields to conquer, they plunged into the Passaic River, swam around the end of the town fence and cavorted happily amid meadowland mire. John Catlin was ordered in April, 1669, to extend the fence by the river to keep the hogs in approved mud.

The original great piece of real estate acquired from the Indians had to be split up, both to satisfy those who had paid taxes for the acquisition and to fix responsibility for property. Land divisions were made several times in the first few years, first through allocations of meadow lots in January, 1669, then through dividing the "salt meadow" in February, 1670. All of the property was assigned by lot.

Three years later, a third drawing acknowledged that a new generation was itching for space. It was agreed that young men must share in the lottery along with older inhabitants. In six years the children of the original colonists were forming new families, the joy of any young community.

Newark was dedicated to aloofness, but commerce began in the burgeoning town. Henry Lyon, town treasurer, wealthy land holder and builder of the town pound, was instructed in 1668 to "keep an ordinary for the entertainment of travellers and strangers." Few strangers ever came, but Lyon had to provide bed and board and a spot of liquid refreshment to anyone happening by his ordinary (or inn).

Two years later, Lyon relinquished the inn to Thomas Johnson, tax collector, father of the town drummer, carpenter on the meeting house, keeper of the pound, and, not the least of his many occupations, town constable. All residents but Johnson were prohibited from "selling any strong liquors by retail under a gallon, unless in case of necessity, and that by license from the Magistrate." Jasper Crane, town magistrate and man of many parts, widened his activity in January of 1673 by securing "liberty to sell liquors in the town." He made the spirits himself, offered them for six shillings a gallon—and gladly took wheat in exchange for his liquors.

All commerce thrived on such barter. Men paid their taxes or bought necessities with what they possessed: the harvests of their fields or the labor they could supply with their muscles, for there was little actual cash in circulation. In his first year in town, Mr. Pierson accepted as part of his salary a house, with the remainder "in several kinds of payments," including "a pound of butter for every milk cow in town." Butter, wheat, corn, milk, boards and nails were all acceptable for either taxes or trade for many years.

Men traded their skills, too. Azariah Bush was given three acres in May, 1669, agreeing to maintain "a good sufficient boat or bigger vessel for the use and commodity of the town as they may need." The same year John Rockwell received six acres for a similar service. Zachariah Burwell and John Baldwin received concessions for sawing wood for a town mill. Others came, offering desired trades, and Newark could not ask them to be both skilled and Puritans. Thus secularization spread.

Newark desperately needed a grist mill. Anyone who built it was assured a fine deal: eighteen acres of upland and six of meadow, the timber necessary for the mill, twenty pounds in pay and the exclusive right to build mills on the brook that flowed through the north end of town. No one accepted.

The town in 1669 offered reliable Samuel Swain, twenty shillings per six-day week, plus "three Pounds over for his skill" to build the mill. As usual, the town fathers showed their parsimonious natures; they said if Swain could see his way to cutting the price, "the town will take it thankfully." Men went forth from the town to search the hills for flat stones for use in grinding.

Even Swain failed, and on August 4, 1670, the town "at length made a full agreement" with Treat and Richard Harrison to build and maintain "a sufficient corn mill***to grind all the town grist into good meal." They agreed to accept 1/12th of all Indian corn and 1/16th of all other grain as their share. They received in advance thirty pounds in "good wheat, pork, beef or one-fourth in Good Indian Corn." That did it; within a year the mill was in full operation.

The years sped by. Families had begun to grow, a second generation was moving on. Many of these clung to the old stern views, for they had been reared in the unrelenting atmosphere of Milford, Guilford and Branford. They went to church, married church members and baptized their children with such good Biblical names as Obadiah, Ephraim, Josiah, Moses, Zebadiah, Caleb, Hannah, Rebecca, Phebe, Rachel and Sarah, plus many a John and Elizabeth.

Increasing numbers of little Obadiahs and Hannahs as well as Josiahs and Sarahs, prompted a concern for education. At first, learning stemmed from the Piersons—the elder Mr. Pierson had brought with him to Newark a library of more than 400 volumes, one of the largest private collections in the New World. Such education emphasized reading from the Scriptures.

Then in November, 1676, the town agreed to hire a school master to "teach the children or servants of those as have subscribed, the reading and writing of English, and also arethmetick if they desire it." He had to give them "as much as they are capable to learn and he capable to teach them."

One interesting clause in the agreement was that concerning servants. These Puritans had hired help, probably indentured or bonded servants. Even the earliest agreement mentioned servants, to be counted, along with children, as worth "Ten Pounds by the Head" for taxing purposes. There is no evidence, however, that any of them had slaves in the early years.

Life was stern and cheerless for the young, and some of them rebelled. Joseph Walters was appointed in November, 1680, "to look after and see that the boys and youth do carry themselves reverently in the time of public Worship upon the Lord's Day and other Days."

Shocked adults pondered this rising generation, which "do misbehave themselves" inside and out of the Meeting House, carrying on by "sleeping, whispering or the like." There were also "grown persons as well as Boys" engaged in such disregard for the teachings and preachings of their elders.

Robert Treat, the staunchest of all early Newark figures left town sometime in the summer of 1672 to return to Connecticut. The date of

As they learned their ABCs, Newark's boys and girls also were given moral lessons.

his leaving is not known; he was too modest to consider it worth recording in the Town Minutes.

Treat lived with distinction for 37 years after leaving Newark. He fought vigorously in King Philip's War, was elected Governor of Connecticut in 1683 and won his colony's lasting gratitude in 1686 when he hid its charter in an oak tree (the Charter Oak) to keep it out of the hands of Sir Edmund Andros, then Governor of New England. The old soldier died in 1710 at the age of eighty-eight—forty-four years after he had helped found Newark.

Time moved on for all the elders who had migrated from Connecticut in 1666 and 1667. The venerable Mr. Pierson survived a withering sickness in 1671 and continued in poor health even with son Abraham Jr. aiding in church duties. When Newark's first minister died in 1678, the son stepped into the pulpit and became the second spiritual leader of a changing town.

Young Mr. Pierson, described as "fleshy, well-favoured and comely-looking," was thirty-three when he succeeded his father in the Newark pulpit. He had been educated at Harvard and returned to Newark after graduation in 1668. He married Miss Abigail Clark, a young woman from his home town of Milford, and in Newark they began their family of four boys and five girls. This Mr. Pierson was different from his father—more liberal, more controversial, more independent, more given to Presbyterian doctrines. His philosophies irritated some strict members of his congregation to the extent that they withheld his salary for a time in 1686, only to restore it fully in January, 1687.

Twenty-one years had passed since 1666, long enough for a baby born that year to have reached legal maturity. Younger people yearned for more liberties, but older heads tightly controlled both church and town affairs. Mr. Pierson stayed for another five years before sailing for Connecticut to become pastor of a church in Killingworth (now Clinton). Ten years later, he became the first president of the College of Connecticut later known as Yale College. So great was his influence that the college was first located in Killingworth to suit Mr. Pierson's convenience.

Statue of the Rev. Abraham Pierson, Newark's second minister, at Yale.

By the time the second Mr. Pierson returned to his boyhood colony, many of the original Newarkers lay beneath sandstone markers in the old graveyard besides the meeting house. Lawrence Ward, Robert Kitchell, Hugh Roberts, Matthew Camfield, Delivered Crane, Stephen Crane, Lawrence Ward, John Harrison and Josiah Ward of the original settlers all had preceded the first Mr. Pierson in death.

As each of the signers of the original compact died, old Newark died a little, too, although its philosophy had been doomed from the start. The time for a rigidly limited theocracy in colonial America had passed even before 1666. A bigger world rubbed against the sound little town on the Passaic. Young people moved off to the hills and away from the church. The gradual involvement with other towns, other personalities, other ideas became important; a "new" Newark—the first of many—was in the offing.

Chapter 4

INTO THE OUTER WORLD

WHEN ROBERT TREAT AND JASPER CRANE headed south across the meadows to Elizabethtown in May, 1668, to attend the first session of the New Jersey Assembly called by Governor Philip Carteret, a bit of the exclusiveness that these Puritans sought slipped away with every step, for in cooperation they yielded independence.

Not that most of the other delegates were in sharp variance with Newark's theocracy. Delegates from Elizabethtown, Woodbridge and Middletown were also transplanted New Englanders with deep Puritan backgrounds. Representatives from the Dutch town of Bergen were not likely to debate matters of conscience in this English-dominated legislature.

Still, the presence of Governor Carteret in Elizabethtown, surrounded by his personal party of courtiers and servants, softened the sharp edge of Puritan ambition. Middletown's delegates represented both the Baptists of Middletown itself and the Quakers of nearby Shrewsbury. In such company there had to be differences of opinion.

A harsh criminal code adopted by the Assembly reflected Puritanical thinking. As in New England, the laws provided death for offenses ranging from burglary to murder and from bearing false witness to being judged a witch. Children over sixteen who attacked or cursed their parents could be executed unless they proved self-defense. Young people on the streets after 9 P.M. faced swift punishment and anyone taking the name of God in vain was to be fined one shilling—half to the informer, half to the town treasury.

Convicted burglars were forced to make restitution and on first arrest had a letter T (for thief) branded on the hand. A second offense meant a letter B (for burglar) burned on the forehead. A third offense meant the gallows. Surprisingly, in view of the New England code, adultery was less severely punished, the New Jersey penalty being divorce, corporal punishment or banishment; or, at the wisdom of the court, all three. Offenders were not branded with an A, as in parts of New England.

Congeniality between Governor and Assembly

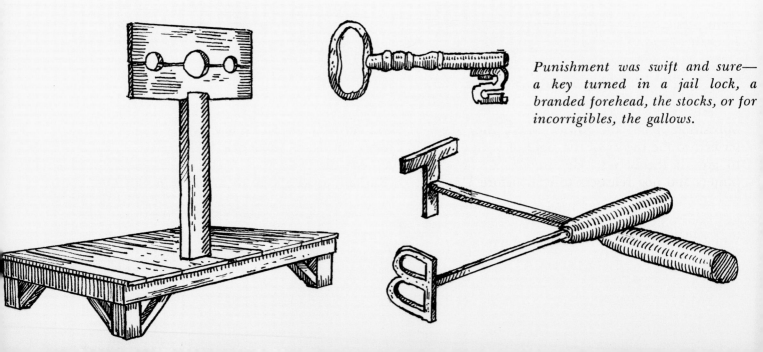

Punishment was swift and sure— a key turned in a jail lock, a branded forehead, the stocks, or for incorrigibles, the gallows.

quickly evaporated after those five days in May, 1668. Carteret refused to sit with the Assemblymen in November of that year, insisting that they submit their suggestions and complaints in writing, ridiculous protocol in a wilderness village where a shout could be heard from one end to the other. Assemblymen retorted that such stiff procedure was "fruitless and endless."

Newarkers sympathized with the dissenters, but as loyal Englishmen they also recognized the duty of the Governor to collect an annual rent of a half penny on every acre of occupied ground for the Lords Proprietors in England.

When rents came due on March 25, 1670, the first day of the New Year under the old calendar, Newark appointed Henry Lyon and Thomas Johnson to "take and receive every man's just share and proportion of wheat for his land," at the rate of four shillings a bushel for winter wheat and five shillings for summer wheat.

Lyon and Johnson hauled the wheat to Elizabethtown, but they appeared before Carteret in lonely dignity. Elizabethtown, Woodbridge, Piscataway, Shrewsbury and Middletown refused to honor the levy, arguing that their land had been granted them before the Proprietors received New Jersey from the Duke of York.

Carteret acted haughtily, apparently refusing to take the "country fare" offered by Newark. He insisted payments be made in gold or silver.

The governor infuriated the townsmen by selling an Elizabethtown house lot to one of his servants without asking town permission, and then stripped two town-appointed militia officers of their commissions. When Carteret gave another servant, Richard Michell, a house and lot, townspeople pulled down a log fence around Michell's house, let wandering hogs through to ruin the garden and ripped clapboards off the house. The Governor was aghast at this protest in the name of home rule.

Carteret's angry retaliation merely solidified opposition in all the towns, where they subscribed to the theory of the right of the people to govern themselves. He brought the fence busters and hog releasers to trial before a jury devoid of townspeople from Newark or Elizabethtown. When his hand-picked panel found the defendants guilty, anger gripped the two towns. Assemblymen gathered in rebellion at

Elizabethtown in May, 1672. Jasper Crane and Samuel Swain had instructions "to consult with the rest of the representatives of the country, to order matters for the safety of the country." However, this latter stemmed more from fear of Indian troubles—already brewing in New England—than from mistrust of Carteret.

After verbally lashing the governor for his violation of Elizabethtown rights, the Assembly adjourned and promptly reconvened "without the knowledge, approbation or consent" of the Governor to elect James Carteret, the dissolute son of George Carteret as the first, and only, "president" of New Jersey. Shocked and frightened, Philip booked quick passage home to report on the mutinous residents in Newark and Elizabethtown.

Fully committed to protest—but still wishing to press for peace through English law—Newarkers enthusiastically agreed at a town meeting on July 1, 1673, to join other towns in petitioning the proprietors "for removing of the grievances incumbent." Jasper Crane headed a five-man committee named to consider sending a messenger to England to present the colonial views.

But the messenger never left, for within the month five Dutch vessels "surrounded" New York. Their guns forced down the English flag on July 30, 1673, and Dutchmen marched gleefully into the village that they had surrendered to England nine years before. New Amsterdam had been renamed "New York;" now the Dutch changed it to New Orange in honor of William of Orange.

Five days after New York's surrender, Newarkers gathered at the meeting house to determine a course of action. The change in government meant little to them. Indeed, in view of their open hatred of King Charles II, manifested a dozen years before when most of them lived in Connecticut, the men of Newark might have welcomed the change. They joined other New Jersey towns in seeking a "privileged county between the two Rivers Passaick and Araritine (Raritan) or with as many as will join us." The venerable Jasper Crane led a party of four to New Orange to seek terms.

The Dutch wanted peace above all and Newark was satisfied there would be no interference in church matters. The Dutch asked that three "schepens" (magistrates) be selected by each town. Newark chose Jasper Crane, Robert Bond and John Ward. Come what may, despised English governor or interloping Dutchmen, Crane always stood ready to serve.

Newark town minutes after August 4 seldom referred to the Dutch rulers as such, although the recorder occasionally mentioned New Orange, and at no time were magistrates called "schepens" in official records. Newark men gathered early in October, 1673, to swear allegiance to "ye authority of the high and mighty Lords the Staets General" and to the schepens of New Orange. A Dutch census showed that Newark had eighty-six men of age, but only seventy-five took the oath. Presumably the missing eleven, seeing no future under the Dutch, found urgent business in the mountains.

Powerful England quickly dislodged the Dutch and within a year "New Orange" was a mere footnote in history. Governor Carteret returned to Elizabethtown, more authoritative than ever. He demanded prompt payment of overdue rents, "of Newark and all other plantations," a strange singling out of the town in view of Newark's willingness to pay from the start. Rents could be paid in "such merchantable pay as the country doth produce," a minor victory for Newark.

Part of the new cordiality between Carteret and the colonists undoubtedly stemmed from a pressing threat to safety. Late in the summer of 1673, Newarkers worried over the possibility of attack by the Indians, already on the warpath throughout New England in the war that the Indian, King Philip, was waging on colonists. Every man, "under sixty and above sixteen," was ordered to appear on October 1 at eight o'clock in the morning, bearing a gun, a half pound of powder and twelve bullets.

Two years later, the town fortified the meeting house against possible enemy attack. Men barricaded the lower half with thin stone and mortar and erected fortifications (called "Palisades" or "Stockades") on two corners of the church. Here people could be safe, but once again some settlers refused to work. The town meeting of September 10, 1675, called for overseers "to take notice who is wanting" in working on the fortification.

As the emergency deepened, John Ward received orders to secure a barrel of powder and sufficient lead for bullets "as reasonably as he can for the town's use". The town agreed to pay him in "corn, fowls, eggs or in any way to satisfy him." Mr. Pierson shared in the appropriation, although normally he was exempted from taxes.

The alert continued through the winter of 1680. Starting in June, 1679, three men stood sentry each night, under orders for "all three of them to be walking" at the next break of day. A half hour after dawn they summoned the drummer to beat the good news that another night had passed without incident. On Sundays, "one fourth part of the town at a time, and so taking their turns, shall carry arms to Meeting on the Lord's Day." No attacker struck at Newark or its environs during the alert. Perhaps the drum echoing each morning through the hillsides warned Indians that Newark stood ready,

Edmund Andros, Governor of New York, caused resentment wherever he went, and his actions against Jerseymen in 1680 stirred even gentle Newarkers close to seething rebellion. Painting by Howard Pyle.

although there is no evidence of an Indian uprising anywhere in New Jersey at the time. Whatever Newarkers feared, they stood ready to meet the test in frontier fashion.

Carteret yielded little to them, but Jerseymen found his disposition improved in comparison with his pre-Dutch days. Thus, when an established court favorite, Edmund Andros, arrived in 1676 to be Governor of New York—and immediately cast envious eyes on New Jersey in the manner of all colonial New York governors—Carteret's subjects rallied to their governor's side in defiance of Andros' pretensions.

Andros was only mildly provocative at first, but on March 8, 1679, he sent Carteret a peremptory note, informing him that New Jersey rightfully belonged under the jurisdiction of New York. Carteret warned Andros not to "molest me as governor, nor the people under my charge." He boldly asserted that New Jersey inhabitants would "defend ourselves and families the best we can."

Newark went on a military footing. It was one thing to submit to amiable Dutchmen, a vastly different matter to crawl before a man they believed to be an English tyrant. On March 22, defense arrangements were voted at the town meeting. The beating of the drum from "Joseph Riggs' gate to Samuel Harrison's gate," followed by "three guns distinctly fired," would be the signal for armed men "forthwith to meet at the Meeting House" fully armed. Let the men of Andros come. Newark would not be caught napping.

A week later, the town meeting informed Andros that Newarkers "give their positive answers to the Governor of York's writ: that they have taken the Oath of Allegiance to the King and fidelity to the present government and until they have sufficient order from his Majesty we will stand by the same."

When Andros struck, he aimed his blow directly at New Jersey's provincial capital, disguising it first in a diplomatic visit. He came to Elizabethtown on April 7, 1680, to read his orders to Carteret and to whomever else they might concern.

Throngs of provincials, including many from Newark, milled inside the stockade to hear Andros demand a New Jersey surrender. When the audience behaved "somewhat churlishly" (in Andros' words), Carteret led the session out into an open field. There the two governors parried, hiding their mounting anger with studied courtesy. Andros even checked his fury when Captain John Berry, whose plantation was in New Barbadoes but under Newark's jurisdiction, told him that his actions would be appealed to England. Indeed, such an appeal already had begun.

Andros left for New York after a sumptuous dinner, but immediately issued a warrant for Carteret's arrest. A few nights later a band of soldiers landed in Elizabethtown, broke into Carteret's darkened house and carried the governor bodily to New York, "all naked as he was." Andros brought Carteret to trial for illegally acting as governor of New Jersey, but juries three times found him not guilty. Ordered back to Elizabethtown, Carteret was enjoined by the jury from assuming "any authority or jurisdiction there, civil or military." Technically, Carteret emerged as victor; actually he had lost.

Andros quietly took over the government of New Jersey, and, if anything, proved less immediately irksome to settlers than Carteret. Newark, for its part, was having internal troubles.

Townspeople had been visiting New York so frequently and for such minor reasons, that the town fathers on February 12, 1679, used "a report that many are sick of the pox at New York" to prohibit anyone from making the trip except on approval of a committee of five elders. Even worse than the running off to New York or the pox were the strangers coming to town.

Strangers, the town records indicate, brought "sundry inconveniences," and that must stop. Gathered together on February 25, 1680, a majority of citizens voted that no one in town could "receive or entertain any man or woman of whatever age or quality soever." Anyone who permitted such "coming and resorting" for a period longer than one month, "without license," was called on to pay a fine of five pounds as well as "all damages that may grow by such entertainments."

The pressures of a slowly expanding and changing population and the conflicts with the outside world were being felt. Trying to expand their boundaries, Newarkers had used temporary Dutch occupation in 1673 to negotiate for purchase of "The Neck," a large piece of real estate across the Passaic River, extending northward from present-day Kearny nearly to Hackensack. Both the law-abiding Dutch and pious Puritans conveniently overlooked the fact that the land already had been given to Captain William Sanford under an English grant. Further, Sanford had purchased the 13,000-acre section from the Indians and had transferred part of it to Major Nathaniel Kingsland, who came, like himself, from the West Indies.

Return of English power voided the deal for The Neck and left the Newark colony frustrated and out of pocket. They appealed bitterly to anyone who would listen, but without success. Rebuffed to the east, they looked to the west, and on March 13, 1678, they extended their western boundaries to the top of the Orange Mountains. Indians named Winocksop and Shenoctos that day traded away about seven square miles, for "two guns, three coats and 13 cans of rum."

This raised Newark's holdings to more than 60 square miles, seemingly enough for the approximately 90 families—about 500 people—in the town in 1680.

Westward lay the course of progress. Surveyors were appointed in December, 1681, "to lay out highways as far as the mountain, if need be." Gradually the young element went that way—the younger Cranes, Harrisons, Bruens, Baldwins, Catlins, Wards, Dodds, Lindsleys, Swains and others, for on the gentle slopes and on the forbidding tops lay a future for impetuous youth. Cattle could be grazed there, supplying both meat and hides that could be tanned and made into the leather clothing worn by men and boys. Up there, too, was water power to run the saw mills and grist mills.

Movement to the hills necessarily proceeded slowly. For one thing, the meeting house in the center of Newark remained the focus of religious life, and to live on the mountains before a church was built there meant arduous Sunday trips to and from meeting. The woods abounded with wolves and occasional bears; as late as 1702 bounties were given for killing either.

Evidence of Newark's emerging influence came in 1682 when the sprawling territories of Newark and Elizabethtown were combined to form the county of Essex, one of the first four

counties of East New Jersey (the others being Bergen, Middlesex and Monmouth). Newark received the courts in 1702 and the county held sessions in the meeting house. Soon after, the Proprietors shifted the seat of East New Jersey government to Perth Amboy and Elizabethtown declined in influence.

County court sessions brought even more strangers into town, and from time to time squatters moved into the territory without consulting authorities, much less paying anyone for their land. Such settlers eventually came to terms, or left quietly, and so the town grew. Slowly, very slowly, the Puritanical hold eased.

Attendance at town meetings became spottier than ever. On January 8, 1686, the few people present at the meeting agreed that all town business could be transacted at quarterly sessions rather than monthly. The practice of a drummer boy's pounding notice of meetings along the muddy streets was also stilled that day. Henceforth a notice tacked on the church door ten days before a town meeting was taken as enough warning.

The apathy of the majority did not lessen the zeal of the civic-minded minority. In 1696, the town's leaders obtained a patent to the Watering Place, the Market Place, the Training Place, the Burying Ground, the highways and about 210 scattered acres known as "The Parsonage Land." This gave all townspeople jurisdiction over town properties—a basic reason for Newark's unusually fine city parks.

A second generation was in power and a third was growing, but the original settlers continued to exercise influence if only through their descendants. The first four trustees of the common lands included John Treat, son of Robert, and Theophilus Pierson, third son of the first pastor, the Rev. Abraham Pierson. Working with Treat and Pierson were John Curtis and Robert Young, relative newcomers.

Such peaceful pursuits as protecting green acres within the town boundaries contrasted with a storm of rebellion about to rise in East New Jersey. The seeds of revolt, planted in 1664 when Governor Robert Nicolls of New York granted land areas within New Jersey without consent of the Proprietors, had sprouted in 1670 when Philip Carteret attempted to collect quit

Still bearing the imprint of its Dutch founders, New York was such a magnet for Newarkers that town fathers in 1679 prohibited travel there except by specific approval.

rents. Those sprouts, in turn, blossomed into fullest flower in 1700, once again directed at Proprietors who attempted to show their power.

Anti-Proprietor factions nailed the door of the Middlesex County court shut on March 4, 1700, and warned the Proprietors' men to stay off the property of the people. A week later a session at the Essex County Court at Elizabethtown broke up in what an eye-witness wrote "seemed rather to look like a rebellion than otherwise." In mid-July, a band of howling dissidents halted a court session in Middletown and threatened the life of Governor Andrew Hamilton when he hastened to the Monmouth County town.

The New Jersey rioters turned their attention to Newark on September 10 for the Essex County quarter session. They crowded into the old meeting house and shouted approvingly when Samuel Carter of Elizabethtown insolently asked the judges by what authority they sat. The answer, "By the King's," merely provoked more disorder.

The first case involved Samuel Burwell of Elizabethtown, accused of not supporting his child, an offense that seldom commanded sympathy. When the judges ordered Burwell taken into custody, Carter and others attacked the constable, pulled the chief judge off his bench, beat him with fists and sticks and broke his sword. They ripped clothing off other justices and turned the supposedly respected court into a shambles.

Two days later, September 12, sixty horsemen galloped across the meadows from Elizabethtown to free an Elizabethtowner named Joseph Parmeter, who had been jailed at Newark. They reined to a halt in front of the home of Justice Theophilus Pierson and demanded the jail keys. The judge appealed to them to respect the courts, then asked by what power they proceeded. Samuel Whitehead of Elizabethtown raised his club and yelled, "By this power!" They forced the sheriff from a nearby house, took his keys and freed Parmeter.

Johnson's mill and farm house, erected in about 1680 on Bound Creek near Elizabeth border. The second mill in town, it ground flour during the Revolution. Proprietor John Johnson dyed cloth in the mill after war, but would not use scarlet because of anti-British bias.

Anarchy stalked New Jersey. Annoyed by the bitter anti-Proprietory demonstrations, Queen Anne heeded the advice of the Lords of Trade and accepted the surrender of governmental authority by the Proprietors in 1702. She then united East and West New Jersey. Rioting, for the time, moved off-stage, but the colony would never be the same. Nor would Newarkers: each year, each act, each defiance, brushed away the old isolation.

Newark still enjoyed wide open spaces. In March, 1704, for example, the town meeting hired a shepherd to guard sheep on the western slopes. Town fences were still a problem. Taxes were still paid in wheat, oats, rye, flax and Indian corn.

Looking westward, Newark gathered in another 13,500 acres in 1702 by purchasing land at the bending of the Passaic River to the northwest. This embraced most of the present area of Caldwell, Roseland and Livingston. Costs were allocated—and land divided—on the basis of individual contributions, in contrast with earlier acquisitions when the town bought the land and then taxed everyone to pay for it. At the price of less than three cents an acre only a foolish or bankrupt man resisted the 1702 offer.

In 1713, as the third generation of Newarkers began to move to the fore, Queen Anne granted Newark a township charter. For the privilege, Newark was to pay a rental of five shillings annually to the English government.

But Newarkers were still obsessed with matters of the pulpit. Changes in town affairs were never so important as to end preoccupation with things of the spirit.

Chapter 5

TOWN IN DIVISION

I RONICALLY, the Rev. Abraham Pierson Jr., first-born son of the Branford minister who shaped Newark's original theocratic and Puritan ways, accelerated the separation of church and state when he ascended the pulpit in 1678. His Presbyterian methods irritated the old guard; they made scant show of regret when he departed for Connecticut in 1692. They chose safely conservative Rev. John Pruden of Connecticut as Pierson's successor.

Mr. Pruden's strictness alienated the more liberal element and his lackluster preaching disappointed those whose stern philosophies he championed. Mr. Pruden surely felt an implicit rebuke in the reduction of his pastoral salary from the longstanding eighty pounds to sixty pounds. He resigned in 1699 and the town meeting accepted—with a hope that Mr. Pruden would continue "preaching the Word to us, till God shall favor us with some other supply."

Newark liked Mr. Pruden as a person and as a consoler; he simply was unable to find any common ground between dissidents in the fast evolving city. As evidence of affection for him, it was ordered that "all persons from sixteen to sixty years of age shall give to Mr. Pruden each of them one load of wood for the year ensuing, whether he serve the town in the ministry another year or no."

The Rev. Jabez Wakeman, twenty-one years old, arrived in November, 1699, as Mr. Pruden's successor. His vigorous sermons and mental capabilities so excited the people that the church increased his salary twenty pounds a year. He moved into the parsonage and in 1701 grateful town fathers granted him ten acres of meadow and sixty acres of upland, unusual generosity for this notably parsimonious settlement.

Empty pews became full, the once-unruly young heeded Wakeman's words, and a gallery had to be added to the church in 1704. Thus, when the twenty-six-year-old minister died suddenly of dysentery on October 8, 1704, Newark went into a state of shock. Three weeks later, two-year-old Samuel Wakeman followed his father to the grave. Grief-stricken Newarkers voted to pay the widow her husband's yearly salary in full. Reliable Mr. Pruden tended Mr. Wakeman in sickness, buried him and his son, comforted his widow, and returned to the church as substitute minister.

Newark's slow metamorphosis from theocracy to full separation of church and civil affairs had picked up pace in Mr. Wakeman's term. He was chosen by a committee of three planters and "such as the church shall appoint" rather than by a town committee. His salary came only from church members rather than from the town at large.

Although the basic outlines were still plain, Newark's second church had a steeple and bell.

A more subtle indicator of lessening church-town inter-twining was the building of the second meeting house sometime between 1708 and 1716, the "sometime" being significant. Details of the first meeting house appeared constantly in early town minutes, but this second meeting house was not mentioned in town records, causing one church historian later to set 1708 as the date of its building and another as "between 1714 and 1716."

Rev. Dr. Alexander Macwhorter, a great Newark preacher of a much later time, believed the date was 1708, and his history gave details of the new stone building, forty-four-foot square and imposing enough to have both steeple and bell. The large size disturbed many church members. Dr. Macwhorter noted:

"It was an exceeding great exertion to erect it; and it was the most elegant edifice for public worship at that time in the colony. There were very considerable difficulties and contentions in the Society to get it as large as it was. It was hardly believed that the inhabitants of the town would ever become so numerous as to fill it."

Time had nearly run out for the sequestered dream of Newark's founders. Many strangers had come to town, from Elizabethtown, from Scotland, from other colonial towns. Some of the original settlers and their children had returned to Connecticut. People were quietly in revolt against strict moral codes as they became more worldly, more materialistic. More than anything

else, Newark's far-flung borders proved to be the eventual undoing of the theocracy.

Newarkers needed the land—or felt that they needed the land—that spread over the mountain top and beyond to the swamps in western Essex County. Out there were swiftly coursing streams to run sawmills. Out there were the woodlots from which to cut the beams, the joists and the shingles for homes and the fuel for fireplaces. Out there were the open spaces needed to supply grazing lands for the cattle whose hides made possible Newark's growing leather industries.

If Newark was to remain a church state, it needed the confinement of a town. People had to be within sight of the church and within earshot of the drum calling them to service. They had to be under the all-watchful eye of the minister, close to where the magistrate could follow his orders to rule them "in matters of Godliness, yea, of all Godliness." That was the way of the manor town in England, the way of life in New England and the transplanted ideal for Newark. Once the second generation began moving westward, the town and church could never again be the sole overseers of all thought and action.

As these young people spread into the open spaces, they became farmers, not members of an agricultural village with carefully regulated duties. They became independent and free. Newark's church remained the spiritual center for the outlanders, but more in a Sunday sense than as an everyday reality. They were not less

Newark as it may have looked in 1708, centered about new church.

religious; they were merely less oriented to church in the sense of a building or minister. First they would attend church less frequently, then found new churches and incorporate new towns. The disintegration had begun.

The frontiersmen still looked to Newark, but their remote settlements needed new roads to maintain the ties. On October 8, 1705, Essex County lawmakers established the routes of twelve new highways. Seven lay solely between villages in the hill country atop Orange Mountain; the rest linked Newark with the outlying settlements. Over these roads went more families to speed settlement of what are now the Oranges, Irvington, Bloomfield, Montclair, Belleville, the Caldwells, Verona, Livingston, and even Whippany, Morristown and other Morris County towns.

Foremost of the highways was "Crane Road," running westward past Jasper Crane's estate near where the courthouse now stands. This eventually became "First Road" all the way to the Orange Mountains. "Crane Road" is today's West Market Street; "First Road" is now Main Street in Orange.

Veering away from Crane Road near Crane's house was "Third Road," now South Orange Avenue, leading out to the center of modern South Orange and up the rising hill beyond. The simply named "Road to Wardsesson" was the first Newark link with what has become Bloomfield, but was then known as Wardses-

son. Roads ran north and south across Orange Mountain itself, one following the path of today's Ridgewood Avenue in South Orange. Two roads led to "Cranetown," settled by the Cranes of Newark. Passing years saw the name Cranetown changed to Montclair.

Calling these narrow dirt pathways "highways" dignified them considerably. They meandered, following specifications to be "as straight as the ground will allow." At best they were wide enough only for one ox-cart or two horses. There were no carriages in America; Newark's streets saw only an occasional team of oxen laboriously drawing roughly built carts. Men and women traveled on horseback, and often husband and wife shared one horse—carrying babes in arms when the family increased.

Such old-line Newark names at Kitchell, Condit, Ball, Lindsley, Baldwin, Williams and others located in the Whippany area in about 1710, answering the call of iron, the "black stone" that Indians claimed could be picked off the earth on the plains.

Enterprising landowners built an iron forge on the Whippany River, bringing iron ore overland in leather bags slung over the backs of horses. Smelted iron was cast into the form of iron bars to fit over the backs of horses and thus taken to Newark or New York for final shipment to England. From the "place of the black stone" to England's treasury—and back—was a long way, but the exchange of Morris County iron for

An early 18th century engraving depicts surface mining of the day, probably the manner in which Newarkers found copper in the 1720s.

English gold was worth the time and effort.

Even more alluring than the Succasunna iron was the hope that the untapped hills might be filled with more precious metals, particularly after 1713 when a slave discovered copper on Arent Schuyler's estate across the Passaic River at what is now Arlington. Tradition says that Schuyler gave the slave his freedom, a dressing robe and all the tobacco he might ever want in his lifetime, then employed more slaves to dig. By 1721, Schuyler sent as many as 110 casks of copper ore to Holland in one shipment.

Prospectors scurried to the mountains. Newarkers discovered a vein of copper in Orange in 1721, on ground they called "Rattlesnake Plain." John Dod, recorded owner of the land, and fellow townsmen named Gideon VanWinkle and Johannes Coeyman took out copper from a 700-foot excavation and the mine was operated until 1755.

Newark even entered officially into the get-rich-quick excitement by agreeing in March, 1732, to "let out the Common or Town's lands or any part thereof to dig for mines." The copper fever lasted at least until December, 1735, when town fathers found "not one person" opposing the lease of town lands for prospecting. Fortunately no one dug on either the military commons or the market place, but even these would not have been safe had anyone suspected copper.

The most radical happening in the town's first six decades, however, was the official switch in church allegiance from Congregational to Presbyterian. It had been long on the way, yet the actual transition did not come until Rev. Joseph Webb, a 1715 graduate of Yale College, became the sixth regular pastor in 1719.

The shift meant little change in the church's moral code. Both religions were strict, unrelenting and dominated by fear of God. The principal difference was in church government. Congregationalists believed each church was sufficient unto itself, without church overlords, while Presbyterians developed a system of cooperating churches. In addition, Presbyterians were not insistent that civil and religious matters be combined.

Affairs quickly revealed the lessened influence of the original meeting house. Families on the Orange hills broke away from the Newark church in 1719 to form the Mountain Society. Distance from Newark was a factor, but there is evidence that the hill people found Newark's shift to Presbyterian doctrine too abrupt. The Mountain Society built its meeting house on First Road (now Main Street) and worshipped in the Congregational fashion.

A third church was established in Second River (now Belleville) by Dutch settlers who had moved within Newark town boundaries. They established a Dutch Church, of course, and shared their minister with Aquackanonck (Passaic). This caused no concern in the church on Broad Street; Newarkers long ago had learned to live with the Hollanders.

New churches raised in the hills or by the Dutch could be accepted without qualms. Such things were inevitable, but just over the horizon was a schism destined to change Newark's church and political pattern forever.

It began simply. Wealthy land holders on the eastern banks of the Passaic across from Newark leaned to the more elaborate ceremony of the Church of England and held such services in the late 1720's. Possibly some Newarkers attended, without fanfare or dispute. Elizabethtown harbored several Church of England families who had invited Rev. Edward Vaughan to hold Episcopal services there in 1708. Mr. Vaughan took Church of England strength in Elizabethtown as a matter of course but was surprised to find supporters "also at Newark, Whippany and in the mountains." The English minister added, in what now seems quaint understatement, that he found in Newark "a general disposition in the people to be instructed and settled in the Christian Faith."

The Newark church serenely steered the course of rigid Presbyterianism. Dissension came not through visiting English divines but unexpectedly from Colonel Josiah Ogden, a leading Presbyterian, a staunch Newarker, colonial legislator, leader among men and son of Elizabeth

Often-used drawing from Atkinson's 1878 history, showing Colonel Josiah Ogden reaping his wheat on Sunday, despite the shocked stares of Presbyterians headed for meeting.

Trinity Church was fully in place by about 1745, when this water color was painted. The steeple gave young Newark its first real "New England" look, since Trinity stood on a small lot that originally was part of the early green set aside for militia drilling. This is believed to be Newark's earliest view, showing not only the church but also the types of homes, the clothing and the dirt road that is now Broad Street.

Swaine, the Branford miss whose heart had been set on being the first ashore in 1666. Elizabeth's first husband had died and David Ogden of Elizabethtown married her and sired four sons, including Josiah.

Practical as well as pious, Ogden fretted during the late summer of 1733 when continuous rains flooded his fields and threatened his wheat, already cut and on the verge of rotting in the muddy earth. Thus, when a warm sun broke through on a Sunday morning and dried his grain, the colonel led his family and his workers into the field and harvested his golden crop. Horrified Presbyterians on the way to meeting could scarcely credit their eyes: Josiah Ogden, harvesting on Sunday!

Church fathers tried Ogden for violating the Lord's Day and rebuked him publicly, a move he deeply resented. Worried Newark elders appealed to the Presbyterian Synod in Philadelphia for support but had their decision reversed. That vindicated Ogden officially, but the harshness of the church trial and the severity of the public rebuke made Ogden feel he had no alternative except to leave the church.

Ogden became a center of controversy. Friend opposed friend, churchman quarreled with churchman, neighbors and relatives took sides. The self-contained, agreeable village was no more. Church dropouts formed a new congregation based on Episcopal principles. They held meetings for at least a decade before being

chartered as Trinity Church in 1746. Trinity's founders insisted on part of the town's public lands for their church, correctly arguing that they were as much descendants of the original settlers as were members of the Presbyterian Church.

Each church appointed members to a committee to work out an agreement. Trinity received a half acre of property at the northern end of the training ground. The church has stood there, to this day.

Work began immediately on the new church. Nearby, stone masons and carpenters began to raise a parsonage on a 4½-acre lot east of the training ground donated by Colonel Peter Schuyler. Funds evaporated quickly; in 1748, the New York *Gazette* announced a lottery "scheme" to raise £337, for Trinity. Three thousand tickets, were offered for fifteen shillings each, with 678 tickets guaranteed to be winners.

Lotteries were common at the time: Trinity's use of one did not indicate any new-found liberality by church members. Up went the stone church, its dimensions of sixty-three-by-forty-five-feet making it much larger than the Presbyterian Church, but inside its straight-backed pews were just as uncomfortable. The ninety-five-foot white steeple dominated the village green and gave Newark an authentic "New England look" in somewhat ironic memory of the town's beginnings.

48

Chapter 6

PURITANISM LINGERS ON

N EWARK'S OFFICIAL ACTIVITY in the first seven decades is relatively easy to discover in the town records: fortunately the Puritan fathers and their sons believed in keeping track of public doings. But little can be found on their private lives, possibly because of losses in the ruinous fire of the Revolution. There are few letters and no diaries. They left neither sketches nor portraits. Not even the plans of their meeting houses have been found.

The Puritans believed in order and in fair sharing of work and taxes, with the richest giving the most in time or money. They carefully allocated land by lot, a seeming contradiction for a people who flatly forbade card playing and dice rolling—but the Scriptures revealed that lots were drawn in Biblical times, and the Scriptures ruled their lives.

They faithfully kept Sunday as a day of rest and contemplation, beginning their Sabbath on Saturday night and continuing through until the sun, or the drummer boy, called them to

Candle making, an art and a vital task, occupied women in the fall, when men were harvesting. (From The Growth of Industrial Art, *1892.)*

Here Lyes ye Body of Samuel Nesbitt Aged 36 years Decd March ye 12th 1732/3

A few worked for others and turned a tidy shilling in the bargain. These included the cider makers; it is recorded that in 1700 "the town of Newark alone in one year made ready a thousand barrels of good cyder out of the orchards of their own planting." Probably some

Tombstones in the Old Burying Ground told a sad story. For every one attaining old age,

work on Monday morning. That Puritan habit persisted when Trinity Church broke away; it remained strong for at least another century and a half and ran through Newark history for at least six generations.

Some of Newark's original settlers lived to see the sorrow of schism. Deacon Azariah Crane, son of the redoubtable Jasper, died in 1730 in his eighty-third year. Three years later, dignified, staid Joseph Johnson died at a similarly ripe old age, and scarcely a man remembered him as young Joe Johnson, Newark's first drummer boy. For every long life, however, the graveyard was strewn with scores of brown sandstone markers that covered the bodies of infants, mothers taken in childbirth and young men and women stricken in their twenties and thirties.

Probably not more than 700 or 800 people lived in the village of Newark in the 1730s. Villagers existed much as their forebears had. They wore simple homespun or leather clothing; made their own candles and soap, fashioned their own tools, tended their flocks, hoed their gardens and found their way quickly to bed at nightfall, weary but pleased with another day's toil. If they were not pleased with work, then generations of descendants who have written about them have been misinformed.

Toil meant tilling the fields with crude wooden plows drawn by lumbering oxen; driving cattle to the meadows in the morning and back at sunset; laboring through ankle-deep mud in the streets in times of extended rains; planting and tending the apple orchards. Toil meant the harvest season, when the whole family labored lest rain, drought or cold ruin the precious crops.

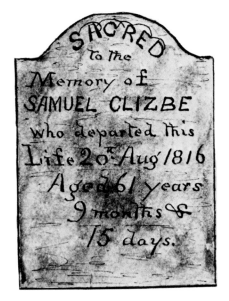

SACRED to the Memory of SAMUEL CLIZBE who departed this Life 20th Aug 1816 Aged 61 years 9 months & 15 days.

of Newark's apple juice either aged into hard cider or was distilled into apple brandy or whiskey.

Others became tanners, and by 1730 they had settled by the "watering place" in Market Street. Millers continued to grind corn for the surrounding environs; builders now specialized in raising houses; stone cutters labored in the quarries that opened about 1720 along the north end of High Street, near the Branch Brook.

Although their religion made all people equal

In Memory of Sally Ann Daur of John & Catharine Roger's died July 20 1805 Aged 1 Year 11 Months & 21 Days

. . . the graveyard had a dozen whose deaths came before they had a chance

before God, an aristocracy developed. At the top was the minister and a few gentlemen; the term "Mr." was reserved for such elite. Then followed the merchants and skilled artisans. Church leaders came from the gentlemen, civic leaders from the artisans—although in a town as compact as Newark the lines were blurred. Sundays revealed status: worshippers were carefully assigned seats according to seniority or position.

Some had wealth for the time, perhaps as much as £1,000 by 1730, and ministers generally stood near the top in personal holdings as well as in prestige. The desire for a compact town lessened the opportunity of amassing a great fortune; it took land out of speculation and prevented the rise of a powerful landed gentry as in New York. The climate had an effect, too: there was no possibility of growing such plantation crops as cotton or tobacco and thus no need for many slaves. Skilled artisans were respected.

They gravitated to this town where they were needed, starting the tradition of capable workmen that one day would enable Newark to attain industrial greatness.

Life revolved around the meeting house, center of government, religion, education and social activities. Worshippers sat in discomfort, listening to torturous sermons condemning them as sinners. They heard that they were doomed by original sin, made worse by human depravity, and dependent solely on God's will for salvation. If a worshipper worried greatly about his worthlessness, it was considered an excellent sign of his piety.

One bright spot was the singing of hymns from the Bay Psalm Book. Since the book gave only the words, the deacon set the musical tone. The result was dismal, at best. A New England source says that any Puritan congregation sounded "like 500 different tunes roared out at the same time," often one or two words apart.

By 1700, Newark "made ready a thousand barrels of good cyder."

Leather was Newark's prime industry from the start. Tanners congregated at the "watering place" near present day Market and Washington Streets to clean their hides and to tan them in vats close to the clear stream.

One delightful story about a near-sighted New England deacon bears retelling, since it could have happened in Newark, or wherever Puritans gathered to sing Psalms.

Failing to make out the first line, the deacon loudly told the congregation, "My eyes, indeed, are very blind."

Faithfully the congregation sang, "My eyes, indeed, are very blind."

The confused deacon exclaimed, "I can not see at all" and the congregation repeated, word for word. "You are bewitched!" accused the deacon. "You are bewitched!" came back the words.

The deacon let out one last shout: "The mischief's in you all!" When the roar came back, "The mischief's in you all!" he sat down and so did the congregation, satisfied that it had performed well.

Although its religious tone remained firm, Newark experienced physical change as prosperity increased. Most of the crude huts of 1670 had disappeared by 1730, either swallowed up in enlargements forced by growing families or torn down and replaced by substantial wooden or stone houses fronting on Broad Street.

Comparative luxury is discerned in a New York *Gazette* advertisement for June 7, 1731, in which one Dr. Schutte offered "a good new stone house, with a lot of six acres of upland and six acres of meadows." The property included five acres of "good bearing young orchard," and as proof of Dr. Schutte's awareness of the medicinal values of alcoholic drink, also featured "a distilling house, with stills, and all conveniences ready for distilling of strong liquors, and especially of syder." As further inducement, the doctor offered instruction "in the art of distilling."

Three years later, the Presbyterians built a handsome stone parsonage on Broad Street, south of the church. It loomed two-and-one-half stories high, with walls two feet thick. Substantial rooms lay to either side of an eight-foot-wide entrance hall that ran to a broad rear piazza overlooking the back lawn. Since congregations tended to grant ministers domiciles less substantial than their own, it must be assumed that the new parsonage was neither unusually large nor comfortable for the Newark of 1734—but by any standard it was a fine home.

Along with such affluence, however, went a rise in poverty, a condition unknown in the halcyon days of 1666. The first attention was paid "the poor" in the early 1690s and by 1700 an overseer of the poor was appointed as regularly as was the keeper of the pound. Then in 1736 the town found a capital means of providing for the poor: it sold "the feed (the hay) from the burying place" for support of the destitute. James Banks, an inn keeper, successfully bid forty shillings for the hay the first year. Seven years later, Isaac Lyon got the hay for eighteen shillings less than Banks paid.

Townsmen conceived another means of raising welfare funds in 1743. Anyone caught cutting "trees, spires or hoop poles" on any of the several parsonage lots without permission faced a fine of twenty shillings—half to go to the informer, half to the poor.

Handsome buildings and higher living standards created a demand for servants, including black slaves. The first families had brought some servants from Connecticut, probably indentured young people with close spiritual or family ties to the founders. When the first blacks arrived is not known but Newark had a few slaves by the 1730s. Most of them lived on the large plantations across the Passaic River, where the Schuyler copper mine operated.

There was no conflict between slavery and Biblical insistence on brotherhood as far as Puritans were concerned. On August 25, 1746, the New York *Evening Post* advertised that

The Plume House, built in 1710, still stands near the Erie-Lackawanna Railroad station. Probably Newark's oldest structure, it is now the House of Prayer rectory. Homer Hill has drawn it in colonial setting.

Joseph Johnson of Newark planned to sell "at publick vendue . . . two Negro men, whome understands mining,"

Slaves chafed under their servitude and some fled their Newark masters as the years rolled on. Emanuel Cocker advertised in the New York *Gazette* of November 28, 1748, for "Charles, aged about 35 years, and speaks broken English." When he fled, Charles wore "a red jacket with white metal buttons, an old felt hat, a new tow shirt and old trowsers." Cocker offered a reward of £3 "and all reasonable charges."

Another fugitive, in 1750, also wore a red coat but took a gun from his master. He was described in advertisements simply as "a Negro with a long face, strait nose, of a middle stature." After that, infrequent announcements of local runaway slaves (indicating that few dwelled in Newark) appeared in New York newspapers.

Crime raised its ugly head, too. John Barnes, alias John Greenwood, alias John Thompson, alias George Brown, robbed Thomas Baily's house three times in 1738 and was sentenced to die in Newark's first public execution. Barnes detailed his life of crime for the Pennsylvania *Gazette* before he climbed the steps of the crude wooden gallows outside the court house on November 17, 1738. His fall from grace began, Barnes said, when he stole a red coat while

Industry was a cardinal virtue, since existence itself depended on everyone's working—father, mother and all the children.

serving His Majesty's army in England; it continued through scores of thefts of everything from horses to clothing, from sheep to silver tankards. Barnes hoped that "all people will take warning by me."

Barnes' execution provided gruesome entertainment as well as an awesome lesson, for in the 1730s a hanging attracted crowds from all the countryside. A family might watch a hanging and remember it forever, presumably "taking warning" as well as experiencing the cold chills of excitement.

Excitement of any kind came seldom enough and when it did had to be savored fully. Generally the big event might be oxen stuck in the mud of Broad Street or the broad-bottomed periaugers being loaded with iron or cider at the town dock. The return of that vessel from New York, with a few spices, a bolt of calico or genuine West Indies molasses, was a topic of conversation for days.

Children lived in strict conformity to church doctrines. The life of a Puritan boy of that time was related in a biography of John Brainerd, a great missionary who labored long among New Jersey's Indians. Young Brainerd grew up in Connecticut, but his training was similar to that of a Newark child. According to the biography:

"A boy was early taught a profound respect for his parents, teachers, and guardians, and implicit, prompt obedience. If he undertook to rebel, 'his will was broken' by persistent and adequate punishment. He was accustomed every morning and evening to bow at the family altar; and the Bible was his ordinary reading-book in school. He was never allowed to close his eyes in sleep without prayer on his pillow.

"At a sufficient age, no caprice, slight illness, nor any condition of roads or weather was allowed to detain him from church. In the sanctuary he was required to be grave, strictly attentive, and able on his return at least to give the text. From sun-down Saturday evening until the Sabbath sunset his sports were all suspended, and all secular reading laid aside; while the *Bible, New-England Primer*, Bunyan's *Pilgrim's Progress*, Baxter's *Saints' Rest*, &c., were commended to his ready attention and cheerfully pored over.

"He was taught that his blessings were abundant and undeserved, his evils relatively few and merited, and that he was not only bound to contentment, but gratitude. He was taught that time was a talent to be always improved; that industry was a cardinal virtue, and laziness the worst form of original sin. Hence he must rise early, and make himself useful before he went to school; must be diligent there in study, and be promptly home to do 'chores' at evening. His whole time out of school must be filled up by some service—such as bringing in fuel for the day, cutting potatoes for the sheep, feeding the swine, watering the horses, picking the berries, gathering the vegetables, spooling the yarn, and running all errands. He was expected never to be reluctant, and not often tired.

"He was taught that it was a sin to find fault with his meals, his apparel, his tasks, or his lot in life. Labor he was not allowed to regard as a burden, nor abstinence from any improper indulgence as a hardship.

"His clothes, woolen and linen, for summer and winter, were mostly spun, woven, and made up by his mother and sisters at home; and, as he saw the whole laborious process of their fabrication, he was jubilant and grateful for two suits, with bright buttons, a year. Rents were carefully closed and holes patched in the 'everyday' dress, and the Sabbath dress always kept new and fresh.

"He was expected early to have the 'stops and marks,' the 'abbreviations,' the 'multiplication table,' the 'ten commandments,' the 'Lord's Prayer,' and the 'Shorter Catechism,' at his tongue's end.

"Courtesy was enjoined as a duty. He must be silent among his superiors. If addressed by older persons, he must respond with a bow. He was to bow as he entered and left the school, and bow to every man or woman, old or young, rich or poor, black or white, whom he met on the road. Special punishment was visited on him if he failed to show respect to the aged, the poor, the colored, or to any persons whatever whom God had visited with infirmities. He was thus taught to stand in awe of the rights of humanity.

"Honesty was urged as a religious duty, and unpaid debts were represented as infamy. He was allowed to be sharp at a bargain, to shudder at dependence, but still to prefer poverty to deception or fraud. His industry was not urged by poverty, but by duty. Those who imposed upon him early responsibility and restraint led the way by their example, and commended this example by the prosperity of their fortunes and the respectability of their position as the result of these virtues. He felt that they governed and restrained him for his good, and not their own."

It was not all sanctity and work. There is as well a touch of nostalgia in Brainerd's final details of that Puritan upbringing:

"He learned to identify himself with the interests he was set to promote. He claimed every acre of his father's ample farm, and every horse and ox and cow and sheep became constructively his, and he had a name for each. The waving harvests, and garnered sheaves, the gathered fruits, were all his own. And besides these, he had his individual treasures. He knew every trout-hole in the streams; he was great in building dams, snaring rabbits, trapping squirrels, and gathering chestnuts and walnuts for winter store. Days of election, training, thanksgiving, and school-intermissions, were bright spots in his life. His long winter evenings, made cheerful by sparkling fires within and cold clear skies and ice-crusted plains and frozen streams for his sled and skates, were full of enjoyment. And then he was loved by those whom he could respect, and cheered by that future for which he was being prepared."

If that sounded idyllic, whether in Connecticut or Newark, it indicated that the Puritan, while assured of man's basic depravity, was not so ascetic that he overlooked the wonders of nature. It also showed that to be young, in any era, was usually enough.

Chapter 7

COLLEGE TOWN

Late in 1736, a twenty-year-old minister named Aaron Burr rode out of the Morris County wilds of Hanover for a preaching engagement at Newark's First Church. He had none of the look of the leader. His thin, fair cheeks bore little more than fuzz and his dark eyes were soft rather than commanding. His short, slender figure scarcely attracted attention —but here was a man for the times.

Youngest of six sons in a Fairfield, Connecticut, family, young Burr went through Yale College with academic distinction, graduating in 1735 at the age of nineteen. During the summer of 1736, he wrote, a religious revival in New Haven made God "open my eyes." He was granted a preaching license that September and soon after came to New Jersey to preach in Hanover's village church.

The First Church congregation, split by the troubles with the Episcopalians, heard of the pulpit eloquence of young Burr, and shortly before Christmas, 1736, asked him to preach in Newark on trial.

Mr. Burr revealed serious doubts about the engagement in his journal:

"***there was scarcely any probability that I should suit the circumstances, being young in standing and trials. I accepted the invitation with a reserve that I did not come with any views of settling."

Mr. Burr's preaching skill and shining intellect made church elders forget his lack of years. They installed him as permanent minister on January 25, 1737, just twenty-one days after his twenty-first birthday.

Sweeping through the Middle Atlantic colonies at that time was a religious fire that has been called "The Great Awakening." Itinerant evangelists rode through the colonies, fervently beseeching audiences to seek God. It was not enough to attend church, they warned; to win salvation, man must commit himself without reservation. He must sense a deep personal experience with God. The "Awakening" divided Presbyterians into the so-called "New Lights" who supported such evangelism and the "Old Lights" who were in opposition.

Presbyterian New Lights rallied behind the Rev. George Whitefield, a remarkable English missionary who traveled through the colonies in 1740, setting town after town aflame with his zeal and his skill in exciting throngs of people.

The Rev. Aaron Burr Sr., pastor of Old First Church from 1737 to 1755 and a founder of the College of New Jersey, the forerunner of Princeton University. He supervised the college in Newark from 1747 until its removal to Princeton in 1756. Burr won fame among all colonial leaders.

Many people dated their "birth" to the day that Mr. Whitefield sent the thrill of fervent religious feeling through their minds.

Mr. Whitefield journeyed from Staten Island to Newark in November, 1740, to preach in Mr. Burr's church. The English missionary struck solidly, recalling in his diary that "the word fell like a hammer and like fire! What a weeping was there! One poor creature in particular was ready to sink into the earth." The ordeal so exhausted Mr. Whitefield that he took to bed.

Newark and Elizabethtown became two main stops on the crusaders' road, and Mr. Burr bluntly refused a sinner "the peace of God until the rebel laid down his arms, and returned to allegiance."

The Newark minister and his Elizabethtown counterpart, the Rev. Jonathan Dickinson, supported a growing demand for a college in the Middle Atlantic colonies to prepare Presbyterian ministers for service in America and to promote the evangelical cause. Harvard and Yale, both distant from New Jersey by colonial travel standards, were also opposed to the radical evangelical spirit manifested by Whitefield and others. Neither could please the New Lights. Mr. Burr and Mr. Dickinson needed a cause on which to pinpoint their efforts.

The opportunity came when the Puritanical Old Light administration of Yale College decided to make an example of David Brainerd, a third-year student and brother of John, a missionary among New Jersey Indians. David

Old Burying Ground markers, now preserved in Fairmount Cemetery crypt.

remarked to a classmate that a certain instructor had "no more grace than a chair." An eavesdropper reported the indiscretion, and when it was learned that evangelical-minded Brainerd also occasionally attended services at a church of different faith, the faculty expelled him.

Such drastic punishment scarcely fit Brainerd's minor crime, but it gave the New Lights a hero. After leaving Yale to serve as a missionary among the Indians along the Delaware River,

he came to Newark on June 12, 1744, to be ordained in a ceremony impressive far beyond that usually accorded a new minister.

Three of Brainerd's most outspoken admirers were Mr. Burr, Mr. Dickinson and the Rev. Jonathan Edwards, the famed Massachusetts preacher. The incident at Yale College reinforced the resolve that a new American college must be founded to train ministers in evangelical Presbyterianism. The College of New Jersey

Here Lyes ye Body of Thoms Ball. Decd Octr ye 18. 1744. in ye 57 year of his Age.

Here Lyes an Aged man of 4 years old Beloved Wife and Children dear Remember now I am gone.

Many Newarkers, like people in other colonies, dated their rebirth to the early 1740s, when missionary spirit swept through the land. Old First Church member Thomas Ball died in 1744, but his tombstone said he was "an aged man of four years old" since being born again.

was the result.

Governor John Hamilton granted the College of New Jersey its charter on October 22, 1746, and classes began in Mr. Dickinson's Elizabethtown parlor the following May. When Mr. Dickinson died within four months, Mr. Burr invited the eight college students to Newark to finish the first year. He found rooms for them in nearby homes and strove to set the bereft college on a firm footing. Mr. Burr divided his time between the church, a private school that he had started in 1746, and college classes in the court room above the county jail on Broad Street.

A second college class entered in May, 1748, after passing examinations that called on them "to render Virgil and Tully's orations into English, turn English into true and grammatical Latin, be so well acquainted with the Greek as to render any part of the four Evangelists in that language into Latin or English and to give the grammatical connexion of the words."

Governor Jonathan Belcher received an honorary degree at the first commencement in Newark on November 9, 1748, staying overnight in the big parsonage where the minister lived alone. The trustees met at the parsonage early in the morning and elected Mr. Burr president of the College of New Jersey.

The six members of the graduating class waited restlessly for exercises to begin, as well they might, for they had earned their diplomas six months before but were forced to wait until King George II signed a new charter and forwarded it to New Jersey for presentation by Governor Belcher.

When the dignitaries emerged from the Burr mansion, the academic procession marched up Broad Street to a marathon commencement in the church. President Burr prayed at length and ordered the assembly to stand up through the long reading of the charter. According to a correspondent of the New York *Gazette,* "The morning being spent, the President signified to

Seal of the College of New Jersey.

Page from Mr. Burr's college account book, showing Newark entries. (Courtesy Princeton University Library).

the assembly that the succeeding acts would be deferred till two o'clock in the afternoon."

That afternoon Mr. Burr opened with a forty-five-minute oration in Latin, declaring his own unworthiness and extolling the virtues of European education in comparison with the ignorance of "the brutish savages of America." Students then spiritedly discussed—in Latin—such questions as "Whether the Liberty of acting according to the Dictates of Conscience, in matters merely religious, ought to be restrained by any human power!" They concluded that liberty ought not to be restrained.

Eventually the president asked the trustees, again in Latin, whether these "young men who had performed the public exercises in disputation, should be admitted to the Degree of Bachelor of arts?" The trustees said aye, and up stepped the happy six: Richard Stockton, Enos Eyres, Benjamin Chestnut, Hugo Henry, Israel Reed and Daniel Thane. All but Stockton became ministers. This scion of a distinguished Princeton family became a lawyer and in 1776 was one of New Jersey's five signers of the Declaration of Independence.

Newark's collegians lived in the parsonage with Mr. Burr or boarded with nearby residents. Their rooms were starkly furnished—a single bed, a chair or two, a plain table for a candle, ink, quill and paper, and a plain chest to hold the few clothes that the young men brought with them. A small shelf held their Latin and Greek lexicons, the Bible and other college texts.

Each day began and ended with prayer, and absence from services at the Presbyterian meeting house on Sundays meant an automatic fine of four pence. Expulsion faced any student so wicked as to "frequent a tavern," to play "cards or dice or any other unlawful game" or to "keep company with persons of known scandalous lives." All of that was spelled out in the rigid college rules.

President Burr did encourage innocent merriment, within limited bounds. When Ezra Stiles visited Newark in 1754, "two young gentlemen of the college acted Tamerlane and Bajazet, etc.," in what must have been Newark's first theatrical performance. That was the extent of undergraduate divertissement; even a trip out of town without permission made a student liable for a five shilling fine.

The president was all things to all students, "beloved as a friend and, like a father, revered and honored," in the words of a 1754 account. He was president, professor, secretary, librarian, purchasing agent and dispenser of funds. His old account book, preserved at Princeton University, includes charges for everything from a copy of Watts' *Logic* to shoes, from tuition to board and from firewood to "books from Boston."

Mr. Burr was college president only when he was not minister of the Newark Presbyterian Church. He held the twin duties for eight years before resigning as pastor in 1755. During his ministry he secured a provincial charter from Governor Belcher on June 7, 1753, for "The First Presbyterian Church," the name that the church still bears.

Mr. Burr electrified the town and college in June, 1752, with an apparently sudden decision to marry. His choice was Miss Esther Edwards, third daughter of Jonathan Edwards, fiery-tongued Massachusetts preacher. Mr. Burr had met Miss Edwards in 1746, when she had barely entered her teens. Six years passed—but let youthful college student John Shippen report that courtship and wedding, as he did in a tart letter to his father on July 6, 1752:

"The best piece of news I have now to furnish you with, is the marriage of our President. As this must come very unexpected to you, I shall give you an account of his proceedings as brief as they were themselves.

"In the latter end of May, he took a journey into New England, and during his absence he made a visit of but three days to the Rev. Mr. Edward's daughter, at Stockbridge; in which short time, though he had no acquaintance with, nor indeed ever saw the lady these six years, I suppose he accomplished the whole design; for it was not above a fortnight after his return here, before he sent a young fellow who came out of college last fall into New England, to conduct her and her mother down here.

"They came to town on Saturday evening, the 27th inst., and on Monday evening following, the nuptial ceremonies were celebrated between Mr. Burr and the young lady. As I have yet no manner of acquaintaince with her, I cannot describe to you her qualifications and properties; however they say she is a very valuable lady.

"I think her a person of great beauty, though I must say that in my opinion she is rather young (being only twenty-one years of age) for the President. This account you'll doubtless communicate to Mammy as I learn she has Mr. Burr's happiness much at heart."

In a postscript, Shippen remarked that the college president was thirty-six years old. He erred in Miss Edwards' age; she was in fact only nineteen. A few weeks later, Shippen wrote his father: "I can't omit acquainting you that our President enjoys all the happiness the married state can afford."

The Burrs lived happily in their parsonage. Two children, Sally and Aaron Burr Jr., were born there. When her son was thirteen months

old, Mrs. Burr wrote in hasty judgment and with what seems too much candor for a mother:

"Aaron is a little, dirty, noisy dog, very different from Sally, almost in every thing. He begins to talk a little, is very sly and mischievous. He has more sprightliness than Sally, and most say he is handsomer, but not so good tempered. He is very resolute and requires a good governor to bring him to terms."

That thirteen-month-old rascal grew up to graduate from the College of New Jersey in 1772 with distinction, to serve honorably in the Revolution and to become Vice President of the United States under Thomas Jefferson. He killed Alexander Hamilton in a duel at Weehawken in 1804 and his career went into a decline, but Aaron Burr Jr., born in a Broad Street parsonage, etched his name indelibly in American history.

Church parsonage where Burrs lived.

Aaron Burr, Jr., born in Broad Street home, was one of Newark's most distinguished native sons. He was graduated from the College of New Jersey with good standing, served honorably in the Revolution and achieved national acclaim in the founding years of America. He met Alexander Hamilton in a duel at Weehawken in 1804, fatally wounding him, and became a fugitive. Young Burr and his sister were orphaned when both parents died in 1757, only a short time after the college moved from Newark to Princeton.

Meanwhile, his father, President Burr, realized that the College of New Jersey could not remain in Newark. Trustees hoped for a more central location, close to Philadelphia and the South. Mr. Burr had removed the second commencement to New Brunswick in September, 1749, possibly hoping that leading New Light leaders there might relocate the college on the banks of the Raritan River. In 1750, college trustees set forth what they required as inducement to settle down: a bond of £1,000, ten acres of cleared ground and 200 acres of woodland. Newark did not respond at all and New Brunswick offended trustees by dallying—for the Raritan was their first choice. Princeton met conditions in 1753.

The College of New Jersey started to build

Connecticut permitted a lottery in 1753 for the college, while it was still in Newark. (Princeton University Library).

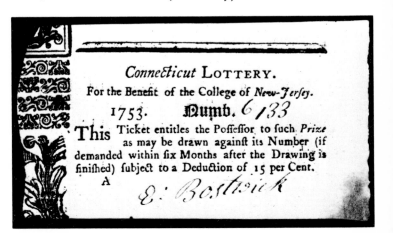

Connecticut LOTTERY.
For the Benefit of the College of *New-Jersey.*
1753. Numb. 6133
This Ticket entitles the Possessor to such *Prize* as may be drawn against its Number (if demanded within six Months after the Drawing is finished) subject to a Deduction of 15 per Cent.
A
E. Bostwick

When trustees of the College of New Jersey finished their Nassau Hall at Princeton in 1756, it was acclaimed throughout the colonies for its size and elegance. This famed Dawkins engraving of 1764 shows Nassau Hall and the president's House. (Library of Congress).

its new home at Princeton in 1753, boasting that it would have "the largest stone building in all the colonies." The trustees asked Governor Belcher's permission to call the structure "Belcher Hall;" he insisted on Nassau Hall, after William III, Prince of Orange-Nassau.

Mr. and Mrs. Burr took their two children, seventy students and the meager effects of the college out of Newark and down to Princeton in November, 1756. "Two large boxes of books" and other items were shipped by water to New Brunswick, then carried overland. Newark lost completely its colonial college tradition; within Princeton grew the college born in Elizabethtown, nurtured through toddling years in Newark, and reared to a maturity as Princeton University.

Newark turned its thoughts elsewhere, but mourned when word came in September, 1757, that Aaron Burr had died in Princeton at the age of 41.

"The fatigue that I have had in the care of

the college this winter has been greater than ever," Burr wrote in February, 1757. Summer found him worn out and ill from multiple college duties and unfit for a series of visits and sermons that he had to make. Late in the summer he undertook an exhausting trip to Philadelphia, returning to Princeton a very sick man racked with fever. When Governor Belcher died suddenly on August 31, Mr. Burr saddled his horse and rode to Elizabeth to preach the funeral oration. That was the last drain on his ebbing strength. Mr. Burr died on September 24, 1757. A few months later, young Mrs. Burr joined her husband in the Princeton cemetery, leaving her two young children.

Only twenty-one years had elapsed between Mr. Burr's coming to Newark and his death in Princeton. His brilliance in the pulpit had made the Newark church stronger than ever— but fully withdrawn from civil affairs. Just in time, too: Newark, and all the colonies, had far more momentous events to face.

Chapter 8
ROAD TO REBELLION

Rebellious Essex County farmers and tradesmen continued to invoke the name of the King. But despite their protestations of loyalty, when they rioted against the East New Jersey Proprietors in the 1740s, they struck at the very foundations of His Majesty's strength in the New World. Their defiance was as real and ugly as that of the rebels who would dump the tea into Boston Harbor two decades later.

Ill feeling against the Proprietors could be traced back to 1670 when Berkeley and Carteret claimed rents due them under the terms of the grant giving them all New Jersey land. The colonists displayed extreme displeasure at that time. Later, in 1700, mobs openly defied the Proprietors, their agents and the King's men and forced the Proprietors to surrender their right to govern.

Now the Proprietors once again had decided to exercise their real estate claims. They had become a large board of powerful men, and in 1744 they assigned three of their number—James Alexander, Robert Hunter Morris and David Ogden—to investigate an area called "Horseneck" in western Essex County. Then part of Newark, the area today embraces the Caldwells, Roseland and Livingston.

Ogden, the only Newarker of the trio, was the son of Josiah Ogden, who had founded Trinity Church after the Presbyterians had persecuted him for working on Sunday. When an open break would come with Great Britain in 1776, most members of the Episcopal Church would remain loyal to King George, and David Ogden would join them.

But in 1745 the matter of splitting with the King was not at issue. Alexander, Morris and Ogden wanted only to convince the back country dwellers that the Proprietors—not the settlers who were building the homes and tilling the soil—owned the land.

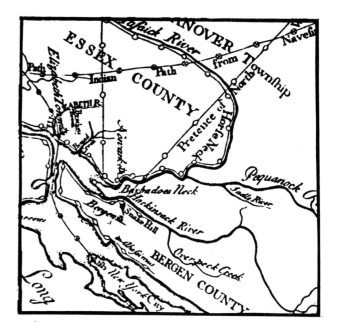

The story of New Jersey's Proprietors began in 1664 when the province was given to Lord Berkeley and Sir George Carteret. The former sold his share in 1673 and Carteret's holdings were sold after he died in 1680. Boards of the West and East New Jersey proprietors eventually included many men whose chief interest was real estate. Governing powers were taken away in 1702. Squatters were at first ignored or tolerated, but as land grew valuable, pressure for rents increased, leading to the Horseneck riots and other clashes. The above is a section of large map drawn in the 1740s for use by the Proprietors in major court action against the alleged squatters.

Those who lived in the "Horseneck Purchase" based their rights on a negotiation with Indians in 1702. They maintained that they could show a deed from the Indians, but by curious coincidence, their purported Indian deed disappeared in a fire that destroyed the Horseneck home of

Artist Homer Hill imagined the scene on Sunday morning, September 19, 1745, when an angry mob stormed the Newark jail, broke down the door and released Samuel Baldwin, who was charged with illegally cutting wood. The September riot inaugurated a long period of anti-Proprietor dissent.

one John Pierson at the time that the Proprietors pressed their suit. Pierson was a great-grandson of Newark's first minister. Nearly all his neighbors were descendants of Newark's earliest settlers.

Alexander, Morris and Ogden began serving eviction notices in the summer of 1745. Then, in early September, they discovered Samuel Baldwin at work in the Horseneck woods, "making great havock with his saw mill of the best timber thereon." They insisted that he was trespassing, but Baldwin countered that the Indian deed was his ticket to the woodlot.

The outraged Proprietors arrested him. Baldwin refused an offer by neighbors to pay his bail, saying that the Proprietors intended to ruin the settlers with expensive law suits. The

woodchopper of Horseneck trudged down the mountain to a cell in the Essex County jail on Broad Street and there he stayed peaceably until Sunday, September 19.

Newark, a sullen, uneasy town after church services that Sabbath, exploded in mid-afternoon when a band of 150 men (according to the sheriff's account) flooded into town armed with clubs, axes and crowbars. They brushed aside the sheriff, broke open the jail door and freed Baldwin, without the nicety of bail. The mob paused only long enough to warn the sheriff that if anyone should be arrested for the caper, they would return "with double the number of men," and might even bring a hundred Indians to help.

Disorder spread to other towns, with the

name of Amos Roberts (or Robards) of Newark appearing often in official records or in the New York press. Roberts, "reverenced as much as if he had been a king," began his rise to power on a cold day in the January following Baldwin's jail break.

Despite the warnings of the Horseneck mob, the Essex sheriff arrested Nehemiah Baldwin, Robert Young and Thomas Sarjeant on January 15, 1745, and jailed them in Newark on charges of being ringleaders in the September riot. He ordered out the militia to guard the prison but not more than fifteen men showed up. Newarkers had little stomach for the task of fighting neighbors, brothers and cousins.

After an uneasy night, the sheriff ordered the militia to help bring the prisoners before a judge, but, as he later recalled, "most of them made frivolous pretenses, as that they had no horses, and could not go." Pleading, threatening, cajoling, the sheriff finally found six townsmen willing to help and off they started to the judge's home with Baldwin in their midst.

A howling throng surrounded the little band and released the prisoner. Undaunted, the sheriff raised a company of twenty-six militia men to take Young and Sarjeant before the judge. More than 200 people blocked the street when the law party left the jail at 2 P.M. The sheriff "asked the meaning of their meeting together in such a manner." They ignored the question, demanding the two prisoners.

Two judges stepped forward and ordered silence. The official report of the day said: "One of them read the Kings Proclamation***against riots and acquainted the people with the bad consequences of such proceedings."

The warning fell on deaf ears. The sheriff sent two captains of Newark militia among the throng, beating drums to call all local militia men to duty. Not one Newarker responded. The drum rolls sounded off the mountain tops, echoed in the valleys, and silence enveloped the Newark streets. Amos Roberts (or Robards) broke the tension with a yell: "Those who are upon my list follow me!" Most of the 300 men now assembled fell in behind his mount.

Within minutes Roberts' army surged forward against the thin rank of soldiers drawn up with firelocks at the ready. A massacre was

in the making, but the order to fire never sounded, for the advancing rioters were neighbors and friends, not an enemy. The mob beat the soldiers with clubs in unneighborly fashion then swarmed toward the beleaguered sheriff, standing alone before the jail door with drawn sword. He made a brave stand, but the crowd overwhelmed him, broke down the jail door and freed the prisoners.

Governor Lewis Morris hastily called the Assembly to consider the desperate situation in Newark. He warned legislators that "so open and avowed an attempt, in defiance of the government and contempt of the laws, if not high treason, makes so nigh an approach to it as seems but too likely to end in rebellion and throwing off His Majesty's authority."

Obviously the Newark riots held an ugly potential far beyond simple land disputes. Disorder spread—to Hunterdon County, to Somerset, to Perth Amboy. Amos Roberts led more than 150 mounted men into Perth Amboy in July, 1747, seeking a prisoner arrested in a Somerset County riot. The invaders attacked the Sheriff, causing a "grievous wound," struck the mayor, "broke one of the constables' head, beat several of the others," freed the prisoner and carried him off "huzzaing."

Roberts denied any intention of disloyalty. In a letter to the New York *Gazette* on January 23, 1749, the Newarker accused the Proprietors of causing "great disorders" and said they offended him by accusing him of treason. He offered a reward of £10 to any man who could prove him a traitor—but said he would continue to free men ejected from their lands. He concluded: "God bless the King that sits upon the British throne."

For all his declarations of loyalty, Roberts fitted the image of a revolutionist. By 1747 he had an illegal kingdom divided into wards, had appointed tax collectors, set up his own courts to settle disputes and organized his own militia. In the spring of 1748 his army threatened to "level Perth Amboy to the ground" and to drive authority "into the sea." That was as daring as anything said in America to that time and as bold as the talk that would later shake Virginia, Massachusetts and all the colonies.

The time for revolution had not yet ripened,

Peter Schuyler

and for the time, a split with Great Britain faded before the major threat that the homeland faced from the French. The possibility that the Continental power might unleash Indian tribes against the American colonies chilled the settlers. By 1755, the dread of Indian raids enveloped Sussex County, and people in the valley east of the Orange Mountains wondered when the savages would strike from the hillside forests. This was no time for a split with the King; the sight of his red coated soldiers was reassuring.

President Aaron Burr of the College of New Jersey spoke fiercely in Newark on New Year's Day, 1755, of the dangers facing the colonies.

He dwelled on France's "treacherous designs upon the British colonies in America." Burr called for "immediate, united and vigorous measures for repelling the insults of our enemies and defending our country and liberties."

Newarkers soon responded, particularly after a law was passed pardoning the Horseneck rioters. England called for 500 volunteers to march northward against the French. Records are vague on the numbers who actually enlisted from Newark, but the town took pride in Colonel Peter Schuyler, always spoken of in the contemporary New York press as being from Newark. Actually, he lived on the estate across the Passaic River near his father's copper mine.

Schuyler led a battalion of 500 men out of Newark in the summer of 1757 to garrison the frontier fort at Oswego, N. Y. The Marquis de Montcalm, French commander, overwhelmed the fort a year later and herded the Americans into prison at Montreal. Schuyler won temporary parole on condition that a French officer of equal rank be exchanged.

Newark prepared a hero's welcome, the first time the town had shed its normally stern reserve to cheer a public figure. Schuyler reached home on Sunday, November 20, and the next night Newarkers roared their pleasure. The New York *Mercury* told of a large bonfire and of houses illuminated the remainder of the evening in honor of Schuyler. Later, "the principal gentlemen of the town met together, where the loyal healths were drank."

When no French officer of colonel rank could be found in exchange, Schuyler dutifully rode back to Montreal to rejoin his men in prison. He spent thousands of dollars of his own money caring for them before all were released in August, 1758.

Despite earlier fears, no Indians swarmed into Essex County and no Frenchmen came by land or by sea. Schuyler took 1,000 men beyond Albany in 1759, led another regiment north in 1760 but was too ill in 1761 to make his annual spring trek to the land of the enemy. A year later, Newark's first military hero died of his sickness.

Peace came in 1763. There is no record of public expression of joy in Newark—no toasts, no firing of cannon, no official notices of thanksgiving. The war had been too remote and confusing for its cessation to be a momentous occasion in Newark in an era of slow communications.

The town rejoiced in other things, particularly in a commerce that was modestly but steadily growing. As early as 1751, John and Uzal Ogden had advertised "a choice assortment of European goods fit for the season" in their Newark store, and in 1759 a family competitor, Gabriel Ogden, offered "a great variety of goods imported in the ship Old Grace and the last vessels from England, to be sold very cheap for ready money." The advertisements appeared in New York papers. Newark had no newspaper, nor was there one in all of New Jersey at the time.

Newark failed to stir visitors to raptures. The Rev. Andrew Burnaby, vicar of Greenwich, England, visited the colonies in 1760 and scrupulously recorded his views. His journal showed that he could pay compliments elsewhere. He extolled New Brunswick for "the number of its beauties," declaring that the town—along with Philadelphia—had "the handsomest women that I saw in America."

When the vicar reached Newark on July 8 in "a small rain," he was impatient to hasten inland to see the mighty Passaic Falls. This is his fleeting impression of Newark:

"I came to a town called Newark, built in an irregular scattered manner, after the fashion of some of our villages in England, near two miles in length. It has a church erected in the Gothic taste with a spire, the first that I had seen in America; and some other inconsiderable public buildings."

That is all. Except for the Trinity Church steeple he saw nothing noteworthy. The square old sandstone Presbyterian Church, while stout and spacious, had no architectural distinction. The county courthouse and riot-scarred jail were not worth noting.

Geographically, Newark was the end of nowhere. The principal pathways between New York and Philadelphia ended at ferry slips in Elizabeth or Perth Amboy. Narrow, rutted roads from the Orange Mountains led only to the Passaic River, where the Mountain Society owned a dock and its own sloop. Population scarcely topped 800 and the only visitors were those hastening elsewhere. The splendid isolation that had pleased the Puritans of 1666 had become an aggravating bind.

Newark needed a road to the east, over the Passaic and Hackensack Rivers and over the marshlands to the ferry at Paulus Hook (later Jersey City). Thus townspeople in 1765 hailed the chartering of "a road from New-Ark to the publick road in the town of Bergen, leading to Paulus Hook." The charter called for ferries over the rivers.

The charter also promised a road "level and good," "very commodious for travelers" and

Enlarged portion of 1777 Faden map shows Newark as a road center.

giving "a short and easy access of a large country to the markets of the city of New York." They expected it to benefit "both to city and country." Nine Newark residents were empowered to raise funds for the road, forming what was probably the first highway corporation in America.

The new road over the rivers and through the marshland came into town over what is now Ferry Street. It connected in Newark with an extension of the Brunswick-Trenton and the Old York roads. For the first time travellers could pass over an all-land (and ferry) route from the Hudson River opposite New York to the Delaware River near Philadelphia. The value to Newark was obvious.

Enterprising Matthias Ward of Newark took advantage of the finished route. He started a stage line to Paulus Hook, prospered so much that he took on a partner, John Thompson, in 1768, and advertised "a new plan for a stage waggon." They prospered, sending off two stages, every day except Sunday, one starting westward from Paulus Hook, the other eastward from the Rising Sun Tavern in Newark. Ward and Thompson advertised trips morning and after-

noon, cautioning passengers to be prompt, "as the waggons must be very exact in meeting Capt. Brown's ferry" at the Hackensack River. Passengers were assured "they may depend (God willing) on constant attendance and good useage."

At least four rival stage lines came into Newark by 1772, their drivers whipping the horses in an effort to maintain the promised two-day trip between New York and Philadelphia. Abraham Skillman boasted that his "Flying Machine" could make it from Paulus Hook, through Newark, to Philadelphia in only a day and a half—plainly the boast of a braggart, his envious rivals insisted, but Skillman kept on schedule much of the time.

The old town picked up pace despite the endless grumbling that the roads to the back country were little better than cattle paths. Uplanders from Horseneck to Newton recognized that if wagons could travel over such paths, so could cattle, and in 1768 Newark established an annual "market or fair," where "horses, horn cattle, sheep or swine" could be bought and sold. Newark promoters correctly, if innocently, declared that the town's chief advantage was "its vicinity to New York."

the Passaic River docks and with their smart militia drilling on the green within shadow of Trinity Church.

Surely most of the drovers stopped by the fancy shops or took in the horse races before heading home. The racing, as well as the finery in the shops, had brought Newark a long way from its Puritan heritage. Horse racing began with a "great race" on September 9, 1767, for a purse of £30. Owners had to prove their animal's good breeding and deposit four dollars to enter a horse. "Common horses" also raced for a prize of a "fine saddle and a good beaver hat."

Thereafter Newark held a "publick market" or fair on the third Wednesday, Thursday and Friday of October. Nothing but livestock could be sold, "except it be for the sale of the products or manufactories of the country," a good bit of license. The town promised exhibitors and sellers "decorum and good order."

The market justly featured some "made in Newark" products by 1768. Ogdens, Laight & Company that year advertised that its Vesuvius Furnace in Newark made iron hollow ware, sold by James Abeel or Edward Laight, merchants, of New York. Abeel sold wherever he could; he advertised in an Albany paper that his hollow ware was "allowed by the best judges to be far preferable to any made in America."

The cattle drovers, pig tenders and iron buyers lingered a while to savor the wonders of Newark, now bearing the look of a lively town. It had two taverns, the *Rising Sun* and the *Eagle,* and ruggedly competitive stage lines. Newarkers were pleased with the increasing bustle down by

Newark shops gradually added luxury items. Garret Thibou in 1775 advertised fine cambric, Irish linen, worsted hose, plaited shoe buckles, ear rings, tea skimmers and other niceties that ladies might not even have mentioned in the town two decades before. Henry Remsen, a rival, showed off swanskin and rose blankets, felt hats, black and colored taffetas and China silk handkerchiefs, as further evidence that self-indulgence was not unknown.

Few travelers ventured across the ague-filled meadows or up into the cold hills—much less on a bone-shaking adventure over the Old York Road—without a pause at the *Eagle* or the *Rising Sun* for a glass of potent Newark cider. Increasingly the taverns were filled with strangers stopping by to exchange gossip picked up at inns from Boston to Charleston.

Plain, outspoken talk of civil war turned smoky tap rooms blue. Treason was brewing. Revolution—brother-against-brother, father-against-son, colony-against-King—was in the air.

*Essex County Court House mural by Francis D. Millett shows grand ju[ry]
boldly rebuking Chief Justice Smythe in Newark for his 1774 remar[ks]
scoffing at colonists for protesting against "imaginary tyranny."*

Chapter 9

"NO FAWNING SERVILITY"

F LEDGLING MINISTER Alexander Macwhorter
rode into Newark in 1759, filled with love
for the new bride who accompanied him and
with a natural hatred for the British. The Macwhorters settled themselves in the pleasant First
Presbyterian Church parsonage on Broad Street
and the 25-year-old minister began to prepare
for leadership among the town revolutionists.

Despising the British came easily to Alexander.
His father, Hugh Macwhorter, emigrated from

the North of Ireland in 1730 and bought the Delaware farm where Alexander was born in 1734. As a child, Alexander heard stories of atrocities inflicted on his ancestors in Ireland and Scotland by the government of King Charles I. Both of his maternal grandparents were hanged from a tree in their front yard by Charles' henchmen. His paternal grandmother was the only member of her family to survive another bloody raid by the King's men.

Newarkers warmed to their new pastor. Their own forebears had been forced to flee the homeland. Many townsmen also remembered Alexander Macwhorter as a rotund, bright student in the College of New Jersey when it held classes in a room above the Newark jail. He was graduated in Princeton in 1757, was licensed to preach in Freehold a year later and there met and married Mary Cumming in 1758.

As an open break with England neared, two camps gradually formed, centering on the Trinity-Presbyterian feud that had been simmering since 1733. When the Declaration of Independence came in 1776, most Presbyterians followed Mr. Macwhorter and other church leaders into the camp of rebellion. Essex County (then also including most of modern Union County) became the New Jersey center of anti-British sentiment. Members of Trinity's congregation generally remained loyal to the King.

Pastor, revolutionist, educator, booster of Newark. All those things describe the Rev. Alexander Macwhorter, who arrived in Newark in 1759 and remained until he died in 1807. He had to flee the town in 1776 before the British, then was present at Washington's council of war that planned the crossing of the Delaware to attack Trenton. His name is sometimes spelled MacWhorter, but he signed it Macwhorter. Not a brilliant preacher, Mr. Macwhorter nevertheless was so esteemed that he often preached at major funerals, including that of Governor William Livingston in 1790.

But the Stamp Act of 1765 tried everyone sorely. They stood together, Episcopalian and Presbyterian, lawyer and client, when His Majesty proposed to tax Americans by revenue stamps on all printed matter—from official documents to newspapers and playing cards. Newark had no newspaper of its own but it warmed to the dissent voiced in New York and Philadelphia papers.

Newarkers joined a throng in Elizabethtown on October 25, 1765, ostensibly to celebrate the fifth anniversary of "the happy accession of his present majesty, King George the Third, to the Throne of Great Britain." A reporter for the New York *Gazette* recognized that the monarch's laws, not his well being, brought the crowd together.

After dutifully saluting King George's health, the crowd got on with the real business. Spokesmen labelled the Stamp Act as an "overthrow of long-enjoyed, boasted and invaluable liberties." The *Gazette* said those present showed their intention to "detest, abhor and hold in the utmost contempt" any "Stamp pimp, informer, favourer and encourager of the execution of the said act."

News of Boston's tea party in December, 1773, evoked warm cheers along Broad Street, and England's hasty closing of the Boston port in March, 1774, gave those eager for rebellion a rallying point. War was near, although no one knew it yet.

Residents eagerly responded to a call in the New York *Journal* of June 9, 1774, for all Essex County "friends of liberty and property in America" to meet at the Newark Courthouse on June 11. One of the two signatures on the notice, that of John De Hart of Elizabethtown, was expected; his revolutionary tendencies were well known. Many eyebrows lifted, however, at the second signature—that of Isaac Ogden, son of David, the power in Trinity Church.

Years later, Isaac explained that he assumed leadership to "stop violent measures." He felt that a lawyer had to stay abreast of the American cause in order to prevent "others from running away with his business." Many fellow Episcopalian loyalists doubted his wisdom in 1774, and most of the revolutionaries questioned his sincerity.

The June meeting was bent on accepting Virginia's call for a Continental Congress. They opened, as usual, by pledging to "ever cheerfully render all due obedience to the Crown." That duty over, they ripped into Parliament for tampering with the rights of English colonists and cheered a resolution to ban purchases of British goods. Quick support was given to corresponding and consulting with other New Jersey counties during the emergency. The assemblage backed a proposal for a congress from all thirteen colonies to "form a general plan of union."

Hostility toward the mother country swelled. Chief Justice Frederick Smyth felt its fury in November, 1774, when he advised a Newark grand jury that protesting colonists were guarding against "imaginary tyranny, three thousand miles distant." He warned the jury that it ought to study "real tyranny at our own doors."

Grand jurors who once sat in awe of a king's judge, stiffly informed Smyth in an official reply: "***We cannot think, Sir, that taxes imposed upon us by our fellow subjects, in a legislature in which we are not represented, is imaginary, but that it is real and actual tyranny. We cannot think, Sir, that depriving us of the inestimable right of trial by jury—seizing our persons, and carrying us for trial to Great Britain, is a tyranny merely imaginary. Nor can we think with your Honor, that destroying charters, and changing our forms of government is a tyranny altogether ideal."

"***In a word, Sir, we cannot persuade ourselves that the fleet now blocking up the Port of Boston, consisting of ships built of real English oak and solid iron, and armed with cannon and ponderous metal, with actual powder and ball, nor the army lodging in the town of Boston, and the fortifications thrown about it are all creatures of the imagination."

The New York *Journal* carried the courtroom exchange in full and reported that it "heard" the chief justice made "a very complaisant and conciliating reply." Judge Smyth's soothing words, if any, have not been preserved. The grand jury's vow that "all honest Americans" would show "no fawning servility towards those in power" remains, clear enough for any one to interpret.

On the 19th of April, 1775, British troops marched out of Boston, headed west for the clashes on the Lexington Green and Concord Bridge. America at last had its image of Redcoats on the march; the dispatch rider who brought the news of the battle to Newark on April 23 was met on Broad Street with cheers.

Painting by Howard Pyle in Book of the American Spirit *portrayed thoughtful men debating the wisdom of rebellion.*

The next day a group of Newarkers declared themselves "willing at this alarming crisis to risk lives and fortunes in support of American liberty."

Militiamen began drilling in lively fashion. Jemima Condict, a lively young miss who lived on the west slope of First Mountain near Eagle Rock, put in her diary in the spring of 1775 a memento of young Americans preparing for battle on one of Newark Township's military greens:

"Monday, which was called Training Day, I rode with my dear father down to see them train, there being several companies met together. I thought it would be a mournful sight to see, if they had been fighting in earnest, & how soon they will be called forth to the field of war we cannot tell, for by what we hear the quarrels are not likely to be made up without blood shed. I have jest now heard say that all hopes of conciliation between Britten & her colonies are at an end, for both the King & his Parliament have announced our destruction; fleets and armies are preparing with utmost diligence for that purpose."

George Washington passed through Newark on June 25, headed for Massachusetts to take command of American forces. Rising early after

Stylized and familiar is this rough woodcut from Atkinson's History of Newark. *All the town turned out as Washington led his bedraggled army of 3,500 men down Broad Street on November 22, 1776.*

a night's lodging in New Brunswick, Washington reached Broad Street at about 9 A.M. Trotting ahead was the Philadelphia City Troop, clad in brown coats, light trousers, high boots and peaked helmets. Washington rode in a handsome phaeton drawn by a team of frisky horses. He tarried briefly for refreshments at the Eagle tavern, where Mr. Macwhorter greeted him warmly, then crossed the meadows to Hoboken.

Each day small bands of armed men hastened through Newark to join Washington near Boston. Some of Newark's militiamen joined them. Others went to do guard duty on Long Island. Early in December Mrs. Washington reached town, accompanied by "most of the principal gentlemen" of Elizabethtown. Newark bells "were set ringing and Col. Allan's company of minute men immediately mounted guard." The general's lady stayed overnight and next morn-

ing "a great number of ladies and gentlemen from Newark" accompanied her as far as Dow's Ferry on the Hackensack.

Anxiety mounted in mid-July when General William Howe sailed one hundred ships past Sandy Hook and landed his Redcoats on Staten Island. War was no longer simply a thing of far-off clashes of arms, of a leader riding north or of brave words in Philadelphia. The British were only a narrow body of water away. Sounds of rifle practice and the booming of cannon told of a mighty army itching for war. Worry gripped Newark; soon those Redcoats might cross the Arthur Kill, overrun Elizabethtown and subdue those who had so loudly espoused liberty. Washington moved his main army from New England to New York but an army in New York would be of little help to Newark if the British struck inland.

Howe decided in August to attack Washington

directly. He ferried his troops to Long Island, routed the Continentals there and pushed into Manhattan in mid-September. Washington slowly retreated northward as far as White Plains before deciding to cross into New Jersey to block Howe's impending march on Philadelphia. If the Americans lost both New York and Philadelphia, the war was as good as over.

Disaster threatened when General (Lord) Charles Cornwallis overwhelmed American defenses at Fort Lee atop the Palisades on November 21. Washington had no alternative but retreat. He led his poorly clothed and equipped troops across the Hackensack River and turned south-eastward to Newark in a driving, cold rainstorm, following the road beside the curving Passaic River.

Newark had been bracing for the worst since November 10, when Dr. William Burnet, chairman of the General Committee, advised the removal of livestock, grains, carriages and all valuables into the hills. Wagons piled high with household goods left Newark daily. Older children drove cattle, sheep and horses up the slopes. On November 21, women and children began to evacuate what they believed to be a doomed town.

Dr. Burnet's warning had to be taken seriously because he was no man to panic. An Elizabethtown native, he had studied at the College of New Jersey in Newark and stayed on to practice medicine after graduation in 1749. He married Mary Camp of Newark in 1754 and they started their family of eleven

children. His stature as a doctor was unquestioned; his enthusiasm for American independence beyond doubt. He had much to lose as a revolutionist. In his eagerness to aid others, Dr. Burnet neglected his own welfare; as the British army forced Washington into Newark, his fifty head of cattle still grazed on his town lot, available to friend or foe.

Cornwallis pursued Washington vigorously— for one day. General Howe inexplicably ordered him to slow pursuit on November 22, the day the American commander led his bedraggled, disheartened army of about 3,500 men into Newark. The main body of the army encamped in the northern and western part of town but Washington continued down Broad Street to temporary headquarters, probably in the Eagle Tavern (although several other locations have been suggested as "Washington's headquarters.")

The plight of the American army was easy to observe. Soldiers slipped away from the encampment, hastening home to protect families and possessions in the impending rout. New Jersey militiamen ignored pleas that they join the cause. When Thomas Paine sat in front of a smoking campfire in Newark and began to write "The American Crisis," he had good reason to note: "These are the times that try men's souls. . ."

Nearly a week of inactivity went by before outlying pickets reported that Cornwallis was again stirring. Washington ordered drummers to sound renewal of the retreat on November 28. The soldiers fell in, straggled down Broad

pproaching British troops sent nilies fleeing. This 1856 engrav- g shows Mrs. Schuyler and helpers rning her wheat. To the right, loaded wagon awaits.

75

Street and out the south end of town just as the handsomely equipped British army marched leisurely into the north side of town. Mr. Macwhorter fled with Washington, aware that staying meant certain imprisonment and possible hanging. His sarcastic words against the British had not gone unnoticed. In addition, he was a close advisor to Washington and took part in councils of war.

Loyalists streamed into the streets, waving kerchiefs and hailing the British as saviors. David Ogden and his followers at last felt free to proclaim aloud their devotion to the King, his officers and his men. Many others, wavering between loyalty and revolution, stood in line to sign a pledge of fidelity to Great Britain.

The Ogden family illustrated the sad choice that had to be made. David Ogden, patriarch of the family, never faltered in his loyalty to King George. Three of his sons, Nicholas, Peter and Isaac—the once radical Isaac—followed his lead. Two other sons, Abraham and Samuel, and a brother, Aaron, actively supported the American cause.

The amnesty offered by the British to all loyal citizens was more observed in promise than in deed. British and Hessian soldiers went amok, pillaging the homes of loyalists, neutrals and revolutionists with impartiality. A contemporary account told the plight of a loyalist:

"There was one Nuttman, who had always been a remarkable Tory, and who met the British troops with huzzas of joy, but had his house plundered of almost everything. He himself had his shoes taken off his feet and threatened to be hanged, so that with difficulty he escaped being murdered by them."

Poor Nuttman! Former militia captain, friend of the British, now grown old in service. His joy at seeing the British turned to bitter disappointment. Later, when the fortunes of war swung the other way, American troops arrested Nuttman and clapped him into jail at Morristown. Either way, he lost.

Cornwallis lingered in Newark from November 28 to December 2, permitting Washington to slip closer and closer to the Delaware River. When the British left the pillaged town, the Americans were on their way to a refuge in Pennsylvania. Cornwallis had no doubts about

the war's end, however. He booked passage on a ship leaving for London, casually promising to return in the springtime if necessary.

Cornwallis never boarded the ship. Washington and his advisers, including Mr. Macwhorter as the only civilian on the inner council,

E. Tisdale   del. et sculp.

The PROCESSION.

*These two 1795 engravings typi_
plight of all Loyalists when th_
tide of war turned. Judged b_*

decided to strike back across the Delaware. The Americans crossed the river on December 25 to overwhelm the Hessians at Trenton. They then stunned the British at Princeton on January 3 and ruined Cornwallis's holiday plans by moving swiftly into winter quarters at

Morristown. Washington thus lay in position to exert pressure on the valley to the east.

Sentiment veered sharply in Newark, for the second time in less than two months. Revolutionaries rejoiced, even as the Ogdens and dozens of other Loyalists raced out of town early in

The TORY'S Day of JUDGMENT,

nfriendly neighbors, they had to
e before their wrath. Dozens left
ewark. (Library of Congress).

January, 1777, to seek safety in New York. With them went the Rev. Isaac Browne, rector of Trinity Church. As Mr. Browne left, Mr. Macwhorter returned to his beloved Newark. He reported his shock in these words:

"Great have been the ravages committed by the British troops in this part of the country. Their footsteps are marked with desolation and ruin of every kind. The murders, ravishments, robbery and insults they were guilty of are dreadful. When I returned to the town, it looked more like the scene of ruin than a pleasant, well-cultivated village. . ."

The minister wrote of families that had been victimized after believing promises of kind treatment. British officers robbed friend and foe alike, packing furniture and silverware on baggage wagons as the army left. Mr. Macwhorter found church records destroyed and his own books mutilated and burned. He continued:

"The mischief committed in the houses forsaken of their inhabitants, the destruction of fences, barns, stables, the breaking of chests of drawers, desks, tables, and other furniture; the burning and carrying away of carpenters' and shoemakers' tools cannot be described. . .

"I might have observed that it was not only the common soldiers that plundered and stole, but also their officers, and not merely low officers and subalterns, but some of high rank were aiding and abetting the profits of this business.

"No less a person than General [William] Erskine, a Knight, who lodged at Daniel Baldwin's, had his room furnished from a neighboring house with mahogany chairs and tables, a considerable part of which was taken away with his baggage when he went to Elizabeth Town. Colonel MacDonald, who made his headquarters at Alexander Robinson's, had his room furnished in the same felonious manner, and the furniture was carried off as if it had been part of his baggage. Another colonel, whose name I have forgot, sent his servants, who took away a sick woman's bed, Mrs. Crane's, from under her, for him to sleep upon."

But Newark had seen the worst. The full impact of war never again touched the town, although two well-planned, major British sorties thoroughly alarmed the townspeople. The first came on September 12, 1777, when a powerful expedition of several thousand men struck from four directions.

Newark had few regulars on duty, but the militia, so disorganized and reluctant in November, 1776, had stiffened after the enemy's viciousness became manifest. Minutemen streamed in from the hills on word of the September attack. They fought delaying skirmishes all day long and confused the British with their hit-and-run tactics. General Henry Clinton neared the center of town at nightfall but decided against remaining for the night, fearful of an unseen enemy lurking on every roof, in every doorway, behind every tree. He pushed northward to camp at Acquackanonck (Passaic).

Next day Clinton called off the foray, but he happily reported to his superiors that he had captured 400 head of cattle, 400 head of sheep and a few horses—and with a loss of only eight men killed, nineteen wounded, ten missing and five known to be captured. If soldiers and livestock could be equated equally, he was away ahead. He also had gained a quickened respect for the "rebels," no matter how much he despised their method of fighting.

Life settled into watchful routine. Dr. Burnet efficiently conducted hospitals in Trinity and

Trinity Church, used as a soldiers hospital by both sides, was badly scarred. From drawing in Urquhart's A Short History of Newark.

First Presbyterian Churches and at the court house and Newark Academy, the latter a substantial stone school building erected in 1774, on the upper green (now Washington Park). Joseph Hedden, Jr., justice of the peace; Samuel Hayes, and Thomas Canfield went about their assignment of confiscating the estates of Loyalists—or Tories—in Newark, and in the process making themselves thoroughly hated among the British and Loyalists in New York.

Hedden's unyielding application to duty brought enemy wrath down on his head on January 25, 1780, in the midst of the coldest winter of the eighteenth century. Temperatures plunged so low that even the Hudson River froze over. Washington's army endured agony in the hills of Morris County, scarcely able to survive, much less wage war. By mid-January, civilians and soldiers on both sides were suffering cruelly from the unceasing cold.

A regiment of 500 English and Hessian soldiers left New York on the night of January 25 under command of Major Lumm, crossed the Hudson River on the ice and proceeded swiftly over solidly frozen marshlands to Newark. The troops marched into town shortly after 10 P.M., posting guards on every main street and surrounding Newark Academy, temporarily used as a barracks. Simultaneously, a detachment of British soldiers walked across the frozen Arthur Kill to attack Elizabethtown. The mission in both cases was the same: plunder and destroy, burn and kill.

The attackers in Newark burned several barns and private dwellings, then set the torch to the Academy after killing seven or eight defenders. As the invaders moved south on Broad Street, the sky across the marshlands in the direction of Elizabethtown glowed red from a British-set fire roaring through the First Presbyterian Church there. The Newark raiders may have mistaken the shooting flames for an American counter attack, for they hastily beat a retreat in the direction of Paulus Hook, herding along thirty-five soldiers captured at Newark Academy.

On the way out of town the Redcoats paused before the home of Judge Hedden, the confiscator of Loyalist estates. He was ill but the British major ordered him out of bed. Mrs. Hedden sought to intervene only to be driven back, her nightdress stained with blood where the soldiers jabbed her with bayonets. Her wounds, though numerous and bloody, were not serious. Hedden was driven into the street clad only in his night clothes and marched to New York at bayonet point. On the way a friend passed him a blanket, and that kept him alive through the bitter night.

Hedden's physical condition deteriorated rapidly during his imprisonment in the New

York Sugar House. When it became evident that he would soon die, British authorities permitted his brothers to take him back to Newark under a flag of truce. There he died on September 27, 1780, in his fifty-second year. Neighbors laid him in the Old Burying Ground, under a brownstone marker which told that he was "Zealous for American liberty in opposition to British tyranny, and at last fell a victim of British cruelty."

Judge Hedden lived long enough to know that the tide of victory had begun to roll in America's direction. He knew that twice in June 1780, Newark militiamen had raced to Connecticut Farms (now Union) and Springfield to help repulse British and Hessian troops trying to force a way through the Short Hills westward to Morristown. He was aware that France had promised powerful support. The judge died knowing that American independence was near.

There would be other minor raids on Newark as British came seeking cattle. There would be alarms in the night, but there would also be the

move toward Yorktown in the fall of 1781. War, with its mingled miseries and triumphs, its heroism and meanness, was on the wane. Newark could begin to move again in peace, counting its dead and wounded and remembering its heroes.

There were names to be recited before fireplaces for years to come: Joseph Hedden, Jr., ever after deemed a martyr; Alexander Macwhorter, one of the Revolution's "fighting parsons"; Dr. William Burnet, surgeon, civic leader, hospital organizer; and William S. Pennington, headed for later mercantile and political success but then an impressive young officer who had won his lieutenant's bars for battlefield gallantry.

Young Pennington found war not altogether depressing; his diary tells of dining with Washington at Morristown on December 26, 1780, and "the pleasure of seeing for the first time, the celebrated Mrs. Washington." The general that day talked not of war but of agriculture, much to Pennington's surprise. Pennington enjoyed his furloughs at home, too. He recorded that on Wednesday, October 16, 1780, "I spent the principal part of the day in Newark, visiting my female acquaintances in this place. The ladies in town, to do them justice, are a very sociable, agreeable set of beings, whose company serves to educate the mind, and in a manner to compensate the toils of military life."

There were others to remember: Mistress Ann Van Wagenen Plume, a slave named Cudjo and Captain Caleb Bruen—people from all walks of life who contributed as best they could.

Mistress Plume watched with dismay as the invaders of November 1776 passed the fine stone Plume house in the northern part of town, but when Hessians disrupted her way of life she put them to rout. She drove the Germans from her parlor where she found them chopping wood; later she locked a stray Hessian in her ice house. American soldiers gave Mistress Plume the Hessian's hat as a memento. Tradition says metal from the hat became a knocker on her front door.

Cudjo, a black slave owned by Benjamin Coe, claimed to be descended from royal African lineage. He went into uniform as a substitute for Coe and fought valiantly (at Monmouth Battlefield in June, 1778, it is believed, as well as on other fields of war.) When Cudjo returned home, Coe gave him his freedom, a house and an acre of ground on High Street.

Caleb Bruen's activities were obscure and confusing. An eager patriot at first, he had risen to the captaincy of an American ordnance company by August, 1776. Then he began acting strangely, at times openly consorting with the British, at times disappearing. His name appeared in Sir Henry Clinton's confidential papers as courier and spy, but, significantly, when Bruen was arrested in 1783 for illicit trading with the enemy, his name was dropped from the record. War's end exposed the secret— Caleb Bruen had spent the war in the most dangerous and least rewarding of all military pursuits: spying on the British for the American cause. He lived to ride in the 1826 Independence Day parade as one of the "Heroes of '76."

Newark's jubilation at victory was tempered by the awareness that many would not return, their Loyalist activities during the war branding them traitors. The Rev. Isaac Browne, the one-time rector of Trinity Church; many of the Ogdens and Longworths, and others of Tory stripe never again could walk the streets of this old town. Most of them went to Nova Scotia or England, including John Edison and his family. Years later, Edison's descendants drifted to Ohio and there a boy named Thomas Alva Edison was born in 1847; he would return the Edison name to Newark in 1871.

Despite the enemy depredations of 1776 and the burning of Newark Academy in 1780, Newark emerged from the war only slightly changed in physical appearance. The streets were wide and dusty, or wide and muddy, depending on the season. The stone buildings along Broad Street were substantial. The two churches stood tall among other structures, although much damaged through their use as hospitals. The loss of the Tories lowered the village population; by 1780 it could not have been more than 850 to 900. Newark town, in truth, still was well off the beaten track.

Finally war was done and soldiers mustered out, stopping by roadside inns as they wandered home. From Pyle, Book of the American Spirit.

Chapter 10

CROSSING THEIR BRIDGES

W AR'S END found Pastor Alexander Macwhorter's fortunes at low ebb. His parsonage had been looted and burned by the British in 1776, and in 1778 a summer bolt of lightning had struck Mrs. Macwhorter, shocking her so badly that although she lived another twenty-nine years, she did not fully recover. Discouraged by life in Newark, the Macwhorters advertised a sale of their worldly goods on October 21, 1779:

"A milch cow, which may easily be made good beef, a half blood colt, a good chest of drawers, a genteel mahogany sofa, very useful for sick families; with tables, chairs, washing tubs and a variety of other articles."

Pastor and Mrs. Macwhorter and their four children headed south, hoping to find peace in Charlotte, North Carolina, described as a "rebel hornet's nest" but seemingly far from the main scene of action. A year later, Lord Cornwallis, the sacker of Newark, stormed into Charlotte. Once again the wandering Macwhorters fled before him, abandoning furniture, books and personal belongings to an avenging army.

Newark Presbyterians invited Mr. Macwhorter back to his old pulpit in 1781 and he accepted gladly. Here he had begun his ministry and here he wanted to spend the rest of his years. The town turned out to welcome back its middle-aged warrior-preacher, cherished both for his anti-British sentiments and his good deeds. Mr. Macwhorter was home to stay.

The marks of war were on the town. Occupation by both British and American troops had damaged both the Presbyterian and Episcopal churches. The burned-out walls of Newark

Academy were a constant reminder of the British raid in early 1780. Here and there a dark ruin marked where a house or a barn had stood.

Physical ruins could be replaced. Mr. Macwhorter worried far more over the ugly dissensions wrought by the war. Gone were the Loyalists, the once-respected town leaders, despised by those who remained to fight the King. More than anything else, the wounds between Trinity Church and the Presbyterian Church had to be healed. Mr. Macwhorter called on the Rev. Uzal Ogden, rector of Trinity, and offered the hand of friendship. Thereafter the names of Alexander Macwhorter and Uzal Ogden appeared often together in public records.

Town meetings were occupied with essentially the same business that they had been wrestling with for more than a century: how to keep wandering livestock out of the streets, how to get laggard landholders to burn the meadows or to work on the streets and how to take care of the poor.

Townspeople constantly discussed the cheapest possible alternatives for handling the increasing numbers of indigents. Year after year they settled for a "poor auction." Bidders lined up the unfortunate, checked their physical condition carefully to see how much work they might do and then estimated the lowest possible cost of maintaining them. The entire group of poor went to the lowest bidder—the one who charged Newark the least to keep them—and off they trudged to aid their new custodian on his farm. The overseers of the poor were supposed to make certain they were not mistreated.

Old First, started by the congregation in 1787, finally stood 204 feet tall.

The poor auctions led to abuses, particularly in the over-working of children. The town meeting of 1794 abandoned the practice and put the needy in the hands of the overseers, "to be taken care of at their discretion." When the auctions resumed briefly in 1804, children were excepted from the bidding.

Pastor Macwhorter at times spoke of Newark as "flourishing in manufactures." The Independence Day parade on July 4, 1788, did show surprising industrial advances. Marching up Broad Street behind the fife and drum were twenty tanners and curriers, fifty cordwainers, eight quarrymen and stone lifters, twelve blacksmiths, four scythe makers, eighteen wheelwrights and turners, six silversmiths, fourteen tailors, eight hatters, plus furnace men, nail makers, millers, tobacconists and many others. Not all of them worked within earshot of Broad and Market Streets. Some came as well from the hills of Orange, the swamps of Caldwell, the plateau of Bloomfield, the quarries of Belleville.

The parade's line of march led past Pastor Macwhorter's pride: the slowly rising, and long-delayed, new Presbyterian Church on the east side of Broad Street. This was the third in the series of edifices built since 1668. Funds had been raised as early as 1774 but the Revolution forced a delay. Fearing enemy thievery, a deacon of the church then had loaded metal for a church bell aboard an ox cart, driven the team across the meadows and buried the treasure in the marshland to await cessation of hostilities.

The church builders assembled on the Broad Street property in September, 1787, and formed a rectangle around a foundation line traced in the dust. Pastor Macwhorter dug the first shovel of dirt and passed the shovel to a deacon, who repeated the symbolic digging. The shovel passed from hand to hand; within a few hours the entire foundation trench had been shaped. Completion of the tall stone building took nearly three years. The steeple rose 204 feet above Broad Street before the official opening day on January 1, 1791. Newark had its most cherished building, then and now. The church remains, its steeple almost eclipsed by surrounding skyscrapers, its clock still keeping watch on Broad Street, its doors still open to those who pass by. This is the enduring monument to Pastor Macwhorter.

A second project could now be faced by the Presbyterian leader: erection of another Newark Academy. The Rev. Uzal Ogden joined Dr. Macwhorter on November 30, 1791, in telling friends and neighbors that it was in "the duty, interest and honor of the town to promote the education of youth by erecting a large and convenient academy for teaching English, the learned Languages and Arts and Sciences."

Some responded with cash. Others bought tickets in a lottery, and St. John's Masonic Lodge (founded in 1761 as New Jersey's first Masonic Lodge) put up one-third of the capital on condition that it could use the third floor as its lodge hall. A Mr. Watts gave "a Negro man, James" as his contribution and the Academy committee empowered Mr. Ogden to offer the slave "for as much money as he will sell for." James brought £40.

Three-story Newark Academy, raised on the corner of Broad and Academy Streets, received its first students early in 1793, with Dr. Macwhorter serving as president. St. John's Lodge opened its third-floor quarters in June, 1795, by entertaining "the brethren of the several lodges in this state and in the city of New York." Visitors marveled at the stunning decorations, including a "superb glass chandelier."

Other private schools followed. Captain Jabez Parkhurst opened his White School in 1797 after a curious fund-raising campaign. He wrote a play starring himself as a campaigner seeking pledges for a new school. His protagonist, in the role of a miserly farmer named "Gripus," refused to contribute. Audiences hissed at such indignant treatment—and enough of them got the point to see the White School through. By 1809, Newark had three other private schools: Market Street School (1804); the Franklin School (1807) on Fair Street and the Union School (1809) on New Street. The town meeting in 1815 also began allocating $500 for "the schooling of poor children."

Newark Academy catered to the sons of the prosperous, including many from the South and West Indies, and after 1802 also accepted "females." It made no pretense of supplying education for all—nor did it need to, in an age when only the well-to-do, and the extremely poor, were assured educations. Schooling for the masses lay in the future, but a concern for the mental development of another group, the town's hard-working apprentices, came from an unexpected source, a clergyman turned shoemaker.

Moses Combs, a minister without a church, began making shoes about 1790 near the Market Street watering place, center of all leather tanning. Combs was short and unprepossessing, but when strangers looked into his glittering black eyes they recognized the zeal that marked his every action, whether sewing uppers or saving souls. Everyone knew him too as a man close with a penny: he refused to have fashionable buttons sewn on the back of his coat because they were "of no use."

Prosperity came to Combs quite by accident. Tradition tells of a Georgia stranger who met the "little black eyed man" in 1790 and ordered 200 pairs of seal-skin shoes sent to Savannah. That opened two doors, one leading to a fortune for Combs, the other inaugurating the extensive trade with the South which seventy years later made Newark industrialists rebel at thoughts of war with the Confederacy.

Combs became the town's leading industrialist.

Newark Academy as it stood on corner of Broad and Academy Streets from 1792 to 1857. Lottery "scheme" for $20,000 in 1793 offered tickets at $4 and listed 427 prizes.

Newark's heralded shoemaking traditions began in uncomplicated surroundings such as this factory depicted in an 18th-century encyclopedia.

Within a few years orders brought him as much as $9,000 each. He made Newark aware that money could be made by serving distant regions.

Fortune and industrial fame brought no relaxation to this man who said that he hoped for "emancipation of the body from slavery and the mind from ignorance and terror." He built a two-story frame building on Market Street, using the lower floor for church services and the upper floor as a school room. There his youthful workers learned to read and to write, to figure and to plan, in what has been called the first apprentice school in the United States.

Many men who later gained success in the leather trade traced their beginnings to an association with Combs—by day at his shoe benches, by night in his school, by Sunday in his church. Praised for his deeds, Combs modestly declared, "Silver showered on me so plentifully that I did not know what else to do with it."

If one year can be singled out as the turning point in a town's history, then 1790 is Newark's point in time. That year Combs opened the Southern markets, and in that year the New Jersey Legislature agreed that the "public good" would be served by building a 64-foot-wide roadway from Newark Court House to Paulus Hook, with wooden drawbridges across the Passaic and Hackensack Rivers.

A leading figure in the project was Mr. Ogden,

the Trinity Church rector, along with commissioners Samuel Tuthill, John Neilson, Robert T. Kemble, William Maxwell and John Pintard. Original funds were raised in a lottery with a top prize of $5,000. Two years later, subscribers eagerly bought out 200 shares of stock at $200 a share.

The commissioners hired the country's chief bridge expert, Josiah Nottage, fresh from a triumphal arching of the Charles River between Boston and Cambridge. In September, 1794, Nottage advertised for "twenty carpenters and a number of labourers," offering cash "weekly, or oftener if required." He also ordered 500 tons of stone from Snake Hill for delivery at the Hackensack bridge site.

Nottage and his carpenters finished both bridges in the summer of 1795. They were magnificent for the day: the Passaic River crossing was 492 feet long and the Hackensack span 980 feet from shore to shore. Connecting the bridges was a road described in *The Traveller's Directory* as "made of logs laid across the road close together, of three or four layers, and covered with the sod and earth dug up on each side; over this is laid gravel."

The road was rough and the draws were too often open, but travelers willingly paid the Passaic bridge tolls: four cents for man and horse; ten cents for horse and chair; twenty-nine cents for coach or light wagon with two horses; thirty-nine cents for vehicles with four horses. Fees were slightly higher on the Hackensack bridge. Dividends to stockholders averaged more than ten per cent annually, causing road users to protest to the state legislature that the tolls were "an intolerable burden on the public." The protests were in vain; the stockholders had a monopoly on the crossings until 1889. Without competition, the rates were not likely to drop.

The transportation pace quickened. Newark was on the high road, at last. Stages rolled constantly into town, clattering over the Passaic River bridge (at what is now Bridge Street), dashing west a short distance to Broad Street and then turning south for the dusty, shouting, noisy run to Archer Gifford's famed tavern on the northeast corner of Broad and Market Streets.

Stage coach drivers were heroes. They reined their steaming horses into Market Street, leather slapping against horse hides, harness ornaments gleaming in the sun. The four or five passengers alighted under the Gifford sign, depicting the end of a fox hunt that underscored the tavern name, "The Hounds and the Horn." They made their way into the august presence of Gifford himself, a rotund, cheerful man who heard all and repeated much. Every seasoned traveler liked Arch Gifford, for his good nature and his fine table. In 1800, he advertised for live quail to dress his menu, offering the princely sum of six cents apiece for the toothsome birds.

"The Hounds and the Horn" was the best known tavern, but others also served as centers of news, gossip, community life and even of government. Captain Parkhurst, the founder of the White School, had an inn on the west side of Broad, three or four doors south of Market. A tavern named "Rising Sun" served patrons near the Passaic bridge, and Stephen and Moses Roff each conducted a tavern on Broad Street. Both Roff taverns served at times as a county court room, polling places, a roof for the Newark Town Meeting and places where corporations and banks were organized. Diagonally across from Moses Roff's inn was Halsey's Tavern. An early account said "the best worn path along the entire length of Broad Street ran from Halsey's Tavern to Roff's."

Visitors often praised Newark. Many diary

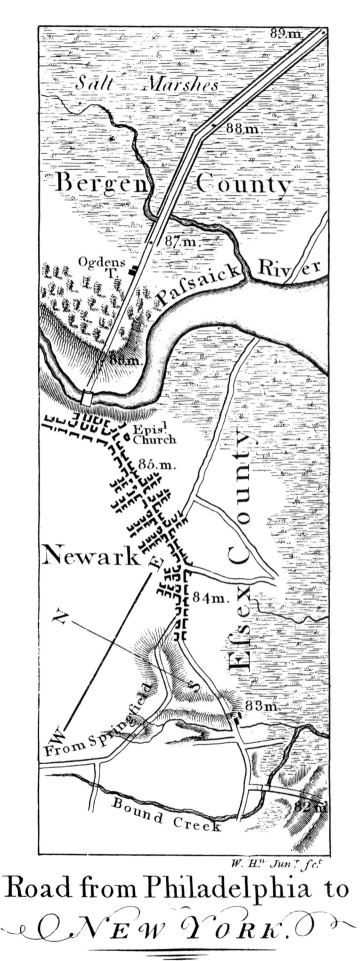

Road from Philadelphia to New York.

View from west, drawn by Archibald Robertson in 1790s, is dominated by Trinity and Old First Church steepl
The artist, apparently overawed by the Passaic River, made it far too prominent.

keepers from foreign countries jotted down impressions between 1794 and 1802—and, for posterity's gain, published them.

Henry Wansey of England saw the town in 1794 just before the bridges were finished. Although mosquitos on the meadows robbed him of so much blood that "they burst from their fulness," he liked this "pleasant little country town." After a "comfortable dish of tea at the Hounds and Horn," he walked throughout the town. First Church he found "peculiarly elegant" and he climbed to its rooftop gallery for a view as far as New York. Except for the practice of white servants insisting that "they shall sit at table with their masters and mistresses," Wansey found Newark altogether heart-warming.

Another Englishman, Thomas Twining, a year later wrote that Newark was "one of the neatest and prettiest towns I had ever seen." He spoke of fine white houses on the western hillside and declared "if I settled in America I should be induced to prefer that spot to any I had seen."

The Duke de la Rochefaucault of France in 1795 called Newark "one of the finest villages in America." He wrote of a shoemaker "who manufactures shoes for exportation" and employed "between three hundred and four hundred workmen." Undoubtedly he meant Moses Combs. John Davis, an Englishman, in 1798 reported that Newark had "probably the largest

cobblers' stall in the United States of America." He, too, referred to Combs.

Yet all was not serene in town. Newark had turned abruptly from its Puritanical doze of a dozen decades. Many were disturbed by the drinking, the carousing, the brashness of newcomers. They were rightfully upset by garbage strewn in the grave yard, by uncollected manure in the streets and by stagecoach drivers who raced wildly down Broad Street. In 1799, one of two racing coaches struck and killed an innocent Newarker. There was genuine sympathy and concern for slaves, for children, for the poor. There was constant threat of fire. Remedial action came in several ways as the century turned.

Newark needed its own newspaper to focus social attention. The town's first journal, founded in 1791 as *Wood's Newark Gazette and New Jersey Advertiser*, hardly did the job: subscriptions in Bergen County outnumbered those in Essex by ten to one. Five years later, Jabez Parkhurst and Samuel Pennington started the *Centinel of Freedom* (using the old-fashioned spelling of "Centinel" at first). Typical of all the uncertainly edited and poorly printed weeklies of the time, the *Centinel* survived. Its heading showed a knight in full armor, defending "The Rights of Man." The editor early spoke out against slavery:

"No longer ought such injustice to be tolerated in a land of liberty. No longer ought the character of American citizens to be tarnished by such an act as this. Shall Americans who nobly resented the first attempts of a designing ministry to enslave them and took up arms to defend their rights, and conquered under the banner of freedom, still continue to hold their fellow-men in thralldom? For shame!"

These were bold words in a day when even clergymen held slaves—and when even advertisements in the *Centinel* offered slaves for sale. One ad on May 1, 1796, told of "a negro man and woman" to be sold, "separately or together as may suit the purchasers." Another offered "a negro man, capable of doing as much work as any man in the State."

Few showed much concern about slavery, but large numbers joined a "Voluntary Association of the people of Newark to observe the Sabbath," founded on July 10, 1798. This type of moral movement was easily understood in a town that still honored Puritan ways. Both Uzal Ogden and Alexander Macwhorter were among the leaders.

The Association decried vice that "like a flood deluges the land," and laid the blame on flagrant breaking of Sunday laws. They agreed, therefore, not to "give nor partake of parties of pleasure" on Sunday, to attend church and to "compel children, apprentices and servants to do the same." They would not countenance "worldly business" on Sundays, and a committee of seven was appointed to aid "the officers of justice" in stopping Sunday violators.

Self-appointed zealots wrecked the association. Some who stopped the mail coach on a Sunday were told by a federal official that such deeds could mean prison. Others removed two French travelers from a stage coach on another Sunday but the Chief Justice of the Supreme Court berated the arresters and let the foreigners proceed. When vigilantes stopped a young Army officer (said to be Winfield Scott of Elizabethtown) riding through town with a "female relative," he did not await court action. He drew a pistol and told his annoyers they were nothing more than bandits. They understood and dropped the reins.

The moralists wore out their welcome and a counter movement gained strength. One Sun-

day enforcer escaped being tarred and feathered only by disguising himself in his mother's hat and cloak. When the Association put up stocks on a lot opposite the Presbyterian Church, possibly to remind themselves of the good old Puritan days, opponents tore down the offensive symbol overnight. Foes derided the Sunday protectors as the "Cold Water Society," and it collapsed by the weight of its own zeal.

Fear of eternal fire had a counterpart in fear of contemporary fire. That fear was highlighted in January, 1797, when Judge Elisha Boudinot's handsome mansion on Park Place caught fire. Within minutes, 500 people surrounded the blazing home but "the want of proper fire implements such as engines, ladders, hooks,

buckets, reservoirs for water, were all discovered when it was too late." The house burned down.

A month later, a Fire Association was formed. It raised $1,000, bought fire hooks, ladders and buckets, and ordered two fire engines from Philadelphia. Nearly a year later one of the engines, a clumsy little tank on wheels, was delivered. Volunteers tried out the engine, ran out of water and lost a barn, although they saved an adjacent house. Fire fighting had far to go. In 1805, the home of Major Samuel Hayes caught fire and burned to the ground when only twenty men showed up with buckets. "The consequence," said the *Centinel of Freedom* "was the ludicrous sight of men snowballing a house to put out a fire."

Not all those who wanted to improve Newark stopped stages on Sunday or snowballed fires. Well-to-do ladies, disturbed by poverty and misery in their midst, organized The Newark Female Charitable Society on January 31, 1803. Each member paid $1 a year, plus "such donations as her benevolence may suggest." Donations took various guises: in 1804, a clergyman's wife donated an extra dollar and urged that it be invested in a New York lottery. The ladies added $5 from the Society treasury to make a $6 investment, but the gamble apparently did not pay off.

The Female Charitable Society helped orphans, old people, the unemployed. They badgered churches into special collections for Christmas. Mrs. Hannah Kinney, first director, recalled in 1816 that for thirteen years the Society had been "feeding the hungry, clothing the naked, and administering comfort to the sick and afflicted."

Growing Newark had other problems. With several leather makers emulating Moses Combs, the first jewelry makers already in town and two or three firms embarked in prosperous carriage making, Newark was hamstrung by the lack of ready capital.

Several Newark financiers gathered in Nathaniel Seabury's inn on April 2, 1804, to organize the Newark Banking and Insurance Company, the first bank in East New Jersey. They convened a month later in Arch Gifford's main dining room to elect Elisha Boudinot president and William Whitehead cashier. Doors opened for business in Smith Burnet's house on Broad Street the next July, with $100,000 in capital, "$40,000 of it paid in."

Newark Banking and Insurance Company issued its own notes, at first unadorned, but later embellished with ornate vignettes of such local landmarks as Israel Crane's quarry and Luther Goble's shoe factory.

Competition was not long in coming. The Legislature in 1812 authorized state banks in Newark, Elizabeth, Camden, Trenton, New Brunswick and Morristown. William S. Pennington, the impressive young war hero of 1780, now grown staid and judicial, headed a group that met in Roff's Tavern on February 8, 1812, to organize Newark State Bank. They

Newark's early banks made their own money.

rented quarters for $275 in a little brick building on Broad, just north of Market Street, despite stock sales so slow that Pennington voluntarily cut his salary from $300 to $250 a year.

Cashiers in both banks "lived in," providing the prudent bankers with both cashier and night watchman for the one salary. They had swords and pistols as ready defenses against robbers, but the only victim was George Herford, cashier of The State Bank, who accidentally killed himself while checking the condition of the pistols in April 1813.

The banks were not prosperous at first. In its early days the "Old Bank," as people called Newark Banking and Insurance Company, often could not discount a note as small as $200. It kept in business by discounting half one day, half the next. Much of the town's financing was underwritten by shrewd Bergen County farmers at interest rates ranging up to seven per cent. Whenever the rural lenders called in a major loan, the two Newark banks pooled their resources to meet the challenge. Both survived as the National Newark and Essex and The First National State banks.

Newark's early history was graphically demonstrated on the map that Charles Basham of the Newark Academy published in 1806. This was called the "Shoemaker Map" because of the shoemaker cartouche in the lower left hand corner. About twenty blocks of varying sizes

Lithograph of 1825 shows Newark east of Mulberry, the street in foreground. Livestock still roamed freely and only a few fenced their land. Road to New York followed Passaic River's bend in the distance. Houses were substantial.

NEW JERSEY HISTORICAL SOCIETY

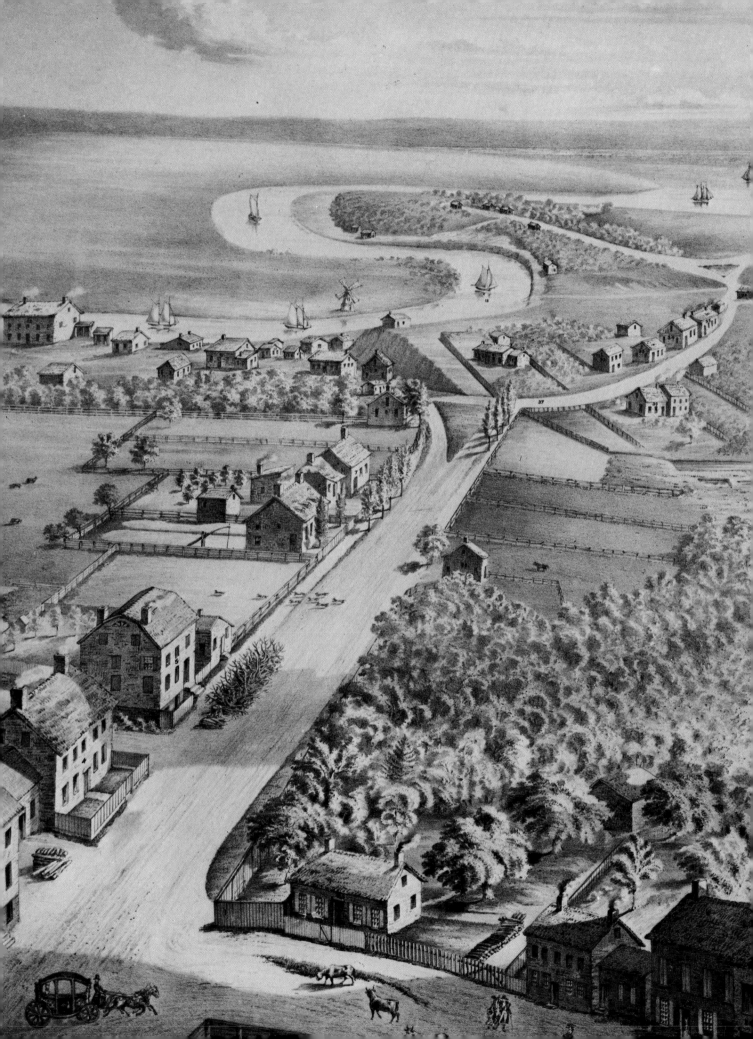

made up Basham's town, with most residences and businesses clustered between Trinity Church on the north and the First Presbyterian Church on the south.

The map bore this legend:

"Newark is one of the most pleasant and flourishing towns in the United States. It is on the main road between NEW YORK and PHIL-ADELPHIA, nine miles from the former and eighty seven from the latter. Its stone quarries are visited by travelers from curiosity. It is noted for its cider, the making of carriages of all sorts, coach lace, men's and women's shoes. In the manufacture of this last article one third of the inhabitants are constantly employed."

The map only partially revealed a larger development—the breakup of the old "Town of Newark" that for more than a century had spread west over the mountains. One section went in 1793 to help form the new municipality of Springfield. A very large parcel left in 1798 when the Caldwell region seceded.

Newark townspeople recognized that growth in outlying regions made it necessary to give them representation on official bodies to insure local road maintenance, proper care of the poor and other local matters. Town meeting alternated the polls between Newark and Orange and divided the region into three taxing districts in 1806. It was all in vain; Orange Township broke away on November 27, 1806, taking all of what is now Orange, East Orange, West Orange and South Orange. This withdrawal heightened impatience elsewhere. The people of the northwest broke away in 1813 to form Bloomfield, which also included today's Montclair and Belleville.

Rivalry continued between Elizabethtown and

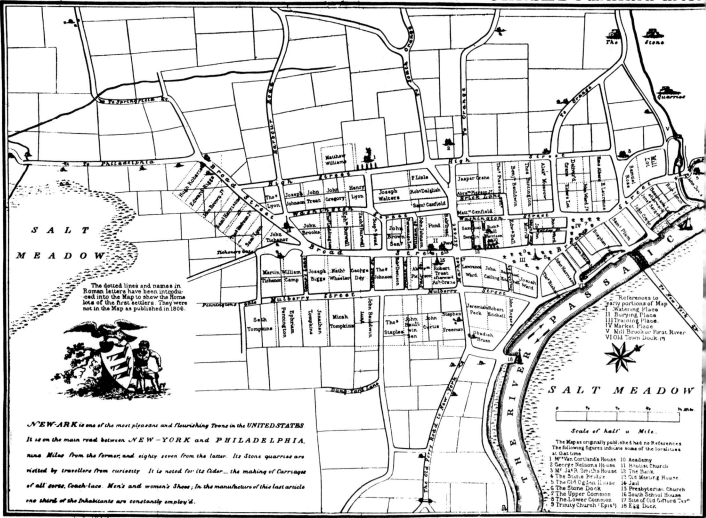

A MAP of the Town of NEW-ARK in the State of NEW-JERSEY Published in 180

Newark, intensified by sordid events in 1807 when voters were asked to choose between Day's Hill (near Elizabethtown) and Newark for the location of a new court house. Three days in February 1807, were set aside for the voting.

Some irregularity took place in the first day's voting at Day's Hill, but the cheating that ensued in Elizabethtown on the second day, according to one account, made the Day's Hill voting "pure and honest by comparison." Elizabethtown and Day's Hill voted heavily against a Newark location.

Newark's turn to register a choice came on the third day. Polls opened at 1 A.M., with people already standing in the darkness waiting to vote. They voted throughout the night and the next day, earnestly—and often.

Women then enjoyed the right to vote in New Jersey, but "enjoyed" is a limited word to describe their enthusiasm in Newark. Eyewitnesses told of women casting ballots as often as six times in various disguises. Men and boys dressed in women's clothing passed unchallenged at the polls.

When the long day came to an end, mobs thronged Broad Street to hear the results. Elizabethtown and Day's Hill voted solidly for their region and Newark cast practically all its votes for itself. Since Newark had the greater number of mischief-makers it won the court house, 7,666 to 6,181. The old town went wild. Torches lit the way for a night of celebration.

The scandal had important repercussions. The State Legislature indignantly took away woman suffrage at the next election (and included foreigners and blacks in the ban for good measure). The denial of the vote to blacks ironically followed closely on an 1804 law providing for the gradual abolition of slavery in New Jersey. By 1814, there were about seventy-five free black men among Newark taxpayers, with businesses of their own. This obvious "taxation without representation" was never mentioned by Independence Day orators. Blacks were generally not permitted to vote in New Jersey until an 1875 amendment to the state constitution was adopted. New Jersey women did not regain suffrage until 1920, 113 years after they lost it in 1807.

Joy at victory over Elizabethtown, by fair means or foul, was dampened five months later when Dr. Alexander Macwhorter, preacher, hero, confidante of Washington, builder, educator and town booster, died at the Presbyterian parsonage on July 20, 1807. His wife and youngest son preceded him in death by a few months. The 73-year-old pastor's passing plunged the entire town into mourning. Dr. Macwhorter had not been a great preacher: even the orator at his funeral said he "never would have gathered laurels in the paths of poetry." But only Aaron Burr, Sr., ranked with him in stature in the town's first century and a quarter. Dr. Macwhorter is remembered today in a street name, and of course, by the imposing church that he built. He also left a slender volume, titled "A Century Sermon," the first history of Newark, written in 1800.

Newarkers grieved, but the town had to get on. The foundations of the new courthouse were dug in 1810 and its doors opened in 1812. New toll roads were built between 1807 and 1812: what is now Springfield Avenue, toward Morristown; today's Mt. Pleasant Avenue through Livingston to Morristown, and present-day Bloomfield Avenue to the northwest. Another ran south to New Brunswick via Elizabethtown.

Down at the docks, swift little sailing vessels sped country produce and a few made-in-Newark goods to New York City. The sloop *Patty* began making trips in 1796 between Newark and Charlestown, North Carolina, to carry shoes and clothing to plantation owners and their slaves. Four years later, the schooner *Louisa* opened service from Newark to Savannah, where by now thousands of well-shod Southerners already wore Moses Combs' creations.

The War of 1812 scarcely interrupted the buoyant mood. The citizens were troubled, of course, at the thought of war bringing England's navy to these shores, possibly even into Newark Bay to hit New Jersey's prime commercial and industrial target. The militia went on the ready in November 1812, "each man having one good blanket and four day's provision, ready cooked," in accordance with state mobilization orders.

British ships never came but Newarkers reacted well when the opportunity arose. They lustily cheered Governor Aaron Ogden, one of the Elizabethtown Ogdens, on November 26,

1812, when he came to Newark to rally the militia and to lead them to a fine repast in Gifford's tavern. In August, 1814, when volunteers were needed to build fortifications at Brooklyn, 200 Newark men marched over the bridges to Paulus Hook and took a ferry to the trouble point. One month later, 800 men volunteered to dig again in Brooklyn, this time with the message, "Don't give up the soil!" sewed on their hats. If not as colorful as Captain James Lawrence's "Don't give up the ship!", the spirit was the same.

Although bankers were ready to flee as far as Morristown with their funds if invaders came, Newark merchants and manufacturers heeded the call of the Army contractor, supplying boots, shoes, harnesses and other supplies. One Robert B. Campfield, a Broad Street contractor, "made an imposing display of patriotism and profit" by arranging in front of his shop fourteen six-pounder cannons, one for each state, that he had made on government contract.

The town hailed peace on February 21, 1815. Gunfire opened and closed the day. Town bells tolled for an hour in the morning and evening. Churches held 11 A.M. services, with special collections for the poor. Hundreds of big tallow candles illuminated churches, homes and main streets that night.

On the move, lively, boisterous and astride the high road linking New York and Philadelphia, a "new" Newark had been born. The town lists still showed many "first family" names but there were sprinklings of "outsiders," too—French refugees who had come in the 1790's, Irish men and women who set up housekeeping before 1800, plus a few Germans and other nationalities. Firmly set for industrial prosperity, Newark opened her arms for those who sought opportunity. It needed them.

Howard Pyle drawing in Book of the American Spirit *shows demure New Jersey women voting, a right they lost after Newark's 1807 election.*

SUMMER HOUSE.
Cockloft Hall.

Washington Irving, from 1809 portrait.

Chapter 11

FAREWELL TO RUSTICITY

NEW YORK CITY PRESSED DOWN on Washington Irving like a "dusty prison." He found himself "immured in the smoky circumference of the city, amid the rattling of carts, the brawling of the multitudes and the variety of unmeaning and discordant sounds that prey insensibly on the nerves." When the young author could stand it no longer he headed for Newark, to "breathe the free air of heaven and enjoy the clear face of nature."

Irving discovered the town about 1807. Industry had not yet brought a "smoky circumference," but the town had shed enough of its Puritanical rigidity to allow Irving and his young literary friends freedom to frolic. A town shepherd still watched the flock on the hills, a town pump stood in the middle of the intersection of Broad and Market Streets and the dead were buried in the plot near the Four Corners.

The "clear face of nature" that Irving praised surrounded the Kemble mansion at what is now Mt. Pleasant Avenue and Gouverneur Street. Isaac Kemble, the builder, named his home "Mount Pleasant," but Irving and associates nicknamed it "Cockloft Hall." They featured the rendezvous in their *Salmagundi Papers,* a series of witty satires that titillated sophisticated New Yorkers.

Calling themselves the "Nine Worthies" or the "Lads of Kilkenny," Irving and his friends rode the stage coach out from Paulus Hook, stopped to pick up spirits in Gifford's tavern and then accompanied Gouverneur Kemble—son of Isaac and one of the "Lads"—northward to

Cockloft Hall. They convened in an elegant summer house, complete with a well-stocked wine cellar.

The fourth of the *Salmagundi Papers* contained these disjointed notes on Newark under Irving's "Memorandums for a Tour; The Stranger in New Jersey":

"Noted for its fine breed of fat mosquitoes, sting through the thickest boot; Archer Gifford and his man Caliban, jolly fat fellows; a knowing traveller always judges everything by the inn-keepers and waiters; set down Newark people all fat as butter; learned dissertations on Archer Gifford's green coat, with philosophical reasons why the Newarkites wear red worsted nightcaps and turn their noses to the south when the wind blows; Newark Academy full of windows; sunshine excellent to make little boys grow."

HAT MANUFACTURERS.

WILLIAM RANKIN, DURYEE & CO.
Wholesale and Retail Hat and Cap Manufacturers, 271 Broad-street

William Rankin, }
John Ogden,
Peter S. Duryee, }
{ J. B. Pinneo,
{ I. N. Rankin.

HAY & AGENS,
Wholesale and Retail Hat and Cap Manufacturers, 244 Broad-street, three doors south of the Canal.
George Hay, }
Thomas Agens. }

RANKIN & LEE,
Wholesale and Retail Hat and Cap Manufacturers, 302 Broad-street, a few doors below Market-street.
Charles W. Rankin, }
William Lee. }

William Rankin, a prominent resident, came to Newark from Elizabeth in 1811 and soon became a noted hat maker. His portrait, above, was painted by Rembrandt Peale, a mark of early 19th century distinction. His youngest children, on right, were painted by Oliver Tarbell Eddy. William's brother, Andrew, also gained success as a hatter. Both had their factories and stores fronting on Broad Street's busy sidewalks.

94

Irving toyed with the truth for the sake of a laugh, but he also revealed his sentimental attachment to the lovely lands overlooking the Passaic. He called it "one of the majestic rivers at the hour of sunset" and wrote:

"The jocund zephyr, full freighted with native fragrance, sues sweetly to the sense; the chirping of the thousand varieties of insects with which our woodlands abound, forms a concert of simple melody; even the barking of the farm dog, the lowing of the cattle, the tinkling of their bells, and the stroke of the woodman's axe from the opposite shore, seem to partake of the softness of the scene and fall tunefully upon the ear; while the voice of the villager, chanting some rustic ballad, swells from a distance in the semblance of the very music of harmonious love."

The Lads of Kilkenny were transients. Other young men, lured by opportunity, came to stay. They came from the Old Country, from New England, from the hills of Morris, where the iron mines had fallen on slack times, and from the farms of Bergen and Somerset. They came from nearby; William and Andrew Rankin left

Boyden, the gaunt, homely New Englander who walked shyly into town in 1815, at about the time that the boisterous Irving was leaving. He brought with him his two most precious possessions: Abigail Sherman Boyden, his bride of one year; and a machine for slitting thick hide into several thin slices. Massachusetts had become too confined for the twenty-seven-year-

Seth Boyden's early factory, above, and a business card drawn by himself, on left.

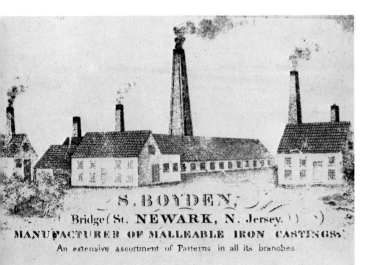

Elizabethtown in 1811 to escape "a depressing aristocratic atmosphere" and became Newark's first hatters. Each built a factory and opened a store, William's close to Trinity Church and Andrew's adjacent to the Old Burying Ground.

Of all the arrivals, no man, young or old, before or since, affected Newark as much as Seth

Newark's prime industrial mover: Seth Boyden.

old Boyden's fertile mind, and he believed that Newark's leather makers would welcome his new machine. He was right.

The Boydens set up housekeeping in a little house on Broad Street, near Bridge, and enjoyed modest success. Mrs. Boyden had reason to expect better times, for she had married a man of brilliance. But for Seth Boyden a problem solved was a solution discarded. He could not stick to anything merely for profit.

Formal education had little to do with Boyden's genius. He attended school in Foxborough, Massachusetts, for two months each year, for only a few years. By age fifteen he repaired watches, engraved labels on steel plates and had rigged up a crude home laboratory to experiment with chemicals and electricity. He built his own high power microscope, invented an air rifle and perfected machines to make wrought-iron nails, tacks and brads.

Boyden's methods quickly became apparent in Newark. He let others have his leather slitter while he developed a successful new way of silver plating buckles and harness ornaments. As that enterprise also prospered, his mind returned to leather, stimulated by an article that he had read on French glazed leather. He searched in New York until he found a sample,

The Bricklayer.

The Brewer.

The Carpenter.

Shipwright.

All illustrations on this page and the next are from The Book of English Trades and Library of the Useful Arts, *printed in London in 1825. There was little variation in methods from country to country, and these show the skills of Newark's craftsmen of the early part of the 19th century.*

The Iron Founder.

Saddler.

The Smith.

Bricklayer, brewer, carpenter, shipwright, iron founder, saddler, smithy, watchmaker, printer, wheelwright—Newark had them all and then some as Seth Boyden and others led the emerging town into industrial greatness. Gradually the old home industries gave way to shops, then to factories. Even at this stage in its development, Newark enjoyed diversified manufactures, a continuing key to its success.

Watch Maker.

Wheelwright.

Letter Press Printer.

the glazed peak of a German military cap, brittle and cracked.

Analyzing the shiny peak, Boyden saw its flaws. By 1818, he had perfected a new method of glazing leather, by applying several layers of varnish. Boyden baked each coat in an oven and polished the last application. Although he called his product "patent leather," Boyden did not apply for a patent. He felt that his discoveries should be public property, a philosophy that would keep him permanently poor as it enriched others.

Sales of patent leather reached $4,521 in 1822 and soared rapidly after that. Boyden looked elsewhere; patent leather and profits bored him. He began experimenting with iron, hoping to make a malleable iron that could be easily worked into forms more complicated than were possible with simple cast iron. He moved temporarily out of the public eye, but all about him Newark was in the midst of metamorphosis.

One victim of progress was the Old Burying Ground in the heart of town. By the early 1820's it had grown unsightly and neglected, a place where cattle grazed, heedless innkeepers dumped garbage and cooks sharpened knives on gravestones. The 1828 Town Meeting authorized purchase of a new town cemetery along the Old Ferry Road on the east end of town. Residents with relatives and friends in the Old Burying Ground were asked to decide whether they wished the bodies moved, "at the town's expense," to some other location. There were few takers.

Industry swept to the fore. The town put on a mighty industrial parade in 1821 to prove the point. Leading the procession were two farmers with sprigs of wheat in their hats, followed by four oxen pulling a plough, a "citizen bearing a stubbing scythe," and a variety of other citizens waving rakes and harvesting cradles to show that rural ways had not vanished.

Along the line of march came Moses Harris and Son, merchant tailors; John Ruckel, baker; Jacob Alyea, blacksmith; Isaac Nichols, carpenter; James Nutman and Nathaniel Canfield, masons; Z. Grant and Sons, stone cutters; E. Meeker and Company, pottery makers; B. Hall, cotton weaver; Messrs. Dey, Tice and others, tanners; Messrs. Goble and Canfield, boot and shoe makers; Andrew Rankin, hatter; Benjamin Cleveland, clock and watch maker; David T. Andruss, plane maker; and Hugh McDougall, cabinet maker.

Then followed David Alling, fancy chairs; D'Coudres and Eagles, tin and copper smiths; Aaron Baldwin, gunsmith; Abner Campbell, tallow chandler; Peter Jacobus, saddle and harness maker; David Beach, coach maker; Jabez Smith, smithy; George Rohde, coach springs; Andrew Wilson, silver plater; William Stevens and Thomas Owens, woolen weavers; Samuel Simpson, stocking weaver; Evans and Owens, chocolate and mustard makers; Peter Tronson, barrel maker; Stephen Cooper, pump maker, and John Paris, hairdresser and wig maker.

Horse-drawn floats displayed the sights and sounds of industry: iron smiting iron, smithy's bellows roaring, tin snips cutting, cabinet makers hammering. Crowds saw clothing made, bread baked, candles dipped on a passing float, silver pitchers being plated, cabinet makers turning out a bureau and bedstead. The line of march represented a directory of town industry —but not a complete one, for there was no float by Epaphras Hinsdale, pioneer jewelry maker; no carriages by James M. Quinby, leader in that field; and no evidence that Seth Boyden even existed.

Newarkers loved parades and celebrations. The Marquis de Lafayette provided two such occasions. His first visit on September 23, 1824, found the town amply prepared. Crowds lined the streets as the esteemed, aging Frenchman made his way from Bridge Street to Military Park. Despite intermittent rains, throngs jammed Military Park to hear the bands play, Theodore Frelinghuysen offer extravagant tribute and to catch a glimpse of Lafayette before he left for Elizabethtown.

Ten months later, in mid-July, the Marquis was back, this time to the town's surprise. His original itinerary called for him to swing through Paterson and Morristown before heading for Elizabethtown. Thus his unexpected detour through Newark found the town, for once, without a parade. Lafayette quietly visited Miss Van Doren's School in the Newark Academy building, had breakfast at Morton's Hotel, inspected the new Third Presbyterian Church, and took his leave.

Newark turned out in force on July 4, 1826, to hail the fiftieth anniversary of the Declaration of Independence. As usual, Seth Boyden did not hear the drums. He was at work in his kitchen, still seeking the secret of malleable iron through the proper refining and annealing of pig iron. He hoped for an easily worked substance that would not be as brittle as cast iron or as costly as wrought iron. He neglected his patent leather business to work on the iron spikes that he was annealing in a small furnace built in his kitchen fireplace.

While Boyden labored on Independence Day, 1826, the town played. The passing of a half century had thinned the ranks of Revolutionary War veterans; the few remaining heroes of '76 rode in carriages, aged and wizened, their heroics a thing of the distant past. Younger men paraded hard and long—the latter necessitated by the expanding length of Broad Street—then wound up their salute to the nation's freedom by drinking potent toasts until long past midnight.

The paraders were gone when Boyden emerged from his kitchen laboratory late that afternoon with the news that he had discovered the secret of malleable iron. Probably no one paid him much attention. Who listened to a tousle-haired, haggard inventor, particularly one attired in leather apron and working clothes on a great holiday? And who trusted a man who turned his back on a fortune in patent leather? But within a few days Boyden began production of malleable iron, the first in this country.

People had more regard for town assessor Isaac Nicholls, who published a census on that July 4. He gave the population as 8,017, more than ten times the 1776 total. He listed seventeen factories, three distilleries, two breweries and two grist mills. A looking glass plant and a tobacco factory were major new additions.

Nicholls found no large factories, for industry was hardly beyond the blacksmith shop stage. Few installations had as many as a dozen hands. The assessor did not list individual shoe manufactories, which was not strange, since most shoemakers still had shops in their homes. He did show that the town had 685 shoemakers, about one-third of the total working force. Nearly 200 worked in various facets of carriage making. Newark already had found one lasting base for industrial prosperity—diversity.

Mural in the former Newarker Restaurant shows Lafayette hailed on his 1824 visit.

Morris Canal, fully completed from Newark to Phillipsburg in 1831, transformed town into bustling center of business activity.

Another base was being formed: transportation on land and water to replace the stage coaches and toll roads.

To the east, John Stevens of Hoboken declared that man might someday speed along in steam-driven carriages at forty or fifty miles an hour. He built America's first steam locomotive in 1825 to prove his point, but it ran only on a circular track in front of his home. Stevens was ridiculed by many as a toy maker.

To the west, a school teacher named George Maculloch and fellow stockholders were planning a canal to link the coal fields of Pennsylvania with the iron mines of Morris County —and the iron mines with the markets of Newark and New York. The fact that Lake

Hopatcong, the main water source, lay 924 feet above sea level at Newark Bay did not deter Maculloch or his engineers. They devised an ingenious system of locks and inclined planes to conquer the mountains.

Investors showed keen interest in Macculloch's scheme. When speculators fought to buy shares, Newark's *Sentinel of Freedom* demanded that those "geniunely interested" get a chance to buy stock, rather than "mere gamblers." With money in hand, the promoters planned their route after listening to Paterson, Newark and Elizabethtown leaders tell why each of their towns deserved to be the eastern terminus. The canal interests compromised by running the canal through both Paterson and Newark—and making Jersey City the eastern terminus.

No Newarker appreciated the ideas of Stevens and Macculloch more than Seth Boyden. He had toyed with steam himself, recognizing that Newark's industry was limited because of its motive power. Most shops and mills still depended on water wheels and some industries drove their machines with oxen, horses—and even dogs—journeying to nowhere on inclined treadmills. Boyden built Newark's first steam engine in 1825, turned out another and made no more. He had conquered steam; that satisfied him.

By 1826, more than 1,100 men and hundreds of mules toiled along the Morris Canal route from Newark to Lake Hopatcong. Surveyors mapped the route on to the Delaware River at what is now Phillipsburg.

Newarkers talked of little else. They watched Irish workers digging the canal bed through the town, only two short blocks north of Broad and Market Streets (along what is now Raymond Boulevard). They marveled at the ingenuity of a lock installed where the canal merged with the Passaic River and enjoyed the workings of another lock atop the hill to the west. They watched in awe while engineers tested the plane by which canal boats soon would climb the hill, riding high above the streets.

Water began to flow through the canal in the summer of 1829. By December of that year, a few boats followed the locks and planes all the way from Newark to Mead's Basin in Morris County. These barges made the trip just in time to escape the first bitter cold snap that froze the canal solid. It became obvious that the canal had at least one major and perhaps fatal weakness: winter.

Such chilling thoughts evaporated with the spring, and completion of the canal from Newark to Phillipsburg in 1831 eased all doubts. The first boat to reach tidewater all the way from Phillipsburg slid down the plane in mid-May, 1832, sloshed into the canal ditch and entered Newark with its load of coal.

The town by then had three newspapers to hail the canal's users. *The New Jersey Eagle* had been founded in 1820 to join the *Sentinel of Freedom* in reporting weekly news, but far more important, the *Newarker Daily Advertiser* made its first appearance on March 1, 1832. George Bush and Company, the publisher, and Amzi Armstrong, the editor, leaned to politics—heavily in favor of the Whigs—but they also hoped that bustling Newark could fill the columns with enough advertising to make Whig propaganda profitable on a day-to-day basis. They succeeded admirably, and gradually increased the space allocated to news.

The editors welcomed the first coal boat and revealed that fifteen or twenty more coal-filled canal barges were on the way from Pennsylvania. Speaking of coal, *The Advertiser* editor urged Newarkers to "provide themselves with this indispensable article at an early period and not defer it till setting in of the winter." Whether townspeople loved coal in May as they would in December is not a matter of record, but ninety to one hundred boats entered Newark every week that summer, half bound east and half bound west.

The canal delighted Newarkers. The noise, bustle and drama of as many as two score boats arriving daily made the coming and going of a half dozen stage coaches seem unimportant. The canal men lolled along the waterway, more friendly than the lordly stage drivers who sat high above their roadside admirers and drove in and out of town in haste. Canalmen told wondrous tales of the New Jersey interior and the adventures that befell canallers in the wilderness.

By 1830, Newark led all New Jersey towns by a wide margin—by any measurement: population, industry, appearance, growth. Its population of nearly 10,000 was double that of any town in the state, and nearly three times as large as its one-time close rival, Elizabethtown. The number and diversity of Newark's industries exceeded those of Paterson, the nearest competitor and a town that had been dedicated to an industrial complex since its founding.

The industries, docks and canals brought large numbers of Irish immigrants to Newark. While they were needed, they were not welcomed. Toleration was limited in the 1830s. Newspapers always added the word (Irish) if it became necessary to mention an immigrant, just as they always put (coloured) after a black's name. The Hibernian newcomers lived in hovels, hastily thrown together to accommodate as many as possible. They drank heartily, laughed boisterously and played with vigor. Altogether, they were considered a nuisance—necessary, but a nuisance. Old-line Newarkers avoided their settlements Down Neck and at the top of the canal plane along Lock Street, near several leather works.

The Irish and other "lower classes" were particularly suspect when Asiatic cholera struck the town in early July 1832. All that spring the dreaded disease had been making its way around the world, killing as it went. Unseen, unchecked, an ugly threat stalked the land.

Discovery of a New York City case spread panic through Newark. Editors urged calm, assuring readers that the disease struck down only the intemperate and the "lower classes." The cholera finally reached Newark on July 6, killing without warning the wife of Captain Tate of the steamer *Newark*. Since she died aboard ship, the *Daily Advertiser* said: "We do not see in it much cause for immediate apprehension."

A week later, with ten dead within town limits, all the papers printed precautionary measures to be taken (principally cleaning sinks and drains with lime). Still the editors showed no alarm, since they could correctly point out that all of the deaths were in or near John Sharkey's house, close to the Centre Street wharf.

The *Sentinel of Freedom* voiced reassurance by declaring that all but two cholera deaths had occurred "in one locality and that the most filthy the town affords." The *Sentinel's* description of Sharkey's abode indicates that slums already had invaded the town:

"In a house containing four rooms not much over ten feet square each, and in a hovel adjoining, were stored nearly thirty individuals, as stated residents. Others, to what numbers unknown, made it a rendezvous for carousels. Among such a community, guilty of all kinds of excesses, and surrounded by filth, it would not be at all surprising that disease should be engendered, even without the assistance of a foreign cause."

Officials forcibly removed twenty-four people from Sharkey's house on July 13, carted them a mile and half away and herded them into a barracks, "to live or to die," as the *Advertiser* editor said. He scolded the officials for such behavior, even in an emergency, calling the action "inhuman and cruel in the extreme, and in the highest degree dangerous to the character of the town." The editor asked, where had the town's conscience fled?

Each day the death toll mounted. The editors dutifully listed (Irish) and (coloured) after the names, sometimes adding "foreigner" after the (Irish). In case after case they reassured the good people of Newark that the departed was "intemperate" or "guilty of some irregularity or imprudence."

By early August, enough temperate people

had also died to make the editors admit that "some of our most respected friends" had become infected. The editorial blame shifted. While not recanting on the intemperate habits of the "lower classes," health officials and editors began to blame the marshes and "animal wastes in the streets." They were not yet aware that polluted wells and lack of sanitary plumbing also spread sickness.

Before the epidemic faded in late August, nearly sixty residents had died in less than two months. A similar ratio of fatalities in modern Newark would mean about 2,000 deaths from a single cause in a period of fifty days.

The cholera horror underscored the fact that Newark was getting crowded, for the disease flourished where people were in close proximity. Cholera unquestionably enjoyed its greatest success in such filthy, crowded places as John Sharkey's hovel. If town leaders could have profited from a lesson, they would have recognized that disease is no respecter of boundaries, real or fancied.

Newark by 1832 could share the reality of Washington Irving's "smoky circumference," the "rattling of carts," the "brawling of the multitudes," the "unmeaning and discordant sounds." The most acute ears could no longer hear a villager "chanting some rustic ballad": The cacaphony of progress was too loud for bucolic sounds.

Painting of Broad and Mar Streets, done by an unkno artist, portrays Newark a appeared in about 1825. foreground, Archer Giffo tavern dominated one cor Town pump is seen in bot of painting. Center portio southeast corner of inte tion, with Presbyterian Ch and graveyard showing upper right.

Chapter 12

BY RAIL AND RUDDER

A CORRESPONDENT WHO signed himself "S.F." wrote to the *Daily Advertiser* in May, 1834, to bemoan what had befallen Newark. He had been away since 1819 and could scarcely believe what had happened to the crossroads village that he had left fifteen years before.

"I feel emotions both of joy and sorrow arising in my breast," wrote S.F. "The numerous streets, spires and wharves, proclaim that the population and commerce have spread further and wider, and the hum of business declares that the march of improvements has not yet ceased." He looked favorably on the canal, the many new churches, the "splendid rows of brick stores and dwellings" and the good stage connections with New York.

"Yet," declared the critic, "with all these I do not feel so much gratified as if I had found it in the same condition as I left it. To be sure, there stands the same church and there runs the same river, but I cannot realize it as my home. The time was when I could call every inhabitant of the town by name. Now I can walk half a mile in the principal street and every face I meet is a stranger."

The returned native found "haunts of dissipation" which destroyed "that innocence and simple beauty" of his boyhood home. Newark lacked public spirit, he felt: "The condition of the roads is bad, the public houses are not of that class which might be expected and numerous other matters of a public nature are not satisfactorily attended to."

S.F. blamed the situation on the fact that most businessmen were natives of other towns. He hoped that "some men of influence may yet arise who will sacrifice themselves a little for the general welfare."

Simultaneously, the noted geographer, Thomas Gordon, visited to gather material for his *Gazetteer of The State of New Jersey* (pub-

lished in 1834). He estimated the population at 15,000 and counted 1,712 buildings, all but 194 of them built of wood. There were fourteen churches—Presbyterian, Episcopal, Baptist, Methodist, Dutch Reformed, Roman Catholic, and two for "coloured persons." The town had three banks, the latest being the Mechanics Bank, founded in 1831.

"The town is remarkable for its manufactures," Gordon said. He told of tanners and leather shapers, coachmakers, and boot and shoe factories. The last-named made $900,000 worth of shoes in 1832, largely to meet widespread demands "in other states." Hat makers hired 487 hands. Two "extensive foundries of malleable iron" showed that Seth Boyden again had shared his secrets. Gordon noted the rapidly growing manufacture of clothing for "home and Southern markets," with 350 tailors employed.

House and furniture shop of David Alling, painted in about 1855, evidenced the prosperity that making fine furniture brought him. Below is a "fancy" side chair attributed to Alling and now part of Newark Museum's furniture collection.

Real estate values were on the rise. The *Gazetteer* told of a property purchased in 1828 for $60 which had sold in 1833 for $10,000—a profit of $9,940 in five years. Small wonder, for Gordon wrote of broad streets, with village greens "shaded by noble trees"; of "wholesome water" brought through seven miles of iron pumps from a clear spring on the mountain, and of "costly, elegant and commodious homes."

Gordon sensed the value of Newark's fine transportation, since "the facilities for communications with New York render the town a suburb of that great city." More than sixty-five vessels made Newark a port of call. Those inbound brought building materials for a growing town; those outbound were filled with coal and iron carried to tidewater by the canal. The steamboat "Newark" churned twice daily to New York, carrying some seventy-five passengers on each trip. Stage coaches hauled upwards of 800 people through town every week. Gordon anticipated the time when Newark would become a port of entry, and expressed even greater hopes for the New Jersey Rail Road, "now rapidly progressing."

Congress made a prophet of Gordon in 1836 by designating Newark as an official port of entry, eligible to receive foreign ships and to clear ships bound for foreign ports. Archer Gifford, nephew and namesake of the noted tavern keeper, was appointed Port Collector. His 1835 report showed that eighty-two vessels and 245 mariners used the port that year, although only nine ships cleared for foreign ports.

One curious part of port business was whaling, first discussed in 1832 and a full actuality in the summer of 1834 when the first whaleboats left port. In anticipation, Stephens, Condit and Wright Whaling and Sealing Company built a major depot for sperm oil and whalebone at the Centre Street dock. Carpenters fitted out the *John Wells* and the *Columbus* as up-to-date whaling vessels and coopers made giant barrels for storing whale oil aboard ship.

The *John Wells* and the *Columbus* cleared the Centre Street wharf in the summer of 1835, each with thirty men and boys aboard. The whalers sailed south to the Gulf of Mexico, rounded Cape Horn, searched the Pacific for their quarry, and then tacked together through the rich whale lands of the Arctic ocean. The *Columbus* smashed into an iceberg, but the *John Wells* crew rescued all hands before the sister ship disappeared in icy waters. Laden with a crew of sixty, the lone whaler scoured the Arctic and filled the hold with 3,000 barrels of oil and heaps of whalebones.

The *John Wells* made three voyages out of Newark; one lives on through a sea-stained log preserved by the New Jersey Historical Society. Uriah Russel, ship master, wrote neatly on the long pages, giving details of the hardships, the fruitless searchings, the excitement and the danger of a whaler at sea. He illustrated success and failure with pen and ink sketches of whales—a full whale for capture, an upended half a whale for sighted but missed.

A few of Russel's entries reveal part of the quest:

"May 7, 1838, at daylight saw school of whales. Lowered. Got one. Got one boat stove in—so ends this day."

Log book of the Newark whaling ship John Wells *for 1838-39 at the New Jersey Historical Society tells of the frustrations and successes of the city's noted whaler.*

The Cooper.

Coopers made huge barrels on Newark docks to store whale oil and cumbersome whalers such as that above called the city home from 1834 until 1839. The John Wells brought in three thousand barrels of oil on one voyage.

"August 13 comes with gale. Saw several right whales but it was too rugged weather to lower. At sunset wind moderated; saw whales and chased. One boat stove and lost a line but got a whale and took it to ship.

"September 7, Elezar Rogers stuck a harpoon through his arm—a dangerous cut. I sewed up arm as well as implements aboard would admit."

"November 8. Two fluke chains in the blubber tore out. The whole ship trembled. It was an earthquake at sea. But when it moderated we hooked onto whale again and cut and boiled."

"January 2, 1839. Ship John Wells bound home around Cape Horn."

"January 20. At 3 P.M. saw sperm whale. Starboard boat first got fast then lost whale. Larboard boat got fast, but whale stove boat and killed Abner Coffin, First officer, aged 26, of Nantucket. At 7 P.M. we took whale."

The last entry was April 9, 1839: "Light breezes. All hands employed all night in beating up through the Narrows." All was serene: the *John Wells* was nearly home.

Whaling couldn't last. Whales were too far away and labor too costly in Newark. The promoters sold the *John Wells* to a whaler in New Bedford, Massachusetts, where experienced crews were easier to recruit than in sophisticated Newark, where the orientation was not to the sea.

Considerably more important was the railroad. When the sons of John Stevens, Hoboken's railroad pioneer, completed the Camden & Amboy Railroad from Bordentown to South Amboy in December, 1832, Newark's leaders fretted at being far off the main line. Passengers and freight sped from New York to Philadelphia in seven hours, even with the long ferry trips on either end. It took no wisdom to see that if Newark tried to pin its future on stage coaches and canal barges, it was doomed to remain a small town.

Newark leaders tried early to get on the track. Townspeople in late January, 1830, rallied behind a proposed New Jersey and Atlantic Railroad from Jersey City to Trenton, via Newark and New Brunswick. Alarmed stockholders of the Camden & Amboy found an ally by convincing the Morris Canal backers that such a line would end the need for slow-moving canal

Steep grades west of the city challenged railroad builders, but versatile Seth Boyden designed two locomotives, the Orange and the Essex, to climb the hills. Within a few years, trains like that on top of the page regularly linked Newark with the south and west.

boats. The two joined forces to "educate" the legislators and defeated the charter bid by two votes. Despite cries of "monopoly," the Legislature stood firm.

Paterson promoters secured a railroad charter on January 21, 1831, and had begun to lay rails between Paterson and Acquackanonck (Passaic) before the Newark railroad backers approached the powerful Camden & Amboy with a compromise: if we run tracks only from Jersey City to New Brunswick, may we have a charter? Camden & Amboy backers approved; they could bring their tracks to New Brunswick, make connection with the proposed line and thus get direct access to the New York Port. The Newarkers secured their charter on March 7, 1832, to organize the New Jersey Rail Road and Transportation Company.

Public enthusiasm evaporated when the railroad offered its stock for sale on May 1. Promoters waited in vain for the anticipated rush, then bought ninety per cent of the shares themselves, prompting the *Sentinel of Freedom* to congratulate them for giving Jerseymen preference in the allotment of stock! Great success was predicted. The *Daily Advertiser* pointed out that the stagecoach traffic between Jersey City and Newark exceeded that of any similar short stretch in the country. Here were potential rail passengers—and Newark industry would fill the freight cars.

Dr. John S. Darcy, a 44-year-old physician, veteran of the war of 1812 and a newcomer from Morris County, was chosen president of the line at the organization meeting in the Eagle Tavern on June 4. Dr. Darcy had been in town only a few months, but his energy and intelligence made him a quick favorite. Later that summer he further endeared himself to all

MORRIS AND ESSEX RAILROAD.

This road was chartered January 29th, 1835, and the Company commenced running their cars by horse power, from Newark to Orange November 19th, 1836, from Newark to Madison by steam power, on Monday the second of October, 1837; and from Newark to Morristown, on the first day of January, 1838; March 1st, 1842, an act was passed by the Legislature for the relief of this road, and on Monday 18th of April, 1842, the road was sold—and the purchasers began to lay the iron rails down the middle of September, and finished the middle of January, 1843, being only eighteen weeks—and the year past, this road has been continued to Dover, and will be ready for use early this spring.

SUMMER ARRANGEMENT
NEW YORK, MORRISTOWN AND SCHOOLEY'S MOUNTAIN.

LEAVE NEW YORK,	LEAVE NEWARK,
8 o'clock, A. M.	9 o'clock, A. M.
4 o'clock, P. M.	2¼ P. M. Freight.
	4¼ o'clock, P. M.

LEAVE MORRISTOWN 7, and 8 Freight A. M., 2 P. M.

Passengers by the Morning train to Morristown, will arrive there at 10½ o'clock, where stages will be in readiness to convey them to Schooley's Mountain, Washington, Belvidere and Easton; also to Stanhope, Sparta, Newton, Milford and Owego.

Passengers from Morristown, will arrive in Newark in time to take the trains for Philadelphia.

William Wright, PRESIDENT,
Beach Vanderpool, *Treasurer,*
J. C. Garthwaite, *Secretary.*
Ira Dodd, *Superintendent.*

After 1838, the Morris & Essex reached west to Morristown and east to Jersey City and New York. Two trains each way served travelers morning and night and freight could be sent once daily.

levels of society by valiant service during the cholera epidemic.

Problems threatened to engulf the railroad builders. The uncertain muck of the Hackensack meadows was bad enough. Contractors dumped thousands of cedar trees and more thousands of carloads of dirt into the morass to make a roadbed—and then did not consider it safe to run a locomotive on the tracks for a full year after completion. Carving through the hard rock of the Palisades to enter Jersey City posed another challenge. As a last burden, the New Jersey Rail Road had to buy out the Hackensack and Passaic Bridge Company, the monopoly of 1795, to insure an unchallenged crossing of the rivers.

Dr. Darcy and his associates conquered all. On September 1, 1834, the horse-drawn passenger car "Washington"—a "splendid and beautiful job of workmanship containing three apartments besides seats on top"—made a trip to Bergen Hill and back. Eight horse-drawn trips were needed to handle the Newark-Jersey City traffic from the beginning. The relatively comfortable ride, the low fare (37½ cents) and the speed (a half hour) appealed to everyone. During the first week 2,026 persons used the railroad and in the second week the total rose to 2,548.

The town exulted on December 2, 1835, when the first locomotive, the "Newark," ran over the New Jersey Rail Road tracks, even though it was only to the foot of Bergen Hill (the deep gash through the hill was not completed until 1838.) Horse drawn cars completed the trip over the hill to Jersey City. Within six months bold passengers were riding across the meadows at thirty-five miles an hour. Disgruntled, envious stage coach owners and tavern proprietors hinted darkly of such dire possibilities as the roadbed's sinking into the soggy marshes or the steam boiler's exploding. But they hinted, and waited, in vain; the railroad was there to stay.

A special New Year's Eve train carried dignitaries, officials and the press to a new connection at Rahway at the close of 1835, racing the eleven and a half miles in about thirty minutes. Cannon boomed a roaring welcome as the train slid beneath a Rahway banner hailing "THE PEOPLE'S RAILROAD." The

first train to New Brunswick left Newark the next July 5 and the entire route from the Hudson to the Delaware was opened on July 7. Passengers knew the thrill of travelling twenty miles per hour: New York suddenly was nearly three hours closer to Philadelphia, through elimination of the tedious New Brunswick to New York Ferry ride.

If one railroad could conquer marshes, why couldn't another climb the hills to the west? Newark and Morristown businessmen joined forces to secure the Morris and Essex Railroad charter on January 29, 1835. They declared

Gash through Bergen Hill, completed in 1838, opened service to Jersey City.

their intent to link their towns by way of the Oranges, or by way of Irvington or any other town, depending on which one showed the most desire—meaning cheap right-of-way grants and stock purchases. The Oranges supplied the land and the proper stockholder interest, so the right-of-way went that way.

Seth Boyden provided the final push over the mountains. Successively wearied of leather slitting, buckle plating, patent leather, steam engines, malleable iron and a half dozen other enterprises, Boyden built a locomotive capable of overcoming the steep grades west of Newark. His six-ton "Orange," with Boyden himself at the throttle, puffed easily over the hills in July, 1837. A month later, two cars carried 200 passengers to Orange and back, prompting newspaper editors to praise the railroad lavishly.

As the railroads accelerated the pace of Newark, leading voices urged that the town be quickly incorporated as a city so that elected officials might have both the power to conduct business and to levy taxes. The simple Town Meeting no longer could cope with the times. Establishment of four town wards in 1833 foreshadowed the transition from town to city government.

The *Daily Advertiser* devoted the entire front page on January 5, 1836, to the full text of the proposed act of incorporation. Such support was extremely unusual, since the paper's front page traditionally was devoted entirely to paid advertisements. Town-wide debate raged as Friday, March 18, 1836, neared. On that day the voters would decide.

Using the usual anonymous letter so common in papers of that era, the *Advertiser* posed "a few plain questions.":

"Do you wish your town to rank among the first for correct internal management, cleanliness, beauty, and good order, as it now does pre-eminently for industry and enterprise? . . . Do you wish an efficient fire department? . . . Do you wish the streets to be paved and otherwise improved, instead of having them a byeword of reproach among visitors and travellers? . . . Do you wish to have an efficient Watch to protect your wives and daughters from insults in the streets? . . . Do you wish to have disturbers of the peace, riotous houses, and all others offending against good order brought to speedy justice?"

The newspaper recommended for anyone answering yes: "Then vote for an Incorporation."

Two days before the election, an *Advertiser* editorial scolded "holders of property" who were mustering to defeat incorporation. Pointing out that many of these opponents had been raised "from comparative poverty to wealth" through Newark's development, the editor expressed

dismay that anyone should oppose "the only measure ever seriously proposed to improve the condition and government of the place."

"What in the name of justice do men expect?" the *Advertiser* spokesman continued. "To live in a civilized state—enjoy all the comforts and advantages of social life—share the fruits of industry and enterprise around and yet shrink from their just measure of taxes? We are almost tempted to say they had better take to all fours and the woods."

Voters crowded the polling booths in four churches, one Baptist and three Presbyterian, on March 18. The simple ballot asked only that they choose between "Corporation" and "No Corporation." Soon after the polls closed at 6 P.M., backers of "Corporation" knew they had won far more than the three-fifths of the votes needed to carry the day. Final returns showed 1,870 for incorporating Newark as a city, only 325 against. Cannon roared through the night and happy crowds gathered in the streets to express their joy.

The *Advertiser* urged that "as we have commenced, so let us continue in the spirit of kindness, conciliation, and disinteredness to act with a single eye to the common interest of the whole."

Harmony continued through the April 11 election when citizens voted for the first city officials. They gave nearly unanimous support to William Halsey as mayor and heavily endorsed these aldermen: *North Ward*, Isaac Meeker, A. W. Kinney, William Lee, John H. Stephens; *East Ward*, William Garthwaite, Joel W. Condit, James Beardsley, James Miller; *West Ward*, James Keen, A. P. Howell, Enoch Bolles, William Rankin; *South Ward*, Isaac Baldwin, T. B. Pierson, Henry L. Parkhurst, Aaron Camp. Abraham Beach defeated T. C. O'Connor by a close 131 votes for city clerk.

Mayor Halsey, a 66-year-old Whig lawyer, inherited good feeling, but he also found himself faced with many city ills. Nine days after his election, the Mayor received a petition for a central market. It cited "the constant assemblage of the great number of fish carts, fruit wagons, and loads of wood on the corners and in the center of Broad and Market Streets, blocking up the way so as to make it nearly impassable." Opening of a new market area late in 1836 temporarily alleviated that problem.

Nocturnal dangers in the new city called for immediate attention. A "night watch" begun in 1834 had served moderately well but the city needed something better. Endeavoring to solve the problem of crime at minimum cost, city officials on May 27, 1836, combined lamplighting and patrol work into a 24-man "Watch and Lamp District." Duties for the watch began each night with lighting the few oil lamps set along Broad Street and ended with turning down the wicks at dawn. Away from the safe glow of the lamps, these first policemen "watched" the dark streets.

Watchmen were expected "faithfully to patrol the streets in said districts, and watch said city; and apprehend and detain until daylight all offenders against the peace, and all suspicious persons they might find walking or lurking about the streets or alleys at late or unseasonable hours of the night." They had to make arrests for "any riots, unlawful assemblies, outcries, noises or other alarm or disturbance whatsoever . . . and in the morning bring such offenders before any Justice of the Peace resident in said city, in order that they might be dealt with according to law."

Twelve watchmen — or policemen — were appointed in June and another four added in July. Council provided each of the lawmen with a thick leather helmet, earning for the watch the hated nickname of "Leatherheads." The watchers also had a shield, for which they paid $1 out of their pay of about $5 a week. They carried no weapons until 1846, when each was given a club.

Mayor Halsey and the council searched for a permanent meeting place, going from the Third Presbyterian Church lecture room to leased quarters in a building at 16 Clinton Street and then to the Old Market House on the South side of Market Street just east of the present Nutria Street. As they moved about, the councilmen negotiated with Essex County Freeholders for space in the new county court house proposed for the triangle where Market Street and Springfield Avenue joined.

A new court house had been in the offing since Saturday night, August 15, 1835, when fire started in the hay barn of Mrs. James A. Brittain,

a widow, whose Broad Street home stood four doors north of the outmoded court house and jail. Flames destroyed Mrs. Brittain's house, spread to Ira Merchant's sash and blind factory and swept through Johnson & Lum's wheelwright and wagon shop before wind-blown sparks set fire to the wooden roof of the stone court house building.

Thirty-two prisoners were taken from the blazing jail, including seven debtors on the top floor, and distributed among neighboring prisons. Volunteer firemen were powerless to save anything but the stone walls and even those collapsed before morning. The nearest hydrant was 500 to 600 feet up Broad Street, effectively pointing up the need for easily available water. The *Advertiser* commented: "$100 for a hydrant might have saved $10,000 or $15,000 in county buildings."

The passing of the county building caused no tears. The *Advertiser* editor summed up the general feeling: "It was an unsightly building and insufficient for its purposes, and the chief cause of regret in its destruction will, we presume, be the loss of its value in money."

The blackened site stood through the winter and spring while Newark and Essex County officials discussed the wisdom and propriety of joining city and county in one building. The two governments agreed on July 5, 1836, to build a $71,000 stone building in Egyptian style, with Newark accepting $29,000 as its share of the cost. Noted Philadelphia architect John Haviland planned the court house plus a $30,000 jail (Newark's share of that was $6,000). Mayor Halsey said at the cornerstone laying in August that the joint venture was "a natural union, like that of parent with a child in its situation, convenient in its construction, and of materials as durable as time."

Both governments moved into the building during January, 1838, and lived happily together for ten years when the parent county bought out the city child and took all the space. City government continued its nomadic existence—to rented rooms on the third floor of Library Hall in Market Street, to the second floor of a new city market erected over the Morris Canal in 1854 and finally, in 1864, into a former old hotel on Broad Street.

William Halsey, 66-year-old lawyer, was Newark's first mayor. He served one year.

All city problems were put aside on Friday afternoon, October 27, 1836. The weather had turned unusually cold and townspeople were laying in stocks of coal from the Morris Canal depots. Workmen hurried to finish the job of laying a connection between the Morris & Essex and the New Jersey Rail Road before winter. Then, at about 3 P.M., a lodger in a German boarding house on East Market Street discovered that the two-story frame house was on fire.

The old wooden building became a torch within minutes. Flames spread to a shop on Market Street and ignited a line of sheds in the rear. Sparks carried the disaster across to Mechanic Street, one block south. The city's five fire departments hauled their pumping engines down Market Street but within minutes their water supply gave out, partly because of the scarcity of hydrants and partly because the hoses on two engines split, spilling water into the streets.

Egyptian style courthouse of 1838 housed both city and county governments for ten years.

The inferno burned uncontrolled for five hours, sweeping up the south side of Market Street, along both sides of Mechanic Street and eventually burning all of the buildings on Broad Street between Market and Mechanic. The New Jersey Rail Road brought in five fire companies from New York on flat cars and volunteer fire fighters from as far away as Rahway hurried to Newark. All stood helplessly by, consoling the Newark laddies that the lack of water was not their fault.

As night fell, the flames roared on. People climbed to surrounding roof tops and stamped out little fires caused by flying sparks, thus preventing the holocaust from spreading to other quarters of the city. Firemen and private citizens successfully kept the flames away from Old First Church and the Newark State Bank on the corner of Broad and Mechanic Streets. The latter was brick and allegedly fire-proof. However, the fire completely destroyed three "fire-proof" buildings in the burned-out block, including the new four-story Washington Hotel.

Heroism and good deeds marked the day. Two Navy Lieutenants from Elizabethtown tried to stem the fire by blowing up several buildings but the flames swept on. Alexander Kirkpatrick earned distinction in the city papers by exposing himself "to billowy sheets of flame" as he poured buckets of water on Asa Torrey's house, saving it. Kirkpatrick modestly refused a reward. Later, a young man dashed up through a burning building to save an 11-year-old boy isolated on a flaming roof. The hero cradled the boy in his arms, jumped two flights to the ground, lifted the lad to his feet and disappeared into the cheering crowd without leaving his name.

The next day the *Advertiser* assessed the damage at about $120,000 but looked on the bright side: no lives had been lost and most of the burned buildings were "old frame workshops and warehouses." Few families had been forced out of their homes. The greatest damage was in temporary loss of jobs in the dozen or so factories leveled by the conflagration.

Fire roaring opposite Trinity Church in 1845 proved weakness of fire fighters.

The loss of jobs was indeed the worst blow, for an economic gloom was deepening across the nation. On the afternoon of the fire the *Advertiser* carried an accolade to the "immense sacrifices of businessmen to realize funds to carry themselves through bad days." The article told of "Southern drafts lately sold to money changers at enormous discounts."

Newark suffered badly in the Panic of 1837. More than 20,000 people now lived in the city, thousands of them attracted by the factories. Industrialists, for their part, had badly over expanded their holdings. The machine—and its operator—were here for good. There could be no easy return to the farm until the depression clouds blew away. Newark was now a factory town, for better in good times, for worse in bad.

One factory that had cost $30,000 fell at sheriff's auction for $1,800. All land values plummeted, ruining speculators. Banks foreclosed on notes and mortgages; it was said that "the notary's clerk, like a newsboy, left notices at almost every store and shop."

Workmen walked the streets that winter of 1836-37. The next spring those who were lucky left to take jobs on outlying farms. The unemployed suffered cruelly, particularly the Irish, the "last hired, first fired" of their day. Many left for greener fields west of the Allegheny Mountains. Newark industry, tied to wheels and engines, came almost to a halt. The burned-out block between Market and Mechanic Streets lay undeveloped for years, mute testimony to empty purses.

When the United States census takers rapped on doors in 1840, they found a population of only 17,202, down at least 2,500 from 1836. The only encouraging thing about the census was this: 11,482 of those Newark residents were under 30 years of age—nearly two out of three. Youth had come seeking the advantages of the city; they would not long be denied.

When E. Whitefield of New York published the lithograph on these tw
pages and the next, Newark was agog over its railroads, the increased s
of its buildings and the paddlewheelers and schooners that filled the Pass
River. Still, the city scarcely reached west of High Street, and on the e
side of the river, cattle grazed close to the railroad tracks. No smoke foul
the air, despite the industry.

Chapter 13

"FROM EVERY DIRECTION"

F EW MEN HAVE LOVED NEWARK more than Benjamin Thompson Pierson, the statistician who brought out Newark's first directory in 1835 and published one annually until consumption felled him in 1862. Pierson constantly roamed the streets, seeking the name, address, color and occupation of every resident. People insulted him and slammed doors in his face but Pierson was not deterred.

Pierson's twenty-six directories are his monument; without them it would be difficult to grasp the sweeping transformation of Newark from the unpretentious town of 1835 to the city alive with a new industrial vigor created by the Civil War.

Names in the first directories had a distinctly "Old Newark" flavor, which satisfied the editor, who traced his ancestry to the Rev. Abraham Pierson, Newark's pioneer minister. There were long lists of Baldwins (seventy-five in the 1835–36 directory) as well as Cranes, Ogdens, Wards and the other names of the town founders.

Later came increasing numbers of Smiths, and as the years rolled on, more Schmitts plus Kellys and Sullivans and an occasional Schoennbrunner.

Sometimes despair and bitterness nearly stifled Pierson. Lingering effects of the depression of 1837 threatened to bring him down; in 1840 he came out "despite the gloom and thick darkness before us." The publisher that year found 110 houses empty but remarked that he was "surprised to find no more were gone, for who can live on the wind?"

An upturn came in 1843, when Pierson reported "many wealthy men are coming who do business in New York." Three years later he found new factories "to make everything from a steam engine to a wooden nutmeg." As evidence of dramatic new industrial power, Pierson also noted in 1846 that Newark now had more than 100 factories driven by steam engines rather than by old-fashioned water wheels.

Benjamin Thompson Pierson, editor and publisher of Newark's first directory and all other editions until 1862. His directories give a clear record of city growth, from names to commerce, as illustrated by directory advertisements on page 117.

115

*Across the Passaic River, a train heads eastward from Newark to Hoboken,
an adventurous trip over the soggy Jersey Meadows.*

Compiling a directory was not easy in a city growing almost chaotically. Pierson discovered new streets cut through without signs: he installed them himself. He found many houses without numbers: he numbered them on his own, only to have his "official" numbers torn down and replaced by whim—the number of children in the family, the number of an insurance policy, and, in one case, the age of a deceased daughter. To aid boy messengers racing from business to business, Pierson introduced a "Runner's Guide" in 1840 with a list of streets and intersections.

Pierson commissioned his own city map in 1836 and updated it as the years passed. Pierson's succession of directory maps vividly illustrate how rapidly the city outgrew even the hopes of leaders when Newark became a city in 1836. The first map showed the original four wards but the map of 1859 contained boundaries of twelve wards, required to recognize sections of the city with spectacular growth.

Streets honeycombed both sides of East Market Street in the "Down Neck" section where the Morris Canal, the broad Passaic River and the open meadows lured industrialists. Immigrants from Ireland and Germany settled in "The Neck," and the section became the traditional home of the newcomer from abroad. New "Down Neck" streets acquired such names as Bremen, Frankfort and Hamburg. Streets were cut through the wide open fields on the hills west of High Street. Other new thoroughfares filled in space in the center of the city, where century-old orchards gave way to homes and shops. By 1848, Pierson's "Runner's Guide" listed 269 streets.

Population soared, from 17,290 in 1840 to 71,941 in 1860, an increase of nearly 55,000 in two decades. Buildings kept pace: between 1836 and 1850 some 2,800 new houses, factories and stores rose in town. Builders increasingly used locally made red brick or the brown sandstone from North Newark quarries, changing the city's face. Steam engines enabled manufacturers to build larger factories, freed from location on water-power, and tied instead to railroad spurs or the Morris Canal, the coal-bringers.

Pierson's directories also provided a means of assessing the early black population. He placed "coloured" or "col'd" after names in early directories—unquestionably indicative at the time of a different social level, but now a valuable record. The first directory listed 112 adult blacks, who in most cases were family heads. They included Henry Drayton, teacher; William Green, barber; John Harris and John Riker, blacksmiths; Abraham King, Henry Ogden and Elijah Smith, carpenters, and John O'Fake, who kept a celebrated oyster and porter

MILLINERS.

BAKER E. D. Milliner, 38 Warren-street.
BEACH ANN E. Milliner, 454 Broad-street.
BOYER CATHARINE, Milliner & Dressm. 115 Market
COOK MARIA, Milliner, 79 Market-street.
COWLAM MRS. Milliner, 296 Broad-street.
CRANE CLARA. Milliner. 327 Broad-street.

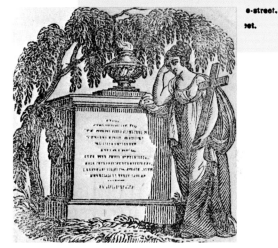

(ale) restaurant near the Eagle Hotel on Broad Street. About a score of the black families owned their own homes.

Pierson seldom indulged his pride for Newark openly, but in the 1849 directory he wrote:

"People appear to be flocking from every direction to share with us in the luxury of living in so pleasant and beautiful a city as Newark, where anyone who is willing to work can earn enough to make both ends meet, and have something left over at the end of the year, if economy is exercised."

Beyond the directory office, Newark was evolving overtly in some ways, subtly in others. A leisure class had risen because of the increasing numbers of immigrants available to do the physical work. A new leadership emerged, based not on church affiliation but on success in law or industry. Manufacturing broadened greatly in scope. Competing for space, labor and economic importance with the old products were vigorous new manufacturers, including zinc, chemicals, rubber, soap, beer, oil, cloth, glue, cutlery and tobacco.

COACH MANUFACTURERS.

D. BEACH,
Coach Depository, 305 Broad-street, near Market.

J. C. HEDENBERG,
Coach Manufacturer, Union Works, foot of the Inclined Plane, Morris Canal.

JAMES TURNBULL,
Coach Manufacturer, 150 Market and 9 Mechanic-street.

JAMES M. QUINBY,
Coach Manufacturer, 325 Broad-st., near First Church.

H. G. VANDERWERKEN,
Coach Manufacturer, near the Railroad Depot,
Foot of Market-street.

JOHN H. STEPHENS, & SON,
Wholesale and Retail Grocers, Wine and Provision Dealers 164 Broad-street, opposite Episcopal Church

JOEL W. CONDIT
Wholesale and Retail Grocer, Liquor and Coal Dealer, and General Provision Store
176 Broad-street, corner of New.

JOHN & J. F. REMER,
Wholesale and Retail Grocers, and Tea Dealers
266 Broad-street, corner of Bank
John Remer,
Jacob F. Remer.

Newark earned a widespread reputation for distinguished legal minds. Young men from afar studied under such eminent lawyers as these: Theodore Frelinghuysen, second mayor of Newark, and a national leader in the temperance, Bible and anti-slavery movements; William Sanford Pennington, Governor of New Jersey in 1812–14; his son, William Pennington, Governor of New Jersey from 1837 to 1843, and Joseph C. Hornblower, whose brilliant legal career was capped by his work as Chief Justice of the New Jersey Supreme Court from 1832 until 1846. The Newark Penningtons, incidentally, were the only father and son ever elected Governors of New Jersey.

Eng.d by Geo. E. Perine N.Y.

The Frelinghuysen name threads boldly through Newark's history. Theodore, above, second mayor of Newark, earned national distinction for work in Bible, temperance and anti-slavery movements. His son, Frederick T., below, became a United States Senator and was Secretary of State in President Chester A. Arthur's adminstration.

NEW JERSEY HISTORICAL SOCIETY

William Pennington, Newark-born Governor of New Jersey from 1837 to 1843. He studied law in Newark, followed his father to the Governor's chair and was named Speaker of the House of Representatives in the tense organization of the House in 1859. Pennington typified Newark's far-famed legal talent.

That first generation of legal eminence spawned equally esteemed lawyers. One year —1839—was exceptional. That year newly licensed lawyers included Joseph P. Bradley, destined to be a United States Supreme Court Justice; Lewis C. Grover, an incorporator of Mutual Benefit Life Insurance Company and its president from 1862 to 1881; Frederick T. Frelinghuysen (son of Theodore), later a United States Senator and President Chester A. Arthur's Secretary of State, and Cortlandt Parker, scion of an old Perth Amboy family who became one of the keenest and most articulate legal figures in New Jersey history.

Newark was agog during the Presidential campaign of 1844 when conscientious Theodore Frelinghuysen won second billing on the national Whig ticket: Henry Clay for President, Frelinghuysen for Vice President. City enthusiasts, reading the *Daily Advertiser,* were misled into thinking that Democratic candidates James K. Polk and George M. Dallas had little chance.

While Frelinghuysen's candidacy itself stirred local pride, Newarkers also liked Clay immensely. He had visited Newark in 1833, and his handsome appearance and Southern charm delighted a town which turned out en masse to greet a national hero. In addition, Clay's congressional exploits in helping to "win the West" had very real impact on Newark.

The West in 1844 included anything west of the Allegheny Mountains, plus Texas. Newarkers and sons of Newarkers were heavily represented among those who helped push the American frontier beyond the mountains. Hundreds of families with Newark connections were among the early settlers of Ohio and Indiana in the first years of the 19th century. Nicholas Longworth, one of the founders of Cincinnati, was a grandson of Thomas Longworth, a Newark Tory during the Revolution. Thomas had fled the town during the war but returned to live out his life.

An even more stimulating "Westerner" was David Gouverneur Burnet, son of the Revolutionary War physician and civil leader, Dr. William Burnet. Young Burnet was born in Newark in 1788, grew up in the little town, then sought his adult fortune in the lands beyond the Mississippi. He settled in Texas in 1831 and played an active part in the Texas rebellion which led to independence from Mexico. He was elected the first President of the Republic of Texas in 1836, while Texas was in effect still an independent nation.

Born in Newark in 1789, David G. Burnet became a South American soldier of fortune at age 16. He wandered afar, then chose Texas in 1831. When Texas won independence in 1836, Burnet was named its first President.

Texas became a burning issue in the 1844 campaign. Clay at first opposed annexation to the United States as "idle and ridiculous," but Polk's outspoken stand for annexation won him growing support. Late in July, 1844, Clay tentatively approved of annexation—only to find that abolitionist-minded Whigs in the North decided to vote for James G. Birney, candidate of the Liberal Party, rather than for either Polk or Clay.

The *Advertiser* editor valiantly defended Frelinghuysen's name in the face of crude and violent attacks in out-of-state papers. The Hartford (Connecticut) *Courant* for example, declared that the Newarker was "nominated to neutralize the stink of Clay's debaucheries and

Newarkers followed this 1844 campaign banner, now in the N. J. Historical Society.

employees to form their own small businesses, the major success stories involved men who came from New England or the Old World, seeking a share of the success beside the Passaic River.

Hanford Smith and William Wright emigrated from Connecticut in 1823 to start a saddlery and harness factory that made them both wealthy. Wright also won political power. Newark elected him mayor in 1841 and sent him to Congress in 1842. The state legislature named him United States Senator in 1853.

Beer-making Peter Ballantine came from Scotland via Albany, New York, where he had landed in 1820. His travels as a malt salesman for an Albany brewing business brought him to the struggling brewery that General John N. Cumming had started in 1805 at High and Orange Streets. Ballantine bought the brewery (then known as Morton's) in 1840.

Ballantine's rich, heavy ale so satisfied the tastes of Newark's hard-working factory hands that aging Scot built a massive new plant on the Passaic River bank near Rector Street in 1847. Ten years later, Peter took his three sons into the firm and bestowed on the company the name—P. Ballantine & Sons.

other crimes." Newark voters gave Clay and Frelinghuysen an Essex County majority of 1,822 and a New Jersey lead of 968 votes but Polk and Dallas won by a slim margin in the national voting. If New York Whigs had not deserted Clay to back abolitionist Birney, Clay probably would have become President—and Newark could have boasted of another Vice President (Aaron Burr, Jr., being the first).

Despite the legal talent, political control rested in the hands of industrialists. It was said that political careers were made or broken in "The Swamp" near Washington and Market Street where leather makers clustered. William Halsey and Theodore Frelinghuysen, Newark's first two mayors, were lawyers, but after that until the Civil War only one other lawyer became mayor, and he for but a single year. All others were of the business or industrial world: coach lace maker, saddle manufacturer, jewelry maker, banker, carriage maker and soap manufacturer.

The bench and the lathe provided the quickest access to riches and prominence. Many Irish immigrants rose from apprenticeships to eminence in the huge leather industry. Trade with the South poured gold into the pockets of Newarkers who made carriages, clothing, boots and shoes. Although young men broke away from

William Wright, leather maker, city mayor and United States Senator from New Jersey.

Hay sellers and lumber dealers gathered beneath Military Park's elms in this 1844 woodcut. Fine homes edged north and east sides of park.

Peter Ballantine dominated Newark brewing for all his life—a long time, since the patriarch reached the age of 92 before he died in 1883. Competition came when an expanding German population demanded light lager beer instead of heavy ale. Several new German-run firms rose before 1852 to satisfy the Teutonic palates: Lorenz & Jacquillard, Schalk, and Braun & Laible. The air was heavy with the sweet smell of fermenting malt.

Another Scot, Thomas B. Peddie, left his heath in 1833 to work for Smith & Wright. Within two years he made leather trunks and traveling bags in his Broad Street basement. He rose from the basement, built a huge factory, was Newark's mayor from 1866 to 1869, and in his halcyon years endowed Peddie School in Hightstown.

Two other Newark leaders, Moses Bigelow and Marcus L. Ward, made their starts in industry and experienced meteoric rises. Varnish maker Bigelow, descendant of a Connecticut family that had been in New Jersey since 1715, became three-time mayor of Newark before and during the Civil War. Ward rose from work in a family soap manufactory, which afforded him

the time and good fortune to be a leading city humanitarian and the Governor of New Jersey in 1866. Both Ward and his wife were descended from original Newark settlers.

Joseph L. Hewes and John M. Phillips, skilled workers in Seth Boyden's employ, founded their own concern in 1846 to make steam engines. The name Hewes & Phillips became nationally celebrated, particularly during the Civil War, when the firm made parts for the *Monitor*. Thomas P. Howell, after serving his apprenticeship, became a partner in his uncle's leather firm and his name became almost a legend among leather makers. J. M. Quinby, another one-time apprentice, took over an old carriage firm in 1834 and won distinction through the eastern United States for the quality and dash of his vehicles.

Newark's industrial power lay in its ability to meet the needs of an altered world. When farmers became more scientific and sought fertilizer for their fields, Alfred and Edward Lister came from England in 1850 and built a major plant on the Passaic River to grind cattle bones into fertilizer. The Listers searched the city and the state, then went to the neighboring states

Early lithographs on this page and the next show scenes of Newark in th 1850s, as published in 150 Views of New York and Environs. *Picture abov shows booming commerce on the Passaic River. On the next page, not the Morris Canal in the foreground. Several factories were four or fiv stories tall, but most buildings were unimpressive.*

for horse and cattle bones. Eventually they had to buy buffalo bones in the West to feed the grinding machines in their "chemical works."

Fertilizer became a Newark byword largely through James Jay Mapes, the energetic proponent of enriched soil. Mapes was a noted New York City professor of chemistry and natural science when he bought an impoverished farm on the southern outskirts of Newark in 1847. The poor soil suited Mapes fine: it was perfect for proving his theories of enrichment.

Soon the Mapes acres were green and fertile. Farmers from afar came to see the farm and to hear Mapes' free-flowing lectures. They rubbed elbows with visitors whose names made history and headlines, including Horace Greeley and William Cullen Bryant. Mapes lectured throughout New Jersey, inviting farmers to come to his demonstration farm. The fact that he hoped to sell superphosphate of lime from his Fertilizer Works did not detract from Mapes' wit and his superior knowledge of agriculture. His magazine, "The Working Farmer," carried his knowledge and advice to farmers everywhere.

When Mapes died in 1866, Greeley said, "American agriculture owes as much to him as any man who lives or has ever lived."

Fertilizer made Newark modern, and so did the start of India rubber manufacture in the early 1840's. India rubber provided waterproof garments for adventurers heading for the Plains, soldiers fighting in the Mexican War, gold diggers in California fields and eventually for Union troops in the Civil War.

While fortune hunters hastened to discover California riches, Edward Balbach came from Germany in 1850 and found his gold in Newark, although not on the streets. He opened a precious metals refinery on River Street, concentrating on recovering the gold and silver from floor sweepings in Newark's many jewelry factories. His methods revolutionized American gold and silver refining.

Jacob Wiss, a Swiss immigrant, stopped by temporarily in 1848 to earn enough money to take him and his two St. Bernard dogs to Texas. Newarkers watched him sharpen scissors and knives on a small grindstone powered by one of the somber St. Bernards on a treadmill. Wiss stayed to found a firm (which still exists) to make quality scissors.

Opportunity often lay simply in asking, "what must people have?" The construction boom prompted builders to seek a durable white paint. In 1850, the New Jersey Zinc Company opened a Newark plant to make America's first white zinc oxide for paint. Furniture and carriage manufacturers sought a clear, lasting finish for their handsome woods; Samuel P. Smith of Newark made this nation's first non-tacky varnish in 1835. Others entered the field, and by Civil War time, Newark was the varnish capital of the United States.

Hand in hand with new industry went financing—money to lend and money to save. The city's prosperity encouraged the founding of two firms with new ideas, Mutual Benefit Life Assurance Society and the Howard Savings Institution.

Mutual Benefit's founders denied charges that life insurance was a wicked gambling with the future when they received a charter in January, 1845. Robert Livingston Patterson, Mutual's moving spirit, insisted instead that his company gave young working fathers a chance to provide for their families. Patterson's directors represented a broad cross-section of Newark: merchant, hardware dealer, harness maker, leather manufacturer, carriage dealer, bankers and lawyers.

Struggling young men could submit a small down payment on a Mutual Benefit policy and promise the remainder in a note. The company rented a $25-a-month room in the *Daily Advertiser* building on the corner of Broad and Market Streets and met with mingled success. The first policy buyer paid nothing. The second, an officer of the company, lived to be 96. Another early client left most of his note unpaid on a $5,000 policy when he died in December, 1845, but the company paid his heirs. Enough policy holders paid their notes and lived long enough to permit Mutual to survive and to move into its own building in 1848. Within five years the company had $15 million worth of policies in force.

Howard Savings Institution similarly based its hopes on the wage earner when it started in May, 1857. The twenty-seven founders hoped that working men would deposit a bit of their earnings in the bank, thus shaping the nest egg that the poor were advised to acquire. The bank accepted any deposit, a relatively novel notion in banking circles, where small accounts

generally were regarded as intolerable nuisances. Even a married woman could deposit money—in her own name, with her husband having no legal claim on the account. Howard weathered rough early years and prospered.

So the city's economy expanded. Steamers on the Passaic carried away Newark-made goods and brought back bones, rubber, iron ore, hides and the variety of raw materials vital to the factories. The Morris Canal teemed with barges loaded with Pennsylvania coal for furnaces and steam engines—hard coal, fortunately, thus sparing Newark the smoky, smelly offensiveness of soft coal, the bane of many 19th century cities.

For all the new smokestacks and for all the new wheels of industry, Pierson was essentially right in 1849 when he used the word "beautiful" in describing his town. Tall elm trees graced the parks and many of the older streets. At Military Park, elm limbs formed a leafy canopy over Park Avenue. Church spires peeped above the topmost leaves, and beneath the elms fine new dwellings of red brick befitted the aristocracy and gave the town a red glow. Newark had risen fully from the ashes of its disastrous fires of the 1830's and 1840's.

City leaders who walked along Broad Street on their way to banks, insurance houses and law offices were resplendent in tall silk hats and formal business clothing. Everyone knew everyone else, at least in that social stratum, and took the time to pause for polite conversation. Even workmen wore high silk hats as they hurried to work at 7 A.M., running lest the owner got there before them, for he usually worked right along with the hands. Some owners rang the plant bell themselves to warn stragglers that man worked from sun up to sun down.

No one questioned the need to get machines humming at 7 A.M., any more than owners questioned workers leaving the plant soon after 4:30 P.M. in winter. All people labored by the sun, on farm and in factory, in home and at the bank. No factory could function by candlelight or whale oil lamp—and most owners and workers shunned gas, even after some houses and a few streets were uncertainly lighted by gas early in 1847. One correspondent, signing himself "Fireman," wrote to the *Advertiser* to ask whether the possible danger from fire out-weighed the pleasure of walking the streets after dark. Walking won: by 1853 the city had installed 337 gas street lamps.

Walking Newark's streets was a mixed experience, by day or by night. Storm-fed streams flowing from the hills at times made Broad Street resemble a muddy, shallow river. There were residents who swore that they caught eels in the flooded main street. Ponds formed near Trinity Church, at South Park and behind the buildings on the west side of Broad Street. Boys aggravated the condition by damming drainage culverts, causing January thaws to overflow the ditches and make small ponds. At the next cold snap, the dam makers skated in the back yards of mid-town businesses.

Frugal Newarkers and their elected officials chose to ignore the muddy or frozen streets. Unexpectedly, a visit by the famed Hungarian patriot Lajos Kossuth in April, 1852, focused attention on the wretched streets.

Kossuth was sought everywhere in America after he led Hungary's battle for liberty from Austria. Newark's turn to honor the freedom fighter came on April 21, 1852, coinciding with the official arrival of an uncertain spring.

Kossuth's train pulled into the Center Street station just as steady April showers turned to torrential rain, but the brass band played on and drenched artillerymen discharged minute salutes from the city's brass cannon. The Hungarian climbed into a carriage for a procession that moved through deepening mud toward city hall. Leading the procession was Colonel A.C.M. Pennington, reasonably resplendent in sodden uniform crowned by a Hungarian military hat and tri-colored scarf.

Kossuth dismounted to review the festivities from the balcony in the old city hall. Across flooded Broad Street the throng clambered aboard parked wagons to view the hero. As excitement mounted, a wagon collapsed and plunged twenty-five people into the ooze and frightened Colonel Pennington's horse. The steed reared wildly, tossing the colonel into the mire. Pennington arose with as much dignity as he could muster and slipped away. One tongue-in-cheek version said "Kossuth was informed these events were not on the regular program."

Embarrassed city officials suffered even more. Mayor J. N. Quinby rose to welcome Kossuth to fair Newark, only to have his words drowned out by a blaring trumpet proclaiming the arrival of "King Mud." Four horses labored down Broad Street, dragging a scow bearing the "king of ooze" and his loyal followers. Waves of mud rolled away from the bow and rippled nearly to city hall. That *was* planned, by aroused citizens tired of mud.

Kossuth's welcome ended on a higher note including speeches in English and German, a dinner at city hall and a reception at which Colonel Pennington spoke, showing no ill effects from his plunge into Broad Street. The next night citizens joined in a torchlight parade on a slightly drier Broad Street. Kossuth left with warm, if muddied, recollections of Newark, and more than $1,000 in a purse given him by sympathetic townspeople.

Advocates of Broad Street paving confronted city officials who long maintained that mud was easier to bear than taxes. The mayor and council quietly began discussing the possibility of laying cobblestones and work began before the end of the year. Broad Street became passable in all kinds of weather, although the rough cobblestones caused some jolted travelers to wonder whether the mud had not been better.

Newark was far ahead of all New Jersey cities, in size, in population, in wealth and in industry just before the Civil War. Farmers from the hinterlands still drove produce-laden wagons into the Broad Street market over the Morris Canal or brought in hay and wood for sale at the upper commons. Newark attracted the old and the young. Many a wide-eyed boy who rode a farm wagon into the city from Morris or Sussex Counties during the 1830's and 1840's returned soon after to clerk in a law office or to become an apprentice in a factory.

All the city's charms, its opportunities and its excitement were forgotten at word of California treasure. Discovery of gold at Sutter's mill in 1848 turned men wild with greed and hope. Some two hundred Newarkers joined an estimated 50,000 fortune hunters who sailed from East Coast ports in 1848 and 1849. Others signed on with the "overland" companies that struck out across unchartered wilderness in hope of shortening the many months usually needed for a sea voyage to California.

As the last weeks of 1848 sped by, the *Daily Advertiser* carried advertisements of "fast schooners" being fitted for the journey around Cape Horn to the golden land. A December 16 offer promised passage to California, food for eighteen months, and a share in the 250-ton, copper-bottomed *Alfred Exall,* all for $500. On December 20, a meeting at Luce's City Hotel organized a "mutual company to proceed to the gold region." Two weeks later ten Newarkers sailed from New York on "the fast bark, *Ocean Bird.*"

The most notable Newark gold hunters were Dr. John S. Darcy, first president of the New Jersey Railroad and hero of the 1832 cholera epidemic, and Seth Boyden, the inventor. Boyden was close to his 60th birthday in 1849 but as hopeful as ever of finding treasure—or at least of having a high time seeking it. He always enjoyed the hunt far more than the catch.

Boyden got away first, leading his two sons and ten other Newarkers aboard the *Falcon* out of New York on February 1, 1849. The speedy *Falcon* made the trip in two months, arriving in San Francisco on April Fool's Day, appropriately enough. Boyden and his dozen associates were digging on April 16, turning up $10 worth of ore the first day. Ten days later the company excitedly counted its worth: $600 in gold—$5 per day per man! By September 8, Seth Boyden was writing that they "did not mine a dollar the past week."

Some of Boyden's men drifted off to other diggings. All yearned for home. Seth himself spent more and more time gathering "seeds, trees and curiosities" before he sailed for home on December 20, 1850. Most of the seeds and trees did not thrive in New Jersey, the curiosities thrilled only a few viewers and Boyden cheer-

THE WAY THEY GO TO CALIFORNIA.

Currier's 1849 lithograph brought laughter, but Newarkers unable to go were envious. Rockets and airliners were suggested alternates.

fully took a minor job in Rankin's hat factory.

Meanwhile, Dr. Darcy's thirty-six adventurers in the "Newark Overland Company" left on March 1, 1849. They crossed the Allegheny Mountains on stagecoaches, then took a steamboat to Pittsburgh, down the Ohio River and up the Mississippi to St. Louis. There, as they sought ox-drawn wagons for the dash across the Plains, they heard fearful tales of warring Indians, limitless open space and treacherous weather. The company began to split up, a few to return home, some to dash ahead on saddle horses.

Westward went Darcy's diminishing company —to Independence, Missouri; to Fort Kearny on the Platte River; over the Rocky Mountains in late June and into Salt Lake City on July 14. A fur hunter misled them for hundreds of miles and they crossed deserts littered with skeletons of those who had gone before. They hove into the gold fields in late August and set to digging. The following February they met a fellow New-

arker, Richard Rankin, who had found a lump of gold weighing fourteen pounds. Rankin and two associates took $4,300 for their find.

Fortune and misfortune hit the Newark Overland Company. William D. Kinney and Dr. Darcy returned with modest wealth. Others came back without even enough gold to pay the expenses of their grueling cross-country trip, much less anything to show for nearly two years of work and hardship. Three of the Overland Company members died in California.

If riches had been their only goal, most of the California adventurers might better have stayed home, where in 1850 the wages were steady and the chances of striking it rich in one's own business were greater than finding gold beside the Pacific. If excitement and challenge were the attraction, most should have found Newark to their liking: The aging town on the Passaic was in the midst of intellectual and emotional ferment to excite anyone's imagination.

Chapter 14

"COME, ALL YE FAITHFUL"

NEWARK'S CHURCHES more than anything else reveal the city's basic character in the six decades before the Civil War. Industry expanded and thrived, streets became too numerous to count, new faces mingled with old—but on Sunday, the old and continuing habit of the town was church attendance.

A writer for the New York *Youth's Companion and Family Visitor* commented on Newark in the issue of August 18, 1832:

"The morality and good order of society is most strikingly evident on the Sabbath. There is a holy hush on hill and plain and street while the solemn bells call to the houses of prayer. The quiet and simplicity of a New England Sabbath may be found here. Thousands of well-dressed and attentive worshippers crowd the churches—and we scarcely know of any city in which may be found a greater or richer variety of ministerial talent."

By 1832, those who responded to the solemn bells of Sunday were a diversified lot. The Puritan, in name at least, had almost vanished, to the extent that a popular song of the period could ask, "The Pilgrim Fathers, Where Are They?" Even the city's oldest churches, First Presbyterian and Trinity, were different from days gone by.

Both of the original congregations worshipped in greater luxury, Old First in its handsome stone structure, finished in 1791, and Trinity in a church completely rebuilt and refurbished in 1810. Trinity's face-lifting included considerable enlargement and costly interior decoration. Only the old tower facing Broad Street remained of the original building; above that to a height of 168 feet rose a white steeple, not as high as Old First's spire but lofty enough.

Despite the architectural changes, Old First remained rigidly Presbyterian, and Trinity continued its Episcopalian rites. The dramatic changes were in other denominations, direct evidence of Newark's new and varied population. Two new denominations, Baptist and Methodist, brought religious forms that contrasted sharply with the staid traditions of the earlier churches.

The Baptists divided from the Lyons Farms Church on the Newark-Elizabeth border in June, 1801, and organized a new congregation.

Smokestacks rose tall, but visitors remembered Newark's many church spires. More than twelve can be seen in this engraving of the 1850s.

Church architecture ranged from the simple mission churches, such as that of Pilgrim Baptist, above, to the stately Gothic of the House of Prayer, left, and the handsome spires of South Baptist Church below.

They staged a baptismal ceremony in the Passaic River that startled Newarkers who watched from the high bank. Joseph Smith, Abigail Hobdey, Reuben Kellam and Jemime Bruen were immersed in the waters in symbolic demonstration of the washing away of sins. That done, the Baptists held services in an old private schoolhouse on the corner of Clinton Avenue and Spruce Street. In 1805, they bought the corner lot at Academy and Halsey for "a meeting house and burial ground." They continued their ceremonial baptisms, attracting thousands to the immersions.

While the Baptists were different, the Methodists were easier to hear. They opened their Wesley Methodist Chapel in Halsey Street in October, 1808. The members erected their own house of worship, one acting as superintendent, another as builder, and held services under the guidance of a circuit-riding preacher who cantered into town on horseback from neighboring counties. Wesley Chapel did not get a full-time pastor until 1818.

The Methodists were vigorously evangelistic, filled with the desire to go among the poor and the needy "and to call sinners to repent." Churchgoers took the pastoral homilies seriously, interrupting often with "Amens," "Hallelujahs" and "yeah, Brothers," to the consternation of non-Methodists. One contemporary chronicler wrote that the responses "very often were louder than absolutely necessary"—occasionally to the point of complete disorder. Methodists loved hell-fire preaching and showed it.

High Street Presbyterian, above, dominated the hill. Grace Church, below, with architect's fees of $11,000, stirred comment, while Catholics built St. Patrick's, right, and St. James, bottom right.

Experiencing severe growing pains, Old First welcomed the plea of members "in the upper part of town" for a new church. Simultaneously, a group living on the south end of Broad Street also sought independence but the north was given priority to split away. The Old First gave the northerners two-sevenths of church holdings, and ninety-three Second Presbyterian Church members laid their cornerstone on a plot facing Washington Park in June, 1810. The peculiar stucco finish of the new edifice gained it the nickname of "the old Blue Church." Services began in September, 1811.

The south end Presbyterians started their church 13 years later. When Old First members wrangled in 1824 over whether to call the Rev. William T. Hamilton as pastor, those opposed to him broke away and built their church close to what is now Lincoln Park. Old First's remaining congregation remained friendly; the dissenters in Third Presbyterian received two-sevenths of church property, the same amount given to the Second Presbyterian "Blue Church."

Divisions within the Presbyterian Church were understandable. So were the coming of rival Protestant denominations, for that matter. Far more disturbing to Newark's Protestant churchgoers was the imminent founding of a Roman Catholic parish. Catholics were generally persona non grata in America.

The arrival of many Irish workers to build the Morris Canal and to work in the city's expanding factories made a Catholic Church inevitable. The Irish held their first Masses in private homes, most notably in Charles Durning's house in Mulberry Street. Sometime in 1826 the Catholics resolved to build a church. In March, 1827, they quietly bought a Mulberry Street lot.

After laying a foundation, the Irish ran out of money. Lotteries, the financial salvation of early Protestant churches and private schools, had been banned. As the future looked bleakest, Trinity Church elders granted the struggling little parish permission to use the Church for a lecture by the Rev. Dr. John Power, eminent Catholic clergyman of St. Peter's Church in New York. Father Power spoke to a full house—at least three-fourths non-Catholic—and his delighted sponsors counted $300 in profits.

As they blessed the Episcopalians, the Catholics neglected to watch their treasurer. He fled town with the $300, leaving the parish rich in ecumenical spirit but poor in purse.

The embezzlement spurred church members to greater efforts, or at least made them willing to underwrite a huge debt. They finished their little church in 1828 and Father Power returned to dedicate it as St. John's Church. Debts piled up and public sale of the building loomed, but a loan of 22,960 francs from the Propagation of the Faith in France saved the church.

Other nationalities, other denominations,

Second Presbyterian Church, nicknamed "Old Blue Church" because of its finish.

other church buildings followed in rapid order. Methodists organized their second church in 1831, holding services in the old court house until they dedicated a new church in Franklin Street five years after the founding. Catholics were not the only ones with financial problems.

A small group of Germans in 1832 organized the city's first Lutheran Church at a carpenter shop in Mechanic Street. That same year, a Scottish Presbyterian Church was founded in the extreme northern end of town, near the Gouvernour Kemble mansion where Washington Irving and his writing friends had frolicked shortly before.

A Dutch Reformed church was started in 1833. Members convened first in various Presbyterian churches and then gathered in a room above the old market in Market Street. They laid a cornerstone at Market and Beaver Streets in July 1834 and moved into a new little brick church the following May.

Of all the new denominations, the most scorned at first was the Universalist Church which began in Fair Street in 1834. The Universalists believed that all mankind would be saved because of the loving kindness of God, the nobility of man and the joy of religious life. This doctrine deeply disturbed the many who believed that only the select could enter Heaven. In a time of fire and brimstone preaching, the Universalists appealed to reason. There were not many Universalists to despise; early meetings in private houses attracted only five or six members.

Shaw's *History of Essex County* told of the memories of one "old and highly respected citizen" who joined the Universalist Church in 1837. "So great was the stigma cast upon the denomination," the citizen recalled, "that no woman would be seen within their congregation in the day time."

Black families originally worshiped with their masters, or, when freed, with families they continued to serve under virtually the same conditions. They sat quietly in balconies or in the rear of churches; one reminiscence by the Rev. Dr. Alexander Macwhorter's daughter told of black servants sitting on the broad window sills of the parsonage while Dr. Macwhorter conducted evening prayers. Many sympathetic young women in the Presbyterian Church established this nation's first Sunday School for blacks in 1815. But black leaders chafed at being members of churches where they were permitted, not invited, to worship.

Christopher Rush, a wealthy black Methodist, established the first formal black church in 1822 in an Academy Street building—the forerunner of the later St. John's Methodist and Clinton Memorial AME Zion churches.

Then, in 1831, a group of blacks withdrew from Old First Church and set up their own Presbyterian mission, determined to have a more active participation in the services. Theo-

dore Frelinghuysen induced several prominent persons to aid in erecting a new church on a Plane Street lot donated by Frelinghuysen. Dedication of this church, the Fourth Presbyterian, was held on May 7, 1835.

Frelinghuysen's interest in black welfare was often misinterpreted, but he was at least sincere. During the Presidential campaign in 1844 Frelinghuysen was scorned by out-of-state newspapers as a "Negro lover." Significantly, within Newark a substantial segment of the black population questioned his activities in the American Colonization Society.

As a founder of the American Colonization Society in 1826, Frelinghuysen unquestionably believed that the Society's aim to resettle American blacks in Africa would be met with enthusiasm. Few of this nation's 300,000 blacks, freed and slave, knew as much about Africa as Frelinghuysen and his earnest cohorts who proclaimed themselves "firm and ardent friends of this unhappy race." Not many blacks accepted the offer to return to a "homeland" that was a century or two in the pasts of most of them.

Peter Johnson and Henry Drayton, both blacks, organized the Anti-Slavery Society in Newark in 1834 to protest slave conditions and the treatment of freed blacks. They were joined by a Presbyterian minister, the Rev. Samuel Cornish, a Newark black who became known throughout the North for his vigorous opposition to African colonization.

Restlessness stirred into bitter disorder in 1833 when a white Presbyterian minister preached in town on "The Sin of Slavery." A white mob stormed the church, seeking to drag off a black worshipper, but he was protected from harm by the white congregation. A few days later another mob threatened a black shopkeeper. When word spread through the crowd that the shopkeeper was armed and determined to sell his life only at high cost, the attackers regained what little sense they had.

Congregations in the older churches showed little zeal for black rights, although individual members in the churches showed compassion in varying degrees. In 1848, when a group of black Episcopalians decided to leave Trinity Church for their own place of worship, they were given land on High Street by William Wright, a leading city industrialist and politician and a Trinity lay leader. The blacks organized St. Philip's Church and built on Wright's donated lots. The Rev. James Tyng, principal of Newark Academy, was the first minister.

Only one white church took an outspoken stand against slavery. That was the Free Presbyterian Church, organized in 1851 to provide religious opportunity to anyone who could not afford to rent a pew, the common money-raising practice in most churches. The Free Presbyterian Church was an outstanding advocate of abolition from the start, and its firm political stand alienated it from other Christian churches.

Church development had become a matter of degree, rather than of kind. Churches sprang up on an average of a new one for each new 1,000 residents until the eve of the Civil War. Churches followed the spreading populace, reaching east of the railroad tracks in the middle 1840's as missions to serve the working classes congregating there. The Methodists followed their tradition of seeking the laboring group by starting services in Union Street in 1847.

Within a year, the Dutch Reformed Church had set up a mission in East Mechanic Street. It finished an impressive brick church in 1849, complete with a 120-foot spire in emulation of more affluent churches near the center of town.

"Down Neck" waited nearly another decade for its most magnificent church building. The St. James' founders, who organized in 1853 as the first Catholic congregation in the industrial neighborhood, promptly started a huge building. It took years to finish the work, but St. James' became the largest church built in Newark before the Civil War, its spire topping all others in the city.

As different denominations reached Down Neck, they also advanced westward to the hill country, where new development proceeded apace. The pattern was essentially the same. Established churches first sent out "missions" or encouraged local congregations to meet in private houses, in Library Hall, in churches, in a carpenter shop, or any place where one might hear the Gospel. Nearly all denominations were involved—Presbyterian, Episcopal, Catholic, Baptist, Methodist—and most followed the same pattern of starting in a frame mission house before building churches of stone or brick.

Life centered about the churches, both in downtown edifices and in countryside missions. Here people gathered to worship, to heed lectures on church-related subjects, to enjoy church choirs and to listen while hometown or visiting divines discussed and debated such moral topics of the day as temperance and slavery.

Temperance was an ever-burning issue. Clergymen preached frequently on the evils of drink and laymen organized societies dedicated to abstinence. Theodore Frelinghuysen was among the top three or four leaders in the national temperance movement and in Newark the voice of the Rev. Patrick Moran inveighed constantly against alcoholic beverages.

Father Moran was probably the most vocal, energetic and influential clergyman in the city just before the Civil War. He ranked with the Rev. Aaron Burr and the Rev. Dr. Alexander Macwhorter among the most memorable of early Newark church figures. Born in Ireland, Father Moran came to America in 1827, was ordained in 1832 and assigned to St. John's Church a year later at the age of thirty-four. He stayed in Newark for his remaining thirty-three years of life.

Hard-driving and forceful, Father Moran rebuilt St. John's two or three times, enlarging the Mulberry Street structure around the original shell. He was his own architect, builder, superintendent and sometimes carpenter and plasterer. Then, in 1848, he spearheaded a drive to build St. Patrick's Church on Central Avenue and Washington Street, buying the land secretly because of anti-Catholic feeling and serving as architect. He planned on a large scale and his young aide, the Rev. Dominic Senez, pushed the work. St. Patrick's held 2,000 people and the brick Gothic structure was a magnificent sight. When the Diocese of Newark was formed in 1853, its first bishop, the Rev. James Roosevelt Bayley, chose it for his cathedral.

Father Moran worked best at his own St. John's steering the day-to-day lives of his Irish parishioners. Combining wit with dedication, he despised both tobacco and alcohol—and never let wayward Irishmen or anyone else forget it. In 1842 he conducted a temperance

*"Signing the Pledge," a popular 1846 lithograph, was widely distributed
by the Washingtonians, one of the active Newark temperance groups.*

campaign, vividly portraying in simple language
the evils of hard liquor. The entire congregation took the pledge of abstinence, and woe
betide the parishioner caught violating it. Hundreds outside Father Moran's parish also heard
him declaim on the evils of drink, and many of
them signed "Father Moran's Pledge."

These were the days of revivals, when people
yearned to be stirred to goodness. Newarkers
often heard clergymen discuss the pitfalls of life
and the fear that salvation might never come.
Orators could leave a congregation weeping in
anguish and despair and vowing eternal self-
reformation. The effect of a powerful voice was
most startlingly shown between late October,
1842 and early 1844.

That was when the Rev. William Miller of
Vermont gripped the nation in his own brand
of terror. The Baptist preacher and prophet of
doom told crowds throughout the East that the
end of the world was fast approaching. When
his followers pressed him for a date he set it as
April 23, 1843.

Newark was tense with anguish and expecta-
tion when Mr. Miller promised to come on
November 4, 1842, to prepare the city for the
approaching destruction. His advance crew set
up a huge tent, 116 feet in diameter, on a vacant
lot off Mulberry Street to insure that those
gathered to hear the word of doom would not
be dampened by rain.

City editors showed scant interest in the portentous tidings of the Millerites. The *Daily Advertiser* allotted one short paragraph to the great tent and the fact that "William Miller and others will show why the Second Advent is coming in 1843." The *Eagle* commented: "The people of Newark take very little interest in this field preaching, and were it not for our proximity to New York, we presume the meetings would be very slim."

The editors erred. Mr. Miller and his fanatic following found many Americans thirsting for salvation and fearful of their times. The sympathetic Newark *Temperance Star* reported that 10,000 to 15,000 people heard the evangelist on Sunday, November 6. The hostile editor of the *Advertiser* admitted only that "the usual quiet of the Sabbath was disturbed by almost continual racing of vehicles through the streets from New York and elsewhere." Upsetting the Sunday calm was nearly as disturbing as the end of the earth to old-line Newarkers.

Mr. Miller departed after ten days, leaving behind the threat of April 23, 1843—and an echoing memory:

"***The end of the world is at hand. The evidence flows in from every quarter. Soon, very soon, God will arise in his anger and the vine of the earth will be reaped. See! See!—the angel with his sharp sickle is about to take the field!"

Newspapers reported a cross on the moon in February. High winds and violent rain engulfed most of the East in mid-April. Believers read the signs of nature and disposed of their worldly possessions. One enterprising merchant posted a sign: "Muslin for ascension robes!"

Millerites donned white gowns and hastened to the hilltops on April 23 despite some hedging on Mr. Miller's part. The April 21 *Advertiser* carried his declaration that if the destruction of the world did not occur on April 23, "then it will come at some future time, not later than the 25th of March, 1844."

The faithful twice went to the hilltops and twice came down, literally poorer if not much wiser. They believed Mr. Miller when he set still a third date with destiny—3 A.M. on October 22, 1844. Newark Millerites that October rented a Baptist Church near the New Jersey Rail Road depot and kept the doors open around the clock. The *Advertiser* reported "numbers constantly on their knees and praying in a manner that is pitiful to hear." Passersby heard voices raised powerfully in the Millerite hymn:

"We are living, we are dwelling
In a grand and awful time;
In an age of ages telling
To be living is sublime.
Hark the onset! Will you fold your
Faith-dead arms in lazy lock?
Up, O, up! thou drowsy soldier—
Worlds are charging to the shock!"

Impressive tent erected in Newark by the Millerites, as sketched for the New York Herald, *November 14, 1842.*

Methodists, at first among the simplest of denominations, finished this showplace at Broad and Marshall Streets in 1856 for $78,248, and the editors of Frank Leslie's Illustrated Newspaper *in New York City were enough impressed to show it in the March 8, 1856, issue.*

Once more a violent storm came, pouring rain on Newark all day October 18. Millerites were sure that perdition was close at hand. The *Sentinel of Freedom* featured an editorial entitled, "The Time Draws Nigh," but it dealt not with the end of the world but rather with the oncoming Presidential election (in which Theodore Frelinghuysen was vying for the Vice Presidency). The "Second Adventers" preferred their *Midnight Cry,* a widely read newspaper printed in New York. That editor said farewell to his readers and predicted: "At 3 o'clock in the morning, He will surely come."

Millerites ascended the hilltops for the third time on October 21 and watched the sun go down. When it rose again next day, the faithful wearily returned home. Newspapers told of personal ruin, of children running in the fields seeking Millerite mothers, and, saddest commentary of all, a Second Advent preacher gone with $1,960 embezzled from his flock. The movement collapsed. A person can experience one "end of the earth" or perhaps two, without disillusionment, but three times were too many.

Clergymen and their congregations could turn their attentions earthward again. Newark entered its most intensive period of church building. Between 1846 and 1854, the city saw twenty-two new edifices rise, eight Presbyterian, six Methodist Episcopal, four Episcopalian, two Catholic and one each of Dutch Reformed and Baptist. The period was marked by an increase in grandeur and a notable rise of

German congregations among all faiths.

Church architecture reflected the desire to "keep up" that overtook most denominations. Grace Episcopal Church set the tone in its new church in 1837 when it paid noted architect Richard Upjohn a fee of $11,000—a sum then enough to build two or three of the typical mission churches. Upjohn designed an English Gothic structure that featured a tower and a turret.

Thirteen years later, the Episcopalians reached into the northern part of the city, and bought the Plume farm on the corner of Broad and State Streets. Although they did not pay a large architectural fee, they raised the House of Prayer in stylish brownstone, added a slate roof and made it "early English," even to the gargoyles on the spire. Surprisingly, it cost only $23,000.

The once parsimonious Methodists entered the architectural competition. Central Methodist dedicated a splendid stone church on Market Street, near Mulberry, on Thanksgiving Day, 1851. Simultaneously, members of St. Paul's Methodist Episcopal Church, met in various public halls to plan a massive brick church "with 1,200 sitting." They finished their showplace at Broad and Marshall Streets in 1856—and announced its cost as $78,248: more than three times that of the House of Prayer.

Catholics could boast of the beauty and opulence of St. John's, St. Patrick's and St. James'. Presbyterians kept in the race with High Street Church, overlooking the city and dedicated in

1852 as "a gem of rare architectural beauty" that cost $43,000. A year later, Presbyterians placed the cornerstone for South Park Church, rejoicing in its emulation of "Grecian Ionic." They said proudly that South Park Church "for comfort and convenience and cheerful effect, was a great advance upon the stiff, cold and repelling specimens of buildings which Presbyterians and some other denominations had been in the habit of favoring."

Dutch Reformed worshippers were a bit late entering into the competition for fine surroundings, but in 1857 they commissioned a new stone building at the corner of Broad and Bridge Streets. Its walls were of brownstone from the Newark and Belleville quarries, and its tower reared 156 feet above Broad Street. The church cost $32,000 but it was worth every penny; immediately the North Reformed Church became known as a place where many of the city's elite gathered on Sunday.

It was recognized that expensive architecture did not always reflect the depth of religious feeling. The editor of the New York *Daily Tribune* looked at Newark's churches in October, 1855, and wondered whether the early settlers "would not declaim against the pride of such elegant churches as the Presbyterians now occupy on High Street and the South Park." He continued:

"And what would the plain old Methodists that worshipped, and sang and shouted in the barn like building called the Wesley Chapel in Halsey Street say should they come to life some Sunday morning and be directed to the beautiful church at the corner of Market and Mulberry Streets, with its fashionable audience, its sold seats, its stained gothic windows and its rich-toned organ? And as they should wander down Broad Street until they stood before the finest stone church in the city, with its magnificent window to the street, would they believe this to be a Methodist Church?"

Had the editor looked more carefully, he would have found that simplicity had not entirely vanished, for thousands still worshipped at inelegant frame churches. This was particularly true of the Germans, whose arrivals had become a flood in the late 1840's and early 1850's when they fled the Fatherland after the thwarted revolutions of 1848–49.

Newark experienced the first impact of a strong German influence that would endure throughout the rest of the 19th century. These newcomers were generally highly literate and strongly vocal. They also were given to beer-drinking and Sunday sports and singing, in defiance of uncompromising local feelings about such things. The Germans were deeply religious, too, but unlike the Irish, they embraced many faiths—Lutheran, Methodist, Presbyterian, Catholic and Hebrew. At least a dozen "German" churches of many faiths sprang up throughout Newark between 1845 and 1860.

Germans joined the Irish as objects of open prejudice. The Irish were scorned mainly because of their faith; Germans because many of them also were Catholic and because their language, their Sunday pleasures and their stubborn belief in freedom of spirit branded them as unmistakably "foreign."

This was time of bitter anti-foreign and anti-Catholic feeling, led by militant Protestant groups. Followers of a so-called "Native American" movement demanded an "America for Americans," urged the use of the Bible in the public schools and demanded a return to the principles of the founding fathers. One Newark minister staged a "mock mass" in church and sent his congregation into howls of laughter. "St. Paddy," was regularly hung in effigy from the steeple of St. John's Catholic Church, but Father Moran ever cautioned his quick-tempered flock to ignore such provocation.

Some Protestants were embarrassed by such excesses, of course, but a majority either silently agreed with or ignored the haters. The fuming, bubbling kettle of bigotry boiled over in 1854 when the American Protestant Association Lodge of New Jersey staged a "grand parade" in Newark on September 5.

A.P.A. lodges from New York, Brooklyn and several parts of New Jersey arrived by train, carrying banners decorated with patriotic insignia. Many held Bibles and, significantly, many also sported pistols in their belts.

The visitors paraded all morning, paused to wine and dine, and resumed marching at 3 P.M. Heading down Broad Street, the parade turned into William Street and past St. Mary's Catholic Church, whose membership was predominately

German. The *Daily Advertiser* the next day insisted that the paraders were "most orderly," but a description of pistols being repeatedly discharged into the air belies that.

Most of the parade had passed St. Mary's when violent fighting erupted. Eyewitness accounts vary sharply. The marchers claimed that stones were thrown at them but "a large crowd of Irishmen" (as the *Advertiser* described them) protested that they watched silently, if not respectfully. Who cast the first stone could never be determined but violence filled the street.

The marchers broke ranks and headed for St. Mary's Church, tearing doors off hinges, shattering windows, destroying the organ, ripping down pictures, overturning pews and reducing statues to rubble. Outside, pistol shots rang out repeatedly, and "an Irishman named Thomas McCarthy" fell fatally wounded. Several others received slight wounds. An attempt to set the church on fire was thwarted by police and by saner heads among both the paraders and the crowd.

Thus, September 5, 1854, was one of Newark's worst days, its nadir in prejudice to that time. City editors tended to side with the A.P.A. in the matter but relented slightly when letter writers of all faiths spoke of the shame for Newark. Bishop James Roosevelt Bayley (first Catholic Bishop in New Jersey) rebuked "bad Catholics" who had been "demoralized by herding together in our large cities," but he also pointed out in a letter in local papers that "every week, almost we hear of some violence committed against Catholic property." He called the St. Mary's episode a "gross outrage" against all of Newark.

Contrastingly, in view of the prejudice they suffered elsewhere, Newark's first Jews experienced little outright intolerance—and certainly none of the violence accorded Catholics. They were far less outspoken than the Irish and much more retiring than most of their fellow Germans.

Newark's first known Jew, Louis Trier, arrived in 1844 to found a tannery on New Jersey Rail Road Avenue. Others followed, many becoming peddlers on Newark streets or in outlying areas. They sold stockings, thread, needles and cheap crockery, quietly accumulating small savings in hopes of buying a horse and wagon or renting a small store. Before 1860, the leading drygoods stores in Newark were owned by Jews, a meteoric rise in fortune in less than fifteen years and a tribute to their enterprise.

One clerk named Benjamin Altman used Ullman & Isaacs' store in Broad Street near New Street as a springboard to success. Customers liked young Altman; encouraged, he left for broader opportunity in New York City. The name, B. Altman & Company, became an enduring hallmark among merchandisers.

Most of Newark's Jews lived in boarding houses near Springfield Avenue and Prince Street on the western edge of town. It is said that they "had little in common except poverty and religion," but they responded to Isaac S. Cohen's call for a congregation in 1847. A year later, on August 20, 1848, they organized the Congregation B'nai Jeshurun, the first in New Jersey, and worshipped in an attic in Catherine (now Arlington) Street. In 1854, when the congregation numbered twenty-two members paying weekly dues of 12½ cents, Rabbi Isaac Schwarz was hired for $300 a year. By 1858, members were affluent enough to build a temple at Washington and William Streets, first in the city.

Congregation B'nai Jeshurun was composed mainly of Germans and Bohemians in the beginning. When increasing numbers of Polish Jews came to Newark, members of the original temple aided the Poles in establishing Congregation B'nai Abraham in 1853. Newark's third Jewish congregation began in 1860 when Oheb Shalom ("Loving Peace") split away from B'nai Jeshurun.

The solid beginnings of Hebrew congregations nearly completed Newark's religious cycle. Now there were Presbyterians, Methodists, Baptists, Catholics, Lutherans, Episcopalians, Dutch Reformed, Jews, Universalists and several free-thinking sects. There were humble wooden meeting houses and mighty palaces of worship; there were churches holding services in attics and store fronts. There were aristocratic churches that still sold pews and there were "free" churches where even the poor could gather and sit wherever they wished. There was prejudice, but there also was tolerance. Newark was maturing in spirit as well as in material things.

Winter stilled the ships on the Passaic River, making it a haven for skaters, ice fishermen and walkers who loved the novelty of crossing on ice. Edward Beuer painted this idyllic scene during the winter of 1852.

Chapter 15

NOT BY BREAD ALONE

MAN COULD NOT LIVE BY BREAD ALONE, nor could the churches suffice to meet the hunger and the need for knowledge that Newarkers faced in the swiftly moving world of the 1840's and 1850's. Man had to improve his mind: the locomotives, steam engines and new industrial processes made the long-accepted standard of educating only the wealthy a luxury that an ambitious city could no longer afford.

The individual and his society had changed. Apprentices no longer expressed the expected extreme gratitude and undying devotion to employers who housed them and taught them trades. Journeymen mechanics boldly stated even in times of depression that they were men, determined to control their own fortunes and destinies. The coming of Irish and German immigrants brought new dimensions in thought to the once isolated town.

Newark also had become a town of young people. The 1850 Census showed that about sixty per cent of the city's 38,894 residents were not yet thirty years old. As a sad corollary, death hit the very young savagely; science could not yet extend or even protect life. In 1840, considerably more than half of all deaths were among children under ten. In 1856, when 1,475 Newarkers died, 1,056 were boys and girls. Longevity was a myth; only about four in every one-hundred lived to be older than sixty by 1850.

Such killers as consumption, scarlet fever and cholera constantly struck a defenseless population. Babies and their mothers died distressingly in childbirth. Newarkers relied heavily on faith —or tried "guaranteed" nostrums advertised in the local press.

Pease's Horehound Candy allegedly cured "coughs, colds, hoarseness, night sweats and all diseases leading to consumption and death." *Sands' Sarsaparilla* took care of "scrofula or King's evil; rheumatism, pimples, chronic sore eyes, ringworm, enlargement of the joints and stubborn ulcers." *Stainburn's Vegetable Extract Pills* supposedly conquered everything from liver complaints to "deplorable debility," while *Sherman's Lozenges* were recommended (by Sherman) for worms, coughs and "all the unpleasant effects arising from the too free use of the brandy bottle."

Sherman's "remedy" met one apparent need in the city. The increased use of all kinds of alcoholic beverages disturbed churchmen and laymen alike in the 1840's and 1850's. Temperance societies fought liquor with fervor, gathering to hear lecturers link alcohol with murder, robbery, insolvency, broken families and juvenile delinquency. Anti-alcohol newspapers in Newark included the *Temperance Star* and the *Temperance Advocate*. Both had their best days in the early 1840's but neither influenced enough subscribers, or advertisers, to last.

Protestant clergymen spoke firmly against John Barleycorn—and the Free Presbyterian Church, organized in 1851, required that all members sign a temperance pledge. Father Moran of St. John's vigorously promoted temperance among the Catholics. Editors of the *Advertiser*, the *Eagle* and the *Sentinel of Freedom* joined in, printing homely little warnings and suggestions for "mechanics and workmen," such as "Abstain from ardent spirits, cordials and malt liquors. Let your drink be that of

Franklin, when he was a printer—pure water."

Newspaper publishers did not refrain from carrying advertisements for "Old Jersey Cider and Boston Rum." Technically, liquor was sold only by the quart, following laws at least a century old, but anyone bent on inebriation could accomplish it by the glass in scores of establishments, including all open-air German beer halls after 1850. Mayor Moses Bigelow bluntly advocated licensing "public houses" in his 1857 annual message:

"The most casual observer cannot fail to see that it (the previous policy of forbidding sales of less than a quart) has not had the effect anticipated—intoxicating drinks now being sold in various parts of the city with impunity. It is not sold with authorized sanction, but it is nevertheless notorious that it is sold by whosoever wishes to engage in that traffic. History and observation alike teach us that legal enactments will not eradicate the great evil."

That year the Common Council authorized "public houses" and heavy imbibing went on as usual, without the added burden of breaking the law. Alcohol was a way of life for some; their need for amusement and companionship was answered in beer halls and saloons.

Home and church had sufficed for most in Newark's first century and a half, but by 1830 cultivated Newarkers were enjoying Oratorios in Trinity Church and the Handel and Haydn Society concerts begun there in 1832. Singing schools flourished. From now until the Civil War the tempo of social life would increase, often combined with adult education. There was a desire to know about other lands and other ideas. Lectures and pseudo-intellectual shows were heavily attended.

John H. Stephens aided the social and intellectual cause in October, 1844, when he opened his third floor Washington Hall on Broad Street, advertised as "larger than any similar salon in New York." Life picked up. The Swiss Bell Ringers entertained in the hall in November, and the following month a grand "Military and Civic Ball" enlivened the grand salon. Itinerant showmen came through and set up in Washington Hall and in vacant stores—exhibiting dioramas, showing strange and wonderful mementoes of far-off lands, talking about gold in

Fairs always provided high entertainment and this State Fair, held at Newark in September, 1856, was sketched for Frank Leslie's Illustrated Newspaper. *The first of the famed Waverly Fairs was held at what is now Weequahic Park in 1867. Fairs continued there until the 1890s.*

California or putting on "a concert of popular Negro music."

Outdoor shows enlivened spring and summer. When Raymond's Menagerie hit town on May 9, 1842, it marched up Broad Street, led by four elephants pulling the music wagon. When the parade reached the arched wooden bridge over the Morris Canal, the elephants refused to cross as a group. Unhitched, they walked across one by one, proving themselves wiser than their keepers.

Glassblowers, magicians, minstrel men and lecturers had varied success. The Rev. Henry Ward Beecher filled a hall with gleeful listeners when he lectured on "Mirthfulness" in 1856, but a speaker on geology expressed keen disappointment the same year at the scant handful who showed up to hear his discourse. One affair, the "First Annual Ball of the Newark Base Ball Club" on February 13, 1856, was typical of a day when each event was hailed in superlatives.

The *Daily Advertiser* assured readers that the baseball party was "the finest of this season." The paper went on:

"The hall, as previously announced, was most tastefully and ornamentally decorated with evergreens, rosettes, flags, paintings, etc. Several of the latter were choice works, and elicited universal attention, particularly a full-length portrait of Washington, at one end of the room. Around the orchestra was a strip of bunting with the words 'Newark Base Ball Club, organized May, 1855'; and around the base were a number of the uniform caps and belts belonging to the Club, immediately over which were two bats crossed, and a ball suspended over all. A number of canary birds in neat and tasty cages were hung around the dome."

The baseball players and their guests had a "handsome supper" at 1 A.M. and danced to the music of John O'Fake's orchestra until 5:30 A.M., when they went home to rest for the long season ahead.

Sleighing parties ventured far out into the country on snow-covered roads. In February, 1856, the Paterson *Guardian* commented on one Newark sleighing crowd that had driven up beside the Passaic River: "We used to think that all the Newark girls had long noses and warts on their lips. The above company, however, contained some of the prettiest girls we ever saw." In summer, Sunday school children rode wagons or walked to picnic grounds in woods on the north side of Newark. Militia companies

and other elite groups boarded Passaic River steamboats for picnics on the Arthur Kill.

But more than anything else, Newark's working class eagerly sought to keep themselves abreast of the knowledge that seemed to be increasing at a pace faster than man could master it. Wise heads among them recognized that they must keep up with advances in their machines. Scientific inquiry was flourishing. Most important, workingmen wanted their children to be eligible for the good things of life which usually seemed to befall only the educated.

The city charter of 1836 provided for public schooling—and the first Council set aside $3,000 as evidence of support for free education. But nothing really changed. Public education was still tied to pauperism. City funds were used to send the offspring of the penniless to classes in private academies. When it became evident that this helped neither the poor, the city nor the academies, the Council established independent schools in 1838. Classes met in damp, dingy church basements or other inadequate facilities. A high school was started on the third floor of a former private school and a "female" school was begun in another out-dated structure. It was free, but such schooling scarcely represented the

right of all children to a dignified chance in life.

The youngsters endured the taunts of more prosperous boys and girls, and increasing numbers of children attended the free schools, inadequate as they were. City-sponsored education limped along, under-financed, out-of-sight and out-of-mind, until 1845, when John Whitehead was appointed to the school committee.

Whitehead later printed a vivid memoir of his fight to improve public education. His fellow committee members were also dedicated, but hamstrung by "city authorities who required us to be as economical as possible in all our expenditures." After attending his first candle-lit meeting in a classroom in the musty basement of a Market Street church, Whitehead set out to look at all the city schools.

One look was enough. Whitehead met with Joseph N. Tuttle, president of the Council, who sympathized but told the school man that education must stand aside while the city sought "an additional supply of water and more policemen." Whitehead retorted that Tuttle "must remember that while the city was providing for a water supply and more policemen, the present generation of youth was fast slipping away from under our control and would soon be taking our

Lyons Farm Schoolhouse, built in south part of Newark in 1784, served more than 100 years. It was moved to the Newark Museum garden in 1938.

places." Whitehead told the Council president that he must decide whether a generation "should grow up uneducated and unfitted for citizenship or whether the city should wait a while for more water and police protection."

Properly stung, Tuttle and eleven other city aldermen crowded aboard a horse-drawn car for a Whitehead-arranged tour of city schools. They saw classrooms so crowded that boys sat on stairways or on the teacher's platform. Whitehead pointed to walls "green with mould," and showed the group one teacher trying to cope with eight grades scattered over two floors. He showed them classes "reciting to student monitors in the open air and in the lobby." A head count showed each teacher responsible for 100 or more children of all ages.

Most of the aldermen had never visited the schools or even inquired about their condition; the tour shocked them into action. That same night the Council unanimously granted the demand for more and better schools.

Three plain, two-story brick structures were built in 1846 and 1847 on State, Commerce and Market Streets. Each cost about $4,000. Three more went up in 1851, when a "colored school" also was started in the basement of the African Presbyterian Church in Plane Street. Newark's first high school opened in January, 1855, in a new building on the corner of Washington and Linden Streets. Classes for boys met on the second floor, but the supposedly weaker girls climbed to the third floor for their lessons. By 1854, more than half of Newark's children were in public schools, a great advance in less than a decade.

None of the buildings could be considered either so handsome as to displease restive taxpayers nor yet so completely cheerless as to discourage attendance. The quality of education was the sore point. Superintendent of Schools Stephen Congar, often called "the father of Newark education," agreed with Dr. John H. Phillips, State Superintendent of Schools, who said of New Jersey teachers in 1853:

"***In a great majority of cases, even those who possess the necessary amount of information are ignorant of the best methods of imparting it to others. Having no experience in conducting a school, they are consequently ignorant of the many thousand avenues to the youthful mind, and consequently labor without method and without success."

New Jersey did not yet have a state teachers

college, but at the same time that legislators established the first one at Trenton in 1855, Congar set up facilities to teach Newark's teachers. He provided a Saturday morning Normal School for all teachers who had not been certified by the president of the Board of Education.

Teachers protested that five days in the classroom were enough, particularly for the pay they were receiving, but the administration stood firm. The Normal School opened in April, 1855, with nine male teachers and thirty-five female teachers from Newark schools among the eighty-five students. Others were would-be teachers, hopeful that the school board would turn to the normal school for its future faculty, as it did. Entrance requirements were simple: about eight years of schooling, with emphasis on the "about."

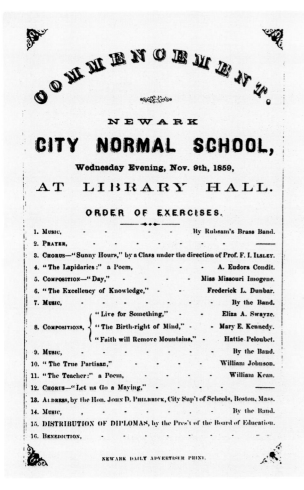

COMMENCEMENT.

NEWARK

CITY NORMAL SCHOOL,

Wednesday Evening, Nov. 9th, 1859,

AT LIBRARY HALL.

ORDER OF EXERCISES.

1. Music, - - - - By Rubsam's Brass Band.
2. Prayer, - - - - - - ———
3. Chorus—"Sunny Hours," by a Class under the direction of Prof. F. I. Ilsley.
4. "The Lapidaries:" a Poem, - - A. Eudora Condit.
5. Composition—"Day," - - Miss Missouri Imogene.
6. "The Excellency of Knowledge," - - Frederick L. Dunbar.
7. Music, - - - - - By the Band.
8. Compositions, { "Live for Something," - - Eliza A. Swayze.
   { "The Birth-right of Mind," - - Mary E. Kennedy.
   { "Faith will Remove Mountains," - Hattie Peloubet.
9. Music, - - - - - By the Band.
10. "The True Partisan," - - - William Johnson.
11. "The Teacher:" a Poem, - - - William Kean.
12. Chorus—"Let us Go a Maying," - - - ———
13. Address, by the Hon. John D. Philbrick, City Sup't of Schools, Boston, Mass.
14. Music, - - - - - By the Band.
15. DISTRIBUTION OF DIPLOMAS, by the Pres't of the Board of Education.
16. Benediction, - - - - - ———

NEWARK DAILY ADVERTISER PRINT.

Teachers trudged to the high school every Saturday from 8:30 A.M. to 12:30 P.M. for classes in spelling, reading, geography, history, etymology, algebra, synonyms, natural philos-

ophy and intellectual philosophy. The school term ran from September through July. Teachers put in about 720 hours in a four-year course to get a certificate. When they finished they might aspire to a salary like that of Isaiah Peckham, principal of Newark High School, who received the princely sum of $19.74 a week. He was New Jersey's highest paid teacher in 1855.

Grumbling about the cost of the expanding school system occasionally broke into the open. Thirty-one residents petitioned in 1856 for elimination of the high school on the ground that it was "aristocratic," but the Council ignored the request. A letter in the *Advertiser* on February 6, 1856, signed "Father," answered the petitioners, pointing out that if there was any aristocracy in the high school, it was the "aristocracy of worth, good behavior, and earnest intellectual diligence."

"Father" checked school records and found about 250 boys enrolled in the high school, thirty of them "the sons of widows." He cited the "intellectual impulse" of the school as being responsible for boys entering the trades or becoming clerks and bookkeepers, steps upward on the work and social scale. He continued, "The children of the artisan and the laborer share the priceless advantages here afforded with those of the cultivated and the wealthy; and by the true process of upward leveling, stand on the same republican equality."

Those who could not attend school were not ignored. City educators opened evening class in 1855 to aid both aspiring boy apprentices and adult workers. But the most significant ventures in adult education were the founding of the Newark Library Association and the New Jersey Historical Society, both part of the spirit of improving the mind.

Newark's interest in books was old, for the Rev. Abraham Pierson had brought 450 volumes with him from Branford in 1667. His son took most of them back to Connecticut—and the collection became the nucleus of the first Yale College library—but Samuel Smith mentioned a library in Newark in his 1765 history of New Jersey. Law students in 1783 pooled their books in the "Institutio Legalis of Newark." Not surprisingly, many who later strongly supported cultural advance in the city gained some experience in that "Institutio."

Industrial expansion brought increasing numbers of boy apprentices to Newark. In 1820, when an estimated 700 apprentices were in town, a private library was started for them to counteract the "unwholesome influence of the streets." Samuel Congar opened the Apprentices' Library every Saturday night and often felt satisfied with the crowd that trooped through before the doors closed at 9 P.M. Shelves were lined with 1,000 volumes of "the most approved works" in everything from art to fiction, but complaints were heard that apprentices turned to "useless trash that is too often thrown in their way."

A library open only one night a week—the night that apprentices might be expected to cut loose after a week of tight restrictions—was not enough. Pressure by newspapers and leading citizens led to formation of a real library in 1845. The founding committee included such men as William A. Wright, industrialist and political leader; Joseph P. Bradley, shining light among lawyers; Frederick T. Frelinghuysen, one

William A. Whitehead, the essence of early Newark intellectual life. He was the spirit of The New Jersey Historical Society, on the boards of Newark Academy and the Normal School, and was president of the Library.

Insurance company and post of, flanked the library in the 1850s

of the city's top legal minds, and William A. Whitehead, the fulcrum of Newark's intellectual life for nearly forty years.

The committee said candidly that the absence of a public library in a community "so intelligent and prosperous" was surprising. It blamed past failures to establish public libraries on "causes that would probably work the failure of any institution founded and sustained as they were." The committee went on:

"It is now proposed to establish one upon

Library Hall offered "halls and rooms to let" and the office of H. C. Parker, "corn and bunion doctor," as well as books.

Self-educated Joseph C. Hornblower became Chief Justice of New Jersey, was active in many church affairs, befriended Newark's black citizens and was first president of The New Jersey Historical Society.

such a broad, liberal, permanent and economical basis that those whose means are limited and those who are wealthy, may alike enjoy its benefits . . . The library is to be composed of books in all departments of useful knowledge, selected with reference to the wants of the whole people, of all classes, ages and avocations, books that will be read, and being read, will give the reader pleasure and profit."

The committee earnestly hoped that "perusal

of such books will direct the young from evil and will cultivate habits of industry, thoughtfulness and independence."

Within a year, $15,000 had been subscribed by selling six hundred shares at $25 apiece, with $5,000 reserved to buy books. Stockholders were given free admission to the library and all library affairs; non-stockholders could borrow books for $2 a year, with minors eligible at half price.

While library promoters vigorously sold shares, another city group earnestly backed formation of the New Jersey Historical Society at Trenton on February 27, 1845. The moving spirit was Whitehead, although a distinguished fellow-Newarker, Joseph C. Hornblower, sixty-eight years old and retired Chief Justice of New Jersey, was named first president. For forty years, William Whitehead was the Society's spirit, its voice and its spark.

Whitehead's value to Newark and New Jersey cannot be overestimated. He keenly supported all educational ventures, serving long terms on the public board of education and as a trustee of both Newark Academy and the Normal School. Whitehead, as secretary of the historical group, easily balanced his interest between it and the Library Association; he was the library's first secretary and its president from 1851 until his death in 1884.

When the Library Association finished its handsome stone building on Market Street in March, 1848, the wisdom and varied interests of Whitehead were evident. The Historical Society had space on the third floor. In the rear, a lecture hall large enough to seat seven hundred was the direct result of Whitehead's insistence that Newark needed a modern public meeting place. Gas lit the building, since Whitehead believed in progress.

The Library Association designed its building shrewdly. It included stores on the ground floor and rented them out; received income from the third floor historians, induced the Common Council to lease space for meetings, was paid a fee by the Fifth Presbyterian Church for use of the lecture hall on Sundays and leased space to the Post Office in 1849. With town government and mailing facilities on the premises, the Library Hall became a prime meeting place. For many years it served as a social and intellectual hub.

Things went well for the library. A month after it opened its doors, Abraham Cross willed his personal library to the association to make the books "available for many people." By May, 1849, so many apprentices used the building that the librarian complained of the "annoyance experienced from the premises being resorted to by numbers of boys at night." Later that year, an assistant librarian was hired to aid head librarian Frederick W. Ricord. The assistant was paid the same salary as the janitor—$150 for one year.

Apprentices continued to be a problem, even with culture made available at low rates. Most of them entered the city as frightened little farm boys but too soon they joined the mischievous crowds that made life difficult for the "leatherheads" on the police force. They represented an era of growing working class restlessness.

The apprentices lived with their employer, subject to his whims and often the victims of the table that his wife set. One apprentice, John Jeliff, fretted at the monotonous and unappetizing breakfast of broiled mackerel and boiled potatoes served each morning by his employer, furniture maker Lemuel Crane. Jeliff penned this prayer and tacked it on the factory door:

"Oh Lord of love, look from above
On us poor cabinet makers,
And send us meat that is fit to eat,
And remove the fish and potatoes."

Either Heaven heard the prayer or the poetic effort touched Mr. Crane's tender side: next morning the apprentices found before them a breakfast more palatable than fish and potatoes. Jeliff survived both poem and food to become one of Newark's foremost furniture manufacturers.

Change overtook the town so rapidly that many found it difficult to follow, much less to comprehend. The Irish and the Germans altered church attitudes, added wit and levity to the somber tone of old Newark and disturbed those who saw evil in anyone who lived differently.

The Germans strengthened the intellectual fiber of the city, for most of them had been well-educated in the Fatherland and saw no reason to abandon in Newark the enjoyment of literature, the arts and music. They founded their own German-language newspapers—*Der Nachbor, The New Jersey Volksman, Die Friedensfeife* and the *Zeitung,* all started between 1850 and 1855. They laughed at their own jokes (two of the newspapers were humorous weeklies) and lustily sang their own songs. In 1853, they urged, unsuccessfully, that town laws be printed in German. Two years later they founded a

German-American School. They were not to be ignored.

When a journalist wrote of Newark for the New York *Daily Tribune* in October, 1855, he showed a deep insight into the transformed city:

"The habits of the people have changed. Very few apprentices now board with their employers, and the many elegant equipages with liveried servants prove that wealth and luxury are more common than in old times. The fast horses which of an afternoon may be seen dashing down Broad Street—a noble street it is—show that Newark has some 'fast young men.' Some of the most elegant new residences and some of the old aristocratic seats in Newark are owned by rich men, who, it is to be hoped, are proud to remember when they handled the hat-block, the awl, the currying-knife, or the jack-plane."

But within the city a sickening poverty also had become entrenched. Newark had known the poor for many decades, but in the Panic of 1837 the jobless found it possible to switch from factory to farm work with more inconvenience than suffering. Now industry had clamped its workers to the work bench and the machine. When prices of food began to rise in 1854, without corresponding increases in pay, the pinch was felt among the working classes. Relief meetings were held in December of 1854: a massive depression was building up across the land and working men would feel it most harshly.

The *Advertiser* in December, 1856, cautioned workers to "live within your means, without emulating your neighbors." Simultaneously, money became scarce. Prime loans in the city commanded one-quarter per cent interest daily —or seven per cent a month. The winter of 1856 was bitterly cold, adding to the general wretchedness. Snow fell as early as October 20, 1856, to foretell worse days for the poor. That autumn money was scarce and prices high; on October 12, more than forty wagons loaded with produce intended for Newark kitchens, rolled back to the country for lack of buyers.

Town leaders called a mass meeting on October 23 to discuss the hard times. "A crushing mass of people of every class and age"

crowded inside and outside of Library Hall that night to hear speakers discuss the economics and philosophy of poverty. It was an evening rich in food for thought but it provided nothing for hungry workers.

By January, 1857, Newark was a stricken city, sharing the stultifying effects of the Panic of 1857 that had engulfed the entire country. Industry collapsed. Beggars combed the streets for small pickings. Each night fifty or sixty indigent men and women filled the cells at the police station, one of the few warm places in town. The Rev. E. A. Osborne started in January to distribute privately contributed funds to starving families and Mayor Bigelow strongly recommended increasing city welfare funds above the $10,000 normally expended.

Interesting schemes were advanced as 1857 neared its end. "A Friend to Education" proposed in a letter to the *Advertiser* on November 2 that the public schools be closed. "Turn the basements into soup establishments," he said, "and the upper stories into sleeping apartments where hundreds may be kept warm." In the same issue, "A Tax Payer" called on the city to use its welfare funds to build public works, thus "preserving their self respect" for laborers and also getting things done at moderate cost.

Two weeks later, more than 2,000 workers gathered in Military Park and appointed a committee "to wait on the city authorities and ask them to give work to the unemployed." They pleaded with anyone in town who had jobs to offer them immediately. As much as anything, that meeting reflected a new attitude by workers —a feeling that they were an integral part of the community, entitled to understanding and opportunity.

The *Advertiser* reported lightheartedly on the opening of a relief food store in Academy Street on November 23. "A half hour's visit is as good as a play," wrote the cynical reporter after watching the poor scramble for groceries. He said Germans were the most numerous, but "the Irish, for some reason, do not muster as strongly as usual. A sprinkling of colored people also gives variety to the complexion of the crowd."

In the store, the *Advertiser* chronicler heard "a confusion of jargon scarcely equalled since

The Four Corners, published by Smith, Fern & Company in 1854, showed city before hard times struck. Above is Broad Street, north to Trinity Church. Below is Market Street westward to the Court House. Top of opposite page is Market Street, east, and the bottom is Broad Street, south. Note width and cleanliness of dirt streets, canopies over storefronts, the slight traffic and a maximum building height of four stories.

the dispersion at Babel." He watched people ordering their relief supplies, with "their wants not only numerous but quite magnificent as regards quantity." Scarcely a moment passed "in which the scoops were not buried in the flour, the meal and bean barrels, and the molasses hogsheads emitted constant streams." Everything seemed to go "with apparent good humor

and considerable confab and mirth," the reporter observed.

The account did not entertain the poor. Even the *Advertiser's* tongue-in-cheek account took notice of "pitiable spectacles of patience—mothers with nursing infants, aged people and the infirm, calmly awaiting their turn."

Sincerely compassionate people kept the relief store shelves stocked. Manufacturers gradually offered old jobs to former employees as things picked up a bit everywhere the following year. Gradually Newark returned to its feet. The city had been through a period of trial, but that trial had come on top of a vigorously strengthened educational system. Even hard times could not take that away.

This Newark home of the Civil War period might have come straight out of Gone With the Wind *except for the white servant holding the horse. John F. Ogden and family posed for the picture in 1863 on the high pillared porch of their home at High Street and Springfield Avenue.*

Chapter 16

TORN BY BLUE AND GRAY

T HE HOLIDAY SEASON OF 1859 represented a significant mid-point for Newark: the clouds of the 1857 depression had rolled away and the shadow of war was not yet visible. Humming factories filled pay envelopes again, sending happy shoppers scurrying along Broad Street to clean the shelves of toys, books and sweets. Most homes and churches were decked with

evergreens and Christmas trees, evidence that German customs already were widespread. Sweet tones from the newly installed St. John's Church chimes, the first in Newark, echoed across the city at midnight of Christmas Eve.

It was a time to remember, for Christmas would never again be the same. The ghost of an appalling Christmas Future already was rising

MECHANICS

AND

WORKING-MEN of NEWARK!

It is well known that Newark owes her prosperity to her manufactories. There are millions of dollars invested in manufacturing in our city, and thousands of men are employed in making all kinds of goods for all sections of our country. Every man in Newark is interested, more or less, in her continued prosperity. That prosperity must cease if the Republican party succeed in carrying out their feelings of hostility to the South. *Even now we feel the effect of a partial withdrawal of Southern trade.* No manufacturing house in Newark is working more than about half the usual force. Should Lincoln be elected, many of our largest factories will be compelled in self-defence to make still less work, *and many mechanics and journeymen will be compelled to face the rigors of winter, and meet the terrible answer everywhere—no work! no work!!*

Workingmen of Newark, I wish not to deceive you. I tell you the plain unvarnished truth. I read every day many letters from all parts of the country. The evidence is overwhelming, that if the Republicans succeed, such a season of dullness and depression of business will be witnessed as has not been seen for years. I ask you are you prepared to vote for that party which will bring all this trouble upon you? Are you prepared to vote for that party which will be the instrument of taking the bread from the mouths of your wives and children? I appeal to you for your own sakes; as you value your own peace; as you love your own homes; as you love your wives and little ones who look to you for their daily bread; I appeal to you to resist this Republican party, by your votes at the polls. I am but a private citizen—have no office to ask—no favors to ask of any. But I see many of you working men—men who depend on their daily toil for their subsistence—being led away to vote for your own destruction—to sign your own death-warrant; and I ask you to pause and reflect. There is but one way to restore peace—but one way to bring success and prosperity back again to our city—that is the defeat of the Republican party. Vote all of you for the UNION DEMOCRATIC TICKET—the UNION ELECTORAL TICKET, and crush out these men who would take from you your very means of subsistence.

I speak to you earnestly and truthfully. Will you heed the voice of   TRUTH.

Probably the work of Edward N. Fuller, editor of the Newark Journal, *this anti-war broadside warned of the severe economic effects that war would have on Newark.*

in Washington, D.C., where Congress had been stalled since December 5 in its normally prosaic chore of choosing a Speaker of the House. Southerners vowed that no "Black Republican" abolitionist would ever be Speaker; Northerners insisted that no pro-slavery Dixie Democrat would get the honor either.

When the decision came finally, on February 1, 1860, after fifty-nine days of bitter debate, Congress chose Newark's William Pennington, an amiable attorney and New Jersey Governor from 1837 to 1843. "The Governor" promised "impartiality and justice for all," declaring that he had "a natural heart, embracing all parts of our blessed Union."

North and South co-existed uneasily, and the 1860 Presidential election brought the issue into the open. Abraham Lincoln, the Republicans' standard bearer, faced three Democratic slates of varied political shades: Douglas and Johnson, Breckinridge and Lane, Bell and Everett. Stephen Douglas, the "Little Giant" who had stood up to "Big Abe" in the Illinois debates, was a popular favorite in Newark, but many in the city favored John C. Breckinridge for his known Southern sympathies.

Newark seethed with campaign excitement. Republican "Wide Awakes" and Democratic "Hickory Men" marched in torchlight parades or listened to impassioned, often vituperative, speeches in halls and in parks. Newspaper partisanship ranged from the Newark *Mercury's* unquestioning support of Lincoln to the *Evening Journal's* scorn for all Republicans. Between them stood the old, calmer *Daily Advertiser*.

Edward N. Fuller, *Journal* editor, insisted that slavery was merely a matter of "state's rights." He expressed astonishment that anyone would wish to upset Newark's booming trade with the South. One unsigned *Journal* letter, perhaps Fuller's own work, declared:

"If Lincoln is elected, many of our journeymen will be compelled to face the rigors of winter and meet the terrible answer everywhere: NO WORK! NO WORK!"

This made economic sense. The South had been Newark's main customer for most of the 19th century; by 1860 about 65 per cent of the city's annual output went below the Mason-Dixon Line. Saddles, boots, shoes, clothing, jewelry and handsomely equipped carriages streamed to Virginia, the Carolinas and Georgia. "South" and "prosperity" were virtually synonyms in the city.

Newarkers generally agreed with the *Journal* that slaves were "property" and therefore the South's own business. All of Newark's blacks were free by 1860, working in jobs ranging from laboring to tending restaurants they owned. Wealthy whites were paternalistic, helping blacks to start churches or aiding them when they grew too old to work. It was not so much a pro-slavery climate as a head-in-the-sand attitude toward the misery of one's fellow man.

Newark voted heavily against Lincoln on November 7, splitting its votes among the three Democratic tickets. Lincoln's loss carried down even Speaker of the House Pennington. "The Governor" won Newark but Hudson and Union Counties—then part of the Fifth Congressional District—gave Nehemiah Perry, Broad Street clothier, the district by 294 votes. Pennington viewed his loss philosophically, but the irate *Mercury* editor wrote the day after election:

Nehemiah Perry, Broad Street clothier, was carried into Congress in 1860 by a strong anti-Lincoln sentiment.

152

THE UNION MUST AND SHALL BE PRESERVED

FREE SPEECH, FREE HOMES, FREE TERRITORY.

PROTECTION TO AMERICAN INDUSTRY

FOR PRESIDENT
ABRAHAM LINCOLN
OF ILLINOIS

FOR VICE PRESIDENT
HANNIBAL HAMLIN
OF MAINE

LITH. BY W.H. REASE

COR. 4TH & CHESTNUT STS. PHILADA.

*Popular lithograph urged Newarkers to back Lincoln and Hamlin in 1860,
but city voters were not convinced. (From the Library of Congress).*

"While Governor Pennington nobly and manfully treats this matter as personal to himself, his friends wish to express their thorough and hearty contempt for the band of mercenary and unprincipled men engaged in the Southern trade, who have been foremost in producing this result.

"If they had been slaves themselves, and every morning had been lashed into humility, they could not have worked more heartily to carry out the wishes of their Southern masters."

Editor Fuller must have been sorely tempted a month later to open his office window overlooking Broad and Market Street and shout, "I told you so!" As he had predicted, the idle walked the frosted cobblestones, vainly looking for work. Lincoln's election had indeed brought economic disaster; machines were idle, smokestacks were cold.

South Carolina seceded from the Union on December 20, edging the nation perilously close to war. The *Journal* urged New Jersey to join forces with the South and thus be "in a position of unexampled prosperity, manufacturing for the Southern trade." Two days after the secession a *Journal* editorial caption said, "Southern Cause Our Cause." Fuller gave thanks to South Carolina for saving the nation from a "worse calamity than disunion—abolitionism!"

The *Journal's* bitterness and the hard times failed to dampen the enthusiasm when Mr. Lincoln arrived in Newark on February 1, headed for Washington to take up his burden. The Presidential train from Jersey City reached the Morris & Essex station in North Broad Street at 9:30 A.M. Despite Lincoln's request that there be "no speeches, introductions or hand-shakings," Mayor Bigelow welcomed the President-elect and told him that Newark's citizens "entertain an ardent hope that your administration will be governed by that wisdom and that discretion which will be the means of transmitting the confederated states as a unit to your successors." Lincoln replied:

"Mr. Mayor, I thank you for this kind reception to your city, and would say in response that my heart is sincerely devoted to the work you desire I should do. With my own ability I cannot hope to succeed, but I trust to be sustained by Divine Providence, and this great, free, happy and intelligent people. Without this I cannot hope to succeed; with it, I cannot fail."

He then stepped into a barouche drawn by four gray horses and the procession moved into Broad Street. An eyewitness wrote that "Men, women and children were temporarily insane. The ladies from their perches scattered flowers and threw kisses; the hoarse throats of the men roared cheer after cheer; all the city was in the streets and the streets could not have known themselves, so wild was the delight. Thousands of feet tramped after the carriage; the esteem of the citizens appeared to amount to worship; men wandered from their wits, and cried they knew not what."

Stores carried welcome signs and bunting, although one storefront showed the President-elect hanged in effigy. Lincoln's party noted that one with distaste, but brightened at the Ninth Ward Public School when children sang "Hail, Columbia" as the procession passed. The tall mid-Westerner rose and solemnly bowed three times to the boys and girls. Near the Chestnut Street station, where Lincoln would take another train to Trenton, the crowd stalled the procession until policemen opened a narrow **path.**

Lincoln boarded the train, paused on the rear platform and briefly thanked the crowd for the enormous tribute. He stepped inside his car, the band played "The Star Spangled Banner" and the train pulled out of the station. Snow fell softly, as if to cloak the littered streets or to brighten the darkness already closing in on the nation.

There could be no turning back. By the time Lincoln moved triumphantly through the city, Mississippi, Florida, Alabama, Louisiana, Georgia and Texas had joined South Carolina in organizing the Confederacy. Most Newarkers would have been content to let them go in peace; war with the prime market was unthinkable.

When telegraph lines south of Washington stopped functioning on April 12, 1861, the *Advertiser* blandly assured readers it was "probably due to a recent storm." The next evening the telegraph ticker corrected that: Confederates had bombed Fort Sumter in the harbor at Charleston, South Carolina. Newarkers thronged the streets hoping for details—with many declaring that the Confederates had telegraphed false reports to alarm the North.

The late afternoon *Advertiser* confirmed the worst fears. Crowds jammed the newspaper office until nearly midnight, eagerly seeking the official word that the South wanted a fight. Two days later the paper gauged that "Whatever may have been the former political divisions, there are but few sympathizers with the rebels in this community." That day—April 15—Lincoln called for troops; Newark men of every age besieged the enlistment offices to sign up for three months' duty. War's beginning came as a relief after months of tension and doubt.

City officials summoned residents to a mass meeting in front of the court house on Monday afternoon, April 22. Speaker after speaker exhorted the great assemblage to support the Union. They represented all segments of the city—industrial, legal, religious, political, the varied nationalities and the militia.

One of the speakers was Theodore Runyon, city counsel and a leading Democrat who had cast one of the four New Jersey votes for Stephen A. Douglas in the Electoral College. He candidly admitted that Lincoln's presence in the White House was not his doing: he had worked

After vowing "to do no more than bow,"
Lincoln warmed to Newark's wild greeting.

to keep him out. Now, Runyon said, he had "no choice but to support Lincoln's government." Five days later, Governor Charles Olden named the 38-year-old Runyon as brigadier general to lead the first contingent of 3,123 New Jersey soldiers to Washington.

Runyon had engaged in many militia activities, although he had never led soldiers in the field. The Newark militia and volunteers rallied heartily behind their hometown general. More than a thousand of them followed Runyon to a Trenton rendezvous on April 30, buoyed on leaving by the sight of "streets, house-tops and windows filled with people." The troops halted at the corner of Washington and Linden Streets while the girls in the high school presented them with a hand stitched flag, then headed for their train.

The departing warriors wore bright, varied militia colors, in keeping with the social club atmosphere that the militia represented. Here was a brigade of Irishmen, a brigade of Germans, a unit of blue bloods, mingled together on the way to war. Runyon's New Jersey units milled about in Trenton, waiting to be issued archaic weapons. Then, on May 3, the Jerseymen boarded slow-moving ferry boats and sailed for Washington.

When the New Jersey Regiment reached the capital on May 7, it created a sensation as the first fully uniformed, fully equipped unit to reach the city. Runyon had performed nobly in welding this unit in less than three weeks. President Lincoln complimented New Jersey—and Newark—on its good looking, well equipped troops.

Two weeks later, on May 24, this elite New Jersey Brigade was secretly routed out of bed at midnight, marched across the Potomac River bridge under heavy guard and sent on the double through the moonlit night to Alexandria, Virginia. They rested on their weapons, ready for anything—and next day they began to dig. They dug from 6 A.M. to 7 P.M. daily for nearly a month, throwing up the capital's first fortifications, appropriately called Fort Runyon. It was not the glory of the battlefield, but it was useful.

The Jerseymen only stood in reserve at the ill-fated Battle of Bull Run on July 21, three days before their ninety-day enlistments expired. Weary from digging, strangers to enemy fire, the First New Jersey returned home on July 25 to a rousing welcome. The fire bell summoned firemen and city residents to the Chestnut Street station to hail the returning heroes.

ort Runyon, named for Newark general.

Men cheered, women waved handkerchiefs or fainted and the soldiers grinned. The joy was complete; not one member of the First New Jersey had been killed or wounded.

War could not continue, however, without drawing more Newark men into the maw. When the first troops came back, the Second New Jersey Regiment, composed mainly of Newarkers, was on its way south to serve for three years. The departure was marred by Captain John Toler's charge that his Montgomery Guards, an Irish unit, had been denied a spot in the regiment because of politics. Toler led the Montgomerys to New York to enlist in the Excelsior Brigade, attracting with him other groups of fighting Irish.

Most of the ninety-day men in the unscathed First Regiment re-enlisted promptly, heading South in September as the Eighth Regiment. War had gone far beyond the onerous chores of digging; these soldiers earned their battle honors —and learned of battle horrors—in the Virginia Peninsula Campaign during the spring of 1862. Newark papers told of battles and casualties: at Yorktown, at Williamsburg, at Fair Oaks, at Seven Pines—a war theater as foreign as Asia to most Newarkers. The *Advertiser* sent its own correspondent to the battlefront to write of the war in "local boy" terms.

The Peninsula campaign gave Newark and New Jersey its first genuine Civil War hero: General Philip Kearny, the one-armed, hard-driving professional soldier who assumed command of the Second Regiment in July, 1861, after the fiasco at Bull Run. Kearny technically was not a Newarker, although he had spent boyhood summers at his grandfather's home in Belleville Avenue (now Broadway). The general's adult home was across the Passaic River in Hudson County, but Newark cherished him and claimed him as its very own.

Kearny took the lackadaisical, independent New Jersey volunteers and bullied them into a hard-bitten and well-disciplined fighting regiment. His Jerseymen fought savagely with him on the Peninsula and followed him when he became a Division commander late in the spring of 1862. The brilliance of Kearny was recognized by both sides in the conflict. Confederates nicknamed him "The One-Armed Devil" in

Philip Kearny, greatest of the volunteers. Opposite, Captain Pennington gave bounty to 12th Infantry recruits.

grudging admiration.

Kearny's star reached its zenith in the late afternoon of September 1, 1862, at Chantilly, Virginia. Wild fighting broke out just as a violent electrical storm swept the area. Kearny rode his sturdy brown horse through the rain, shouting orders, rallying his men. He charged to the front lines and disappeared into the murky twilight in the direction of the Confederate lines, whether in confusion or in daring has never been made clear.

Across the field a half dozen musket flashes were seen in the dusk, then nothing. A Southern bullet had stilled him; Phil Kearny was dead. He lay in the Virginia mud, a fury while living, a legend when dead. Distinguished Northern and Southern leaders alike sent regrets to his young widow. Newark mourned— and the war went on.

Phil Kearny's flashing course across Virginia made the headlines, but Newark interest that summer centered on Camp Frelinghuysen, established to muster northern New Jersey volunteers into service. The huge camp sprawled westward from what is now Branch Brook Park, and extended from the tracks of the Morris & Essex Railroad toward Bloomfield Avenue.

Mothers, wives and sweethearts trudged daily to the camp over dusty roads to carry baskets of food to the soldiers.

Volunteers gathered at Camp Frelinghuysen in July, 1862, to form the Thirteenth Regiment. The unit was at full strength on August 28, 1862, when the Rev. Dr. E. M. Levy and several ladies of the South Baptist Church stopped by for the afternoon retreat parade and presented a regimental flag stitched by the ladies. The troops stood at attention as Dr. Levy said:

"This flag . . . is not made for holiday uses, nor to float in the quiet breezes of home. It is intended for the smoke of battle, the rallying object in the hour when you and the enemy will meet face to face. . . . Be assured, colonel, female patriotism still survives; and while your regiment is far away from home and loved ones, tender hearts will be praying for your success, and gentle hands will be preparing to wreath your brows with honors, or to strew your graves with flowers."

Colonel Ezra A. Carman accepted the flag and promised that the Thirteenth would "follow it to the battlefield, fight under it, and, if need be, die beneath its folds."

While the men of the Thirteenth might have been ready to die on some distant battlefield, in Newark they wanted to live. When officers cancelled a promised overnight leave just before departure, a thousand men stampeded through the camp barriers. Guards stuck their rifles into the ground and joined the overnight AWOLs for a night at home or on the town. Dismayed officers forgave everyone when the soldiers returned the next day. They marched in dignity down Broad Street to the train on August 31, resting in Washington Park. The Second Presbyterian Church minister dismissed the congregation when he heard the troops across the street, and the worshippers mingled with the soldiers.

Less than three weeks later, the promise to "die beneath the folds" of the South Baptist Church banner was fulfilled. On September 17, the green troops fought at Antietam and suffered cruel losses. When coffins came back to Newark, the ladies remembered their vow to strew "your grave with flowers." The Thirteenth fought on —through Virginia, at Gettysburg, on Sherman's march to the sea, and beyond to war's end.

The war had turned grim. The casualty lists, the funerals and the sight of empty sleeves in blue uniforms made the gaiety of flag presentations a mockery. On the home front, industrial depression lingered and added to the gloom. The Newark Female Charitable Society reported late in 1861:

"At this moment a portion of our poor find temporary employment in the Governmental requisitions of the war. But the wheels of healthful industry stand still. Our women are plying with hurt hands the sail needle, and our little boys are stitching at those melancholy knapsacks. The home guard is becoming small.

"You enter a poor man's premises now (especially among our foreign population) and he is not there. You miss the din of his hammer and the wreath of smoke from his pipe, and all the cheerful concomitants of his simple enjoyment. The wife weeps and fails to make you understand what has happened, but the children tell you that 'Father has gone to the war.' And from the many applications made to us recently, we ascertain that the *brothers* are also gone; and that women, many of whom cannot speak a word of English, and pitiful children alone remain, to bar the door against coming storms."

Lilly Martin Spencer, who lived in Newark during the war, painted this poignant scene of children playing at soldiering while adults grieved over headlines telling of death and ruin.

The N. Y. Illustrated News *on June 21, 1862, showed wounded soldiers being treated in a Center Street warehouse that had been hastily converted into a government hospital.*

Depression, at least, would pass away. War's insatiable appetite transformed industry to meet demands that had never been known before. Hewes & Phillips made vital gun parts and furnished the turret rings for the iron-clad *Monitor* (conqueror of the South's *Merrimac*) and parts of other war ships. Thomas B. Peddie's trunk factory manufactured cartridge boxes and knapsacks. Nehemiah Perry, Pennington's successor in Congress, switched his production to army uniforms. J. M. Quinby's esteemed old carriage factory put together field ambulances and gun carriages. The problem was not contracts, but manpower to fulfill them, for Newark's 1860 population of 71,941 had sagged to 68,000 in 1863. Then it began to rise sharply as newcomers streamed in to take advantage of the war-inspired opportunities. By 1865, 87,413 people lived in the city, despite the absence of some 10,000 men who had gone off to war.

Booming factories underscored the fact that this had become a war of attrition and sacrifice, a far cry from the carefree days of 1861. The lure of factory pay envelopes was powerful, but the glory of war faded when casualty lists were tacked on the elm trees along Broad Street.

Abraham Lincoln made it clear on September 22, 1862, that slavery *was* an issue. That day he gave warning that within 100 days he would issue an Emancipation Proclamation—declaring slaves free.

Editor Fuller of the *Journal* called Lincoln's decree "as absurd as it is fanatical." The *Advertiser* was guarded: "Whether it will be productive of good or evil only time will reveal," but the editor insisted that Lincoln had "discharged a delicate and difficult task . . . with singular tact and rare moderation."

Nehemiah Perry urged his fellow Congressmen to keep the Constitution "safe from the insidious attacks of these abolition doctrines" of emancipation. He declared: "If you love your country better than the Negro, the Union better than party, drop these diverting, ruinous measures . . . Millions for the Union, not one cent for abolition."

One direct victim of Lincoln's emancipation warning was Marcus L. Ward of Newark, Republican candidate for Governor and a man who endeared himself to servicemen and their families.

Ward had helped soldiers get their pay home to families without cost and had secured pensions for the wounded or for the families of the dead. When trains began on May 10, 1862, to bring back the first wounded of the Peninsular Campaign, Ward scurried through the city to find them temporary rooms in private homes and hotels. The next day he sought and received state funds to start the city's first hospital. Before the day was finished Ward had leased a four-story brick warehouse on Center

Street, between the railroad and the river. As workers scrubbed and fumigated the second and third floors, he lined up volunteer surgeons, purchased and borrowed beds and linen, and had the hospital ready on May 13—in less than two days!

Forty-six wounded or disease-ridden soldiers reached Newark on the night that Ward's hospital opened. Within a month federal authorities took over the institution, staffed it and assumed control. Hundreds of casualties streamed into the Ward United States General Hospital every month, totaling 2,800 men by December 1. Demand grew so great that nearby buildings had to be acquired.

Simultaneously, Ward, the "Soldiers' Friend," was running an election campaign against Democrat Joel Parker of Monmouth County. Democrats launched a smashing attack on all Republicans after the Lincoln emancipation warning. Ward fell before Parker in a statewide Democratic romp that political sages attributed to the Lincoln "error." The Emancipation Proclamation on January 1, 1863, seemed an anti-climax; the *Journal* dismissed it as "of little importance in its practical bearings upon the existing revolution."

The last of the genuine volunteers were preparing for war during the 1862 political campaign. These were "draft avoiders"—decidedly different from draft dodgers, since these soldiers had rushed to enlist for nine-month terms in the summer of 1862 before Lincoln ordered a New Jersey draft. One of five such volunteer New Jersey units was the Twenty-Sixth Regiment, raised and equipped at Camp Frelinghuysen.

Newark furnished six of the ten companies in the regiment, others coming from nearby Essex County towns. Admirers called it "the flower of Essex County," but the Twenty-Sixth earned mixed distinction. It listed twenty-four deserters before it left the city in late September, then learned to drill on the battlefield. Matched against hardened Confederate units at Fredericksburg on December 12 and 13, 1862, the Twenty-Sixth Regiment showed its mettle. Southern fire decimated the ranks, inflicting 123 casualties.

Nine months passed. Men in the ranks of the Twenty-Sixth believed that their enlistments ended on June 3 but federal officers insisted the date was June 18, the nine-month anniversary of the day that a federal (rather than a state) officer had sworn them in. On June 5, when most of the regiment thought they should be homeward bound, they were still on the Rappahannock River below Fredericksburg.

Officers that day ordered the storming of a strong Southern position across the river. Soldiers of the Twenty-Sixth vied with the Fifth Vermont Regiment for the honor of leading the attack and both units rowed across the Rappahannock to silence the enemy battery. In fifteen minutes of bitter fighting the Essex regiment lost fourteen men killed or wounded. Across the river, a number of laggards "fell behind, not through cowardice or inability to keep up, but deliberately, because they felt there was no obligation to fight after the 3rd of June."

A week later, all were headed north; on June 19, the Twenty-Sixth marched proudly through the city. Spectators put on "a grand demonstration" for Rappahannock hero and laggard alike. If the "flower of Essex County" was slightly wilted, bystanders chose to ignore it.

"Grand demonstrations" could not put down the restlessness and anguish building up in the city. Southern soldiers advanced relentlessly into Pennsylvania in late June and early July. Newarkers realized that the unchecked Confederate advances would open the way to Philadelphia and New York, with Newark as an interlude on the way.

Telegraph messages brought grim word that fighting had begun at Gettysburg on July 1. Despair gripped Newark on July 3; conflicting reports from Pennsylvania added to the gloom. In Central Methodist Church on July 4, as a large congregation observed Independence Day, the program was halted by a man hastening up the aisle. He handed a paper to the speaker, who became too dazed to read it. A second man snatched the paper to shout that a Southern cavalry charge had been repulsed at Gettysburg. The invaders were in retreat. The congregation burst into "Praise God, From Whom All Blessings Flow" and streamed into the open air to join a celebration starting near the telegraph office at Broad and Market, where news of Gettysburg victory was sounding on the telegraph.

Cheers turned into protests nine days later, on July 13, 1863, when Lincoln announced a draft of able-bodied young men. Crowd leaders began suggesting that Newark should emulate the protest riots in New York. Words gave way to action. A downtown mob pelted the office of the pro-Lincoln *Mercury* with stones and ripped off the front door. Police Sergeant Henry Haury saved the day by standing in the door defying the mob. The angry crowd turned on Provost Marshal E. N. Miller's home nearby. Warned, Miller had moved out his family; the crowd showered his home with rocks.

Alderman N. C. Ball, acting mayor in place of the absent Moses Bigelow, talked the crowd into dispersing. Next day he urged all residents to stay home after sundown. Ignoring the plea, the mob surged into the streets again, but Mayor Bigelow, back in town, calmed them. Violence had been avoided and Newarkers accepted the draft. They entered service if absolutely necessary, secured a substitute if they could afford one or simply "skedaddled" beyond the reach of searching army officers.

While rioters were protesting, Camp Freling-huysen continued receiving men to fill the ranks of a new outfit being assembled by a remarkable nineteen-year-old colonel, George W. Mindil, about as dashing and capable a young commander as the Union army could boast. Mindil entered service in 1861 at age eighteen, was one of General Kearny's aides, and impressed superiors with his flamboyance and skill.

Mindil commanded the volunteer Thirty-Third Regiment, composed mainly of active veterans attracted back to the ranks by the promise of further glory and/or the prospect of a bonus for re-enlisting. About half of the troops came from Newark. Mindil decked his regiment in gaudy blue Zouave jackets and vests, red pantaloons and tasseled fezzes, in imitation of the Zouaves who had fought in the Crimean War.

The Thirty-Third needed guards to get all of the regiment out of town, since soldiers everywhere often took to the hills after receiving a bonus. Once the hard-bitten Mindil weeded out the loafers and the slackers, the Thirty-

Third became a storied regiment. The teen-age colonel took his no-nonsense Zouaves on a trail of glory and savagery, storming Chattanooga, marching with Sherman to the sea, fighting homeward through Georgia and the Carolinas. Colonel Mindil was promoted to major general before he was twenty-two, after leading the Thirty-Third over 2,500 miles—including 1,700 on foot—and into eight major battles.

Slowly the South gave ground, but Abraham Lincoln was genuinely concerned when he stood for re-election in the fall of 1864. He recognized that New Jersey probably would turn against him again to support General George B. McClellan, the deposed Union commander who now lived in West Orange. Popular "Little Mac" stood a good chance to win the nation for the Democrats.

Editor Edward Fuller of the *Journal* over-reached himself during the 1864 Presidential campaign. He said editorially of President Lincoln's July 19, 1864, draft call for 500,000 men: "Those who desire to be butchered please step forward at once." Fuller called the President of the United States "that smutty joker." Even for the *Journal* that was strong language.

Federal officials arrested Fuller on July 21, charging him with counselling persons to resist the draft and with inciting insurrection against the United States. The editor first sought refuge in freedom of the press, then pleaded guilty on February 15, 1865, and paid a $100 fine. He returned to his editor's chair overlooking Broad and Market Streets.

Fuller's attacks were more cutting than crippling. Sherman's advance through Georgia and successes in the Shenandoah Valley had changed the war's course. McClellan's possibility of becoming President faded with each victory. Record crowds voted in a pouring rain on November 8. Essex County surprisingly backed Lincoln, but McClellan carried New Jersey by a 7,000 vote majority, winning all seven electoral votes.

Thousands of Republicans stood throughout the night in the drizzling rain near Broad and Market Streets to await election results. New Jersey saddened them, but when the ticker confirmed Lincoln's national victory, the crowd lit a bonfire in the center of the city and danced about it.

The war was nearly over now. Down went the Confederacy, torn to shreds in The Wilderness, beaten soundly at Petersburg, surrendered

Descendant of one of Newark's founders, prosperous in city industry and dedicated to human welfare, Marcus L. Ward, opposite page, was a great Civil War leader. His handsome home in Washington Street, now the site of Newark Museum, was a center of social and political life, and there Lilly Martin Spencer painted his four children in the early years of the Civil War. Untiring work for servicemen earned Ward the title of "Soldier's Friend" and it became a campaign song when he successfully ran for Governor of New Jersey in 1866.

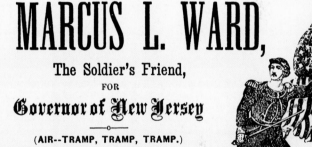

MARCUS L. WARD,

The Soldier's Friend,

FOR

Governor of New Jersey

(AIR--TRAMP, TRAMP, TRAMP.)

Written by R. B. NICOL, author and publisher of a choice collection of Popular Songs—printed on fine note paper, and sent to any part of the United States, postage free, on receipt of price.

Terms—14 copies, 50 cts.; 30 copies $1; or $25 per 1,000.

Address—R. B. NICOL, care of Gibson Brothers, printers, 271 Penna. Avenue, Washington, D. C.

From the battle-fields we come,
With our Banners soiled and torn,
To our peaceful homes on Jersey's tranquil shore.
We have fought a valiant fight
Many hardships we have borne,
Now we claim the rights of Citizens once more.

CHORUS.

Tramp, tramp, tramp, the boys are marching,
Cheer up, Marcus, we will come,
And a helping hand shall lend
To elect "The Soldier's Friend,"
And defeat the trait'rous Copperheads at home.

In the battle front we fought
During all the great campaign,
Till the Rebels and Rebellion met their doom;
So we'll rally to the Polls,
And a victory will gain
O'er the Copperheads, our *enemies*, at home.

Chorus.

How those trait'rous hounds rejoiced,
When our cause looked dark and drear,
Is well known to every son of Liberty;
During all the tug of war
They were fighting in our rear—
But we soon shall gain a final victory.

Chorus.

We are marshalled for the strife,
And we come with all our might,
To maintain the cause which traitors would subdue;
Then three cheers for Mr. Ward,
For the Union and our Rights,
For New Jersey and her Bonny Boys in Blue.

NEW JERSEY RAILROAD & TRANSPORTATION CO.

SPECIAL ARRANGEMENT

FOR THE TRANSPORTATION OF THE REMAINS OF THE LATE

PRESIDENT ABRAHAM LINCOLN,

OVER THE NEW JERSEY RAILROAD,

On Monday, April 24, 1865,

UNDER INSTRUCTIONS FROM THE WAR DEPARTMENT.

A Pilot Engine will precede the Special Train, leaving each Station 10 minutes in advance of that train.

THE SPECIAL TRAIN WILL BE RUN AS FOLLOWS:

STATIONS	TIME	SPECIAL INSTRUCTIONS
Leave New Brunswick at	7 55 A. M.	No Train or Engine (except the Pilot Engine) must enter on the main Track for New York, or leave any Station within 20 minutes in advance of the Special Train.
Leave Metuchen at	8 07 A. M.	
Leave Rahway at	8 35 A. M.	No Train or Engine must enter on the main track, or leave any station until 20 minutes after the Special Train has passed.
Leave Elizabeth at	8 55 A. M.	
Leave Newark at	9.20 A. M.	No Train or Engine must pass over Passaic Bridge, either way, between 9 05 A. M. and 10 00 A. M., unless both the Pilot Engine and Special Train have passed.
Arrive at Jersey City at	9.50 A. M.	
Due at New York (by Ferry Boat) at	10.00 A. M.	Telegraph Operators must be at their stations and report the arrival and departure of the Special train to all stations.

A Pilot Engine will precede the Special Train, leaving each Station 10 minutes in advance of that train.

F. WOLCOTT JACKSON, Gen'l Sup't.

J. W. WOODRUFF, Ass't Sup't.

Shocked Newarkers began mourning even as President Lincoln lay near death in Washington on the Easter weekend. One week later a black-edged broadside gave the times when his funeral train would pass through towns from New Brunswick to Jersey City.

at Appomattox. The casualty lists mounted, but peace was near.

Newarkers began to remember their dead: General Philip Kearny, felled at Chantilly; Major Peter M. Ryerson, former wealthy iron maker who volunteered in 1861 at the age of sixty-four and died at Williamsburg; his son, Lieutenant Peter Ryerson, twenty-two, killed at Kenesaw Mountain fighting with the Thirteenth Regiment; Lieutenant-Colonel Charles Wiebecke, pride of the German community, slain at Spottsylvania. They remembered other privates and corporals and sergeants—their sons and husbands and lovers, who died by the hundreds unheralded on battlefields or in prison camps. They saw the fresh mounds in their cemeteries and knew some of their young had come home to die of wounds or disease.

Mayor Theodore Runyon, the general of 1861, received word of General Robert E. Lee's surrender on Sunday, April 9, and ordered a celebration the next day. Church bells and factory whistles sounded late in the afternoon of April 10. People ran through the streets, blowing horns, firing sidearms, yelling, and hugging one another. A Broad Street merchant placed a bar of steel in front of his store and banged it wildly with a hammer. Flags flew from every building. The town gunners fired the city's brass cannon at the corner of Broad and Mechanic every minute, until one of them forgot to remove the ramrod and sent it whizzing along Broad Street, wounding several. The carnival of joy reached a climax when thousands crowded into and around the Library Hall for an evening jubilee mass meeting to express their delight.

The rejoicing went on all week before voices gave out. Normalcy returned in the rush of preparations for the Easter weekend.

Word swept through town on Saturday morning that President Lincoln had been shot on Good Friday night in the Ford Theater in Washington and was near death. Next day, Easter Sunday, the gaunt, lonely President died. Newark, city of bells and whistles only six days before, became a city in deep mourning. Flags dropped to half mast; city buildings, firehouses, police stations and private buildings were draped in black.

On April 20, when funeral services were held in Washington, Newark conducted a similar rite. Down Broad Street crept the funeral procession, cloaked in a silence that was broken at regular intervals by a tolling bell and a booming minute gun. Otherwise, only the soft clop of horses' hoofs, the squeaking of carriage wheels, the flapping of muffled banners and the shuffling of feet could be heard. Marching were invalid soldiers from the Ward Hospital, veterans, civic clubs, town officials and German and Irish societies. Honorary pallbearers, the city's top citizens, walked beside an empty hearse decked in red, white and blue and drawn by six horses swathed in heavy black palls.

The last bitter scene came on the morning of April 24, when the funeral train bearing the President's remains passed through town on the way to burial in Illinois. A multitude moved somberly toward the Chestnut Railroad depot before 7 A.M., hoping for even a glimpse of the black-draped car. They filled the street, clambered on fences and rooftops and waited in silence. When the funeral train stopped at about 9 A.M., even the church bells were still and the soft sobbing of thousands could be heard above the steaming and hiss of the locomotive. The engineer pulled the throttle, the train moved on and Mr. Lincoln was headed home forever.

Lincoln, in death, had conquered Newark more surely than in life.

But the War Between the States had come to a close. The Union was saved. That was something to be thankful for, even though the causes of the war had not been settled.

Civil War veterans, industrialists, bandsmen and city leaders paraded down Broad Street on May 17, 1866, to mark Newark's 200th anniversary. A artist sketched this scene for Frank Leslie's Illustrated Weekly.

Chapter 17

A CITY TURNS 200

Townspeople seemed anxious to get on with the peace, and the industrial boom that it spurred. They paused only briefly in their daily occupations of 1866 to mark the two-hundredth anniversary of the city's founding. William A. Whitehead, secretary of the New Jersey Historical Society, tried as early as May, 1865, to stir Newark's officials into observing the bi-centennial but met only apathy. He then planned a Historical Society observance in Old First Church for May 17, 1866.

One month before that date, the Common Council belatedly voted funds for a traditional city parade on the same day. That seemed right: a city-sponsored parade in the morning and the Historical Society's oratorical observance in the afternoon. In case of bad weather, the parade would be postponed until May 22. Whitehead announced that the Historical Society program would go on, rain or shine.

Rain fell steadily as May 17 dawned, creating doubts about the parade. Colonel Joseph W. Plume, grand marshal, assumed that the procession was called off and took his usual train to

New York. Rain splashed on Broad Street's cobblestones throughout the morning. Red, white and blue decorations on store fronts turned soggy, but when the downpour changed to a drizzle, city officials announced that the parade would step off at 2 P.M. It was five hours late and at the precise time set for the start of the Historical Society program.

Bugles sounded and marchers moved through the mist, led by Governor Marcus L. Ward, pride of Newark. The Governor walked as far as First Church, where he left the line of march to join the historians and their guests. The marchers continued noisily by on Broad Street, forcing speakers in the church to compete with the brass bands.

Whitehead opened the proceedings with a 10,000-word "Historical Memoir of the Circum-

stances Leading to and Connected with the Settlement of Newark, May, 1666." Dr. Thomas Ward followed with a long, rambling "lyrical poem."

William B. Kinney, former editor of the *Daily Advertiser* and more recently the U. S. minister to Sardinia, valiantly began his long, polished main address, replete with classical and poetic references. He gave up when a brass band outside broke into the rousing strains of "Rally 'Round the Flag Boys."

The two-hundredth anniversary memory persists, thanks largely to Whitehead. He edited and published for the New Jersey Historical Society the *Records of the Town of Newark from 1666 to 1836*, a document that remains the basis for nearly all understanding of Newark's colonial history. He also published the full proceedings of the 1866 program, covering 104 pages.

Old Newark took due pride in its two hundred years. Only New York and Boston among major American cities could boast of greater age. Few had retained such charm. An 1865 account says that forty of the original sixty-four founding families had direct descendants living in Newark or the adjacent suburbs.

Newcomers continued to crowd in, as they had for thirty years. By 1866 some 90,000 people lived in Newark and by 1870 the total climbed officially to 105,059. Industry's gains were evident. Sunday afternoon walkers could see the huge plants huddled by the Passaic. Lovers strolling on High Street could look eastward over the towering smokestacks and church steeples set throughout the town.

Yet, the city retained its small town atmosphere. Two articles on Newark in the *Northern Monthly* for September and November of 1867 provided a vivid glimpse of a municipality on the edge of startling change. Newarkers read and nodded agreement as the September article began:

"The average citizen knows less about Newark than he does about any point of equal interest in the United States. He does not even know that Newark possesses any interest . . . He will demand to know what there is worth of interest in a little suburban city, or village—if it is a village; he is not entirely certain on that point

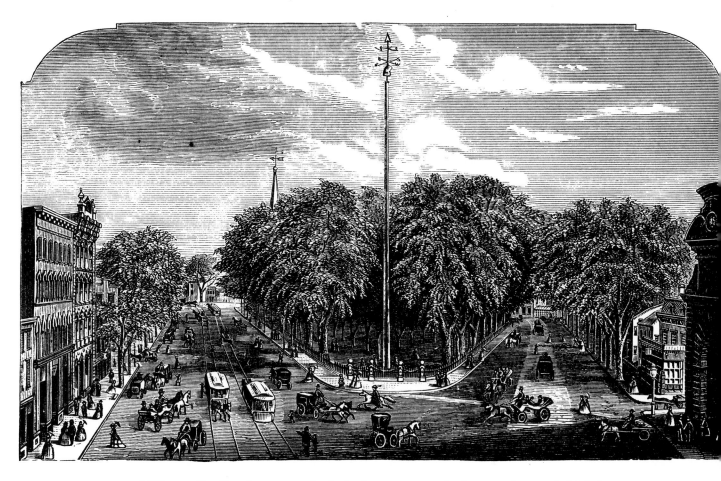

Military Park's elm trees shaded the green and almost obscured Trinity Church spire. Liberty pole stood at south edge of park, behind a fence. Horse cars plodded along Broad Street in this engraving of 1874, and the Morris Canal passed under Broad Street just south of this point.

—nine or ten miles from the great American metropolis, and used principally as an out-of-town residence for New Yorkers."

The writer took readers on a detailed word tour of the city. He tramped in and out of factories, rode carriages past fine estates, walked through the city's "seven handsome cemeteries," visited the churches and strolled through the shops.

Sundays in Newark, he found, still reflected the Puritan traditions:

"A sacred stillness broods over the town; no petty shops are open; no horsecars tinkle their bells through the shaded streets; the profane locomotive shrieks not. There is even very little private riding or driving in the smoothly graded thoroughfares, so strongly does public opinion set against the practice."

Desiring a panoramic view, the *Northern Monthly* writer climbed ten flights of stairs in the Fagin & Company flour mill on the banks of

the Passaic River. While he climbed to what he called "the Alpine height," he learned that the mill turned out two thousand barrels of flour every twenty-four hours. Its mighty engines were made by a noted neighbor, Hewes & Phillips. Fagin & Company's representatives told him that they liked Newark, for "here they get out of the crowd."

From atop the high flour mill, the writer saw Newark "grand as every hive of industry is grand from such an outlook, beautiful as few cities are —and surrounded by reaches of hill and dale, of grove and broad-spreading plain." He became quite poetic:

"The city is almost embowered with green. It is said there is not a street in all Newark that is not adorned with shade trees. They cluster about the very factory doors; they line the busiest thoroughfares; the Broadway of the town (Broad Street) is thick with them from end to end. The smokes of forges and engine-fires float up from amid the foliage, and the drayman's wheels mingle their rattle with the musical rustling of the leaves. New Haven, the 'city of elms,' has not within its borders so many elms as Newark . . .

"The next peculiarity of the scene is the great number of church steeples in it. Brooklyn, the 'city of churches,' has not so good a title to that sobriquet as Newark has, for there are more churches here than there, in proportion to the population. This in spite of the fact that Brooklyn is emphatically a *residence* city, while Newark is emphatically a manufacturing town . . . The longer you look, the thicker the steeples seem to grow."

He stressed the absence of smoke (due to the burning of hard coal rather than soft). Thus he could see the "glassy bosom of the Morris Canal but a pebble-toss away" and "aristocratic High Street overlooking the town." Immediately below was "a schooner on the stocks, ready to be launched." Tied up at the Fagin dock were the *Magenta* and *Thomas P. Way*, famed party boats. Steamboats puffed on the Passaic. Trains "a half mile in length" slid along the railroad tracks.

Newarkers long had debated whether High or Broad was the best street in town. The *Northern Monthly* reporter boldly entered the argument:

"High Street is certainly a very handsome avenue. But I must confess I consider Broad

The Northern Monthly's *scribe climbed ten flights of stairs in Fagin & Company mill for a view of Newark, "beautiful as few cities are."*

The Album of Newark, *handsome little picture book published in 1881, featured this panorama "from VanVliet's malt house." On left is the Passaic River, lined by industry and busy docks. Right side shows Morris Canal (upper center) and the railroads crossing the river.*

Street to be one of the finest streets in the United States . . . When the long shadows of the later afternoon cover it, pen can not paint the brilliant scene here presented—the fashionable turnouts, the fast trotters; the beauty, elegance, and wealth displayed on wheels and on horseback."

Laden with coal barges is the Morris Canal, in this photograph of late 1860s. In foreground, the canal passes under the N. J. Railroad, aided by a lock clearly visible beyond the tracks.

After he had surveyed the streets, the churches and the industry, the writer took time to visit Seth Boyden, the man always credited with turning Newark toward industrial greatness.

Despite Boyden's 79 years, the journalist found him "really a most extra-ordinary character, and his memory is a well-stocked storehouse, from which he draws liberally for the entertainment of his visitors. His rugged face is deeply seamed with the marks of time and toil; but many a man of fifty might envy him his clear head, his sound digestion and his strong arms."

"Shade, shade, everywhere!" exclaimed the impressed *Northern Monthly* writer. "Whether on the edges of town or in the heart of it, you can not 'escape the all-prevailing shade trees of Newark."

In November, the *Northern Monthly* scribe concentrated on Newark's industrial prowess. He recited statistics—"Newark is the third city of the Union in manufacturing importance, employing a capital of ten or eleven millions of dollars and turning out annually manufactures to the value of twenty-one millions." Admitting

himself at a loss in trying to describe the varied industries, he turned alphabetical:

"Here are manufactured agricultural implements and axles; baskets, belting leather, bedsteads, bits and spurs, blank books, Britannia ware, brooms, brushes, beer and buttons; carpet-bag frames, carpets, carriage cloth, carriages and coaches, casters, chairs, children's perambulators, cider and vinegar, cloak and dress trimmings, clothing, combs, confectionery, cords and tassels, cradles, cribs, and curled hair;

"Drain pipes, edged tools, enameled leather, fans, files and rasps, fire-engines, flour, furniture and gas; gig-saddles and pads, gig-trees and ornamental glass, globes and glue, gold pens and hair-cloth, hairwork and homes, harness mountings and hats, hoopskirt trimmings and hatchecks, ink and iron in a thousand shapes; jewelry, jewelers' tools, lasts, leather, locks, lounges, matches, morocco, magazines, mustard, nails and needles.

"Here we pause to breathe but the list is only fairly begun.

"Shall we begin again? There are newspapers manufactured here also, and oil-cloth, and paper-boxes, and patent leather; patterns and models, piano fortes, plows, and rope and twine; saddles

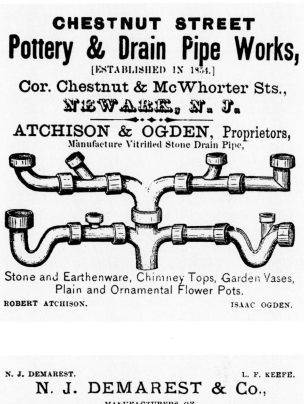

Newarkers made everything: baby carriages, engines, harness, plumbing and a thousand and one other things—and advertised their goods.

and harness and saddlers' and harness-makers' tools; saddle trees, sash and blinds, scales, segar boxes, shears, shirt-bosoms and shirts; silk, skates and skirts; spokes, springs, and soap; straw goods, thread, and trunk-frames; varnish, wagons, and watch-case springs; wax and whips and wires and wrenches, and so on to the end of the alphabet."

The *Northern Monthly* visitor left impressed, but despite the industrial prosperity and diversity evident to him, few Newarkers appreciated the extent of the manufactures in their 200-year-old community. There were two main reasons. The average employee worked from dawn to sunset, leaving him little time to know or care what his neighbor did for a living. For their part, factory owners believed that world-wide customers respected only one label: MADE IN NEW YORK—and that was stamped on many Newark products.

The editor of the *Advertiser* approved of that. On December 13, 1870, he urged Newarkers: "Let us abandon the notion that we are a warehouse; we are only a workshop, a community of manufacturers rather than merchants. The transfer of trade must be made mainly in New York, which is our national exchange. Our streets will never be crowded with buyers, but will be with hurrying wagons of goods already sold."

The Newark Industrial Exposition that opened on August 20, 1872, at the old skating rink on Washington Street was a red-letter occasion. It offered manufacturers a chance to display their wares, and it also gave Newarkers a panoramic view of their industrial diversity. No other American city had ever held an exhibit of only its own wares.

Opening night vindicated Arthur M. Holbrook, publisher of the city directory since Benjamin T. Pierson's death in 1862. Convinced that no place surpassed Newark in manufacturing skills, Holbrook proposed an industrial exposition, but, in his words, "men were found who ridiculed the idea, called it quixotic and said it had better not be attempted."

Holbrook insisted that Newark was known, "not as a city which had worked out successfully the problem of life, but as a suburb of New York, dependent solely upon the latter city for the prosperity it enjoyed." He prodded the Board of Trade, founded in 1868 to promote industrial interests, until members fell in line. Prominent men accepted positions on the exposition board (Marcus L. Ward was its president).

On opening night, J. H. G. Hawes set up a calcium light at the corner of Broad and Marshall Streets to direct "an immense throng" to the exposition. Nearly three thousand people crowded into the rink when the doors were opened at 7 P.M. The *Advertiser* described the scene:

"Somehow the manufactured articles had a different appearance from that which they wore in the factory when seen amid the dust and debris necessary to their creation. The eyes of the men who made them beheld with a keener appreciation the beautiful things that their hands had wrought, as they walked up and down the avenues attended by their wives and sweethearts.

"It was a proud night for our mechanics, as they pointed out the lines they had traced, the shapes they had moulded, the delicate pieces they had polished during the heat and burthen of the day."

Hundreds of gas jets, shaded by opal globes, turned the old rink into a fairyland of light. French, German, English and American flags waved over a marble and silver fountain in the center of the rink. "Reinhard's band never played better," the *Advertiser* reported. "They seemed determined to show what a Newark band could do, and played *Yankee Doodle* and *The Star Spangled Banner* as these old National airs are seldom played."

Ex-Governor Ward opened the show by extolling both manufacturers and "that great body of skillful mechanics and artisans with which our city abounds." He said that "even those among us who have been most familiar with our manufactures will be astonished at the variety and beauty of this exposition."

General Theodore Runyon, former mayor and Civil War general, pointed out that Newark's early industrial strength stemmed from leather, carriages, silver plating, beer, jewelry, hats, clothing, varnish, malleable iron, boots and shoes. The city still made all of those, Runyon said, but had lately added chemicals, hardware,

e great Industrial Exhibition, running from August to
ober, 1872, in the one-time skating rink, gave workers
owners alike a chance to show their industrial might.

cotton and silk thread, enameled goods and
dozens of other products—in more than "two
hundred different branches of manufactures."
Runyon estimated that Newark factories employed "over 30,000 hands" at average annual
wages of $500 a man (about $10 a week).

The Industrial Exposition continued until
October 11, attracting more than 130,000 people
and winning praise from editors as far away as
New York, Philadelphia and Scranton. Horace
Greeley and U. S. Grant, rival candidates for the
United States Presidency, both paid visits. As
the *Daily Journal* said, "The wealthiest and the
lowliest mingled together with good old democratic freedom."

Visitors saw a glittering array of Newark
products. They saw harnesses valued at $10,000,
gold-plated sleighbells worth up to $200 a set,
one hundred styles of table oilcloth, books
printed in Newark, pearl buttons, ribbons and
a hundred varieties of paint. They saw buggies,
walnut bird cages, ink, rosettes, steam fire
engines, gold pens, chalk, tools, toys, malleable

iron castings, telegraph instruments and clocks.
They marveled at a trunk "that could be converted, by a very simple process, into a baby's
cradle and bath-tub." It was easy to believe that
Newark mechanics could make anything.

October 2 was "Secretary's Night" in honor
of Arthur M. Holbrook. He received "the best
watch and chain that Newark could produce"
and Mrs. Holbrook was given a morocco case
containing $125 worth of Newark-made jewelry.
Significantly, the attendance "was nearly as large
as it was upon the occasion of General Grant's
visit."

Holbrook and his associates repeated the
Exposition in 1873, 1874 and 1875 but gave up
in 1876 when industrialists turned attention to
the Philadelphia Industrial Exposition. Four
years of Newark's Exposition did more to boost
city pride than all the advertising, all the boasting, all the parades, all the talk of Puritan heritage and all the speech making that had gone
before. Newark knew its claim to glory: the
variety of the goods pouring from her shops.

Chapter 18

AN AGE OF GIANTS

"H E PASSED ALONG OUR STREETS intent upon his thoughts, seemingly remarking nothing of all that was going on around him, unobservant apparently even of the evidences of prosperity to which his patient research, and his days and nights of toil, had contributed so much . . . It is eminently fitting that this city of artisans should honor the memory and seek to perpetuate the name of her Master-Mechanic . . ."

General Theodore Runyon spoke thus in the Newark Opera House on May 22, 1872, and well he might, for his subject was the late Seth Boyden. His audience knew that they would be asked to contribute to a statue of their incomparable "uncommercial inventor," known in his last days as much for his poverty as for his inventions. He had been experimenting with giant strawberries when he died on March 31, 1870, at the age of eighty-two. Near his end Boyden expressed regrets: he had enough experiments in mind to last through two more lifetimes.

Runyon stirred the Opera House audience with tales of the inventor's useful life—and with the reminder that Boyden's discovery of patent leather alone meant an annual $6,000,000 to the city's economy. This citizen deserved lasting honor, Runyon said, for he was Newark's "representative man." Since Boyden would take nothing in life (he had rejected with embarrassment an offer of financial aid in his last years), then Newark must honor him in death.

Local industrialists finally raised the statue, twenty years after Boyden's death and eighteen years after Runyon's plea. Tradition holds that the bronze likeness of Boyden unveiled in Washington Park in 1890 was the first American statue dedicated to a workingman.

Seth Boyden would have liked that, for he always considered himself a workingman. And he would have been pleased that the sculptor portrayed him wearing his familiar old leather apron and standing in front of an anvil. The likeness of Boyden was a good one—tousle-haired, strong, sad-faced, homely, and dignified through his work.

Boyden died just as Newark began to emerge into genuine industrial greatness. Visiting journalists and the Industrial Exposition depicted Made-in-Newark diversity and showed the extra-

Ballantine's Brewery, founded in 1840, as it appeared in 1905.

Lister Brothers chemical works, above, converted bones into fertilizer, and Hewes & Phillips, left, were major machine makers in these 1872 sketches.

175

ordinary craftsmanship of the city's mechanics. But there was much more to the industrial saga. This was an age of giants in America: of intellectuals such as Thomas Edison, Edward Weston and John Wesley Hyatt, all of whom flowered in Newark; and of capitalists, who raised giant plants where once blacksmiths had toiled.

Now, as the nation embraced new inventions and streams of immigrants came to occupy the old cities of the East Coast, production moved into high gear. Except for patent leather, Newark had no single type of industry to accord it international fame—such as the stockyards of Chicago, the steel furnaces of Pittsburgh or the flour mills of Rochester. But there was no question that expansion was the watchword.

Peter Ballantine & Sons steadily enlarged their riverfront brewery at the foot of Fulton Street. Hewes & Phillips, forced into rapid growth by a flood of Civil War contracts, was spreading its buildings over two and a half acres of ground. New Jersey Zinc Company enlarged at the foot of River Street. Lister Brothers made so much fertilizer that by 1873 their bone-grinding plant on the Passaic River included more than fifteen buildings. Edward Balbach Jr., who refined the sweepings from jewelry house floors, invented in 1865 a method of rapid separation of precious metals from base ores; within ten years his huge plant was refining more than $5,000,000 worth of precious metals annually. Balbach vied with the United States Mint in producing gold and silver bars.

George A. Clark, a Scot who arrived in Newark in 1864 to found the Clark Thread Works, typified the bigness. Clark decidedly was not in the fictional mold of the "poor but proud" immigrant intent on making a fortune in America. He brought with him from Scotland both capital and an industrial background, for his family had been making cotton sewing thread in Paisley since 1812.

Clark started in a rented building on Fulton Street. By 1866 he had completed a huge new plant in the northern part of the city along the Passaic River. By 1870 more than one thousand men and women worked for Clark Thread Company. Later, when the company opened additional buildings in East Newark, Kearny and Harrison, it hired thousands more. Clark's

O.N.T. ("Our New Thread," not "Our Newark Thread" as the initials were sometimes mistakenly translated) became known wherever American woman stitched.

Expansion was the easy-to-see facet of Newark's industry. Less obvious was the unusual interdependency of factories within the city.

Leather tanners gave rise to shoemakers—and it must be remembered that it was leather that enticed Seth Boyden from New England to Newark. He, in turn, gave the city patent leather. By 1875, leather waste went to the glue works and leather splits found a ready market in the trunk factories. Shoemakers bought larger trimmings for insoles. Hide shavings went to chemical makers for prussite of potash. Harness, saddles, trunks and traveling bags all followed the fundamental leather tanning.

Balbach's jewelry sweeping success encouraged other refiners to locate nearby. Their combined successes made Newark a center of electrolytic refining and electro plating. The latter, in turn, eventually gave impetus to electrical experiments and manufacture.

Carriage makers needed a good varnish; that industry rose in the 1840s to satisfy the need and was of major importance by 1875. The presence of the New Jersey Zinc Company and Balbach's refinery unquestionably lured paint makers to Newark, since the Zinc Company furnished zinc oxide and Balbach's supplied pure lead, both basic paint ingredients. A tiny chemical firm, Heller & Merz, grew to major size after it began making pigments—particularly ultramarine blue—for the paint trade in 1880.

The city had an unusual number of tinkerers and improvisors and on-the-spot inventors in its shops. Its machinists could turn out tools and machines and any kind of weird device on order. In an age of innovation and invention, Newark had an abundance of clever hands, skilled by tooling leather, making jewelry or tinkering with obstinate steam engines. Inventors and men with new products and novel ideas naturally gravitated to the city.

Edison, Weston and Hyatt came for the simplest of reasons. Here they could find the mental stimulation that new ideas needed—and skilled workers to translate ideas into reality.

Edison arrived in Newark in the winter of 1871 at the age of twenty-four, bringing with him a modest reputation as an inventor and $40,000 that Western Union had paid him for an improved stock ticker. Needing space to manufacture 1,200 tickers immediately, Edison leased the top floor of a four-story building at 4–6 Ward Street. Within thirty days he had spent nearly all his capital on machinery.

Edison's improved stock ticker.

Mary Stillwell, Edison's first wife, who married the inventor in Newark on Christmas Day, 1871. Their two children were born here.

Thomas A. Edison, whose major inventing period began in Newark in 1871. He put together here the team that served in Menlo Park.

More than seventy men worked for Edison by the end of 1873 and about half of them posed for this picture taken outside the Ward Street factory late that year.

Edison's advertisements for men with "light fingers" intrigued many who were making clocks or small machines. He began putting together in Newark the team of dreamers and craftsmen for the "invention factory" he would open at Menlo Park in 1876. Edison's Newark years were his time of consolidation. Here he perfected his concept of inventions "on order."

John Ott, a twenty-one-year-old Jersey City youth, assembled an assortment of parts into a ticker on a "don't pay me if I don't succeed" offer. Edison made him his assistant on the spot. Others whose names and fortunes rose with Edison after being hired in Newark were Charles Batchelor, the black-bearded young Englishman who had been a machinist at the Clark Thread Works; John Kreusi, a Swiss clockmaker, and Sigmund Bergmann, a newly arrived German whose English was so bad that Edison said "his work speaks for him." By the end of 1873 Edison had seventy workers on the payroll.

Edison's Newark work was mainly for Western Union, then being fought over by New York capitalists. Caught in the middle of the ferocious economic maneuverings of the "Robber Barons" of Wall Street—Jay Gould, Jim Fisk and others—Edison was broke and dispirited much of the time. Still, he did invent in Newark the quadruplex telegraph, which permitted the sending of many messages over the same wire. Other inventors came to the Ward Street plant to seek his advice. He helped a Milwaukee inventor named Christopher Sholes to perfect the country's first typewriter. And, toward the latter part of 1875 he invented a device for multiplying copies of letters, which he called the Mimeograph. He assigned it for a modest sum to A. B. Dick, of Chicago.

Edison met his first wife in Newark. She was Mary Stilwell, sixteen years old, "tall and full of figure, with a great pompadour of hair," and they were wed on Christmas Day, 1871. Two of their three children were born in the city. Edison nicknamed his daughter Marion, "Dot," and his son Thomas Jr., "Dash," so complete was his preoccupation with sounds of the telegraph and stock tickers.

Edison left Newark for a quiet Menlo Park hillside in 1876. But another rising young inventor, Edward Weston, moved into the bustling city and stayed the rest of his life.

Weston emigrated from England to New York in 1870, took a job with the American Nickel Plating Company and thoroughly revamped the company's processes. In less than a year, Weston, at the age of twenty-one, was the foremost expert among American nickel platers. He developed a dynamo to give steady current to his electroplater and had it built in Newark. King of the electroplaters and leader among dynamo makers, young Weston settled permanently in Newark in 1875, possibly influenced by Edison's fame, certainly influenced by Balbach's reputation among metal refiners and undoubtedly hopeful that his dynamos would find acceptance. He acquired a former synagogue on Washington Street in 1877 and established the nation's first electrical machinery plant.

Many of the great minds of the day worked simultaneously to develop a practical, safe system of electrical lighting. Electric carbon arc lamps were well known but women complained that the garish blue light made them "look dead." By adding metal salts to the carbon, Weston could change the flame to any desired color (red was most popular), making complexions pleasing and the glow less flickering. He mounted one of his improved arc lights at the corner of Washington and Market Streets in 1877. Its light was so brilliant that Weston had to notify the fire alarm tower anytime that he turned on the current.

The City Council let Weston put up an arc lamp in Military Park in the summer of 1878, provided that he furnish both lamp and power free. The lamp equalled the light of seven thousand candles and drew public attention and "millions of bugs." Weston lamps soon gleamed —on free trial—in Boston's Forest Garden, at a Fort Lee amusement center, at a Rockaway Beach hotel, on Coney Island's Iron Pier and in other places.

Newark gave Weston a contract for arc lights on five posts in Military Park in May, 1881— the country's first municipal underwriting of electrical street lighting. It took courage for Mayor William Fiedler and the Council to approve carbon arc street lights in a time when many believed electricity was not even possible, much less necessary. The courage was limited to "not more than $300."

Weston's great coup was lighting the Brooklyn Bridge with arc lamps. A journalist declared on opening night in May, 1883, that the fireworks paled in comparison "with the miracle light of eighty powerful electric lamps strung along the arching roadway."

Electric carbon arc lamp of the type that Edward Weston used in lighting Military Park in 1878. Ten years later he perfected his portable volt meter and won fame in electrical measurement.

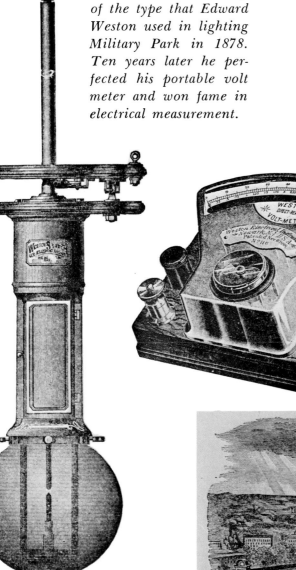

Edward Weston's inventive genius rivalled Edison's. He came to Newark in 1875, noted as an electroplater, and began working with electricity, where he gained enduring credit. Below is his factory at Plane and Orange Streets.

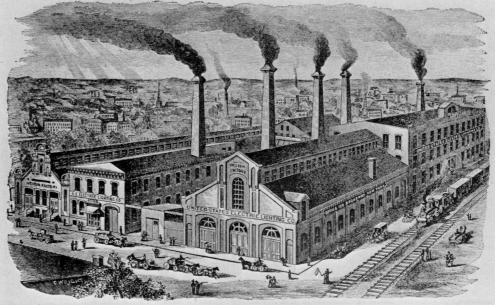

There was no stopping Weston now. His inventive genius rivalled that of Edison. By the middle of 1884 his patents covered the entire electrical field from motors and generators to underground cables, batteries and fuses. He took over a big plant at Plane and Orange Streets for manufacturing and started the Newark Electric Light & Power Company in Mechanic Street in 1882 for street lighting. He turned back a gas company bid for a monopoly on city street illumination—but just barely, for city fathers felt that Weston's charge of one dollar to light one arc lamp through a night was too high.

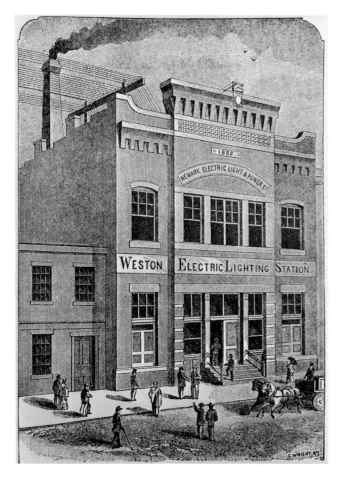

Weston's Mechanic Street "Central station," opened in 1882 to light street lamps.

Weston quietly veered from the illumination field in 1886 to pioneer in electrical measurement. Instruments used to measure electricity were so delicate and uncertain that the iron buttons on a passerby's suspenders or the wires of a lady's hoop skirt could alter measurements radically. Weston had little scientific data available; he was like a man trying to build an automobile before the motor had been invented.

He made the first permanent magnet, previously considered an impossibility by the scientific world. He developed two new alloys, *Constantin* and *Manganin*, both fundamental in electrical measurement. He perfected a new copperbase alloy to use in the delicate springs of his meters. He had invented his own basic tools; now he could fashion his instruments and measuring devices.

Weston's greatest scientific contribution was his "Normal Cell," the first stable standard for the volt, the basic unit of electromotive force. He revealed it in 1893 but dissenting leaders in the competitive and disorganized electrical world waited until 1908 to concede that the Weston Normal Cell was indeed the international standard.

Electricity was no more than a curiosity in the 1880s, despite its fascinating potential. Quicker to achieve popularity was Celluloid—the first commercially successful synthetic plastic. It had an odd origin.

In 1869, a New York billiard supply house, suffering from a shortage of elephant tusks, offered $10,000 for a synthetic pool ball. John Wesley Hyatt, an Albany, N. Y., printer, decided to try for the prize. Working at night in the kitchen of his unenthusiastic Albany landlady, Hyatt experimented by combining pyroxylin with camphor.

Since pyroxylin is principally highly explosive nitro-celluose, Hyatt's use of heat and pressure placed his life, and his landlady's kitchen, in constant peril. Aided by a fellow printer named James Brown, Hyatt produced an ivory-like plastic that he called "Celluloid." He won the prize and began making excellent, if volatile, pool balls.

Celluloid's healthy pink color suggested to Hyatt its use as a "gum" in dental plates. He later added knife handles, piano keys and assorted novelties to his line of artificial teeth and billiard balls, then accepted the offer of New York financiers to transfer his operation from Albany to a new five-story plant in Mechanic Street in Newark. Wealthy Marshall

Lefferts, head of Western Union and Edison's early financial backer, named himself president of the Celluloid Manufacturing Company—but Hyatt cannily retained his patent.

Three Newark concerns soon used Celluloid for harness trimmings, mirror backs, buttons, shirt collars and cuffs, truss pads, napkin-rings and scores of flashy, inexpensive items. Hyatt and an aide named Charles Burroughs made the world's first injection molding machine in 1878 to turn out harness buckles, buttons, combs and shaving brush handles.

Celluloid could also be rolled into sheets of thin plastic, causing the Rev. Hannibal Goodwin, rector of The House of Prayer, to pioneer in the development of flexible photographic film. His despair at a series of broken glass stereoptican slides of Bible stories started Mr. Goodwin's search for a substitute film.

He succeeded in making emulsion stick to the Celluloid sheets and applied for a patent in 1887. As the patent application dragged on, George Eastman of Rochester pursued the same quest for flexible film. Two years after Goodwin's documented discovery, Eastman sent Edison some film for use in his movie work. The courts upheld Mr. Goodwin's basic patents in 1914—long after the minister's death—and his widow was paid a substantial sum by Eastman in legal agreement that flexible film had first been made in a Newark rectory.

The billiard ball synthetic prompted Hyatt to invent a lathe for turning perfect spheres. In 1885, he used the lathe to perfect a roller bearing capable of standing the pounding abuse of sugar grinders. That bearing, useful in many

Synthetic billiard balls accidentally led John Wesley Hyatt to Celluloid, the first commercially successful plastic. Hyatt, above, was at the height of a diversified Celluloid business when he perfected the lathe to make roller bearings, just in time for the oncoming automobile age.

kinds of machinery, became the basis for the smooth ride that Americans demanded when they reached the automobile age. An order from the Olds Company in 1900 for one-hundred-twenty rear axle bearings made Hyatt the greatest name in automobile roller bearings.

New companies and new notions held great promise for the city's future, but every census of manufactures from 1870 to 1910 showed the oldest of Newark products—leather—to be number one. Leather makers in 1870 made $8,600,000 worth of products and forty years later the figure reached nearly $21,000,000, both far in front of all other Newark-made goods.

Newark's tanneries could handle any kind of hide. By 1870, they produced 90 per cent of all patent leather made in America. George and John Dougherty became the nation's prime producer of Morocco leather after the Civil War. T. P. Howell, biggest of the patent leather tycoons, tanned this country's first Russia leather in 1873, using three barrels of birch oil sent him by the United States Minister to Russia. Daniel Kaufherr's acceptance of alligator and reptile skins in 1880 made him the first United States tanner to do so. R. G. Salomon introduced the manufacture of cordovan leather in America, and by the middle 1880s was also the nation's leading tanner of alligator skins. That tanning of unusual hides became a continuing Newark specialty.

One name to remember among Newark leather men was Martin Dennis, who developed the "one bath" system of chrome tanning. Chrome, used as early as 1858, gave excellent results but was extremely difficult to handle because it required a series of complex immersions. Dennis revolutionized the industry in 1893 with a simple "one bath" treatment, as easy to handle as the familiar old bark tanning processes.

Newark leather went everywhere. Parisian women delicately encased their feet in Newark-made shoes. Emperor William of Germany chose fine leather from the city for his carriage of state. Most Presidents of the United States had shoes custom made by Newark's Johnston & Murphy, and free-spending Diamond Jim Brady found Johnston & Murphy shoes fit his feet as well as his personality—although he

substituted diamonds for the relatively staid pearl buttons that the Newark firm attached to its usual uppers.

Jewelry ranked among Newark's top three industries between 1880 and 1910, although self-concious local manufacturers often stamped "London" on their gold rings and brooches. Fine ladies, it was said, "spelled 'imported' with capital letters."

James Madison Durand, who rose from an apprentice's bench to head his own Newark jewelry company, and Aaron Carter, another ex-apprentice, excelled in promoting both their wares and the city's name. Joseph Atkinson could report in his 1878 *History of Newark* that "the eyes of the blind have been opened and dazzled by the brilliancy of Newark workmanship, as displayed at Tiffany's and other great bazaars of New York and elsewhere."

Jewelry was not merely glittering ornaments; it could be as practical as gold watch cases and fittings. Throughout the 1890s nearly all American-made watch case material came from Newark. Crescent Watch Case Company, which moved to the Roseville section from Chicago in 1891, claimed to be America's number one watch encaser. When a Victorian male reached for a gold collar button, it was ninety-nine to one that it came from the second floor factory that George Krementz had opened in 1866. Krementz advertised: "We will pay the cost of assay and furnish one dozen Krementz One-Piece Collar Buttons for every one which falls below the standard stamped upon it."

Other precious metals were not overlooked. Tiffany's of New York—a name that made fine ladies preen—located its sterling silver manufacturing in a new plant in North Newark in 1896. Tiffany's placed its operations behind a twenty-one-inch-thick wall made with bricks imported from England. The building, complete with turrets, looked more like a castle than a factory.

Two platinum refiners both found Newark ideal for their purposes in 1875, probably because of the city's refining know-how and jewelry trade but also because burgeoning electrical and chemical experiments needed platinum. Daniel W. Baker started Baker & Company and Charles Engelhard founded the American Platinum Works on New Jersey Railroad Avenue. Newark became the heart of the platinum industry. Later, Baker and Englehard combined into one company and the distinction persisted.

Changing habits and increasing prosperity brought some alterations in the industrial pattern. Trunk manufacture, the third most important industry in 1870, was nearly gone by 1890. Foundry and machine products moved upward after 1880 and in 1910 stood second only to leather. Drugs and chemicals, nowhere among the leaders in 1870, were eighth in importance in 1910. Electrical machinery, appearing on the list in 1910 for the first time, was seventh, turning out $5,616,000 in products that year. Commercial bakeries indicated the growing numbers of working wives and mothers, plus immigrants who were used to bakeries in their home cities. Scarcely known until the late 1880s, commercial bread and cake makers in 1910 sold $4,627,000 of their wares. Varnish and paint manufacturers, modestly noted before 1900, made up the city's fifth most important industry in 1910.

One old steady—beer—flowed constantly upward in both importance and volume. It was not solely a matter of "German beer drinkers" or German brewers. Germans had the most breweries, but the venerable Scot, Peter Ballantine, easily occupied top position.

Ballantine concentrated on heavy ale, suited to the tastes of most workmen in the factories and along the docks in Newark and Hudson County. The Germans brewed their popular light lager beer in small, local plants; names like Schalk, Lorenz & Jacquillard, Braun and Laible and Peter Hauck meant much to Essex County Germans by 1850.

Then the Germans who would make Newark beer famous started to arrive. Joseph Hensler journeyed from the Fatherland in 1850 to work for Lorenz & Jacquillard. He opened his own brewery in 1860, and built his home next door, the better to watch the hops and malt bubbling in his vats. In those days, men who made beer lived close to their source of wealth.

Gottfried Krueger, 16 years old and wearing wooden shoes when he arrived in Newark in

Tiffany & Company's factory was such a wonder that it appeared on this postcard of 1900. Corner turret and 21-inch thick walls gave it the look of a castle.

1854, began his career in his uncle John Laible's brewery. Gottfried donned a leather apron and began "learning the business by sweeping floors." The boy learned, saved most of his monthly salary of $5 (plus room and board) and by 1865 owned the brewery.

Such success stories made America a magnet. A year after Krueger became master of his own brewery, another young German, Christian Feigenspan, started his apprenticeship with Laible. The story was repeated: sweeping, scrimping and watching, Feigenspan saved enough and learned enough to start his own brewery in 1875. George H. Weidenmeyer took over his father's long-established Newark City Brewery in 1879 and enlarged its capacity. Those were the "big five" among brewers: Ballantine, Hensler, Krueger, Feigenspan and Weidenmeyer.

Peter Ballantine was not about to let German beer makers outdo him in sales to the big Teutonic population, even if his heart was given to ale. When the depression of 1873 hit Newark, it left Schalk Brothers, makers of lager beer, distraught and with a large bill due Ballantine's.

Peter ignored the conservative objections of his three sons, absorbed Schalk's and added lager beer to his honored ale. If Newarkers wanted German beer, Peter Ballantine would oblige and profit thereby.

Prosperous brewers worked hard for the city. Hensler served three terms on the City Council, and Krueger became Essex County Freeholder and a State Assemblyman. Krueger lived next door to his brewery and in 1865 turned one of his rooms into a show place tavern, where a nickel beer and free lunch attracted crowds. He encouraged German songfests by building Saenger (Singers) Hall near the brewery. Weidenmeyer served as an assemblyman and alderman and provided a field for the baseball team. Christian Feigenspan, after building a fine new brewery in 1891, showed his appreciation to the city by labeling his beer "P.O.N."—the Pride of Newark. The Ballantine family served Newark civic enterprises well for several generations.

All of the industrial stability and prosperity promised just after the Civil War had come true by 1900. Newarkers understood their industrial might, and knew well the importance of the city's factories and mills. They recognized the value of having manufacturing diversified through hundreds of products and in hundreds of factories. They could tolerate the smokestacks and the industrial smells and the crowded streets. Those were the sights and smells and impact of industry, the symbols of men at work. They were accepted as disagreeable but inevitable.

Industry had created problems undreamed of in 1870. The sweet Passaic River had turned sour and filthy, despoiled by man. The creeks and marshes were redolent with sewage. Water became nearly as precious as gold—and often as tainted and foul as the sewage-infested Passaic. Streets were often nightmares of congestion and confusion, clogged with wagons and horse-drawn street cars. Dimly lit streets were not always known for quiet, peace or general safety.

The time had come for conservative old Newark to face up to its problems. It was no longer a case of attracting industry or of making townspeople aware of its value, but rather of keeping the city from being ruined by its own progress.

Christian Feigenspan's brewery, opened in 1891, was so modern and gleaming he called his beer the "Pride of Newark."

Chapter 19

INDUSTRY GAINS ALLIES

I F BELCHING SMOKESTACKS beside the railroads, imposing brick factories in all parts of town and streams of workmen hurrying morning and night along the streets did not convey the message that Newark was an industrial city, then the Board of Trade and the local newspapers did. When the Board of Trade advertised in 1890 that among all cities there was "None Bigger, None Brighter, None Busier," it rested its case largely on industry.

Yet, Newark by 1890 included far more than an industrial complex. It was also New Jersey's hub of finance, its center of commerce and the merging point of communications. Streetcars linked suburbs to the city and railways joined the city to the world.

Money—big money—made the world go. Once, by dint of hard work and good luck, a man could rise from kitchen workshop or corner smithy to control hundreds of workmen and to life in a fine mansion near his factory. Seth Boyden began that way, although he did not seek power or fine mansions. By 1890 John Wesley Hyatt's rise from an Albany kitchen to Newark riches in Celluloid was an American saga. But in 1890 the hardest fact of industrial life was not genius, but capital.

Banks could not, or would not, heed the urgent calls to underwrite business and industrial ventures. Traditionally the banks loaned money on such highly conservative terms that would-be borrowers said, not always in jest, that "the only way to get money was to prove that you did not need it." Well-established manufacturers and merchants organized the banks, served on the boards and passed on all loans. As they saw it, their duty was principally to finance their own businesses.

When William H. Shaw published his *History of Essex and Hudson Counties* in 1884, Newark had ten banks and five savings institutions.

State Bank money issued in 1864 showed Old First Church and the bank side by side.

Shaw said all were strong and had weathered the Panic of 1873 without disaster. Their conservatism had proved so worthy in the panic that hard-pressed New York banks several times had borrowed Newark money to keep solvent.

Their very staunchness kept the banks small and ingrown, scarcely the agencies to finance large expansion. Into the void stepped Newark's insurance companies, so fabulously successful that by 1895 the city ranked fourth nationally in insurance assets, topped only by Hartford, Philadelphia and New York.

Money flowed freely into and out of the insurance firms, generally carefully controlled, but in such quantity as to astound local bankers who believed that a million dollars was impressive capital. When Shaw described Mutual Benefit Life Insurance Company in 1884, he used terminology that possibly led readers to believe it was a charitable institution. His high-flown, involved style could not cloak the dollar impact:

"The power which the company has exerted in the cause of that truest benevolence, the protection of the widow and the fatherless, is shown by the fact that it already has paid over eleven thousand death claims, aggregating thirty-eight millions of dollars. It has also paid directly to its members for annuities and matured endowments over three millions; for dividends, over thirty-one millions and for surrendered policies over ten millions, making in all, payments to its policy holders or their direct representatives, aggregating over eighty-three millions of dollars."

Eighty-three million dollars moving in and through Newark in the thirty-nine years since Mutual's founding in 1845 represented tremendous fiscal strength. Much of the money flowed outward to the widows and the fatherless, but while the insurance dollars awaited bereavement, they created marvelous assets for favored banks and other institutions or projects in which Mutual invested funds.

Shaw briefly described other insurance firms: Newark Mutual Fire Assurance Company, the oldest in the city, founded in 1810; The Firemen's Insurance Company, with 1884 assets of $1,409,941; The Merchants Insurance Company, the New Jersey Plate Glass Insurance Company (proof that storefronts had taken on a glassy look), the Germania Insurance Company, and lastly, the Prudential Insurance Company of America.

Prudential deserved the least attention in 1884, despite the fact that it already had issued over 900,000 policies since its founding in 1873. The company appealed to the low-paid common man, and all of its policies added up to a relatively small $580,100 in assets.

John Fairfield Dryden, Prudential's founder, nicely fitted the classic 19th century mold of the giant who rose from poverty.

Born in 1839 on a rundown Maine farm, Dryden lost his father at age thirteen. He entered Yale in 1861, working his way until he became desperately ill in his last term. In his junior year he married the daughter of a New Haven boarding house keeper and the young couple went to Ohio in 1864, as penniless as only a sickly and unemployed college senior can be.

Dryden twice failed in Ohio insurance ventures, then came east hoping to establish an industrial insurance firm patterned after the Prudential Assurance Company of England. New York state refused him a charter on the grounds that the risk was too great. Almost as a last resort, Dryden turned to Newark to found the Widows and Orphans Friendly Society in 1873.

Poor himself when he reached Newark, Dryden was appalled by the workingman's lot. The worker, achieving little in life, left his survivors destitute when he died. Scraping together a capital of $30,000 from various sources, Dryden rented a basement in the National State Bank building on Broad Street and began selling "cheap" or "industrial" insurance on "healthy lives." Other major life insurance companies boasted of millionaire clients; Dryden linked his future to the downtrodden.

Anyone from age one to seventy-five could buy policies, and get from $10 to $500 in benefits. Dryden or an agent collected small weekly premiums, often a few pennies, at homes of policy holders. He promised payment of benefits in the day that he received proof of death—and he never failed to live up to that promise. When he ran out of Newark workers to insure, Dryden expanded to Paterson, Jersey City and other New Jersey factory towns.

The Widows and Orphans Friendly Society assumed the more dignified title of Prudential Friendly Society in 1875. It continued in the bank basement, paying $116.67 monthly and feeling the pinch so much that Dryden sublet the back room and rented desk space in his own office. The firm received a charter to sell anywhere in the United States in 1879 and Dryden moved the firm out of the basement to larger quarters.

Prudential sold more than one million policies by 1890, more than four million by 1900 and more than eleven million by 1912. Action in 1912 amounted to more than $311 million in death benefits, and annual premium payments amounted to more than $80 million.

Dryden continued to serve the little man, but his firm left its bargain basement birth far behind in 1892, the year that Prudential finished its imposing gray stone castle on Broad Street.

Mutual Benefit was the center of this full-[ ] spread in the New York Daily Graphic *for Ma[y] 1874, showing the city's "principal banking [and] insurance buildings." Banks were ornate Victo[rian] structures, but some insurance companies car[ried] on business in narrow buildings sandwiched [in] the commercial district on Broad Street.*

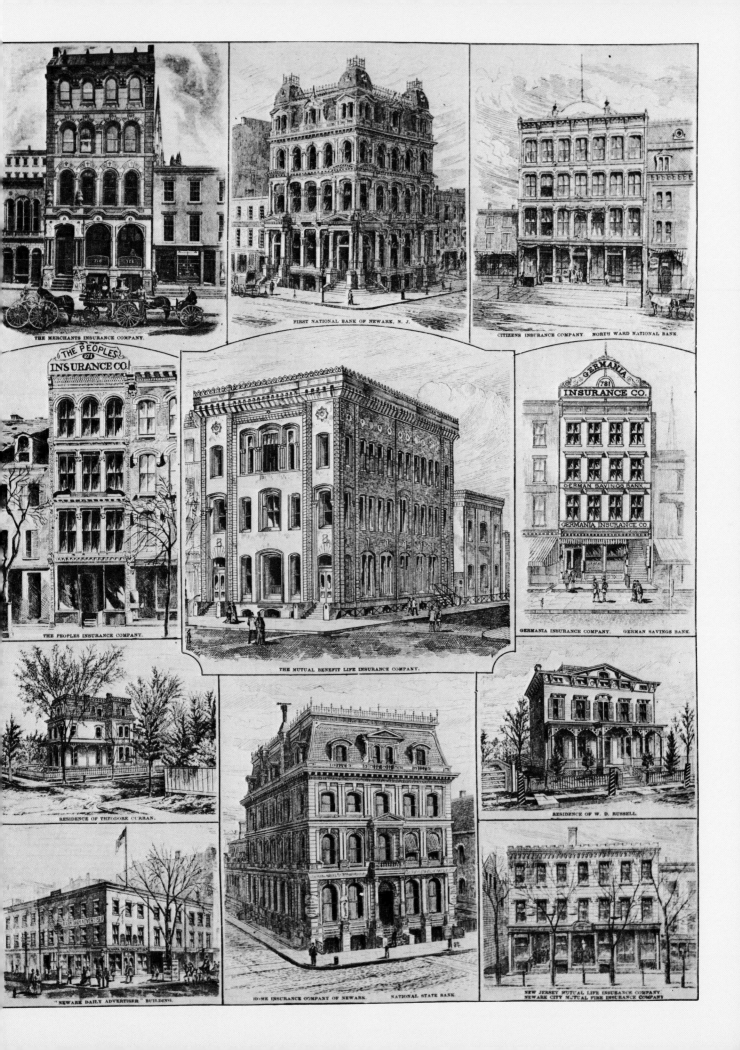

THE MERCHANTS INSURANCE COMPANY.

FIRST NATIONAL BANK OF NEWARK, N. J.

CITIZENS INSURANCE COMPANY.   NORTH WARD NATIONAL BANK.

THE PEOPLES INSURANCE COMPANY.

THE MUTUAL BENEFIT LIFE INSURANCE COMPANY.

GERMANIA INSURANCE COMPANY.   GERMAN SAVINGS BANK.

RESIDENCE OF THEODORE CURRAN.

RESIDENCE OF W. D. RUSSELL.

"NEWARK DAILY ADVERTISER" BUILDING.

HOME INSURANCE COMPANY OF NEWARK.   NATIONAL STATE BANK.

NEW JERSEY MUTUAL LIFE INSURANCE COMPANY.
NEWARK CITY MUTUAL FIRE INSURANCE COMPANY.

Architects came from afar to study the Romanesque lines. Bystanders marveled at the massive proportions that dwarfed everything else ever built on Broad Street. Artists sketched its towers and turrets and gargoyles. Called "A monument to the prosperity and thrift of the American people," the structure was the biggest in New Jersey. It had to be; by 1892 the "Pru" employed 4,000 people to back its trade mark as the "Rock of Gibraltar" among insurance companies.

The prosperity and thrift of the American people served Dryden and his associates well. Prudential's top men received salaries and dividends worthy of the baronial size of their Newark headquarters. Dryden helped found Fidelity Trust Company, a major factor in Newark financial circles, and Prudential supplied much of the capital when the giant Public Service Corporation was founded in 1903. When he bought a Bernardsville estate in 1903, Dryden left far behind the house that he had rented in Woodside, north of Newark, in 1873. An influential figure in Republican Party circles, Dryden was elected United States Senator from New Jersey in 1902. His early associates, Dr. Leslie Ward, ex-pharmacist, and Noah Blanchard, former leather manufacturer, shared as well in the wealth.

Prudential's new headquarters manifested the sweeping material changes overtaking America. Every room had a telephone. Electric lights sparkled from basement to tenth floor, and elevators whisked people skyward at the rate of 500 feet a minute. At that time, few concerns of any kind claimed even one telephone, much less electric lights or elevators.

Newarkers of 1892 stood in the midst of a transformed city. Within the two decades, from 1870 to 1890, new elements of metropolitan success emerged—and in this period Newark welcomed not only such things as the telephone, but also its first major newspapers, a satisfactory (if often confusing) system of street railways and its first major department stores.

Prudential Insurance Company exuded opulence when it finished its new home in 1892. Medieval trimmings, such as gargoyles and the fountain above, were in vogue.

Fancy trimmings did not extend to this plain room set aside sometime during the 1890s for the Prudential's women policy writers.

Telephones came simply enough after Alexander Graham Bell showed off his talking "electrical toy" at the Philadelphia Centennial in 1876. Within three years two competitors—Bell's own company and Western Union—vied for Newark telephone subscribers.

John J. Ghegan of Western Union, demonstrated the instrument's value by installing one at the Pennsylvania Railroad depot and another at Hickey's Drug Store at Market and Mulberry Streets, thus enabling the station agent to announce arrival of freight destined for the Four Corners. The achievement was a modest one (an errand boy could have run from depot to drug store in two or three minutes), and Ghegan had to offer free service to the first fifty customers. He set up a switchboard on May 1, 1879 (the sixth switchboard in the country), and quickly felt the competition from Bell.

Ghegan's rivals held a Bell franchise, and they also had as a sponsor Edward Weston, the noted electrical wizard. Weston helped organize the Newark Domestic Telephone and Telegraph Company in Jabez and Fred Feary's cigar store in the center of town. Feary's store lured Civil War veterans, reporters, editors and financiers during the downtown lunch hour, and served as an unofficial civic clearing house and idea center. There Feary and Weston promoted the telephone in 1880 and many leading citizens invested in the noisy, if useful, device.

Competition continued for two years until Western Union lawyers in 1881 recognized in court that Bell's patents were tamper-proof. In a compromise, Western Union agreed to drop out of the telephone business and Bell agreed to eschew telegraphing messages. The peace was quickly consummated in Newark, since the rivals were back-to-back neighbors. They simply cut a hole in the wall between offices, thus effecting the quickest merger in the entire system.

Telephone usage came slowly. When businessman Samuel Crump insisted on a line between his Montclair, Newark and New York offices in 1883, the company grudgingly strung a single iron wire across the meadows. It worked reasonably well, particularly on wet or foggy days, when the moisture cut atmospheric disturbances on the iron strand to a minimum.

Thus plugged in to the outside world, Newark had an improved means of learning the truth about the world. Now it needed a good local newspaper, for residents could scarcely rely on their newspapers either for information or for wide circulation of advertising materials.

The *Daily Advertiser,* founded in 1832 as New Jersey's oldest daily, and its wholly-owned subsidiary, the weekly *Sentinel of Freedom,* Newark's oldest newspaper in continuous circulation, led the field as the 1870's began. Unimaginative in format and thin in coverage, both papers also showed an unabashed bias for the Republican Party and for the lingering conservative tone that threatened to stifle the city. Neither paper represented, nor reflected, Newark as it stood on the threshhold of incredible transformation.

The *Advertiser* claimed a circulation of 7,000 in 1870 and the *Sentinel of Freedom,* 2,500.

The Advertiser *still claimed to be New Jersey's "leading newspaper" when this photograph was made in about 1900, but the city's oldest daily paper already was eclipsed by bright new rivals.*

NEWARK PUBLIC LIBRARY

189

They led other papers, such as the violently Democratic *Evening Journal* and various struggling weeklies, but such leadership was practically by default. The newspapers made no effort to appeal to the large German population, leaving that field to the popular *Freie Zeitung* and lesser German-language papers.

Thus, the arrival of the *Sunday Call* and the *Evening News* revolutionized newspaper publishing in Newark—and the success of both proved that old-line publishers had completely overlooked the potential of bright, independent pages.

Openly flirting with the Republican Party when it started in 1872 as the city's only Sunday newspaper, and flouting the old Sabbath customs, the *Call* nearly went down in the Panic of 1873. Circulation dipped to 1,100 subscribers and advertising dropped to less than two columns of advertising per issue.

Once the *Call* management showed independent thinking in its editorials, circulation increased rapidly. The *Sunday Call* editors shrewdly recognized that Newark was the core of an urban-suburban complex, not merely an overgrown factory town. Issues ran to sixty or more pages by 1900 and *Call* readers enjoyed columns on sports, the theater, fashions, food, women's news as well as sprightly feature stories on off-beat Newarkers and spots of interest in the city or within reach by train or trolley. The *Call*'s circulation had soared to 36,000 by 1910.

The *Call*'s success did not stir the *Advertiser* or *Journal* to betterment. The appearance on September 1, 1883, of Wallace M. Scudder's *Evening News* caught Newark—and rival editors—by surprise. The first editorial dedicated the *News* to being "bright, outspoken, enterprising, independent and newsy," qualities which other daily editors thought quixotic.

Scudder expressed the opinion (or the hope) that "there is a wide and inviting field in this busy city for a bright, independent newspaper, untrammeled in politics and unhampered by corporate affiliations."

He was right. The original four-page *News* reached a circulation of more than 8,000 within a year and 30,000 in ten years. One editor and two reporters gathered and wrote all city and county news in the beginning, working a twelve-hour day to feed the appetite of the little gasoline-powered press. All type was set by hand—and the *News* initially required eight printers to handle the output of its three-man staff. By 1910, the *News* sold more than 70,000 papers daily.

Overwhelmed by such competition, the *Sentinel of Freedom* died in 1895 after ninety-nine years of publication, and the *Daily Advertiser* succumbed in 1906 after seventy-four years. The *Advertiser*'s publisher changed the name to the *Star*, avowed political independence, printed morning and evening editions, and by 1910 had built the circulation to 65,000 (compared with the *Advertiser*'s 14,000 in 1900). The old *Advertiser*, re-named the *Star*, subsequently merged and remerged and is today's *The Star Ledger*.

The publishers saw that Newark's future lay not with political parties but in improved transportation links to Vailsburg, Woodside, Clinton, the Oranges and other suburbs. They knew that street car railways had changed Newark from a limited Broad Street shopping center, serving only local customers, to a commercial center for all of northern New Jersey.

Street car service began with horse-drawn vehicles in June, 1860, and by 1880 cars radiated outward along nearly all the main thoroughfares. City ordinance restricted speeds to six miles an hour, which was easy to enforce, since horses drawing heavy cars could barely plod along at four miles an hour on the level. The clop of horses' hoofs could be heard on Broad Street cobblestones as early as 5:06 A.M. (for the Irvington Line) and as late as midnight on the Orange line and the Broad Street tracks. Hills slowed traffic westbound, requiring extra horses to help pull heavy loads over the hills.

Horse drawn streetcars were near the end when the above picture was taken in front of the old City Hall (on left) in 1890. Horse and conductor posed, lower left, in 1893 on South Broad, and below is an 1876 horsecar schedule.

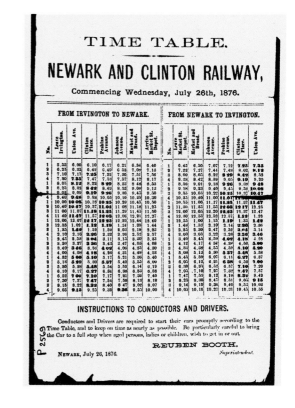

TIME TABLE.

NEWARK AND CLINTON RAILWAY,

Commencing Wednesday, July 26th, 1876.

FROM IRVINGTON TO NEWARK.							FROM NEWARK TO IRVINGTON.						
No.	Leave Irvington	Union Ave.	Clinton Place	Prohine Avenue	Johnson Avenue	Market and Broad	Arrive Market St. Depot	No.	Leave Market St. Depot	Market and Broad	Johnson Avenue	Prohine Avenue	Clinton Place	Union Ave.

INSTRUCTIONS TO CONDUCTORS AND DRIVERS.

Conductors and Drivers are required to start their cars promptly according to the Time Table, and to keep on time as nearly as possible. Be particularly careful to bring the Car to a full stop when aged persons, ladies or children, wish to get in or out.

REUBEN BOOTH, *Superintendent.*

NEWARK, July 26, 1876.

191

Horse cars offered scant comfort. Passengers nearly froze in winter and roasted in summer. Addition of pot stoves in the 1880s did little to improve things. Those near the stove constantly feared asphyxiation and those farther away felt colder than ever. Outside on his platform, the driver braved the elements in two overcoats, several pairs of mittens, a long scarf, arctics and a cap that covered head, ears and most of the face.

hauling picnickers to the country on Sundays. Newark's boundaries followed the street cars outward. City fathers took in part of Clinton Township in 1869, added Woodside in 1871, enveloped the remainder of Clinton Township in 1897 and 1902 and annexed Vailsburg in 1905. During the early 1890s there was constant talk that Harrison and Kearny soon would be within the Newark orbit. Harrison and Kearny were willing at the time, but Newark dallied

One of Newark's first trolley cars, pictured in about 1895 as it stopped to pick up passengers near Lincoln Park.

Newark's several traction companies in 1880 reported that 1,546,362 passengers had paid five cents each during the year for one-way rides. Horse cars prompted thousands of Newarkers to desert the downtown tenements in favor of little houses in outlying wards, well away from Broad Street's sound and bustle. The *Sentinel of Freedom* reported in April, 1878, that real estate promoters were turning their "cabbage patches into city lots," foretelling suburbia.

The street cars filled many needs, carrying workers and bosses between home and work and

too long. By the time annexation plans solidified, the two Hudson County towns had industrial strength of their own and spurned the wooing of the great metropolis across the Passaic.

Newarkers knew their horse cars by color: dark orange for Springfield Avenue and Irvington, blue for South Orange Avenue, red to Woodside, yellow to South Broad and Elizabeth, green to Roseville and white to the smoke-tinged East Side. Horses became known by name and disposition. Drivers were hailed as noble individuals on their daily rounds. But the most

devoted horse enthusiast knew that Newark's transportation needed something better than raw horsepower.

The Newark & Irvington Street Railway Company suggested one possible answer in January, 1888—a moving cable from the Pennsylvania Station, along Market Street, up the hill by the court house and beyond to the Irvington car barns. The endless cable, a few inches beneath the surface in an open trench, would be kept moving at steady pace by steam engines. All the

The time: turn of the century. Only horse-drawn vehicles and one trolley car offered obstacles to pedestrians crossing at the corner of Springfield and Belmont Avenues.

Trolley cars quickly became more than a means of inter-city travel. They carried city dwellers to country picnics and sometimes, decked in bright lights, rode through dark streets on romantic excursions.

car operator had to do was manipulate a claw so that it gripped the cable. By releasing the claw and applying the brakes, the car could be stopped anywhere. So much for theory.

Tests began in April, 1888. Motormen found gripping the moving cable was easy. Releasing it caused the trouble. Often the cable cars careened past irate waiting customers as the claw refused to unlock. Motormen then leaped from the car, dashed ahead to one of the infrequent telephones and asked the power station to stop the cable. When the cable halted, every car on the line stopped. Few mourned the end of the cable experiment in December.

Electricity had to be the solution. Cleveland, Ohio, had been testing electric street cars since 1883, while Atlantic City and several Passaic County towns had electric service before 1890. Newark street railway promoters dared not delay longer, despite their great investment in horsepower. Workmen began stringing overhead trolley wires along Market Street in the summer of 1890 and newspapers announced that electrified car No. 1 would roll up the Court House hill on October 4, 1890, without benefit of horse or cable.

Crowds lined Market Street on that October Saturday, skeptically awaiting the experiment and in fear of possible shocks and lightning bolts. Apprehensive city officials boarded the 34-passenger "Irvington" at Pennsylvania Station and rode triumphantly to the end, gaining

confidence with each passing minute. A reporter at Court House hill wrote:

"People stood fixed in their tracks, gaping with open eyes and mouths at the wonderful thing with no apparent power. 'No pushee, no pullee,' as the Chinaman said."

Three weeks later a Central Avenue trolley followed its electrical impulses to 18th Avenue. Fears of electrical doom apparently had vanished, but a newspaperman wrote in 1890 of juvenile delinquents:

"Boys welcomed the cars as a source of sport and irritated the conductor by stealing rides. Some of the more daring stretched full length on the tracks, jumping up as the motorman ground on his brakes and the crowd gasped. A casualty is threatened unless a restraining influence is brought to bear."

No question about it now: the horse had lost. Horsepowered street cars stopped altogether in 1893. Traction companies hastened to electrify their lines and the City Council passed out franchises with little thought of the tangled mess of tracks and overhead wires it was creating. By 1895, the Board of Trade complained that "the best streets have been given up to the trolley syndicates, by which large fortunes have been made without corresponding benefits to the city or county treasuries and without the people obtaining the best results obtainable from rapid transit."

Few residents cared about such things as trolley syndicates. They could see the mass of overhead wires stringing the city like a giant, unplanned cobweb, as trolley wires were threaded among telephone and telegraph strands and electric light wires. But the benefits of the trolleys outweighed their ugliness.

Electric power sped the movement to the undeveloped fringes of the city. Better-paid bosses and foremen took their families to Woodside, Vailsburg or Clinton Hill for a permanent supply of fresh air. As they moved out of their downtown flats, they left the doors open for streams of immigrants. Values of downtown real estate skyrocketed and merchants stopped living over their stores. They converted their flats to offices, built on the upland and rode the trolley to and from work. It was pleasant and quick. The South Orange Avenue line to Vailsburg, for example, cut running time to Broad and Market Streets to twenty minutes—at a fare of six cents for adults, three cents for children.

Working people found country joys delightfully close. Each Sunday a parade of trolleys left Newark bound for the picnic spots, the German songfests and the amusement parks on the Orange Mountains. Eagle Rock and Electric Park attracted thousands of Newarkers westward every weekend. Passengers jammed every seat of the open cars, stood in the aisles or clung to outside running boards. According to a contemporary account, a conductor "had to be an acrobat to travel from one end of the car to the other to collect the fares and an optimist to expect to get all of them!"

Trolleys were much more than a means of transportation: for thirty years they offered as well a chief source of recreation. Cyclists bound for the last trolley stop begged for (and got) special outside racks for their wheels. For that privilege the cyclist paid two fares: one for himself, one for his bicycle. Long trolley trips became a Sunday passion, intriguing adventurers with pockets full of nickels and a willingness to transfer from line to line in an effort to pile up mileage and see the sights.

Trolley cars built up the suburbs and increased Sunday attendance at amusement areas

and had a direct impact on Newark's economy. Transportation became big business in itself, creating jobs, increasing capital and making vast fortunes for early investors. Also, the swift, comfortable trolleys attracted increasing numbers of shoppers to downtown stores.

Until the 1870s, Newarkers, like shoppers everywhere, depended on specialty stores. If they wanted shoes, they went to a shoe store. If they wanted a man's suit, they frequented a draper. So it went with corsets, candy, books, novelties, food and nearly every consumer article. There were no ready-to-wear garments. Men had their clothing tailor-made (or homemade) and women went to dressmakers or fashioned their own wardrobes.

The quickened manufacturing and buying pace pushed down prices. Sweat shops and cheap clothing factories marketed inexpensive apparel to be bought off the racks. Increased volume and lower prices, combined with expanding payrolls, called for dramatic new selling techniques. The finest department stores appeared.

Many factors combined to make department stores possible. Improved transportation brought in the customers. Electricity brought multistory buildings, since buyers could be whisked to upper floors by electrical elevator. Electric lights supplanted gas lamps. Electric ventilators cleared the air in tall buildings. Basement departments were traceable directly to electric lights (gas lamps in windowless basements could cause sickness and death—and the flickering flames constituted a constant fire hazard).

Newark's "big three" department stores, Hahne & Company, L.S. Plaut & Company and L. Bamberger & Company, were thriving before 1895. Customers came in from the suburbs, shopped all morning, lunched in a restaurant, shopped again in the afternoon and occasionally stayed in town for a dinner and theatrical show. The dollars they left in town added up to a big business, completely unanticipated two decades before.

Hahne's, oldest of the department stores, started as a bird cage store in 1858, expanded to general merchandise in the 1870s and when it opened its new building on Labor Day in 1901 its clientele included many of Newark's

wealthiest families. Customers drew up to Hahne's in handsome carriages, lending an air of dignity and approval to such merchandising. A generation earlier, those wealthy customers might have sniffed at an "all under one roof" establishment. Now they welcomed it.

Next came L. S. Plaut, founded in 1870 by a Connecticut Yankee, L. Simon Plaut, and his senior partner, Leopold Fox. Their "Bee Hive"

beside the Morris Canal prospered, although the economy-minded partners at first slept in the store to stretch their funds. Plaut's one-price policy, without rebates or gifts as premiums, kept the firm busy. The "Bee Hive" was a top Newark name until 1923, when Sebastian Kresge bought the establishment and rebuilt it into the well-known Kresge Department Store.

The last of the three major department stores was L. Bamberger & Company. Louis Bamberger purchased the bankrupt stock of Hill & Craig late in 1892, found himself short of both money and time. He enlisted a brother-in-law, Louis M. Frank, and a young rubber goods salesman, Felix Fuld, to help him unload the bankrupt stock. They opened their doors on December 13, 1892, and sold out the merchandise so quickly that they decided to stay in business. Friends counseled them against it: Market Street was too far off the beaten track (Had Hill & Craig succeeded?).

Borrowing Plaut's fixed price custom and firmly sticking to a "customer is always right" policy, Bamberger's proved the skeptics wrong. Salesladies in long, black aprons and floor walkers in Prince Albert coats gave the store an elite air. By 1898 the firm needed all six floors in its original building and had spread to an adjacent building. Bamberger's put up a new store before 1912 on the present Washington and Market site.

L. S. Plaut's "Bee Hive," Bamberger's and Hahne's dominated all department stores. Bam's soon outgrew its first corner, top, opposite page. Plaut's became Kresge's and Chase in time, but Hahne's kept the name it had in 1858 when it began. Above, Christmas decorations in Hahne's, and below, workers posed amid wrappings at the furniture warehouse.

Trolley riders coursing in and out of town felt that thriving Newark had gone about as far as it could go. Industry hummed. Prudential experienced such growth that each year it added hundreds to the payroll. Mutual Benefit Life Insurance Company, while not nearly as energetic as Prudential, felt sufficiently secure in 1905 to begin work on a quietly conservative seven-story white granite and marble edifice at the corner of Broad and Clinton Streets.

Banks' assets swelled. Resources of commercial banks, $22 million in 1892, jumped to $97 million in 1909—a rise of nearly four-and-a-half times in sixteen years. Savings banks saw their deposits nearly triple in the same period, from $11 million to $32 million. A new type of financial system—the building and loan association—emerged to help finance the thousands of one- and two-family dwellings built Down Neck and in the western and northern parts of the city between 1890 and 1910.

The transformation was not easily accomplished. Trolley riders coming in to shop or to work at the "Pru" could see that the old tenements were more populated than ever. The Prudential did not have to reach for more "poor" customers. They lived in those tenements—but these were newcomers from another world, unused to urban prosperity, perplexed by city ways. These were foreigners, the latest in a long line to see in Newark the hope of a Promised Land.

Chapter 20

THE OLD ORDER CHANGETH

"THE OLD AGITATION in regard to the Sunday laws is revived afresh, but with more than the usual bitterness," the editor of the *Sentinel of Freedom* warned his readers on April 22, 1879. He agreed that the Sunday laws needed revision, but cautioned that revamping "ought to be done entirely outside of politics."

He cautioned too late. Sunday laws already had become the prime issue in that year's mayoralty campaign. Bitterness over rigid controls had been rampant in Newark for decades, but now it was complicated by temperance views, powerful anti-foreign attitudes and inter-party political scheming.

New people in town caused the trouble, some said. "New" people had always caused trouble. That is why the Indians looked askance at the Connecticut interlopers, why the Puritan founders sought to keep intruders out of town, and why antagonisms against the Irish Catholics of the 1820s and the free-thinking Germans of the 1840s flared into open conflict.

Calm still descended so regularly along Broad Street every Sunday that it astonished visitors and journalists just after the Civil War. However, up on the hill to the west, where the Germans lived along both sides of Springfield Avenue west of Belmont, families gathered after Sunday services to sing, dance and play games. The men openly drank lager beer.

A writer named Martha Lamb praised these Teutonic newcomers in *Harper's Magazine* for October, 1876: "A wondrous tide of Germans has flooded Newark, dropping into all the vacant lots and spreading itself over the flats to the east and the hills south and west, until it numbers one third of the voting population. The German quarter on the hill is one of the interesting features of the city. A section nearly two miles square is a snug, compact, well-paved city within a city, giving evidence of neither poverty nor riches. The Germans who dwell here are chiefly employed in the factories and nearly all own their own houses. They live economically and save money. German habits and German customs appear on every side . . ."

The frugal Germans had adapted so well to America that they now owned major breweries and leather factories. Some had organized a bank and an insurance company (particularly because established financial houses usually looked askance at foreign business). Others had taken the lead in introducing good music and literature to the city. Several were leading physicians. They were solid citizens, vitally interested in individual liberties.

The Germans drank beer on Sunday, despite the laws, which plainly forbade it. Since police

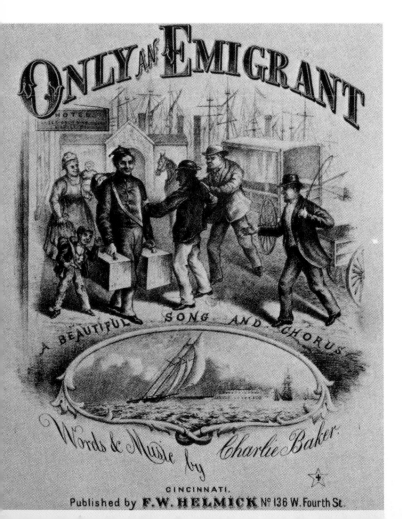

The immigrant was still a sentimental subject in 1879 when this popular ballad was published. (Library of Congress).

Harper's Magazine *used "a bit of German-town" in its October, 1879, issue to illustrate Martha Lamb's article on Newark.*

felt that they did not disturb the peace, they looked the other way. But determined to stamp out such lawlessness, the Ninth Ward Sunday Movement in 1870 demanded the closing of saloons and beer gardens. Although reluctant to take a stand at first, the city attorney finally agreed to prosecute Sunday violators. He announced pointedly that if the Germans did not like the laws, they could "go back to the Fatherland."

Enforcement of Sunday laws picked up pace, for a time. Saloon keepers cheerfully paid the nominal $10 fine, since they made four or five times that sum by keeping the swinging doors open on the Sabbath. Frederick Waldmann, owner of a German beer garden announced a "Sunday Concert" at his place. A large crowd clearly enjoyed the "Concert" and the beer that went with it.

When prominent clergymen and other citizens formed the Newark Law and Order League in 1877, German saloon keepers organized the Citizens' Protective Association. On two Sundays in the spring of 1879 they successfully stopped all city activity—street cars, milk deliveries and all industry, no matter how vital—to prove that enforcing the Sunday law would "destroy Newark as a monster workshop."

The election of 1879 presented the issue squarely. Republican Theodore Macknet, prominent hardware dealer, banker and insurance executive, was committed to strict enforcement of the Sunday laws; Democrat William Fiedler, German businessman, was pledged to act "in the interests of those who place me in nomination," meaning the open Sunday group.

The election of Democrat Joseph E. Haynes as mayor of Newark in 1885 represented a blow to old-time conservatives. A veteran principal of Morton Street School, Haynes relied heavily on support from workingmen and the large Irish population. Haynes was re-elected for ten consecutive years and unquestionably was one of Newark's greatest mayors. Scornful opponents tried to dismiss him as "Picnic Joe" because of his fondness for country outings, but Haynes fought back in witty, intelligent speeches. His proposal to tap the Pequannock River watershed for water in 1886 brought on a storm of abuse. Enemies hanged him in effigy in front of the City Hall but the mayor induced the council to adopt a far-seeing plan that is the basis for today's exceptional supply of good water.

Fiedler defeated Macknet by 3,367 votes, largely because of a switch of normally Republican German voters. His victory was doubly important: it showed clear-cut sentiment against the 200-year-old Puritanical laws, and it elevated a member of the German community to city leadership. Two years later, apparently satisfied that they had made their point, Germans on the hill returned to Republican ranks and repulsed Fiedler's bid for re-election.

Conservatives suffered another blow in 1885 when Democrat Joseph E. Haynes, long-time principal of Morton Street School, was elected mayor through support of the large working class. The *Daily Advertiser* chided him for support from "the undesirable elements." When he was re-elected in 1887 (he held the mayor's post for ten years), Haynes told an appreciative crowd:

"Two years ago the *Daily Advertiser* said: 'Joseph E. Haynes has been elected Mayor by the undesirable elements,' and I am proud to see among the sea of upturned faces before me

the same men who voted for me before . . . I am proud to be the choice for Mayor of that class of men whose skill and industry have made Newark the chief manufacturing city of the Union, and I am free to say that in the future, as in the past, I shall be glad to participate with them in their festivals and excursions, for I recognize the importance of such recreation to them and myself."

Argumentative, headstrong and colorful, Joseph Haynes became one of Newark's greatest mayors. He forced through sewer, street and water reforms (as will be related in the next chapter) and his free-flowing, humorous annual addresses delighted his supporters and dismayed his foes.

The smoldering resentment against freethinkers flared into the open in June, 1891, when the German community announced that the sixteenth Great German *Saengerfest* (song festival) would be staged in Newark from July 3 to July 7. The *Saengerfest* brought together choral groups from nearly all principal German-speaking communities in the United States, and many cities vied for the honor (and the business) accruing to the host. Mayor Haynes issued a proclamation hailing the festival. City store owners decked their shop fronts in red, white and blue to welcome the visitors.

Nearly five thousand German singers converged on the city for the start of festivities on Friday, July 3. On Sunday, July 5, the program included a Wagnerian concert and a performance of ballet music from *Samson and Delilah*, followed by a singing contest. Spectators felt the day was dignified and appropriate. Germans beamed happily, both on one another and on the crowd of non-German spectators. Most of the latter beamed back, but the Sunday singing was resented in some quarters.

The Rev. James Boyd Brady, pastor of the Franklin Street Methodist Episcopal Church, saw Wagnerian music and ballet strains on a Sunday afternoon as a "great menacing, living, curse." Sunday after Sunday, for fifteen consecutive weeks, he hurled inflamed words at Newark's Germans, vowing that he would not allow their breaking of Sabbath laws "to pass unnoticed by any clear-eyed, single hearted, watchmen on the Wall of Zion."

The minister had praise for early colonists ("nearly all Englishmen," he emphasized), for French settlers and for Spanish colonizers, "treacherous as they are." He felt that "Irish Presbyterians have done much for the country, and so did the Italians." As for Germans, Mr. Brady asked rhetorically:

"What have the Germans done? They walk around the streets, sell beer and gamble as though they owned the whole country and the Constitution. They march through the streets as though nobody had a right but they. We have some rights, too, and they are going to be respected."

Such pointed thrusts won approval in a congregation already committed to Mr. Brady's views, but his words failed to influence the community, and the city's 1,300 saloon keepers operated as they pleased.

The rising population made prejudiced criticism of Germans pointless. The tides of Irish and German immigration had transformed Newark between 1830 to 1880, but the waves now rolling in came mainly from Southern and Eastern Europe, bringing Italians, Poles, Hungarians, Russians, Lithuanians, Greeks and others to Newark's shores.

The Census of 1880 found 136,508 people in the city. That soared to 181,830 in 1890 and to 246,070 in 1900—a jump of 100,000 people in twenty years. Between 1900 and 1910, another 101,000 residents flocked to Newark, boosting the population to 347,469.

There was no mystery about why these newcomers were fleeing their homelands. Italians endured the indignities of steerage to escape the grinding poverty of homeland farms. Eastern Europeans sought to cast off both poverty and the yoke of increasing political and religious oppression. Those reasons for migration had a familiar ring to the Irish and Germans already dominant in Newark.

Newark offered what the immigrants needed most: work. As Irish immigrants, or their sons, rose to positions of leadership in the building trades and among street paving and railroad contractors, they needed workers for the menial tasks that once had been assigned to them. Italians took backbreaking, laboring jobs. Greek boys eagerly shined shoes. Hungarians and Poles labored long hours in the mills without complaint. Russian Jews roamed from the city into the suburbs as peddlers or supervised their families in tedious, eye-straining sewing in the home.

The *Sunday Call* highlighted the labor situation on May 19, 1889, when the sweep of Southern and Eastern Europeans into Newark was just beginning. Under the headline, "Irish Laborers no Longer Available," the *Call* said: "Italians have taken their place because the Irishmen have found something better to do."

The *Call* cited an unidentified Irish employer who recalled that his fellow Hibernians "were an independent lot of workmen, and at times difficult to manage, but that was only when an employer was too exacting and demanded too much of them." He regarded any Irishman as "better than two first-class Italian laborers."

Bernard M. Shanley, a Newark contractor who hired a thousand laborers to maintain the railroad tracks between New York and Philadelphia, told the *Call* that "where formerly our force

Lonely and bewildered, immigrants waited outside the labor exchange [at?] New York's Castle Garden. Hope kept them going, but many in [the?] country bitterly opposed their arrival, as depicted (opposite page) in Les[lie's?] for September 8, 1888. Titled "The Last Yankee," it sought to warn t[hat?] foreigners would shove "Americans" off the land.

of laborers consisted entirely of Irish and Germans, it now contains only about fifty per cent of those nationalities and the other fifty per cent is made up of Italians." He found Italians "slow but intelligent" and "better than the Hungarians, Poles and Swedes."

Shanley explained the drop in available Irish labor this way:

"The man who comes over from Ireland now, as a rule, has friends here with whom he has been in communication, and it is on their advice, and frequently on their money, that he comes over. This invitation is not extended until arrangements have been made to start him at work as soon as he arrives . . . and in nine cases out of ten his friends have taken care to provide him with work in a shop or some place where he can learn a trade and earn more money than he could as a laborer."

Those who made little of Italians, Hungarians, Poles, Russian Jews, Greeks and other non Anglo-Saxon immigrants, overlooked the fact that no friends stood on the docks to welcome these aliens with pre-arranged jobs. No established churches held services in their native tongues. No clubs had signs over their doors in the languages of Southern and Eastern Europe. The Census of 1880 showed only 407 Italians in Newark, a mere sixty-one Russians, sixty-nine Hungarians and 274 Austrians. Newark was an Anglo-Saxon town.

Thirty years later the Census showed 20,943 Italian-born residents, 21,192 Russians, 6,029 Hungarians and 12,963 Austrians. These figures do not disclose the fact that many of the immigrants, particularly Italians, stayed only a few years before returning home or moving elsewhere. Only the Russian Jews generally came as a complete family. Others, if they did not go back, sent for their families after a few years.

At first, immigrants lived on the outskirts of

the town. Land on the periphery was cheap and factories generally were close by. The Germans occupied the section along Clinton Avenue near the southwestern edge of town, a mile and a half from Broad and Market Streets. Poorer Germans shared Down Neck land, close to both factories and the malaria infested marshes, with the struggling Irish.

Desirable residential land lay close to Broad Street. Wealthy financiers, merchants and industrialists built fine homes along the streets sur-rounding Washington and Military Parks or facing South Broad Street. High Street lured those who wanted a fine view overlooking the workshops and storefronts, yet within walking distance. The key was proximity to work, and in the waning days of the 19th century business executives gave close personal attention to their firms. Well-to-do factory owners built homes as close as possible to their enterprises, the better to supervise them twenty-four hours a day.

Street cars changed that pattern of living

drastically after 1880, except for the heart of the city, where the very wealthy still lived across from the parks. Better paid workers went out to Roseville, Woodside, Forest Hill and eventually to Vailsburg. Some built or rented single-family houses; many rented half of the increasingly popular two-family units. As they left downtown tenements, immigrants moved in. As the pace of immigration quickened, the rush to the suburbs picked up, creating more vacancies for Southern and Eastern Europeans.

The immigrant area pushed slowly westward up the hill, street by street, but space became more difficult to get. The new arrivals were forced to crowd together—with as many as four or five families occupying a single apartment. As many as sixty to seventy families lived in buildings designed for sixteen.

Add to regular residents the visiting relatives, immigrant friends "stopping by" until they could find space in another apartment and boarders, and some notion of the crammed quarters can be gathered. The dwellings available to the immigrants were already deteriorated when they moved in. Inevitably they became dirty, rat-infested slums, neglected by both the tenants and the owners who profited from them.

Since many of the immigrants were young, single men, they slept where they could. Greek shoeshine boys, brought to America by "patrons" on contract and forced to work until they paid off their passage money, offered a pathetic example. A youthful-looking, Greek-speaking investigator for the North American Civic League for Immigrants took a job in a Newark shoe-shine parlor in 1910 and described what he found:

"In the morning we were called at 5:30 and were served breakfast at 6:15, which consisted of tea sweetened but without milk, and an unlimited supply of Italian bread. At ten (A.M.) we went back to the house and had another meal of bread, olives and oil . . . Dinner was served at four o'clock and consisted of a dish of rice, meat and bread with water to drink. At ten o'clock when we returned for the night, we were again served with olives, oil and bread.

"These meals were served in a basement kitchen which was also used as a washroom for the rags which the boys used in the shoeshine

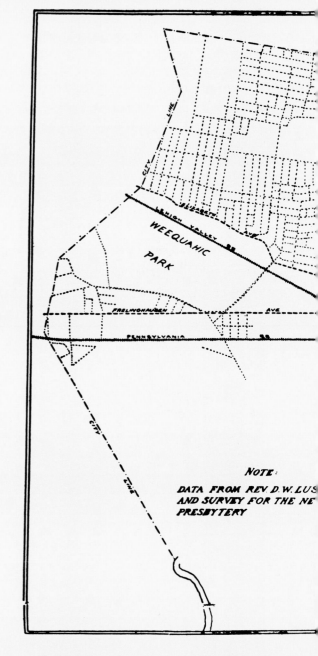

A Directory of Social Agencies, *issued in 1912, mapped areas of foreign born.*

parlor. This room was lighted by two windows. It was very damp and unhealthy.

"After the ten o'clock supper we went directly to our sleeping quarters which were situated on the third floor. The room which I slept in was a large one and contained three full-sized beds. It was lighted by an oil lamp. I slept in one of the beds which was without pillows and I used my coat and trousers for this purpose. I

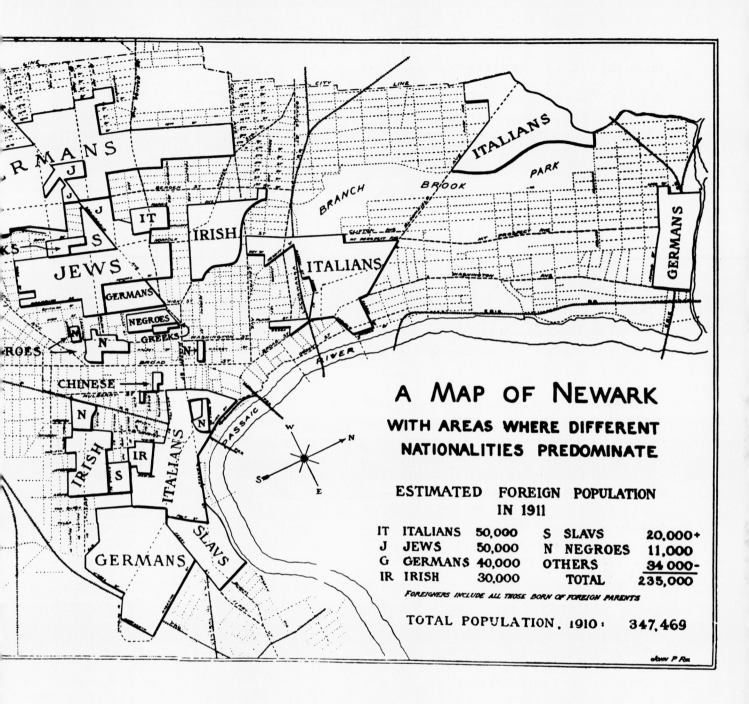

A MAP OF NEWARK

WITH AREAS WHERE DIFFERENT
NATIONALITIES PREDOMINATE

ESTIMATED FOREIGN POPULATION
IN 1911

IT	ITALIANS	50,000	S	SLAVS	20,000+
J	JEWS	50,000	N	NEGROES	11,000
G	GERMANS	40,000		OTHERS	34,000-
IR	IRISH	30,000		TOTAL	235,000

FOREIGNERS INCLUDE ALL THOSE BORN OF FOREIGN PARENTS

TOTAL POPULATION, 1910: 347,469

was informed by the boys that in the busy season when there are many more boys, there are always two and sometimes three in each bed, and that even now in the day time, men who are employed on night duty in a lunch-room owned by the proprietor of the shoe-shining parlor, sleep in these same beds."

The Greek boys worked seven days a week, twelve to fourteen hours a day. Their lack of English kept them tied to the shining cloth while their patron—or owner—often made as much as $500 profit a year on each of them. Incredibly, the boys saved money, picked up through tips or small handouts, to send home to bring other relatives to America.

Italian laborers fared little better. Usually hampered by meager education, even in their native tongue, they fell victim to all kinds of

exploitation. If Irish employers of labor gangs did not keep down their wages, shrewd Italian Padrones kept the hapless immigrants in line.

Acting as liaison between employers and immigrants, Padrones supplied labor gangs on contract. When the Pennsylvania Railroad was building new tracks across the meadows from Newark in the late 1880s, it hired about fifty Padrones, each of whom supplied a hundred or more workers. Each laborer was assessed an initial fee of three dollars and then paid the Padrone a dollar a month. Monthly wages were $24.75—meaning that each immigrant worked more than a day to line the Padrone's pockets.

Immigrants were fleeced in many ways. Land-lords overcharged them. Padrones bound them tightly to laboring jobs. Hastily organized "immigrant banks" depended only on the uncertain integrity of the proprietor. Fly-by-night employment agencies took fees for non-existent jobs. Saloon keepers victimized those who stopped by to drown their sorrows or to seek information. Politicians led them to the polls, often without the formality of citizenship.

The evils perpetrated on the newcomers in all of New Jersey were brought to light in a 1914 report of a state-appointed Commission of Immigration. However, the evils were perhaps more shocking to the social workers than to the immigrants.

Photographs on these two pages show how immigrant muscles helped transform Newark—digging the ditches, laying the trolley tracks, repairing the wretched streets and laboring in the factories.

For all its faults, the immigrant saw America as the land of shining opportunity, far better than his worn-out farm on the edge of the Mediterranean and much preferred over czarist persecutions. These were farm people, ill prepared for urban life. They came without education, money or friends, because America represented a chance. They took the dirtiest jobs, eager to prove themselves in the land of the free.

The few with skills found that Newark had need for them. Italians quickly displaced Germans as barbers and the vaunted Italian knowledge of masonry was invaluable in a growing city. Both Italians and Russians turned to clothing manufacture, at dreadfully low income. Some jewelry makers or leather tanners found work in those trades. But most of the immigrants found only menial work—on the railroad tracks, the streets, in the sewers.

Russian Jews had some help from established Jewish residents, although earlier Jews had come mainly from Germany and Poland. The language and economic barriers that separated the

Russian Jew from German Jew also separated Italian Catholic from Irish Catholic.

The Irish controlled Newark's Catholic churches until 1881, when strong German pressures resulted in the naming of Father Winand Michael Wigger (of German descent) as third bishop of Newark. This disconcerted Irish clergymen, but when Bishop Wigger named an Italian, the Rev. Januarius de Concilio, as his vicar-general, such protest erupted that the bishop withdrew the nomination and named instead an Irishman.

Italians desperately needed church services in their own language. Bishop Wigger established an Italian mission in 1882 in St. John's School hall, and by 1886 Newark had enough Italians to prompt the Vatican to send the Rev. Conrad Schotthoefer, an Italian-speaking priest, to give them leadership.

Father Schotthoefer organized an Italian congregation in St. Philip Neri Church on Court House Place in 1887. Two years later, he bought the Second Reformed Church building

207

on Edison Place, changed its name to Our Lady of Mt. Carmel Church and began services in Italian. Newark's first Italian pastor arrived in 1893 to take over the latter church with its typically "New England meeting house" look. Other Italian-oriented parishes sprang up. St. Lucy's, organized in Sheffield Street in 1891, and St. Rocco's, organized in 1899 at Morris Avenue and 14th Street, were two. St. Rocco's indicated that at least modest wealth had come to some Italians in Newark, since the handsome altar of Carrara marble was the gift of a parishioner.

Other Catholics from Eastern Europe quickly followed suit in establishing churches. Polish immigrants in a colony near the eastern end of South Orange Avenue founded St. Stanislaus's Church in Belmont Avenue in 1889. A Polish colony in the Ironbound section in 1908 organized St. Casimir's. Lithuanians who clustered in the Ironbound along Adams and Warwick Streets founded the Sacred Heart of Jesus Church in 1894 and eight years later built a new church, which they called Holy Trinity. Slovaks organized St. Stephen's Church in 1902, and Hungarians established the Church of the Assumption in 1911, buying the former Free Methodist Church as their sanctuary.

Protestants also were busy among the foreigners. They had already established Bethel Mission in the Ironbound in 1850 in the effort to reach boatmen and dock workers. Presbyterians started the First Italian Presbyterian Church in 1891. Other national groups, such as Poles and Hungarians, included Protestants in their ranks. Russian Jews joined existing congregations or set up their own struggling little synagogues.

Churches exerted great influence, although a leading Catholic historian in 1908 bemoaned the fact that in Italian church matters "so many of the men are lukewarm, indifferent to the practice of their religion, and are seemingly contented to let their wives and daughters do all the praying."

The saloon often exerted a stronger pull than the altar. Willard D. Price, a social worker in The Neighborhood House, surveyed the Ironbound district early in 1912 and found that 114 of 122 saloons had "tables and chairs for social purposes." Price declared:

Immigrants haggled in the market place in 1878 sketch of Newark, exchanging their vegetables for man-made goods.

"The men, after eating a hasty supper in a dirty, crowded home or boarding house, quite naturally leave such unattractive surroundings to spend the evening playing cards and drinking in a warm, well lighted saloon. Friends find it a convenient meeting place, work and wages are discussed, political arguments are frequent, and recent immigrants discover it an admirable school in which to learn English rapidly and gain an acquaintance with things American. Some of the saloons run saving banks. Many of them serve as club rooms for various social and political associations.

"The saloons fill a real and vital social need—the need of fairly agreeable surroundings and congenial companionship. Until other social agencies equip themselves to fill that need as extensively, the popularity of the saloon is secure."

Price found the saloons encouraged games of chance. He told of "real nice girls" who went to dances in the saloons, "not because it is their ideal place of recreation, but because it is a question of choosing between it and nothing." He saw girls dancing the "grizzly bear" but found "little distinctly immoral dancing in the halls, and practically no good dancing."

He also told of rundown houses, dirty streets, inadequate sewer facilities, scant recreational opportunities and exploitation of workers by industry. He listed gambling dens and dance halls by name. More than anything, he pleaded for additional recreational facilities in an area that had 140 saloons, dance halls and gambling dens—and only four churches.

Industrialists answered Price in a pamphlet of their own, warning bluntly that social agencies such as the Neighborhood House might find themselves without funds if they continued criticizing "the large manufacturing concerns of this part of the city upon which social workers find themselves financially dependent." The pamphlet did not deny any of Price's allegations. Instead, it prefaced words of praise from clergymen and others with an excuse:

"Every large city in the world has its poor district to which present day social workers affix the term 'The Slums.' Cities where industries flourish are more subject to these so-called slum districts than cities of residential pretension . . ."

The industrialists' view of the Ironbound found "contentment" among residents who lived "amid the drum and grind of industries, smoking chimneys, the dust-laden atmosphere and all the other elements that make up the neighborhood." These were industry's own words for the dwelling place of a large segment of Newark's newest immigrants. The pamphlet advised:

Prince Street, just before World War I, demonstrated that street markets still appealed to the foreign-born.

"Social workers in their zeal to spread their gospel of social adjustment forget that the greatest Social Worker of All said: 'The poor ye have always with you.' "

The impoverished immigrants *did* seem to enjoy life, at least in the side that they showed to the public. Italians, like the Germans, loved colorful, noisy picnics and celebrated feast days with gaiety. To the consternation of the diminishing numbers of rigid traditionalists, they revived homeland religious customs by parading their church statues in the streets on holy days.

Immigrants seemed always ready to parade. The Irish had been marching up Broad Street in honor of St. Patrick ever since the 1830s. Germans marched in honor of Fatherland holidays or to celebrate German military victories. Italians joined the paraders on Columbus's birthday in 1892 when they hiked proudly up Broad Street to celebrate the 400th anniversary of the discovery of America.

The foreigners made the best of their lot. They danced their mazurkas and polkas. They dug their gardens and planted vegetables with strange, exotic names. They cooked foods with tantalizing odors so appealing to the palate that native Newarkers soon patronized downtown Italian spaghetti houses or Greek restaurants specializing in beef recipes. They spoke in many tongues, tried to laugh at their tormentors and endured wretched homes and low wages. But they lived in hope. If this was America, they would try to taste its sweetest fruits—and, as history has proved, in the cases of a great many of these "new" Newarkers, they did. In time they rose to political and industrial power, to places of honor and trust, to positions of wealth.

They had help. Not all Newarkers believed that slums, disease, illiteracy and unsafe working conditions were the inevitable by-product of industry. Many, like young Willard Price, were seeking to change things in the waning days of the 19th and the early years of the 20th century. This was a time to establish schools and recreation centers, to start a public library, to open playgrounds and to pioneer in health activity. The immigrants benefitted greatly whenever they took advantage of educational and other opportunties. So did all of Newark, young and old, "foreign" and "native-born."

America's growing labor movement, evident in Newark's "Great Labor Parade" in 1892, aided immigrant workers' quest for equality.

Chapter 21

"ALL EAGER TO LEARN"

THE TIDES OF HUMANITY flooding into Newark between 1870 and 1910 needed help. Any time that 242,000 new people pour into a small area, as they did into Newark in these forty years, educational complications of major proportions necessarily ensue. The fact that Newark's arrivals were mostly immigrants aggravated the situation.

Coincidentally, knowledge also had taken giant strides between 1870 and 1910. These were the discovery years of the telephone, the electric light, plastics and the automobile. By 1910, man had soared on motor-driven wings. He had sent his voice through space by wireless. Doctors discussed the possibility of conquering malaria, typhoid fever, diphtheria, cholera, and other scourges of mankind. Education that was satisfactory in 1870 had become archaic by 1900.

Progressives demanded that this city (and all America) make education widely available. Often they battled apathy and hostility. In 1870, when about 8,000 pupils attended public schools —and only about fifty Newarkers attended college in any given year—many prominent citizens protested constantly that education took about twenty per cent of all annual tax money.

In 1870, the average teacher faced fifty-eight pupils in her classroom, and some taught more than one hundred in a room. Most of the teachers were young girls rushed through high school and then appointed to handle classes of seventy-five or more children. They could then sharpen their teaching skills in Saturday Normal School. Salaries seldom rose above $500 a year.

Few boys of 1870 went beyond the fourth or fifth grade. High school offered no lure for most males in a time when a factory job was a major goal. Educators stressed a classical education in the top grades, thus pressuring girls into teaching careers. The high school curriculum was expanded in 1872 to include "commercial" sub-

NEWARK PUBLIC LIBRARY

Interior of Newark Public Library shortly after it was founded in 1888 to meet city need for intellectual improvement.

jects, but bookkeeping appealed even less to boys than Latin and English literature.

The *Sunday Call* editor on May 13, 1883, described high school training as a "hollow show" given to fostering "that counterfeit gentility which has become so pernicious in American social life." He added:

"We have maintained for years that the present system of high school training has no place whatever in public education and should not be tolerated, since it also serves to divert a large proportion of the funds intended for the elemental education of all to the apparent benefit of the few."

". . . Scholars are turned out half-baked, unfit either for mechanical or professional pursuits and far too advanced to begin, as they ought

The first home of Newark Technical School, forerunner of Newark College of Engineering, at 21 West Park Street was too narrow for all students to pose in front.

to, in the first stages of a business career. The *Call* has always deprecated the maintenance of the high school, with its pretentious class distinctions . . ."

Schools Superintendent William N. Barringer replied in his 1883 annual report:

"This institution (the high school) never was more prosperous than it is now; never more valuable to our system of public instruction than now; never exerted so wide and healthful an influence."

Barringer recognized that schools should help train youth for industry. About him stirred winds of change, set in motion by the passage of a state industrial educational law in 1881. The measure authorized the state to give from $3,000 to $5,000 to aid a municipality in establishing a technical school—provided the municipality matched the state grant.

Newark's Board of Trade campaigned for a matching fund of $5,000 from private donations. Late in December, 1883, the total reached $4,583. Then the Common Council put the drive over the top by voting $500 in city money for the technical institution. The city allocated $500 annually until 1888, when someone either deviously or accidentally inserted $5,000 in the budget. The councilmen voted "aye," and two-thirds of them, according to a newspaper account, "thought $5,000 was the regular fee." Once raised, the fee remained at $5,000.

A joint state-city board of trustees adopted a technical school curriculum of drawing, physics, algebra, trigonometry, and mathematics, despite *Sunday Call* admonitions not to "place the school on too high a plane." Professor Charles A. Colton accepted the directorship in 1884 and forty-six young men began studies in a three-story building in West Park Street the following February. They met three hours nightly for three to five years before graduating.

Professor Colton bought "the Hedges place" on High Street in 1890 and moved the school there for both day and night classes. Six years later, he built a "grand hall of technical education" named Weston Hall to honor Edward Weston, Newark inventor and benefactor of the school from its earliest days.

Professor Colton guided the institution for thirty-four years, remaining long enough to see the technical school's graduates rise to prominence in the city—and to see Newark Technical School become Newark College of Engineering in 1919, on the same High Street site.

Evening schools were a Newark educational tradition. By 1890, nearly 3,500 pupils trekked to classrooms after dark and that year the city opened its first night high school. Seven years later, Schools Superintendent Charles B. Gilbert reported:

"This is emphatically a city for evening schools. The adult population is so largely of foreign birth and ignorant of the English language that it is quite important that the city furnish facilities for their education."

The foreign born were getting attention, yet, in emphasizing their impact, educators and editors sometimes overlooked the fact that sheer numbers of people, rather than immigrants, had forced the city's school system into near crisis.

Every classroom was desperately overcrowded. Census figures for 1890 showed 25,500 pupils enrolled in a system where only about 23,000 seats were available. The high school in 1895 had 700 pupils jammed into facilities meant for 500. About twenty-five per cent of school age children apparently never attended classes, a truancy that was good for space, if bad for them.

When Gilbert became superintendent in 1896, he wrote that "good work has been hindered and many children injured physically and mentally by sadly over-crowded and unhygienic conditions prevailing in our schools." He hired nearly a hundred more teachers, boosting the

city total to 861 in 1897, and cut average class size to forty-eight pupils. He started a crash building program, adding nine thousand seats, but when the work was finished in 1900, swelling numbers of new residents in Newark caused enrollment to outstrip seats by 3,500 boys and girls. This had all the earmarks of a hopeless treadmill.

The worst was yet to come. Population increased by 110,000 between 1900 and 1910. In that same decade, the minimum age for leaving school was raised from twelve to fourteen. Desperate school officials hastily started new schools, including the new high school near Branch Brook Park, finished in 1899 (and named for Schools Superintendent Barringer in 1907). The building program boosted the seating capacity of schools to 47,840 in 1910—a commendable jump of 16,500 over 1900—but the net result was only a continuing shortage. In 1910, there were 10,000 more pupils than seats!

Many parents sent their children to private or parochial schools rather than inferior public schools. In 1910, some 25,000 Newark children were being privately educated, including those in parochial schools.

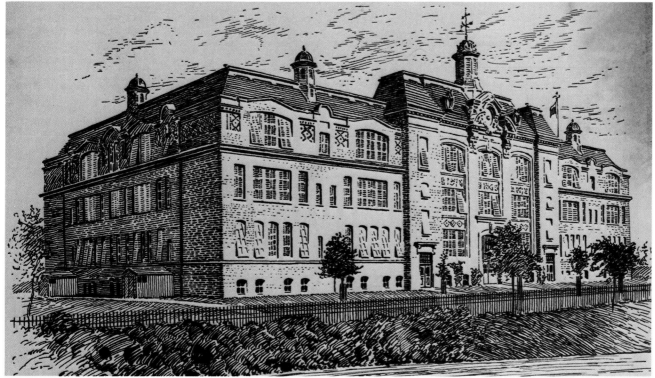

Early sketch of new high school (now Barringer) built close to Branch Brook Park in 1899. Students soon packed it to full capacity of 1,500 and the city was forced to rush plans for more high schools.

*Females outnumbered males when Newark High School's Class of 1899
posed for a formal portrait. Girls appeared in ruffles and bows, while boys
sported stiff collars and plastered-down hair. J. LeRoy Baxter, son of the
famed black Newark educator, was on left of rear row.*

Educational emphasis always had been strong among Newark Catholics. Most parishes quickly opened parochial schools; by 1870, nearly seventy per cent of all churches had schools. Some were very large. St. Patrick's Cathedral School, for example, had more than 1,100 pupils before 1900, and St. James Church School had about 1,000 boys and girls. Many Catholic parishes were predominantly Italian or Polish, and so were their schools.

Staid old Newark Academy provided an academic shelter for the sons of the wealthy. It had moved out of the center of town in 1857 to occupy a building at High and William Streets. Generations of Newark families supported the private school, which was under the direction of Dr. Samuel A. Farrand, headmaster, from 1859 to 1901. His son, Wilson Farrand, succeeded him. Most Newarkers who went to college in 1900 were Newark Academy graduates, although Newark High School (Barringer) sent many graduates to college, including

Arthur Vanderbilt, later Chief Justice of the New Jersey Supreme Court.

Newark public schools performed well in aiding the foreign born. In several elementary schools whose neighborhoods were predominantly Italian or Russian Jewish, curriculums emphasized the teaching of English. Dr. Addison B. Poland, who became superintendent in 1901, urged that the blighted areas where foreigners lived be given schools of "especial excellence." He said:

"There is no other factor in our American political or social life that equals a good public school in democratizing, socializing, and, in general, Americanizing our foreign population, old as well as young . . . Good schools cost money. Crime, poverty, ignorance and vice also cost money, both to prevent and to punish."

Adult immigrants dragged themselves to classrooms after a hard day's work. In 1906 an observer wrote:

"In the classrooms set aside for their use,

Straw hats and derbies, plus high lapels and high button shoes, were the mode when Newark Academy's Class of 1887 sat stiffly for the annual picture. Generations of wealthy Newark families supported the old school and sent their sons to its classes at High and William Streets.

these adults study lessons that the smallest children in the day schools would look upon with disdain. But they are so much in earnest that the awareness of this fact is never permitted to interfere with their quest for knowledge. Visitors to the evening school will see bearded men, women well advanced in years, married couples, prosperous looking men, and those who are evidently familiar with poverty . . . all eager to learn the ways of the country of their adoption and to benefit from its free evening schools."

The concern of city educators for the immigrants generally was not matched by a similar regard for the education of black people, who had not yet become a major factor in the city. In 1910 only 6,700 blacks lived in Newark— about three per cent of the population.

Despite the city's 1872 edict banning segregation in the public schools, the "Colored School" of pre-Civil War days lingered on in 1900. It used the same textbooks as other schools, but the course of study was "as the

acquisition of the pupils demand." The lowest salaries in the entire system were paid to "Colored School" teachers.

Black children owed whatever educational equality they had to James M. Baxter, who came from Philadelphia to Newark in October 1864 as a 19-year-old black teacher hired for the Colored School. He worked to improve the quality of education for black children. When he died in 1909 his battle for open schools was nearly won.

Baxter fought against constant prejudice. When he urged a talented black girl, Irene Pataquam, to enter the high school in the early 1870s, an opponent bluntly declared that "if the high school is opened to Ethiopians, all schools will be opened to them." Baxter was unrelenting. He won his point, Miss Pataquam was admitted, and by 1908 about 1,000 black children were attending formerly "white" schools. When Baxter began his forty-fifth and last year of teaching in September 1908, there were still

James M. Baxter, invited to Newark in 1864 to head the Negro School, fought constantly against school segregation. A black girl was admitted to Newark High School in the 1870s, and when Baxter died in 1909, all schools had been desegregated.

about 150 pupils in his Market Street Colored School, most of them because of the regard that parents held for the principal. All five of Baxter's children were graduated from Newark High School and went on to college and professional careers.

A radical turning point was due in public education. It came in 1907, when voters replaced the unwieldy school board of thirty members (two elected from each ward) with a board of nine men appointed by the mayor. The Board of Trade, composed of the city's leading businessmen, backed a small board, maintaining that it would be more efficient and that each member would have fixed responsibilities. Trustees too often had backed school improvements for their own wards at the expense of an overall plan. Newarkers approved the change, but only by a small margin.

Public education moved rapidly ahead in the next decade—but it had a long way to go.

The new high school built near Branch Brook Park in 1899 soon was packed to its full capacity of 1,500. By 1910, the city had three high school "annexes" to accommodate the crowd. Every grammar school was overcrowded. Teacher training had not been improved by the shifting of normal school classes to the old high school, which was abandoned when the new school opened.

Dr. Poland declared in 1907 that the conditions that had made the old high school unsuited for young minds made it as unsuitable as a training school for teachers. "In summer time," he said, "when the windows are necessarily raised, the noise is frequently so deafening that the work has to be stopped every few minutes until a trolley car has passed."

A 1909 report by the Russell Sage Foundation was deeply disturbing. It showed that of every one hundred children who started school in Newark, seventy-two left before the eighth grade. The biggest dropout year was in the fifth grade, when many children went to work. The Russell Sage report stressed that children dropped out partly because of limited opportunities in high school courses, but principally because their families needed financial help.

Once city leaders decided to meet the situation, new schools rose in all parts of town. Between 1909 and 1913, fifteen approved schools were built or entirely rebuilt at a cost of $2.7 million. The buildings provided for 15,000 more pupils, and included such "frills" as thirteen new gymnasiums and thirteen new auditoriums.

The new buildings included three high schools —Central Commercial and Manual Training High School, opened in 1912 in High Street next to Newark Tech; East Side Commercial and Manual Training School, opened in 1912 in VanBuren Street, and South Side High School, opened in 1913 at Johnson Avenue and Alpine Street. Within two years high school enrollment jumped from about 2,500 to nearly 5,000—proving the value of conveniently located buildings.

The faculty also won improvements. Despite opposition from both the Board of Education

St. Benedict's College on High Street, as it appeared in 1892, next door to St. Mary's Church. Benedictine monks founded the college in 1868, in a time of growing Catholic demands for parochial education.

and the Board of Trade, teachers won Civil Service protection in 1899 and added tenure in 1909. Salaries rose gradually, although not fast enough to attract many new male teachers to the system. The biggest boost to the teacher corps came in 1913 when an impressive new Newark Normal School was opened on Broadway in the secluded northern section, far from the city's noise. Its architecture represented both the Jacobean and the Elizabethan periods, including a sunken garden. This training center befitted the newly won stature of teachers, offering both beauty and an expanded two-year course.

Many still left school early or seldom attended classes despite the pleas of teachers and the

threats of truant officers. Nearly all Newark children labored at bench or machine by age 14.

The need for a public library was apparent. The Board of Trade in 1887 urged such an institution to aid "the artisan and the poor who desire to improve themselves." Voters overwhelmingly approved the establishment of a free library later that year. When its board of trustees met for the first time in May, 1888, the *Sunday Call* declared:

"It should be known from the start that this is to be a people's library, and that the struggling artisan is to be as welcome to its precincts and its privileges as the scholar and the millionaire."

The library trustees leased the handsome

Central Commercial and Manual Training High School, from architect's rendering in 1911. The school was opened the following year and still is an important part of the city system. Started in the same year was what is today's East Side High School. South Side High received its first students in 1913. The three new high schools dramatically increased attendance. By 1915, about 5,000 students were enrolled in the city's four high schools—compared with a 1912 attendance of 2,500.

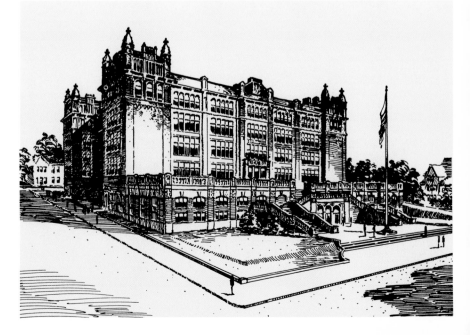

brownstone Park Theater building that the privately financed Newark Library Association was then remodeling on West Park Street. Visitors on opening day, October 17, 1889, were delighted with the marble floors, solid oak trim and 246 blazing electric lights. A New York journalist declared it "the prettiest library in the country, save St. Louis."

The library earned a reputation for service equal to its appearance. Librarian Frank Hill introduced open stacks where users could browse; paid special attention to children's needs and started placing city-owned library books in the public schools. He also supervised the building of the new granite and marble library on Washington Street between 1897 and 1901. Ex-State Legislator John M. Burnett complained that this "white elephant" was "too far away," but the library became the intellectual center of Newark.

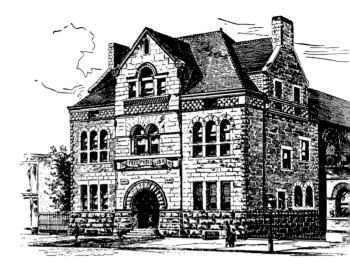

The one-time Park Theater (above) became Newark Public Library's first home. Visitors agreed it was among the most handsome in the country, but by 1901 pressures for service forced completion of the new granite and marble structure on Washington Street, still the library's main building. Note the Bull's Head stable next door.

Newark Museum, 1911, with visitors posed at opening of a photo exhibit. John Cotton Dana, below, one of the greatest librarians in American history, sought to banish exclusiveness. His goal was books for every taste.

ead, read, read: Invitations from the brary went out in pre-war years in Italian, olish, Yiddish, Ruthenian, Russian, and erman as well as in English.

Despite Hill's distinguished achievements, the most memorable name at Newark Library is that of John Cotton Dana, truly one of the foremost Newarkers and probably the most famous public librarian this country has known.

Dana made the Newark Library a vital force. He flooded the newspapers with materials on reading and books. He distributed reading lists throughout the city. He excited Newarkers about their library, their streets, their neighborhoods, their city, their state and their world. He put business books in an annex in the downtown office section in 1904, thus founding the world's first business library.

Constantly goading, pleading and educating, Dana worked for a better Newark through enlightenment. He urged the teaching of Newark history and civic responsibility in all schools —and when no such local text was available, he supervised the preparation of one.

Many bemoaned the influx of foreigners, but the fact that seventy per cent of Newarkers in 1910 were foreign-born or children of foreigners was to Dana an irresistible challenge. He added to the shelves many books in French, German, Polish, Lithuanian and Italian and issued reading lists in Yiddish, Ruthenian, Polish, Russian, German and Italian.

The chief contact between the library and the foreigners was the Hayes Street Branch, set in a neighborhood that was eighty-five per cent foreign. Nearly 70,000 immigrants lived in a section from High Street on the east, South Tenth Street on the west, Waverly Avenue on the south and Central Avenue on the north. They were both the trial and joy of every librarian who worked in the branch.

Hayes Street librarians seldom knew a quiet moment. Every evening and Saturday afternoon people stood in line for books. Often a hundred or more waited patiently for a chance to get inside the building. Each child of foreign-born parents was offered two books, one in English for himself and one in the native language of his parents. The impact of this practice on Newark history can not be statistically evaluated, but there is clear evidence that good citizenship began for thousands of Newarkers through the services of the Newark library.

Dana's awareness of the wonders of the world prompted the founding of Newark Museum in April, 1909. Before then he had sponsored small exhibits of paintings, prints and art objects, but the museum grew directly from a 1908 show of Japanese prints, silks and porcelains. When the owner, George T. Rockwell, a Newark pharmacist, offered to sell the collection for the low price of $10,000, Dana jumped at the chance. He induced the city to put up the money and persuaded fifty leading citizens to serve as Museum trustees.

Museum activities started on the fourth floor of Newark Library. The Newark *News* hailed the venture seriously but added a puckish note in a poem entitled "Art for Newark," which began:

"I s'pose she does need culture,
for she had a backward start
And never found much time to
spend in getting next to Art.
Her best approach to Latin is
the kind her aliens speak,
She is better off in German than
in Sanskrit or in Greek . . ."

Dana encouraged avant garde artists, particularly those in "The Eight," a group of controversial Philadelphians. Scoffers referred to them as the "Ashcan School" because they portrayed everyday life rather than in traditional landscapes or stylized portraits. He did not like modern art, Dana admitted, but he felt that it must be given a showing. He said, "there is always hope that the new is good and helpful and let us help it to find itself."

Newark Museum became a vital center in the city, along with the Library. Schools flourished, knowledge became more widespread, and before World War I the critics of such use of public monies had been hushed.

Newark's 19th century literary traditions sp
the city's name far. Perhaps the best-known
created by a Newarker was Hans Brinker, or
Silver Skates, by Mary Mapes Dodge. Red B
of Courage established an enduring niche
Stephen Crane, the pensive young man on
opposite page. At top is William Henry Her
better known as Frank Forester, when he live
The Cedars, on bottom of page. As Foreste
won a wide audience for his books on sport

BOBBETT & EDMONDS

Yr truly
Henry Wm Herbert
The Cedars

Chapter 22
GOOD FOR NEWARK

PETER J. LEARY, who prepared a "souvenir" *Illustrated History of Essex County* for the Board of Trade in 1891, was enchanted by his "great city," now so built up that he found it difficult to tell "where Newark ends and the townships begin." Yet Leary recognized that Newark was a sleeping—and often much abused —giant.

"It is only of late years," he wrote, "that Newarkers themselves have begun to awaken to a realization of what their city really is, and of its magnificent possibilities . . .

"Indeed, twenty years ago, Newark was anything but an attractive place. Providence, it is true, had done much for the place in the way of scenery, giving it a beautiful river along its eastern and southeastern front . . . a rolling country composed of hill and valley, that suggested to the lover of nature grand possibilities for laying out a beautiful city, and to the sanitary engineer superb opportunities for drainage and sewerage. The early settlers had laid out the town in a manner that afforded great possibilities for its future development, but their descendants had grown careless of their glorious heritage."

Leary correctly attributed Newark's new-found success in coping with growing pains to the Board of Trade, founded in 1868 when the city was little more than an overgrown country village. The Board became Newark's goad and its financial watchdog for more than a half century.

Although it sometimes opposed city improvement on the narrow ground of tax costs alone, the Board of Trade generally followed the principle that what was good for Newark had to be good for industry and business. On that basis it fought for better streets, improved sanitation, better schools, good parks, rapid transportation, adequate hospitals and sound public welfare measures.

Every American city endured expansion pains between 1870 and 1920. In most of them unscrupulous political machines feasted on the taxpayers, in the manner of New York's notorious Tweed Ring. Despite its mushrooming growth, Newark was surprisingly free of graft and corruption at this time. The Board of Trade watched every expenditure closely and the newspapers detailed costs.

Fortunately, too, Newark enjoyed a highly dedicated citizenry. Most of its top business and industrial leaders continued to live downtown, unlike lesser executives who had begun the flight to the suburbs. The business leaders ran for office, served on citizen boards and worked for and through the Board of Trade. Newark was their pride.

Despite such civic interest, the city was on the edge of chaos. When Leary wrote his *Illustrated History*, many problems beset the city. He told of a wild, disorderly spread between 1870 and 1890:

". . . Improvements ran mad for want of proper men to control them. Streets were laid out in pasture lands where they would not be needed for many years to come, with more benefit to the land owners than to the city. Sewers were built in streets that were not graded, and while all this was going on, the center of the city was neglected."

The panic of 1873 was a cruel blow, depressing property values to the point where many property owners in the outlying wards despaired even of giving away their holdings. Streets lay muddy and neglected. Sewers fouled vacant lots and marshland. Polluted water from the Passaic River ran through city water pipes. Police and fire departments were dangerously undermanned and subjected to such petty political control that they verged often on the edge of breakdown.

Leary lived to see a change, and to exult:

"The growth of Newark within the last five

years has been most remarkable. Property on Broad Street, near Market, now [1891] sells for $3,000 a foot, and all along that street it brings thousands, where it brought hundreds a few years ago. Old rookeries are being torn down . . . A new water supply is about to be introduced . . . A public park is under consideration . . . Handsome bridges span the river . . . A free public library with thousands of volumes and a noble building has been established in West Park Street . . ."

There were other improvements cited by Leary: four hospitals, a "large technical school" on High Street (the forerunner of today's N.J. Institute of Technology), a public school system that was "the best in the state." and the prospect that Newark might at last have a first-class hotel for the first time in its history.

Such praise normally could be discounted. Leary glossed over the miserable streets, the decline of the Morris Canal and the dangerous grade crossings on the railroads. Raw sewage still floated in the streams. The schools might have been "the best," but every classroom was overcrowded and teachers were underpaid. Overhead, electric and telephone wires were enmeshing the city in a copper cobweb.

Nevertheless, Newark was on the move, thanks in large measure to outspoken, courageous Mayor Joseph E. Haynes. The working class swept ex-school teacher Haynes into office in 1883 and he stayed there for ten years to fight for civic improvement on every front. His lasting monument is the city's water system. All Newark civic accomplishment of the late 19th century pales beside it—both because of the need for water and the daring solution that Haynes supported at the risk of political ruin.

Water was the difference between a progressive city and one in decline. City fathers began worrying about a municipal supply in 1851, and in 1860 bought out the Newark Aqueduct Com-

Traffic chaos at the Four Corners is nothing new. This scene, taken sometime in the late 1880s before electric trolleys had chased many of the horses away, shows horsecars, lumber wagons and people tangled at Broad and Market Streets—probably soon after a street parade.

Lock Number 17 on the Morris Canal, just above High Street in 1895.

pany for $150,000, despite Mayor Moses Bigelow's recognition that the facilities even then were "notoriously insufficient."

The city turned to the Passaic River in 1870, deluding itself that the stream flowed as sweet and fresh as in Puritan days. An intake at Belleville pumped river water into a city reservoir on the heights of Belleville and into Newark homes.

Official reports in 1872 and 1873 spoke of water "highly offensive to both smell and taste," "a shocking degree of contamination," and "filthy appearance," but the city drank on. Carbolic acid dumped into the river by a Nutley paper mill made the water even more offensive to taste and smell. The indictment of the acid dumpers did not materially improve the water's quality.

Newark blamed Paterson, Passaic and other up-river towns whose sewers and cesspools drained into the stream. But an 1882 study revealed that Newark wastes spoiled the water even more. Newark had only sixty miles of sewers but every line emptied directly into the Passaic River. Incoming tides picked up Newark sewage and swept it upstream. Outgoing tides carried the foul wastes into the Newark intake at Belleville.

Year after year, typhoid plagued the city. The Board of Trade referred to this in 1875, saying that everything depended on "the health of our city." Business was endangered. The prosperous

brewing industry, with an annual production of 600,000 barrels, relied heavily on a pure water supply.

Wealthy residents dug their own wells or bought bottled water brought in from the country rather than use the Passaic's tainted offerings. Proposals to use the Morris Canal as a water supply were dismissed since anyone could see the infestation in that slack waterway. A new reservoir in Clifton Avenue, filled for the first time in the fall of 1873, developed leaks—and did not stop leaking until 1895, when ironically, it became part of Branch Brook Park (it is now the skating area.)

In the face of pollution, an engineering firm recommended in 1879 that Newark look to the hills of Passaic County, where the Pequannock River bubbled in pristine beauty. Newark Mayor Henry J. Yates suggested that several Passaic River cities might cooperate in developing a joint supply. That progressive idea was squelched temporarily by the State Legislature's quick approval of a private company to develop the Pequannock watershed.

Matters grew worse. An 1885 survey showed that seventy-five per cent of all private wells in the city were polluted. Even the town pump at the corner of Broad and Orange Streets, long a favorite with parched street car riders and pedestrians, was found unfit.

Mayor Haynes stepped boldly into the controversy. He said in his 1886 report: "The importance of an abundant supply of pure water cannot be overestimated. That from the Pequannock seems the most feasible and best adapted to meet the requirements of our city for the present and having a due regard for the future." A year later he warned: "The time has come to act."

Late in 1888, the East Jersey Water Company approached Haynes with a proposition to provide fifty million gallons of water daily at a cost of $6 million. The offer called for East Jersey to build three reservoirs, at Oak Ridge, Clinton and Macopin, and to lay twenty-one miles of forty-eight-inch steel pipe from the upland reservoirs to Newark's storage area in Belleville.

That was a bargain, but a swirl of protest and vituperation swelled against "Haynes' Folly." Opponents assailed the mayor as "Picnic Joe," said to be so influenced by trips to "the lager parks and target shoots" that he was carried away by the thought of water from the country. Extremists hanged him in effigy and a noose was suspended in front of city hall to remind Haynes that his neck was away out.

The mayor met his opponents in an open session on June 5, 1889. He entered the council chambers, "looking quite gallant with a big, blood-red rose on his coat." He swallowed a glass of water (contaminated by the Passaic) and faced his critics, who included Dr. H. C. H. Herold of the Board of Health. Dr. Herold insisted that "zymotic diseases" could be caused by water "subject to fermentation" in reservoirs. Haynes countered with his own facts and figures and his own fervent belief in the project. The contract was read, debated and approved.

The first Pequannock water flowed into Newark in January, 1892. Haynes reminisced in his 1892 message about "the filthy waters of the Passaic" and said: "If a single death of a human could have been traced to the use of the Passaic water, my opponents would have clamored—and justly—for my indictment for murder . . .

"Today the number of opponents of the new water supply bears about the same relative proportion to our entire city population that the number of inmates of the County Jail holds to the entire population of Essex County."

By the end of 1892 only Pequannock water flowed from city faucets—and deaths from typhoid fever dropped seventy per cent! Memories of the foul old days were revived in 1899 when a temporary water shortage forced the city again to introduce Passaic River water into the city system. Epidemics of typhoid fever, dysen-

Idyllic calm surrounded Newark's reservoir at Belleville in 1881 view, but the water was dangerously polluted.

Reservoir at South Orange Avenue in the 1890s, after supplies had been improved by tapping Pequannock River.

tery and diarrhea engulfed the city and fifty deaths were traced directly to use of Passaic River water. Quickly the city contracted to buy additional water from East Jersey Water Company. Installation of meters in the same year reduced consumption of water by six million gallons daily.

Improvements to the water system forced substational outlays of money until by 1905 the cost had risen to $11,977,000. There was little grumbling, since the utility was so well administered that it showed a profit. In addition, the Board of Trade pointed out that a good water supply stepped up fire fighting efficiency and thus reduced fire insurance rates.

Water was the vital need but Newarkers had much else to do. They had to dispose of their waste, systematically and with as little pollution of the Passaic River as possible. Garbage removal began in 1872, street cleaning became a matter of growing concern after 1890, and by 1900 city officials had tackled the disposal of sewage with some success.

The increased awareness of the relation between pollution and disease led the city to build thirty-six miles of sewers between 1870 and 1880 (compared with a total of twelve miles of sewer lines in all the city in 1870). Construction was haphazard and most sewer lines emptied into the meadowlands, transferring pollution from uptown lots to the marshes. The Board of Trade warned in 1883:

"Stagnant water and filth raise the death rate, and all this, besides distress and sorrow, means injury to our reputation as a healthful city, and inflicts damage and loss to property interests many times over the cost of applying the remedy."

More dollars were poured into sewer construction, until by 1910 Newark had 310 miles of lines, nearly ten times the 1880 total. That did not end pollution of the Passaic River; Paterson, Passaic and other towns still dumped their refuse into the stream. Factory owners in Newark, in turn, increased their disposal of sewage into the river after the city abandoned the Passaic as a water supply in 1889. Newark and seven sister cities started a joint sewer system in 1898. Newark paid most of the initial appropriation of $11,250,000, but the city desperately

needed relief from the noisome condition of the Passaic River.

A surprising number of Newarkers managed to disregard the filth in the Passaic. Boating clubs continued throughout the 1880s and 1890s, but by 1900 only the most enthusiastic rowers could stand the polluted river. The May 30, 1901, regatta of the Passaic River Amateur Rowing Association was the last major boating affair on the river. (Rowing was resumed on a lesser scale after the joint sewer became fully operative in 1924.)

Streets were wretched. Newark had only twenty-seven miles of paved streets in 1870—out of a total of 621 miles—or about four per cent. Only twenty-two more miles were paved between 1870 and 1890, at a time when Newark's borders were expanding and when 75,000 more residents were added to city rolls. The 1890s started with 181,000 people in town, with factories and businesses booming, and the streets were no better than in 1871, when the *Sentinel of Freedom* had declared:

"There is hardly an acre of natural road-bed soil within the bounds of Newark, and the only alternative is between pavements and the worst kind of mud. It cuts up in the fall rains, only to freeze into horrible ruts in the winter, to be worn down at heavy cost of wear and tear of vehicles; breaks up and freezes again at intervals through the cold season, furnishes another epoch of mud in the spring and closes out with clouds of dust in the summer. And, finally, the more the roads are worked, the worse they are."

Once more the Board of Trade led the fight for city betterment. Businessmen backed German-born Julius A. Lebkuecher, wealthy jewelry maker, in his successful bid for mayor in 1893. Lebkuecher set out to beautify Newark, keeping an eye at the same time on efficiency and economy.

Sixty miles of streets had been paved in the sixty years before Lebkuecher's administration. He paved thirty miles of streets in his two-year term and started Newark on a program that by 1910 saw all but eighty-five miles of city thoroughfares paved. Brick and granite block replaced cobblestones, and by 1910 more than fifty miles of streets were paved with smooth asphalt. Newark filled its ruts just in time. By 1910,

Cleaning Market Street's rough stone surface at the turn of the century was hard, but white-garbed sweepers kept just ahead of trolleys.

the automobile honked and chugged along the streets—and owners of horseless carriages could not tolerate the jolts that their buggy-driving fathers had endured.

Much more perplexing were the disorder and confusion that the electrical age inflicted. Electricity brought the telegraph, telephone, lights and power. It brought street cars to whisk people magically about. It also brought a maze of overhead wires and a snarl of trolley traffic. And, wherever the street cars crossed the grade level tracks of the railroads, disaster constantly threatened.

The joy over rapid transit diminished soon after the first electric street cars ran in 1892, since the Common Council failed to regulate trolley franchises. Builders strung their wires above the streets to add to the casually growing webs of electric and telephone lines.

Street car companies made little effort to keep schedules or to control traffic. By 1900, more than 300 trolley cars were scheduled to pass Broad and Market Streets every hour. The slightest breakdown—or even a horse-drawn funeral crossing the tracks—brought on a nightmare of clanging trolley bells, neighing horses, shouting drivers, angry passengers and frustrated pedestrians. The city government felt powerless to ameliorate the situation.

Day after day, a trolley might ram a passing beer wagon or buggy. Day after day, railroad engineers and street car drivers fenced with one another at grade level crossings. The possibility of tragedy prompted the *Sunday Call* to editorialize on September 2, 1900:

"Three hundred cases of typhoid and fifty deaths were necessary to make Newark adopt a meter system which would check extravagant use of water . . . The killing of half a dozen prominent residents by a railroad train will be the signal for the removal of grade crossings."

Pennsylvania and Jersey Central railroads soon started to eliminate more than two dozen grade crossings within the city, but the Lackawanna delayed. Determined prodding by Mayor James Seymour, a pioneer in the elimination of grade crossings, brought the Lackawanna in line on December 26, 1901. The *Evening News* declared that disappearance of the Lackawanna crossings would remove "a shackle that long has fettered the city's growth and hindered its development . . ."

Work proceeded slowly, and on February 19, 1903, the *Call's* warning came true, but it was not a "half a dozen prominent residents" who were sacrificed. Rather, nine Barringer High School students died that day in a trolley-train crash that ranks among Newark's most shocking tragedies.

More than 120 riders, mostly high school students, were packed aboard the North Jersey Street Railway Company trolley when it headed north in Clinton Avenue from the Orange Street stop at about 8:45 A.M. Joyful students filled the crisp February morning air with song as the trolley started down a slope in Clifton Avenue toward the Lackawanna tracks. To the west, the speeding Bernardsville Special whistled its approach to Newark.

The gate went down as usual, and the motorman applied his brakes as he had countless times before. The trolley slid on. It crashed

Meeker Avenue's ruts and mud made even horse and buggy travel difficult in 1895, when a photographer snapped this pastoral scene.

through the gates and the singing changed to shrieks of horror as the packed passengers saw the train bearing down on them. The huge locomotive shattered the trolley, strewing bodies along the tracks. In view of the crushing impact and the fact that few passengers had a chance to jump, casualties were relatively light. Nine died and about 30 sustained injuries—and all the dead and most of the hurt were young. Their deaths forced both city and railroad officials to face the cost of negligence.

A coroner's jury blamed the trolley company for the crash, charging that nothing had been done to clear snow and ice from the tracks. Sand meant for scattering on the tracks was found frozen in the box. The railroad company was reprimanded for operating at a higher rate of speed than was permitted in the city, but the jury agreed that the speed "did not directly contribute to the disaster."

In the aftermath of the trolley tragedy, work was accelerated on elevating railroad tracks, and by 1904 the Lackawanna had joined other railroads in removing many death traps.

Trolley companies had fallen on hard times. High costs had forced smaller companies into a series of mergers that had brought most streetcar service under control of the North Jersey Traction Company, dominated by Philadelphia interests. Disenchantment within Newark was at a peak. The *Advertiser* on March 23, 1903, said the city's liberal franchise grants

had brought "positive ingratitude by creatures she (the city) has encouraged and fostered and done so much to build up." The Board of Trade asked the courts to regulate the Traction Company.

Newark-born Thomas N. McCarter Jr., a distinguished, wealthy lawyer-politician, stepped into the deteriorating trolley situation in the summer of 1903. He organized the Public Service Corporation of New Jersey with the support of the Prudential Insurance Company and the Fidelity Union Bank. Public Service used its $10 million in capital to acquire street railways, gas companies and struggling little electric light and power companies.

Narrow dirt paths on either side of streetca[r] tracks were good enough for wagons o[n] Richelieu Terrace in 1915, but increasin[g] numbers of motorists found them wretched

The new company did not immediately accomplish miracles in bettering streetcar service. McCarter himself admitted in 1910 that the situation at the Four Corners was intolerable; by then, 552 trolleys were scheduled to pass Broad and Market Streets every hour. Declaring that the situation "will become worse instead of better," McCarter suggested abandoning the nearly defunct Morris Canal and building an open air subway in its bed. Public Service would be willing to build a subway or would lease one from the city, if the latter preferred to underwrite the project, McCarter said.

Nothing was done. The debris-cluttered, brackish Morris Canal continued to flow through the city. Its days were numbered, but 1910 was not the year to eliminate the outmoded facility. An occasional canal boat still meandered through the city, along what is now Raymond Boulevard, under Broad Street, past Plaut's Department Store and up the long inclined plane to the west.

In time, Public Service brought financial stability to the streetcar lines. It introduced efficiency to its electric power lines—and when prodded by such threats as the opening of the city-owned electrical power company in May 1908, lowered its rates. It began to bury some of its wires, as the telephone company did, and the whimsical threat of a city being snared in a cobweb lessened.

Looking west on Market Street in about 1900 (above), Newark appeared much like a city caught under an ever-expanding cobweb of copper telephone, telegraph and electrical wires. At a Lackawanna Railroad crossing at Clifton Avenue (below), a train speeds west. In February 1903, a trolley crashed through the gates, hitting a train and killing nine high school students. Thirty others were injured.

Lackawanna Railroad station, just after tracks were elevated over Broad Street.

Out of the turbulence a city changed into a metropolis, willing to face its tasks. Taxes rose but services improved: streets were smoother and cleaner, water was pure and plentiful, sewer disposal facilities leaped from 17th century improvisations to reasonable, early 20th century standards. If this was not the best of all possible cities, certainly the strides since 1880 had been significant.

First office of the Public Service Corporation, near The Four Corners.

THWARTERS OF DEATH

Pure water, improved sewers, cleaner street these were manifestations that mankind ha begun to recognize the correlation betwee disease and dirt—and the fact that death coul be thwarted, at least in the early years. Add tionally, Newark physicians led a fight betwee 1865 and 1910 to make their city healthy.

Hospitals were recognized as the first bulwar against sickness, but they were only slow established in Newark. Gov. Marcus L. Ward hospital for wounded Civil War soldiers was th city's first. After the war, St. Michael's, S Barnabas and the German Hospital (now Cla Maass Hospital) were started between 1865 an 1868. The City Hospital was organized 1882, and it first operated in the wing of t alms house as evidence that it was viewed mo in terms of charity than science.

Medicine in the late nineteenth century sto on the threshold of dramatic advances, but su diseases as diphtheria, smallpox, tuberculo and typhoid fever raged unabated year aft year. Particularly endangered were the po who lived in crowded tenements and all ch dren younger than two years, whether rich poor. In 1870, fifty per cent of all the dea in the city were among children less than t years old.

The United States Census of 1890 revea a shocking fact: Newark had the highest de rate among all the twenty-eight cities in United States with populations of more th 100,000. The city's death rate had even beca a factor in politics, and in 1883 a Democra sweep was attributed largely to a decline public sanitation under Republican rule.

Working to overcome the city's unheal reputation was a growing corps of dedicated brilliant doctors, young and old. Dr. Cha J. Kipp, founder in 1880 of the Eye and Infirmary, was a pioneer in the prevention infant blindness through use of precauti immediately after birth. Dr. C. H. Her crusaded against diphtheria and, as a pu health leader, quickly used diphtheria a toxin in the city after its discovery.

Dr. Edward Zeh Hawkes, a Newark surg and gynecologist for 60 years, gained fame new operating room techniques. In 1902, became the first doctor in New Jersey to u

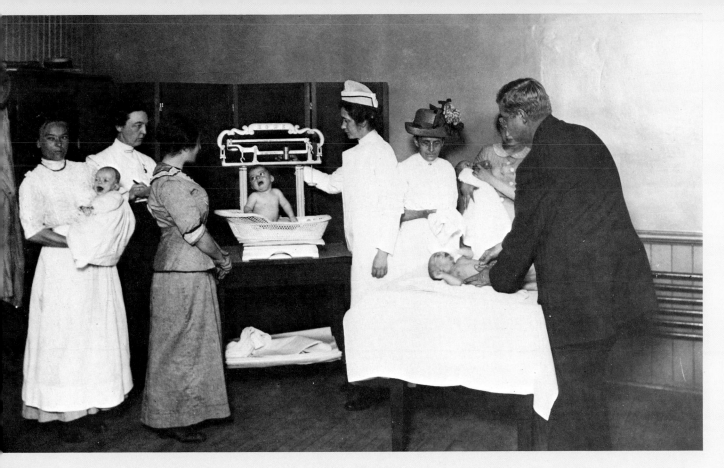

Vital in the city's improved health were the "Baby Keep Well" stations. Dr. Henry L. Coit is in foreground.

spinal anesthetic, for an operation in a farm house in what is now Branch Brook Park. He and Dr. Edward Sprague, also a noted Newark surgeon, administered the state's first blood transfusion in St. James' Hospital in 1908. Another city gynecologist, Dr. Edward J. Ill, began practice in 1883. During his long life he gained international acclaim for his gynecological surgical techniques. Colleagues often referred to Dr. Ill as the "father of medicine and surgery in New Jersey."

In the forefront of the fight against childhood killers was Dr. Henry L. Coit. He began a life-long crusade for better infant feeding and for clean milk after his first son died at the age of two of an intestinal disease.

Dr. Coit centered his attention on milk, then commonly sold by peddlers who plunged unwashed dippers into forty-quart cans to fill containers brought by purchasers. The fact that they wiped their hands on their dirty coats while handling the milk did not disturb most customers. Dr. Coit outlined a program of milk purification in 1892 and soon after the State Legislature adopted a law to supervise the handling of milk from dairy to the dealer. In May, 1893, the world's first bottle of certified milk,

handled entirely under medical supervision, was delivered to Dr. Coit.

Dr. Coit helped found Babies Hospital in 1896 at a meeting in Dr. Kipp's office. It was the second such hospital in the United States. The public knew Dr. Coit even better through the "Baby Keep Well" stations which he established to encourage mothers to bring healthy babies for periodic checks.

By 1910, Newark, which twenty years before had the nation's highest death rate, stood sixth among cities with the lowest rates.

The year 1883 was a significant date in Newark medicine, for Drs. Herold, Ill and Coit all began practice in the city that year. Coincidentally, Harrison A. Martland was born in 1883—and he lived to become possibly Newark's best-known doctor.

A full generation before the atom bomb, Dr. Martland demonstrated the lethal danger of radiation by examining dying workers who had tipped brushes in their lips while painting luminous watch dials with radium at an Orange factory. His many contributions to medical thought as Essex County Medical Examiner prompted Newark to name its new high rise medical center in his honor.

231

*Newark had no place to go but up. Next to Old First Church, Nation[e]
State Bank rose ten stories high. Up Broad Street, in this photo made i[n]
about 1912, the Kinney Building of twelve stories and the Firemen['s]
Insurance Company home, sixteen stories, dominated the Four Corner[s]*

Chapter 23

TRULY A GOLDEN AGE

IF A GOLDEN AGE is when buildings of distinction are raised, parks created and statues commemorating men of old erected; or when people find life simple and business proceeds in courtly dignity, then Newark enjoyed such an age between 1900 and 1916.

Early 20th century Newark was a compact city at its center. Downtown businessmen had no way to go but up. Real estate values within four or five blocks of the Four Corners had risen so high they were measured by the foot rather than the acre. By 1910 a foot of property fronting on Broad Street near the Four Corners was worth upwards of $5,000. Rambling three or four-story brick buildings gave way to tall, slim giants of granite or limestone.

The Firemen's Insurance Company set the pace. It surprised the city by a decision to rip

The Firemen's Insurance Company decision to build a skyscraper doomed this sturdy old Victorian structure on the northeast corner of Broad and Market Streets, and meant the end for the familiar statue of the fireman atop the ornamented roof.

Looking west from roof of one of the skyscrapers, the new Court House was one sign of progress, and the sign in foreground urged young marrieds to build new homes.

down its staid and perfectly sound Victorian stone home office on the northeast corner of Broad and Market Streets. In 1910, the company's new sixteen-story building towered over all. This was Newark's first skyscraper, and on its small lot the gleaming white structure looked taller and thinner than it really was.

Across the street, on the southeast corner, the twelve-story Kinney Building was finished in 1912, obliterating all evidence that this had been Robert Treat's home lot in colonial times. A bronze plaque was placed on the building to remember Treat.

Prudential was thinking big in 1916, when an architect rendered this dream of a forty-five story tower on the northwest corner of Broad and Market Streets. The plan carried out the powerful look of the company's buildings already in place. In the foreground, the architect visioned an underground walkway beneath the Four Corners. The grand plan was never carried out. NEWARK PUBLIC LIBRARY

Slightly to the northwest, the Prudential Insurance Company's stone fortress dominated Broad Street, putting even the completely re-modelled edifice of Mutual Benefit into the shade. In 1916, the Prudential was planning a forty-five-story tower on the northwest corner of Broad and Market, but that project never left the drawing board. Prudential remained in its complex of three buildings erected between 1892 and 1909.

Southward, National State Bank replaced its little 19th century home at Broad and Mechanic Streets with a ten-story building. This new-comer looked slender in comparison with its predecessor because the bank had available only forty-nine feet of frontage on Broad. Next door, the Old First Presbyterian Church kept the bank in its confined space, and even when the new building was finished it was no higher than the old church steeple. Newarkers began to appreciate the towering majesty of that steeple raised 120 years before.

Swarms of workmen were always digging in the streets, laying sewers, burying electric cables, ripping up old trolley tracks or laying down new ones. Men and horses dug and scraped in lots along the streets to prepare the way for new buildings. Newark was alive with prosperity.

Amid the whirl of vehicles and pedestrians a kind of order bordering on stateliness emerged. Powerful horses clomped majestically over the cobblestones and Belgian blocks, tugging color-ful beer wagons. The sleek carriages of the wealthy slid through the traffic, carrying finan-cial barons to their offices or transporting well-dressed ladies on genteel shopping expeditions.

Postcard from the Vailsburg track, above, and the unidentified Newark cyclists poised for a spin in about 1900, below, gave proof that cycling was a sport for all.

Bicycling was an inexpensive means of trans-portation and an exhilarating new way of life. Young men set off on Sunday mornings on long "runs" along the dusty roads to outlying coun-ties. Others rode westward on South Orange Avenue to watch such cycling greats as Frank Kramer at Vailsburg Veledrome. The bicycle opened new vistas to middle class city dwellers, carrying them to amusement parks, to picnic grounds and on courting missions. A bicycle was a cherished thing, earned only after months of saving.

236

3437

Young bicyclists pedalled everywhere, recklessly darting between trolley cars. Bank clerks and mechanics cycled to work. The Newark Library had to install bicycle stands for its borrowers. Frank P. Hill, the first librarian, pedaled to work, and his young assistant, Miss Beatrice Winser, rode her wheel down from Forest Hill.

The cyclists faced the snorting, fuming horseless carriages that could frighten man and beast alike, while their lordly drivers rode proudly in their goggles and dusters. By 1900, there were enough drivers in and near the city to organize the New Jersey Automobile Club, with such names on its roster as Thomas A. Edison, Christian A. Feigenspan, Edward Weston, Felix Fuld and Dr. Edward J. Ill (the last four all from Newark).

More than 8,000 crowded Vailsburg's Electric Park for the opening of the city's first automobile show on Washington's Birthday in 1908. They wandered among the shiny, brass-trimmed run-abouts and touring cars. (Squeeze-bulb horns and acetylene gas headlights were available for an extra price). Automobile shows were

held every year thereafter—usually at the Sussex Avenue Armory—until World War II.

There were many skeptics when the police department bought its first automobiles in 1910 and when the first motor driven fire engine rolled the following year. The vaunted gasoline motors never truly replaced the spectacle of a steamer drawn wildly down Broad Street by sweating, straining horses. But by World War I the fire department horse, along with other vehicular horses, was doomed.

Amid the 20th century transformations, some of the old held firm. Old First and Trinity Churches were of such religious and historical significance that no one dared suggest that they make way for progress. Other churches along Broad and Market also assumed a patina of antiquity to insure their preservation. The old Plume House beside the Lackawanna Railroad tracks quietly turned 200 years old in 1910.

Onrushing time had doomed the original burying ground on the southwest corner of Broad and Market. It was not simply impatience with the past: the desecration of the ceme-

Powerful horses racing through city streets with a steamer in tow created powerful excitement, but even the most nostalgic agreed that Newark Fire Department vastly improved its efficiency when it turned to gasoline power in 1911. Amazing changes ensued from the time firemen in what became the Vailsburg section of Newark posed outside their firehouse in about 1895 (below) and twenty years later when the department was motorized.

Newark government wandered from place to place—to five churches, upstairs over two market places, in quarters with county offices and in rented rooms of Library Hall—before old MacGregor House at the corner of Market and William Streets was bought in 1863 and converted into a City Hall. Mushrooming city business forced city fathers to begin thinking of a new building in the 1890s. A row of unsightly stores and dwellings, opposite page, top, was bought and razed in 1899 to permit a start on the present City Hall. The building was nearly completed when the bottom photo was taken in 1906, and advertisements fully covered the temporary wooden fence. The new municipal building cost $2,000,000 but the marble pillars and spacious rotunda inside made taxpayers happy. A prediction that the new building would serve for a century did not hold true. By 1926, the first addition was completed.

tery by builders, garbage tossers and vandals had been common a century before. By the Civil War, headstones were crumbling. When the bones and tombstones of the city's founders finally were gathered together in 1887 and placed in a crypt in Fairmount Cemetery, they received more respectful attention than they had gotten in years. As for the old burying ground, a fire house stood at its Broad Street entrance and Branford Place was soon dug across its once hallowed acres.

Sentiment also gave way to practicality in the City Hall and the Essex County Court House. The brownstone Egyptian-style Court House at the corner of Market Street and Springfield Avenue no longer could accommodate county business. A converted hotel on the corner of Broad and William Streets had served well since 1864 as the City Hall, but it creaked with age.

Although they planned to erect new buildings at the same time, city and county fathers rejected grouping of them to give Newark a governmental complex worthy of New Jersey's most important city.

Work began first on the City Hall. Contractors razed a row of nondescript stores and houses along Broad Street and turned the blueprints of John H. and Wilson Ely into an impressive

edifice encased in New England granite and decorated inside with marble. The core was an imposing rotunda, seventy-seven feet high and surrounded with balconies. Atop the Hall was a great dome, reminiscent of the Capitol in Washington.

Slightly more than $2 million was spent on the land and construction. More than half the financing came from selling the Old Burying Ground and other city-owned real estate. This structure, said proponents, would serve all Newark governmental needs for a century to come. (It served, actually, for less than twenty years before additions were made.) But when city workers moved into their five-story home just before Christmas in 1906, this was a gift of magnificent proportions.

A year after construction started on the City Hall, Essex County began raising its new Court House. Cass Gilbert, one of the country's '

The new Essex County Court House, built at a cost of nearly $2,000,000, as it appeared soon after dedication in October, 1907.

ing architects (whose work included the Woolworth Building in New York), designed a noble mass, featuring a facade of double Corinthian columns and a series of steps leading to the entrance. The Court House cost nearly two million dollars. On dedication day, in October, 1907, everyone agreed it was worth it.

The new Court House rose behind the old, which stood until all business could be transferred. Despite hopes to preserve the 1838 Court House by moving it, wreckers leveled the handsome building. There were cries of anguish at the loss of the rare architectural gem, but the fine murals, the statuary and majestic appearance of the new seat of county business helped to mitigate the pain.

Visitors to Newark were impressed by the skyscrapers, the new public buildings, the fine library and the strenuous efforts to build enough schools to cope with the rising population. They commented favorably, as well, on the growing number of parks and the numerous statues of figures notable in the city's and the nation's history.

In 1895, Essex established the first county park system in the country. The Park Commission engaged Olmstead Brothers, designers of New York City's Central Park, to transform a region of north Newark from monotonous flats and ill-used land into Branch Brook Park. Eventually, its beautiful landscaping, lawn tennis courts, open air band concerts and a lake for boating and fishing won nationwide praise from park planners and city designers. On the southern edge of Newark, in the swamps of Weequahic and on the old Waverly Fair grounds, the Essex park builders created a lake

Newark was fortunate in having foresighted leaders who believed in parks. When boys in knickers and caps skated alongside young men in derbies and young ladies in daringly short skirts, their pond was Blue Jay Swamp. It became part of Branch Brook Park in the Essex County Park System, first in the nation. Below, Military Park in 1913 was a refreshing bit of green that stemmed from colonial days.

surrounded by wide open playgrounds set under fine trees.

City fathers also saw the need for small municipal parks. They retained the shady atmosphere of the colonial parks—Washington, Military and Lincoln—and added small plots of greenery in other parts of town. These they called "the lungs of the city," where residents might breathe freely.

Statues were in vogue. Newark was busy dedicating monuments to its heroes. In 1880, it had placed a life-sized figure of Major General Philip Kearny in Military Park, with General Ulysses S. Grant and other dignitaries present. Seth Boyden was honored in Washington Park, Frederick T. Frelinghuysen in Military Park and Msgr. George Hobart Doane in a little triangle just north of Trinity Church. Christian Feigenspan, Newark banker and son of the noted brewer, sponsored the Colleoni in Clinton Park, a copy of what John Ruskin called the world's finest equestrian statue.

The two greatest of American heroes—Lincoln and Washington—assumed fixed images in the city thanks to the will of Amos VanHorn, a local furniture dealer. Gutzon Borglum, one of the country's greatest sculptors, fashioned the statue of Lincoln, seated in front of the Court House. Dedicated in 1911 by President Theodore Roosevelt, the Lincoln masterpiece has been one of the city's prides ever since. Washington, sculpted by J. Massey Rhind, took an enduring pose beside his horse in Washington Park in 1912. The vigorous likeness overlooks Broad Street, down which Washington's dispirited troops had retreated in 1776.

VanHorn's will also provided for a memorial to the nation's servicemen. This was not completed until 1926, when the Wars of America Monument, another Borglum creation, was dedicated in Military Park on Memorial Day.

Newark's social and business leaders clustered near the parks, as they had been doing for a half century. Lincoln Park's neighbors included the McCarters, leaders in Public Service and Fidelity Union Bank, and Franklin Murphy, varnish maker, ex-mayor and ex-Governor. Northward, such leading families as the Ballantines and Wards lived in mansions fronting on either Military Park or Washington

Park. Handsome homes stood along much of High Street and dozens of well-to-do citizens had small estates in the Forest Hill and Mt. Prospect sections.

Some of the newer citizens were living well, too, particularly the German beer makers. Christian Feigenspan employed an architect to design a magnificent Victorian mansion built in 1906. He embellished the High Street home with paneled walls and stained glass windows. In recent years the Feigenspan mansion has housed the Newark Chapter of the American Red Cross. Nearby on High Street, another distinguished brewer, Gottfried Krueger, built a much-admired showplace.

Newark's social pace was set mainly by the debutantes and their beaux who lived near the downtown greens. They gathered often for glittering parties in the gaslit brownstones, but the most brilliant affair was the annual Assembly Ball, started by the Essex Club and carried on by committees of socially prominent young men. The Assembly Balls were bright and exclusive, frequented by the Keasbeys, the Plumes, the Dennises, the Bradleys, the Emorys, the Giffords, the Frelinghuysens, the Symingtons, the Ballantines and others of social prominence.

Daughters of these families attended either Miss Frances Whitmore's Newark Seminary or Miss Margaretta Craven's School (later the Prospect Hill Country Day School). The boys went to Newark Academy. Boys and girls

Seven hunters, or at least men with guns, gave an air of authenticity to a posed picture of the Active Gun Club at its South Orange Avenue headquarters in the 1890s.

he Triton Rowing Club on the Passaic iver in 1884, when a regular program river racing drew large crowds.

Horse racing was a popular sport at the Waverly Fair Grounds, at what is today's Weequahic Park, throughout the 1890s.

Boating on the Passaic,
from a 1909 post card.

alike attended dancing classes taught by Peter P. O'Fake, a talented black whose brother John was a leading music teacher and orchestra leader.

Wealthy boys went to college while their sisters stayed home to prepare for their debuts and for coveted marriages to those in their own set. Every debut and society wedding was certain of an extended, flattering description in the press. Between debuts and marriages, the society crowd danced and dined for charity, for show, and, sometimes, just for fun.

Elsewhere, the "neighborhoods" had taken on distinctive colorations. The city was really a conglomeration of small, self-contained towns—

Vailsburg, Roseville, Forest Hill, Woodside, Clinton Hill, Down Neck (or The Ironbound) and the beginnings of the Weequahic section. Each community had its own stores, taverns, churches—its own pride and its own way of life. Roseville was as far removed in atmosphere from Down Neck as Newark itself was from Milwaukee.

There were some common bonds. The downtown department stores brought neighborhood shoppers together. The Essex County parks brought young people together in track meets, field days and all sorts of informal recreation. Newark High School united young intellectuals.

Churches also tended to unite Newarkers on a social as well as a religious basis. Trinity, Old First, North Reformed, Peddie Memorial, the House of prayer, Second Presbyterian and other

School children brought their own tools to clean up a Belleville Avenue (now Broadway) playground in 1913. Proud mothers looked on and a father supplied the wagon.

Park Place depot of the Hudson Tubes, finished in 1911, offered Newarkers a swift, safe and inexpensive ride to downtown New York City.

Hudson & Manhattan Station, Newark, N. J.

downtown Protestant churches were discreetly proud of the town leaders who each Sunday occupied their pews. Catholics scattered through many parishes took pride in the huge new Cathedral of the Sacred Heart overlooking Branch Brook Lake. Work had begun in 1899 and by 1902 the granite walls of the Cathedral were fifty feet high. By 1910, the front wall and towers stood ninety-eight feet above the ground. But the magnificent Cathedral actually was not completed until the middle 1950s.

There were theaters aplenty before 1910—Waldmann's Opera House, Fox's Washington Street Theater, the Empire on Washington Street, and Henry C. Miner's theater on Market Street, to name only a few. Stock companies were tremendously popular and such stage greats as Lillian Russell, Chauncey Olcott, Maude Adams, Edwin Booth, Joseph Jefferson and other stars made Newark a regular stop.

The city's numerous taverns underscored the fact that it was a man's world. No lady ever set foot across the saloon sill or even peered through a swinging door. If she had, she might have been envious.

Inside, tasty free lunches could be had for the price of a nickel schooner of beer. Hard boiled eggs, pigs' knuckles, roast beef, pickles,

olives, cheeses and cold cuts tempted the beer drinkers. In some places on the "Hill," where Germans congregated, beer cost only three cents a schooner, astounding out-of-town visitors.

Several of the places were justly famed: Charley Charles' tavern, where only straight whiskey was served; Ludwig Achtel-Stetter's restaurant and bar on Broad Street, specializing in fine German cooking; Mrs. Louisa Aab's place on the site of the present City Hall, the hangout for politicians; Simonson's on Broad Street, the most noted oyster house in town; Jake Holtzman's bar on Market Street, worthy beneficiary of the Court House trade, and Murray's on Market Street, which served up both roast beef and the latest baseball scores in front of glittering mirrors.

Newarkers admired their city and began to look ahead to 1916, when the town on the Passaic would be 250 years old. But before it could call itself modern, Newark needed a rapid transit tie with New York City and a port from which it could send its products abroad.

Rapid transit came first, and in double measure. The Pennsylvania Railroad started its tunnel under the Hudson River in 1902. Simultaneously, it built a new double track line across the Meadows from just east of Newark. The job

The meadows presented a bleak prospect in 1915, as work proceeded on the new port.

was done in 1910, giving Newark (and all of the United States west of it), a quick run into midtown New York.

Closer to Newark's heart was the Hudson & Manhattan Railroad tunnel that young engineer William Gibbs McAdoo set out to complete in 1900. McAdoo was courageous. The tunnel under the Hudson, started in the 1870s, had twice ruined contractors and took the lives of twenty men in an 1880 cave-in. About 3,600 feet of tunnel had been dug by the original contractor, who found himself out of cash and faith in the venture.

McAdoo took what had been called "that dead thing, laid away in the cemetery of unworkable ideas," and rammed it from bank to bank through the mud and rock under the river. He linked Hoboken and 19th Street in New York by underground railroad in 1908, built westward to Jersey City and on to Newark by the fall of 1911. His men put the finishing touches on a station on Park Place, facing the fashionable homes across from Military Park.

Regular travel began with little fanfare at 12:01 A.M. on December 20, 1911, when a train left Hudson Terminal in downtown New York for Newark. Newspapers hailed the ride the next morning. The New York *Times* declared the H. & M. line to be "virtually a private one for the benefit of Newark and the thickly settled districts between that city and New York." Newark and New York were now only twenty minutes apart, and downtown Newark was much closer to downtown New York, the *Times* declared, than much of Manhattan.

In succeeding days Newark residents jammed the new facility. Officials reported that more than 100 fifty-trip tickets were sold to commuters the first day they were offered. The *News* reported that heretofore quiet Park Place "bore a steady stream of people and vehicles."

People quickly nicknamed the H. & M. "the Tubes." The Park Place depot was referred to always as "the Tube station." By any name, the new facility quickened Newark's pace. It enticed New Yorkers to live in Newark or its suburbs, and it helped bring new residents to surrounding areas. Commuters rode in to Newark by trolley, automobile, and, later, by bus to board the tubes for New York.

Now joined to its powerful neighbors by a high speed system, Newark yearned for a union with the world. Since earliest times the wide bay and the broad river had held forth the hope that Newark might achieve a maritime reputation. The hope had not materialized. The high land of Newark, where the first settlers touched shore, was some four miles inland from Newark Bay by way of the Passaic River. Unstable muck sloped off from the meadows where Newark land touched the bay.

A ship channel had to be the answer. Early in the 1870s there was talk of a waterway that would run nearly three miles inland from Newark Bay to within six or seven blocks of South Park (Lincoln Park). A ship canal, featuring five or six huge docking areas, can be seen on city maps of the day.

That canal was never built, but the pressure for an easy shipping access to the outside world could not be put aside. The Board of Works quietly began acquiring meadowland property off Newark Bay in 1911. Clear title was difficult to get, since many pieces of property had been unused and forgotten since the founding days of the 17th century. Despite a barrage of criticism because no plan had been announced for the new property, the city spent nearly $1 million to acquire titles by 1911. A year later, it authorized another $1 million to dig a channel, 300 feet wide, twenty feet deep, from Newark Bay into the oozy meadowlands. The first spadeful of earth was removed on New Year's Day, 1914, and dredges the next day began biting at the bottom of Peddie Ditch.

Those dredges were opening up a swampland comprising almost one-third of the city. Despite its pleasant name of The Meadows, the section had been unloved and untouched since colonial days except for an occasional herd of wandering cattle or the muskrats and mosquitoes who found the dampness to their liking.

Newarkers were invited to "Port Newark Terminal Day" on October 20, 1915, to see where their millions were going. More than 10,000 people made their way to the soggy meadows, by train, boat and automobile. They saw a channel extending nearly a mile over the meadows, complete with a 500-foot wide turning basin near the Jersey Central tracks. The Newark *News* reported:

Arrival of tug bearing city officials signified the Port's opening in October, 1915, and officials traipsing pipe line (below) to avoid the mire felt assured of Newark's shipping future.

Combining artistic fancy with symbols of its industrial might, Newark invited the world to the 1916 birthday party.

"When the tug *Henriette,* with Mayor Thomas L. Raymond, the Board of Works commissioners and other city officials, steamed up the inland channel where once Peddie ditch flowed odorously to the sea, visitors had an ocular demonstration of what can happen all over this spacious bay front. The boat tied up to a dock nearly a mile in length, which is but the first of a chain of docks that will form many miles of accommodations for shipping, if Port Newark lives up to its expectations."

As the *News* said, "it was easy for visitors to see that what has been done with a few acres can be done for all." And it came to pass, in

time. Port Newark became a great port, although nearly another year elapsed before the first commercial ship, the schooner *A. J. West,* tied up with a cargo of mahogany from Manila.

The opening of Port Newark gave strength to the momentum gathering for the city's observance of its 250th anniversary. Mayor Jacob Haussling named a Committee of One Hundred in July, 1915, headed by ex-Governor Franklin Murphy. Naturally, John Cotton Dana, the ebullient librarian, worked hard for the anniversary. Newark was about to prove his declaration: "I am a citizen of no mean city."

But preparations bogged down in argument. Dana and Murphy clashed over the location of a proposed $1.5 million memorial building. A month after voters approved a bond issue for the memorial building in November, 1915, the site committee approved purchase of a lot at the corner of Broad and Camp Streets, across from Lincoln Park. Fronting on Broad Street for 185 feet, it cost $285,000.

Dana promptly resigned, charging that the site was too far removed from the center of population. When the Newark *News* assailed the purchase as ill-advised Murphy withdrew. Wallace Scudder, publisher of the *News,* then resigned from the committee to permit himself and his paper freedom of expression. Later Murphy and Scudder returned to action, but Dana refused to end his opposition. The memorial building was never built.

Everything else proceeded quite smoothly. Ceremonies began on May 1 with cannon salutes, pealing church bells and ceremonies in Proctor's Palace Theater. Hundreds of thousands of people streamed in and out of the city for the next few weeks to watch parades, see the pageant in Weequahic Park and cheer athletic events and baby parades. Nearly all nationality groups paraded. Thousands of school children marched in their own parade in June.

Honors for top billing had to be shared between the Founders Day Parade on May 17 and the pageant that was presented for four nights at the end of May and the beginning of June. The parade moved up Broad Street past four tall pylons erected near City Hall. A few days after the parade, Mrs. Chester F. Williams, dressed in flowing white robes as "Miss Newark," floated above Broad Street on wires to advertise the pageant.

The pageant's cast included thousands of Newarkers, young and old. The budget of $50,-000 allowed for ninety-two speaking parts, more than 4,000 performers and the cooperation of more than forty clubs and organizations. A specially constructed amphitheater in Weequahic Park faced a water-filled moat on which "Robert Treat and the Founding Fathers" re-enacted Newark's founding. Crowds of 50,000 attended the performances.

Poets were invited to submit verses. Some 900 entries were received from forty-two states and five foreign countries. Seldom have so many poets put forth so much effort for a top award of only $250. First prize went to Clement Wood of New York for his *The Smith of God,* which began:

> *"I am Newark, forger of men,*
> *Forger of men, forger of men—*
> *Here at a smithy God wrought, and flung*
> *Earthward, down to this rolling shore,*
> *God's mighty hammer I have swung,*
> *With crushing blows that thunder and*
> *roar . . ."*

There were protests from disappointed bards, but the winning poem rather well summed up the character of a city welded together by industry.

The most permanent effects of the celebration were two major buildings dedicated on Park Street in the anniversary year. One was the Robert Treat Hotel, the first truly good hotel in the city. The name was chosen after a special committee rejected such alternates as "The McCarter," "The New Ark," and "The Military Plaza." Nearby, Public Service Corporation completed its $5 million terminal in 1916. The seven-story steel, limestone and terra cotta home office of the power company became the North Jersey center for city and suburban transit.

The 250th anniversary celebration had stirred the city to a high peak of enthusiasm. Young and old, immigrant and member of the "first families," shared a warm feeling for Newark. Truly this was a golden age. The war in Europe was only a small cloud on the horizon— although each day the newspaper headlines loomed darker. The war was an ocean away. Could it mean anything to the United States, or to Newark?

Spring had only begun to touch the trees in this moody photograph of Newarkers striding briskly through Military Park on April 1, 1916.

Chapter 24

SOLDIERS, SHIPS AND FLU

GERMANY HAD OVERRUN the Lowlands and France and Italy were in constant fear. Great Britain was fighting desperately for its life. On the seas, the Kaiser's U-boats struck terror into the hearts of all voyagers. In America, the factories hummed.

At first, Newarkers followed the war with considerable detachment, although for a time in May, 1915, the sinking of the *Lusitania* by a U-boat had evoked anti-German sentiment. There was no thought of America's participating in the conflict—the general reaction from President Woodrow Wilson down. The war was, for the time being, Europe's problem.

The big German population in Newark at first felt no need to hide its exultation over the Fatherland's successes. The large Irish population, if not openly favoring a German victory, felt no cause to weep for England's difficulties.

More than 6,000 Newarkers of German ancestry marched up Broad Street on June 10, 1916, as part of the city's 250th anniversary celebration despite protests that the show interfered with the parade of Spanish-American War veterans scheduled for the same day. The protests were not anti-German in nature, but directed rather at the poor timing. The veterans also marched, but only a thousand were in line.

The Stars and Stripes were carried by all the German units. Since Germany and the United States were not at war, the marchers saw this as logical. One float showed Germania and Columbia greeting one another in friendship. Newspapers reported many small German and Irish flags in the hands of paraders and spectators.

Ten days later, when uniformed soldiers of the First Regiment stepped briskly along Broad Street, Germany still was not the American

Camp Frederick Funston in Douglas, Arizona, home of the First New Jersey Brigade for July and August of 1916. The dusty camp ground would turn to mud in a rain and the smelting works in the rear blew acrid odors through the tents. Newarkers were delighted to get home.

1ST "NEW JERSEY" BRIGADE
ON THE BORDER
BRIG. GEN. EDWIN W. HINE COMMANDING
CAMP FREDERICK FUNSTON
DOUGLAS ARIZ - 1916

enemy. These soldiers were on the way to the Mexican border to punish the revolutionist bandit named Pancho Villa for mistreating American citizens south of the border.

The New Jersey troops reached a mesquite-covered camping ground near Douglas, Arizona, on July 4 and stayed there for more than two months. They endured temperatures as high as 115 degrees, intermittent torrents of rain that turned their dusty field into steaming mud, sickening odors from a nearby smelting works and alkali drinking water that made thirst almost preferable. But they never saw Villa, their phantom enemy. When they returned home in October they had only sunburned faces, upset stomachs and Mexican souvenirs to prove they were veterans of the border war.

Newark buzzed with industrial activity that summer. The Sunday *Call* estimated in June, 1916, that nearly $20 million had been invested in new Down Neck factories since early in 1915. Some of the activity could be attributed to the opening of Port Newark, but the *Call* observed that the European battleground was the prime reason. Every factory of any consequence in the city knew the pleasant jingle of foreign dollars seeking the tools of war.

So many new chemical makers had crowded into the meadows that Avenue R was called "Chemical Row." Maas and Waldstein, a new company, hired more than a thousand to make cellulose, acids and other war material. Acrid fumes hung low over the meadows surrounding the plant, but three shifts of workers chose to ignore that nuisance.

More than 3,000 new jobs had been created in the meadowland since January, 1915. Any skilled worker could demand premium wages, with electricians in particular demand. A competent electrician could earn from $60 to $80 a week by working twenty hours overtime. Unskilled electrician's helpers carried home as much as $40 a week, a very high wage for the time.

Employers found a scarcity of unskilled labor. Immigration had dwindled to a trickle and many immigrants had returned home to fight for their native lands. Laborers demanded at least $4 a day and floated from job to job. Often forty to fifty of them would quit simultaneously for a better offer. Many skilled workers quit their trades to take up the temporarily lucrative career of laborer.

The boom had its annoying side effects. Trolley cars were jammed to capacity and Public Service showed scant concern when William J. Morgan began touring the streets in a tiny bus in the summer of 1914, picking up passengers at five cents a ride. A five-cent piece was called a "jitney" and the buses received that nickname. Within a few days, Morgan's brisk business inspired competitors. By June, 1916, more than

What is believed to be the city's first jitney appears on the right in this Springfield Avenue photograph taken in 1915.

200 of them roamed the streets, run by chauffeurs who protested that their pay of thirty cents an hour was too low. Jitney owners, in turn, complained that they made little, since gasoline cost $4.50 a day and oil $1 for each vehicle. By mid-1916, there were so many jitneys that the city licensed them.

Housing shortages increased sharply as out-of-towners came to seek work in the factories. A 1915 survey had found ninety-six "To Let" signs in one street. In April 1917 there was not a vacant room in the same block. Speculators hastily built brick apartment buildings in several sections of the town.

Early in 1917, the Board of Health estimated that between 27,000 and 30,000 blacks now lived in town, most of them just up from the farms of Georgia or Alabama, where they had been recruited by industry in need of muscle. This marked the beginning of major migrations of black laborers to Newark.

Employers eagerly hired blacks to perform the heavy work that traditionally had been assigned to the Italians, Irish, Poles and Hungarians. But work and good living were not one for these new arrivals. W. H. Young of the city's sanitary division said in a 1917 report:

"The main difficulty is the shortage of adequate accommodations for families. No white landlord seems to want this class of tenant at all, especially in any modern house, with the result that much overcrowding was unavoidable. There are simply not enough good houses to go around. The result is a living condition contrary to all good sanitary laws.

"At the same time the white landlords take the opportunity of extorting high rents for miserable shacks, cellars and basements, some of those renting for $15 and $16 a month.

"When found living under such conditions, the Department has immediately ordered their discontinuance, a practice which seems to drive the families from one undesirable place to another. In some instance improved quarters have been found, and it has been our observation that when these people are given a better class of dwelling their habits of living and cleanliness are improved."

Young concluded:

"There is only one way to solve the very pressing problem of Negro housing and that is to build wooden houses for their accommodation, give them a chance and treat them like human beings. There must be in the city some capitalists who are willing to meet this great emergency by providing the money to build modern colored apartments."

There were no such capitalists, then or for many years afterwards. As more black workers sought jobs in Newark's war plants, the housing situation deteriorated drastically. Black leaders in 1917 started the New Jersey Welfare League under William M. Ashby (still an active social worker in 1966) in an effort to cope with the many miseries of a black rural populace suddenly cast into urban living.

But overriding all problems was the imminent involvement of the United States in the war. Stories of German atrocities filled newspaper columns. Woodrow Wilson cautiously advocated a peaceful settlement of the conflict, while privately admitting sympathy for the Allies. Then, in January 1917, Germany warned the United States that unlimited submarine warfare would begin February 1. This country, Germany said, would be permitted to send only one ship a week on a specified route to Falmouth, England, providing it carried no contraband.

Indignation swept the land. Most Germans discreetly put away their Fatherland flags. When U-boats sank three United States ships in March, full participation in the war was inevitable.

Wilson called for "war without hate" on April 2. Four days later, throngs of Easter shoppers and workers on their way home from a Saturday of toil in Newark factories learned that Con-

Uncle Sam said I WANT YOU on posters everywhere in town and Newarkers followed orders. Below are candidates for the First Regiment, labeled "Newark's Own," lined up before the Army's recruiting team. All ages were eager to enlist in March, 1917, when this was snapped.

gress had declared war on Germany. The next day nearly all clergymen in the city injected a strongly martial tone into their Easter Sunday sermons. Newark was ready to fight.

War demanded manpower. The National Guard had been called out in February to patrol armories, arsenals and storehouses and on April 1 the First Infantry was summoned to guard tunnels, bridges and factories between Newark and Jersey City. Military leaders knew that a few well-placed bombs in the railroad yards in and near Newark could create havoc.

Recruiting agents set up shop immediately, appealing to young men in Military Park, in theaters and churches, the schools and in Olympic Park. Many enlisted under the banner of the First Regiment.

places, warned that all males between twenty and thirty must register for the draft.

On Registration Day eve, June 4, the First Regiment held a recruiting session along Broad Street. A chorus sang patriotic songs on the steps of City Hall and Mayor Thomas L. Raymond addressed a crowd of 15,000 that stopped all traffic. That night the First Regiment was dubbed "Newark's Own." Scores of young men rushed to enlist.

Church bells rang on Registration Day, a legal holiday. By 7 A.M. long lines had formed and parades rattled through the streets in the morning and afternoon. Before the day ended, more than 50,000 had registered in Newark—rich and poor, clerk and laborer, descendants of the Founders and sons of immigrants.

Enlistments failed to supply enough men. Aware of the draft riots that had shaken New York and other cities, including Newark, during the Civil War, President Wilson reluctantly called for conscription. Congress enacted a draft law on May 23 after heated debate.

Trouble was expected on Registration Day, June 5, between 7 A.M. and 7 P.M. A massive propaganda campaign urged all young men to recognize their obligations to their country. Posters in many languages, placed in all public

Every train leaving from the Central Railroad station, whether loaded with draftees or regulars, brought crowds down to see the boys off to war.

Draft boards began to choose those needed to fill Newark's first draft quota of 2,537.

The First Regiment formed on the afternoon of September 4 to entrain for Camp McClellan in Anniston, Alabama, where the regiment would be merged into the 29th Division. Governor Walter E. Edge and Mayor Raymond said farewell at City Hall before the soldiers marched on to troop trains waiting in the Jersey Central Railroad yards.

Warren P. Coon, chaplain of "Newark's Own" told of the departure:

"Patriotic impulses actuated every spectator and tears mingled with cheers. The crowd streamed past police lines to its heart's content, while the police, moved by the same emotions as governed the crowd, used judgement and tact and were not too strict in holding the crowd in check.

". . . As the trains pulled out in the fading twilight, the last word spoken, the last kiss given, the crowd of parents and children wended their way homeward with no less brave a spirit than the lads speeding southward to prepare for entering the greatest war the world has ever seen."

Already at Camp Dix was a small advance party of Newarkers to prepare for the 1,055 drafted men set to depart on September 19. These civilian soldiers obeyed the instructions to "wear old clothing, carry no luggage." Eventually, 9,591 Newarkers were called under the first draft. Hundreds more went from the second draft call on September 12, 1918, (for those between the ages of 18 and 45). The second draft registration brought the total of Newarkers registered for the draft to about 60,000.

War was still something of a lark. The newspapers carried cartoons and humorous letters about such things of the military life as kitchen police, ill-fitting uniforms, teachers who worked as truck drivers (and vice versa), ever-present mud, bumbling second lieutenants and forced marches that led nowhere.

Those at home enjoyed the levity because they worked hard, too. Wages in the round-the-clock factory shifts were far better than Army pay, but the workers were assured that they were just as vital to the war effort as the uniformed men. This war would be won by raw industrial power as much as by those in the trenches.

Newark's vaunted reputation for making almost everything brought the city a variety of war contracts—for hardware, munitions, paint, clothing, blankets, machine parts, truck components, chemicals and scores of other needs. All industry kept busy, but the major World War industrial story unfolded on the docks at Port Newark.

Manpower was the key, ranging from a matter of getting draft "greetings" as above or working in the shipyards. Below, the Agawam, *first of the scores of ships built at Port Newark, slides down the way on Memorial Day, 1918.*

Rumors of a major shipbuilding role for Newark were heard in June, 1917. They came true on September 14, when the Submarine Boat Company announced that it had received an $18 million contract to build fifty ships at Port Newark. The city was incredulous: Port Newark was not much more than a wide muddy ditch surrounded by swamps.

Henry R. Sutphen of Morristown, head of the Submarine Boat Company, brought novel shipbuilding ideas to Newark. His method was simple. He first built a model exact to every screw, then took it apart to standardize each part. He had built cargo ships by that method for Canada

keel five days before Christmas, 1917. The first fabricated ship, the *Agawam*, slid off the ways into Newark Bay on Memorial Day, 1918. As it hit the water, John P. Nicholas, purchasing agent for the company, turned to general manager B. L. Worden and cried out, "Oh, the damned thing floats!"

Sutphen launched three ships simultaneously on July 4, 1918. On Memorial Day, 1919, the company's fifty-second ship was launched, setting a record of one a week. The program of 118 emergency freighters, started in 1918, was completed in January, 1920, a year before the much-publicized Hog Island yard near Philadelphia

Women workers proudly marched up Broad Street in all of Newark's many parades, and they correctly boasted of their role in winning the war.

before the United States entered the war.

Forty thousand piles were sunk into the swamp to support warehouses and the twenty-eight ways on which the ships were to be built. A new town rose on the marshes, complete with police and fire departments, mess halls and cafeterias for the 15,000 to 17,000 employees who eventually swarmed over the grounds. Newly constructed railroad tracks and a trolley line carried workers to and from Newark and surrounding towns.

Sutphen wasted little time. He laid the first

finished its 122 freighters. Thanks to Submarine Boat Company, Newark led all American cities in shipbuilding tonnage in 1919.

Women assumed new importance, for the first time becoming involved in outside activities. They became motor mechanics and took up other skills previously reserved for men. They toiled in home gardens or worked on nearby farms. The Submarine Boat Company hired them in droves for jobs ranging from riveters to tool sharpeners, and publicized their dependability (only one per cent of female employees

Women volunteers attended evening classes to learn wireless telegraphy in case they were called on to replace male operators.

were absent more than two consecutive days). By the spring of 1918, newspaper ads offered women all kinds of work. When they started training as trolley conductors in May, 1918, men had the uneasy feeling that the world would never again be the same.

Life was full for those left behind, whether or not they were engaged in such glamorous activities as shipbuilding or street car conducting. Both men and women devoted countless hours to the Red Cross, YMCA, Salvation Army, various government bureaus, church groups and other civilian efforts designed to aid the fighting men. City Hall became a town meeting house, the center of nearly all war and civil activity.

Children played their part, too. They gathered peach pits, which were ground into bits for use in gas masks. More than 3,500 children enrolled

in the Home Gardens Division of the Junior Industrial Army, working to ease the food shortage. In the summer of 1917, the Essex County Park Commission converted thirty acres of park land into gardens to be planted and harvested by children. High school boys drilled in school units and boys and girls alike took part in Liberty Loan Drives.

These drives had an emotional appeal that was missing from such commonplace efforts as vegetable gardening or collecting peach pits. Noted stars, including Irving Berlin and Irish tenor John McCormick, came to Newark to rouse support for the Liberty Loans.

Newark responded well to Liberty Loan appeals. Five times it was asked to subscribe designated amounts and each time the quota was oversubscribed, by amounts ranging from $2½ million to $22 million. The September to October Loan drive in 1918, Newark's fourth, carried a quota of $38 million; Newarkers bought more than $60 million in bonds.

Shortages appeared by the end of 1917 as food and other products went to Army camps and to foreign shores in ever-increasing supply. A lack of coal caused suffering when sharp winds drove the temperatures down to near zero through much of January, 1918. The Fuel Administration permitted lights to glow only on Saturday nights to save coal.

Newarkers learned to live with wheatless Mondays and Wednesdays, meatless Tuesdays, porkless Thursdays and Saturdays and "Over the Top bread," made partly of bran and wheatgrain rather than white flour. Gasless Sundays for motorists started in September, 1918.

*Save, work together, and win: Those became
more than slogans. One of the most enjoyed
volunteer duties was entertaining service men.
They could get lodging and breakfast for 35
cents at St. Paul's Methodist Church or could
relax at a High Street canteen.*

Amid the fervor and the sacrifice there were
instances of misguided patriotism. Librarian
John Cotton Dana was visited in December,
1917, by a group of self-styled "vigilantes interested in vigorous Americanism" who ordered
him to remove eight books from his shelves because they were "war propaganda."

Dana refused, saying: "I came to the conclu-
sion many years ago that liberty of thought is a
very desirable thing for the world and that
liberty of thought can only be maintained by
those who have free access to opinion."

This obstinate stand irked the New York
Journal into an editorial declaring that Dana
was entitled to the Iron Cross. The librarian
ignored the taunt.

City commissioners got into the "patriotic"
act. On June 27, 1918, they changed Berlin
Street to Rome Street, Hamburg Place to Wil-

Together you will win!

NATIONAL SERVICE SECTION
UNITED STATES SHIPPING BOARD · · · EMERGENCY FLEET CORPORATION

son Avenue and Bismarck Avenue to Pershing Avenue. Dresden Street became London; Bremen Street, Marne; German Street, Belgium; Frankfort Street, Paris, and Frederick Street, Somme. Strangely, Berlin Street was changed to Rome only as far as St. Charles Street, leaving one part of the thoroughfare with a German accent.

It was a time when "patriotism" ran to such ends as changing the name of sauerkraut to Liberty Cabbage. Germans necessarily sought to blend into the scene. The Deutsche Club changed its name to the Abraham Lincoln Association and the Germania Fire Insurance Company took the more acceptable title of National Liberty Insurance Company.

Newarkers from the front pages of newspapers on October 21. After first being rejected as too young and too short, he had finally enlisted at the recruiting station in Park Place on March 29, 1917, four days before his eighteenth birthday.

More casualties would come soon. The First Regiment regulars and the Fort Dix draftees moved across the Atlantic after long training periods. Ironically, the draftees moved first, embarking from Hoboken on May 20, 1918, as part of the 78th (Lightning) Division. The regulars

Dancing time at National Service League's headquarters on Broad Street in 1918.

The city was shocked by the report of the first local man killed in action. He was Joseph Desmond McKinney of 136 Pennington Street, second class seaman aboard the Transport *Antilla,* sunk October, 1917, by a German torpedo in mid-Atlantic.

Young McKinney's picture stared out at

did not leave until June 15, when they boarded transports at Newport News, Virginia, with the 29th (Blue and Gray) Division.

Newarkers in the Lightning Division were thrown against the Germans at St. Mihiel in France on September 16 and moved steadily forward. The regulars in the Blue and Gray Divi-

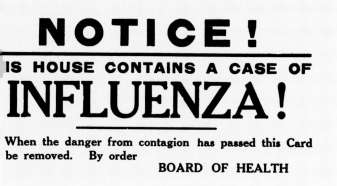

sion met the enemy at Verdun on October 8.

The lists of dead and injured grew, but they were tempered by news of Allied victories in every sector. The end of the war was in sight by mid-September of 1918. The Army closed its recruiting office in the city in September and a false report on Saturday night, October 5, of Germany's surrender inspired an impromptu parade.

The celebration masked a spectre more dreadful than German guns. It had been stalking Newark since mid-September, when the first case of influenza was reported. The dreaded sickness was seeping insidiously around the world, killing as it went. Newark's turn had come.

Sixteen cases and one death on September 27 marked the start of the epidemic in the city. On October 4, the one-day case total rose over the 700 mark; health officials knew that real trouble had come. New cases topped 1,200 on October 8 and a peak was reached on October 14 with a total of 1,626 new victims that day.

Schools and theaters were closed. Barbers were ordered to cover their faces and clerks in City Hall wore masks when they collected taxes. There was a bit of grim humor in that, at least. When Newark saloons were closed, inveterate drinkers crossed the river to Harrison, where bars remained open.

The epidemic overwhelmed the city's medical facilities. With so many doctors in service (almost 175), those left worked constantly to stem the attack, often falling victims to the disease themselves or collapsing from overwork. Since hospitals could not handle all the stricken, Mayor Gillen converted a vacant building at the corner of Broad Street and Central Avenue into an emergency hospital and recruited a force of volunteer nurses. Thousands were cared for in the temporary hospital.

Often the dead remained unburied for days

(and even weeks) because of the lack of men to inter them. City employees were sometimes used for grave digging and a hundred firemen volunteered for the task on one occasion. Teams of horses were used in several cemeteries to plough trenches, in which influenza victims were buried in long rows. When 140 unburied bodies crowded Holy Sepulcher Cemetery at once, the city hired laborers—at high wages—to perform the corporal work of mercy.

Newark's insurance companies were hit hard. The Prudential reported its agents to be "harrassed and sleepless" as they struggled to handle 85,000 influenza death applications totaling more than $20 million. Claimants stood in long lines outside the Newark offices while agents, wearing masks, interviewed them. Claims received through the mail were fumigated before being opened. Prudential went on a seven-day week, with days lasting twelve to fifteen hours, to meet the emergency.

Frederick Frelinghuysen, president of Mutual Benefit, admitted the influenza epidemic had "tested the stability" of his company. During the last three months of 1918 the company paid nearly $3 million for 874 death claims.

The trend was downward after mid-October, although 973 cases were reported on October 22, followed by 850 the next day. When the epidemic was declared over on November 12, a total of 26,235 residents had been felled. Of those, 1,133 died. Another 614 died in October and November from pneumonia attributed to influenza.

In contrast, 120 Newarkers were killed in action with another 135 dead from wounds or other causes. The total Newark war casualties, killed, wounded and missing were 1,152 in nineteen months—*only nineteen more than the number who died of influenza in Newark between September 27 and November 12—a mere forty-seven days!*

Gradually the epidemic faded. October turned into November and every day held the promise that World War I soon would end.

On November 7, 1918, newspapers carried an erroneous United Press report that the war was over. The news raced through the city. Workers left desks and benches. Pupils and teachers raced from classrooms. Wives and mothers darted from homes. All converged on the Four Corners to unleash pent-up joy by dancing in the streets.

Later, papers carrying a denial of the report were seized by the revelers and torn to shreds. All afternoon and late into the night the crowds celebrated. The saloons profitably kept the binge going. The next day street cleaners swept up the shredded newspapers while Newarkers went back to waiting for official word of peace.

It took the Germans four more days to admit defeat. When the armistice was announced in Newark at 2:45 A.M. on Monday, November 11, the scenes of November 7 were repeated and then some. By 5 A.M., before the sun had risen, the throng at the Four Corners was immense. Sirens blew, church bells rang, people screamed for joy. By 8 o'clock, nothing on wheels moved. Strangers kissed and embraced in the streets and vented their joy with as much noise, laughter and tears as they could muster. The victory party continued until dawn of the next day.

While they waited for the boys to come home (some 20,876 Newarkers saw active service before war's end), those at home kept working. They still filled war orders and ships kept sliding down the ways at Port Newark.

Another winter without coal was the prospect in late 1918. Those with a sweet tooth faced the bitterness of more sugarless months. Mayor Gillen announced the issuance of coal and sugar tickets on November 26, making Newark the first city in the nation with an organized distribution. Sugar could be had by showing tickets at precinct police stations. Coal was sold by the bushel. On the first day of rationing, more than 500 people showed up at coal depots with baby carriages, boxes, wheel barrows and wagons to get their share at thirty-five cents a bushel. Mayor Gillen himself appeared at the depots to load bushel baskets. The situation was serious; at one time the thermometer hit thirteen degrees below zero.

Spirits were lightened by thoughts of the soldiers homeward bound. Every troop ship bearing Newark soldiers was met in the New York harbor by city officials and the Police Band. The former First Regiment, "Newark's Own," (renamed the 113th Regiment in the 29th Division), set the city wild when it marched into Newark on May 20. More than 500,000 jammed Broad Street to cheer the steel-helmeted veterans.

The others came home in turn—the 312th Infantry, the draftees turned into hardened soldiers; units of other regiments and, day after day, those detached from scattered units came one by one. They returned quietly, many of them spending time at the Soldiers and Sailors retreat on High Street, then fading back into the homes and jobs that they had left.

Newark's form of government had changed while the soldiers were away. The old system of a mayor and councilmen representing the various wards, in vogue since the city was chartered in 1836, had grown unresponsive and cumbersome (there were thirty-two councilmen by 1917). Voters approved a change to a five-man City Commission by a vote of 19,069 to 6,053 on October 9, 1917.

Five weeks later, eighty-one candidates vied for the five commission seats. Charles P. Gillen, an Irish-born independent, whose leanings were Democratic, topped all candidates. Other winners were Archibald Alexander, William J. Brennan, Thomas L. Raymond and John F. Monahan. Gillen was named mayor at the Commission's first session.

Housing was the city's most serious problem. Gillen ordered city workers to erect National Guard tents on a lot in Hawthorne Avenue at Fabyan Place in April, 1919, as a temporary housing measure. Only a few homeless people took advantage of these.

The next spring, Gillen shifted his tent project to Vailsburg Park. The canvas homes were placed on wooden floors and linked to water, sewers and electricity. At its most crowded, "Tentville" (or "Camp Gillen") housed fifty-eight persons in fifty tents. One baby born in the settlement, to Mr. and Mrs. Samuel McCully, was named Charles P. Gillen McCully.

Many of the families stayed on through the fall, requiring extra blankets from City Hospital for the cold nights under canvas. December's chill cut the tenants cruelly, and finally, on Christmas Eve, 1920, the last of the families was moved from Tentville into permanent quarters found for them by the city.

So, the war was over. Newark had to find what it could in the peace, prosperity and problems that swept the nation.

Newark Evening News.

LAST EDITION

subscription rates: 50 cents a month, 12 cents for postage, including war tax; $6.00 a year, $1.50 for postage, including war tax—Entered as second-class matter, September 11th, 1883, at the Post Office at Newark, New Jersey, under the Act of March 3d, 1879.

ght by The Evening News Publishing Co. of Newark, N. J., 1918.

NEWARK, N. J., MONDAY, NOVEMBER 11, 1918.—24 PAGES.

215-217 Market St., Newark, N. J., Daily, Except Sundays.

TWO CENTS.

d War Is Brought to End by Armistice
n Terms that Amount to Abject Surrender
Newark Explodes in Tumult of Celebration

**Whistles Sound Victory
Everyone Declares Holiday
bilates Accordingly.**

des Continuous Parade of Triumph

ty Departments Close---Industrial Plants,

**Pacific Mail, United Fruit
Ships Reported Taken Over**

WASHINGTON, Nov. 11.—The United States Shipping Board, it is said, has commandeered all ships belonging to the Pacific Mail Steamship Company and the United Fruit Line. These boats, which are now in transpacific and South American service, respectively, will be placed in transatlantic service immediately.

Officials declared that the expected withdrawal of British and other tonnage now forces this government to take extreme measures in obtaining tonnage to supply her army. The reported commandeering of the ships is said to have taken place on request of

**Wilson Goes to Congress
and Announces Terms
of Armistice.**

Must Retire Across Rhine

**German Armies Have Fourteen
Days to Get Out of France
and Belgium.**

**Another Attempt on Life of
Prince Henry Is Reported**

COPENHAGEN, Sunday (By the Associated Press).—Another attempt on the life of Prince Henry of Prussia has been made at Flensburg, where he was in seclusion in a villa. The result of the attempt is not known, but it is believed that he escaped.

Prince Henry, brother of the one-time Kaiser, was attacked by marines while fleeing from Kiel in an automobile flying a red flag on Wednesday last. A dozen shots were fired at him, and his chauffeur was wounded.

**President Announces Conditions
Laid Down by Victorious Allies at
Joint Congress Session.**

Fleet and Army Rendered Impotent

"Newark Explodes" said the headline on Armistice Day, and week after week the city turned out in Broad Street to welcome back its men.

Chapter 25

UP FROM BROAD STREET

IN THE SPRING OF 1917, the Carteret Book Club, a group of distinguished Newarkers, invited author Walter Pritchard Eaton to the city. He was asked to write about a town which librarian John Cotton Dana declared had been transformed since 1900 from a "huge, uncouth and unthinking industrial Frankenstein monster" into a place of refinement.

Eaton's text, illustrated by Rudolph Ruzicka's etchings, appeared in a handsome, limited edition volume late in 1917. Eaton noted the bulky gas storage tanks near the Passaic, the city "smooched with smoke" and a waterfront "picturesque in its chaos." He chided the city

for the brownstone grave markers crumbling in the Old First Cemetery and the rows of decrepit tenements on the hills west of High Street.

He told of the big orange-yellow trolley cars, the trees shading the three Broad Street parks, the stretch of unspoiled riverbank near Mt. Pleasant Cemetery and the mysterious meadows, unconquered despite the new ship channel. He detected a new spirit of feminine independence in the "short-skirted laughing girls, deliciously self-reliant and alive to the life about them . . . They will have more to say about the future than their Puritan mothers did."

Eaton fell victim to Broad Street's charm, although he termed the new tall buildings "a rather pathetic imitation of New York." The writer asked, in what now seems a farewell to yesterday:

"If it is a crime for a stable-keeper to let loose a string of flies to walk across your butter and introduce germs into your system, is it not also a crime for a real estate operator to erect a fifteen-story building on this street, where it will break the peaceful perspective, cut off a part of the sunlight, put you out of the mind of serenity into the mood of hurry, poison your soul?"

Already the Broad Street that Eaton found so charming was clogged with traffic. City leaders pointed with somewhat perverse pride to studies that showed the Four Corners to be one of the busiest—perhaps *the* busiest—intersection in the country. A Public Service check in 1915 had counted 280,000 pedestrians crossing the intersection during one thirteen-hour period.

Newark's prosperity depended on its ties with the outside, both the nearby suburban towns and world markets that could be reached by rail, ships and the much-debated airplanes beginning to appear.

Rudolph Ruzicka's 1916 engraving of Broad Street, Trinity Church and Military Park.

World War I had fastened the jitney, or motorbus, to the Newark scene. By 1923, buses hauled an average of 200,000 passengers through the city daily. Twenty-two trolley lines at the same time averaged 330,000 passengers a day. Many thousands more used the trains and the Hudson & Manhattan tubes.

More troublesome was the automobile traffic, swollen far beyond the control of police officers standing in the middle of the streets with STOP and GO signs. The city erected a stone and bronze traffic tower in the center of Broad and Market Streets in July, 1925, dedicating it by raising the American flag while the police band played the Star Spangled Banner.

Christmas business was good in 1925, when crowds thronged Broad and Market Streets.

Located on the spot where the town pump stood in colonial days, the tower looked down on a teeming scene. A twelve-hour traffic check by the State Motor Vehicle Department at the Four Corners on October 2, 1926, counted 2,644 trolleys, 4,098 buses, 2,657 taxicabs, 3,474 commercial vehicles, 23,581 automobiles and 124 horse-drawn wagons. A New York survey firm promptly labeled the intersection "the busiest traffic center in the world."

Trolley aisles, jitneys and horses were part of the Four Corners scene in 1920.

Traffic was so brisk at Central Avenue and High
Street in 1922 that two officers, one on a motor-
cycle, were needed. Below, smiling policeman was
a fixture at the Four Corners, controlling automobiles with a "GO GO" sign. But when the
intersection was labeled "the busiest in the world,"
humans gave way to the picturesque tower that
endured from 1925 until 1939.

Newarkers felt themselves in tune with the 20th century on June 1, 1921, when a little 100-watt transmitter was licensed to send radio programs from the city under the call letters of Station WJZ.

One month and one day later, Major J. Andrew White was at the microphone in Boyle's Thirty Acres in Jersey City, announcing the Dempsey-Carpentier heavyweight championship fight live over WJZ and a temporary station called WJY. This championship bout, viewed by 90,000 people, established WJZ as a major station, ranked only behind Pittsburgh's pioneering KDKA.

WJZ brought the World Series between the Yankees and Giants into Newark area homes the following October. Gus Falzer and Sanford Hunt of the *Sunday Call* telephoned the play-by-play from New York to an announcer in a studio located in a former women's rest room at the Westinghouse plant at Plane and Orange Street, WJZ's home office. He re-created the game for his unseen audience.

Election returns were announced by WJZ on Tuesday, November 8, and the following Saturday the *Sunday Call* sponsored a broadcast of the Princeton-Yale football game from Palmer Stadium in Princeton. Regulations demanded that all broadcasts be suspended for two minutes every hour to listen for distress signals from the sea, regardless of the nature of the program or the location of the ball on the field.

Before it moved to New York in 1923, WJZ offered such stars as Vincent Lopez and the "Happiness Boys," Billy Jones and Ernie Hare. It also featured Bill McNeary and his *Man in the Moon* stories for children. Miss Josephine Lawrence of the *Call* wrote the tales, remembering to put special stars over the homes of deserving boys and girls. WJZ also hired such unknowns as Milton Cross, Graham McNamee and Ted Husing, all of whom became celebrities. In 1922, Gus Falzer broadcast the Princeton-Chicago game from Chicago's Soldier's Field. Newarkers heard his voice over three speakers installed in Military Park.

Radio was not new to Newark. A. Frederick Collins had been pioneering with wireless broadcasts in the city as early as 1909. In June of that year, Collins linked Governor J. Franklin Fort and Newark Mayor Jacob Haussling in a wireless telephone conversation. He transmitted from the L. S. Plaut store and by 1912 had been heard in Philadelphia. He was a decade too early. By World War I his business had failed.

Young John B. Gambling, whose mixture of exercises, news, weather and chatting helped millions to awaken.

Newark's chief venture in early big time radio, however, was WOR, the 1,000-watt station that went on the air from Bamberger's in February, 1922. The first studio was in a corner of the department store's sixth floor radio and sporting goods section.

Bamberger advertised that WOR programs reached as far as Staten Island, Asbury Park and other shore towns. The station gained national attention in January, 1924, when a WOR announcer helped to guide the dirigible *Shenandoah*, adrift and lost in a storm, back to its base in Lakehurst.

Station WOR had its "name" performers too, but one of its best known emerged purely by accident. He was John B. Gambling, a young British recruit who started as an engineer in 1925. He substituted as an announcer for an early morning gym class, scored a hit and stayed on until his retirement—long after his program had given up gymnastics.

Radio became an important new business. By the end of 1922, Newark was one of the nation's major makers of radio equipment. Splitdorf and Jewett led local manufacturers, who combined to make more than 1,500 receivers daily. General Electric and Westinghouse that year stepped up production of radio tubes to 175,000 a month in their Newark plants. Other firms fabricated variable condensers, cabinets, tuning coils and crystal sets.

A companion 20th century innovation was the airplane. Late in 1919, local business leaders sought $25,000 in public subscription to build an airport. They raised only $7,000, enough to clear a field and build a cinder-covered runway on the edge of the Forest Hill Golf Club. The crude strip was given the dignified name of Heller Field, for the north Newark family whose tool factory and real estate development had done much for the area.

Pilot Walter H. Stevens fought his way through a snowstorm from Washington, D.C., on December 6, 1919, to land 700 pounds of mail at Heller Field in a flight that took one hour and fifty-nine minutes. Thereafter, a fearless band of pilots, wearing the helmets and goggles that were standard for the day, flew in and out of the Heller Field obstacle course.

They dodged trees, buildings, railroad tracks and telegraph wires until the government withdrew the mail service in May, 1920.

Heller Field's failure underscored the need for a metropolitan airport. A few Newark enthusiasts who insisted that the meadowlands offered the best possible site stepped up their campaign when work advanced on the Holland Tunnel in the mid-1920s. That tunnel, they argued, would make an airport on Newark's meadowland only minutes from New York City.

Mayor Thomas L. Raymond and his four fellow City Commissioners at first felt that the meadows had too much industrial potential to waste on such a chimerical scheme. Then, in

...er since open cockpit biplanes had flown in and ...t of Heller Field (bottom, opposite page) in a ...carious operation of 1919 and 1920, leading ...warkers dreamed of having their own airport. A ...rt of New York Authority report in July 1927, ...ced Newark next to last of a list of desirable air ...s, but Mayor Thomas L. Raymond, right, en-...usiastically pressed on. The mayor died two days ...ore dedication in October, 1928. Others lived ...see the single hangar on the edge of a muddy ...adowland field become one of the nation's ...atest airports. By 1929, when George A. Brad-...w drew his impression of the facility (top of ...ge), Newark had become the eastern airmail ter-...nal and some four thousand passenger flights ...re booked for the year. The Ford Tri-Motor in ...foreground of Bradshaw's drawing was the ...est in speed and comfort for commercial travel, ...t daring young speed enthusiasts such as Howard ...ghes and Captain Eddie Rickenbacker were ...ng Newark for coast-to-coast racing exploits.

May, 1927, Charles A. Lindbergh flew alone in his *Spirit of St. Louis* from New York to Paris and the airplane came of age.

Newspaper accounts differ on how Mayor Raymond changed his mind. One reported that the mayor was overwhelmed by the thought of an airport when shaving one morning, a month after the Lindbergh feat. He rushed downtown and excitedly announced, "We will build an airport!" Another account attributed these more restrained words to Raymond:

"This young man has demonstrated it is possible to leave one field and reach another thousands of miles away without mishap. We might as well make up our minds to build an airport."

The newly created Port of New York Authority did not share Newark's enthusiasm. It surveyed ten potential airport sites in the New York area and placed Newark ninth on the list. Four days later, on July 18, 1927, the Assistant Secretary of Commerce for Aeronautics sent word from Washington that he felt Newark should go ahead. Early in 1928, a study commission appointed by President Herbert Hoover reported that Newark was best able to handle air traffic from the south and west.

Newark already was in motion. The City Commission voted $5.5 million for the airport, declaring discreetly that if the airport failed, the site would be excellent for industrial use. Work began in January, 1928. Fortunately the city was deepening its ship channel through Newark Bay and engineers ingeniously piped the dredged material three miles to the airport site. Eventually they spread a small mountain of one and a half million cubic yards of wet fill, twelve feet high, on the tract.

The first truckload of dry earth was dumped atop the wet fill on April 1. Rain fell on thirty-three of the days between April 1 and July 15. Each rainy day set the job back a day or two, but eighty trucks fought through the muck to dump the million cubic yards of dry fill needed to bring the land up to grade.

By mid-summer, the outlines of a 1,600-foot runway were clearly visible, and within a few weeks an asphalt-treated cinder strip was in place—the first hard-surfaced commercial landing site in the United States. Raymond's "vision of 1927" had become a reality; sixty-eight acres of land were developed, with another 180 held in reserve.

Ironically, the man who worked most feverishly to finish the airport for dedication on October 10 inadvertently delayed the formal opening. Mayor Raymond died on October 7. His funeral in Trinity Church on October 10 set the dedication back two days.

A vigorous city-sponsored publicity program insured the airport's success. The federal government designated Newark Airport as the eastern airmail terminal. Commercial flights began in 1929; that year more than 4,000 planes took off on passenger runs. Acclaimed in 1931 as the busiest airport in the world, Newark had 120 scheduled flights daily from 5 A.M. until 10 P.M. More than two million pounds of airmail also cleared the airport that year.

The facility was used by such airlines as Canadian Colonial, Martz and Transcontinental & Western. Transcontinental & Western advertised the first all-air passenger service to the West Coast in 1930, assuring customers that they could make the journey in only thirty-six hours.

Four years later, Captain Eddie Rickenbacker flew a passenger transport from Los Angeles to Newark in thirteen hours, three minutes. Howard Hughes set aviation circles buzzing in 1936 by flying from California to Newark in seven hours, twenty-nine seconds.

The aviation records meant less to most Newarkers than two exciting transportation developments closer at hand. Within the city, the old Morris Canal was being transformed into a subway and automobile boulevard. On the outskirts, Pulaski Skyway was being built to bring New York within easy driving distance.

The passing of the Morris Canal saddened a few who loved the waterway coursing under Broad Street and westward past Branch Brook Park. But the canal had been outmoded for at least thirty years. Few boats used it and the water was weed-infested and garbage-strewn. Proposals for developing the canal as a recreational facility were brushed aside.

The waterway was abandoned in 1924, and three years later the city bought the canal bed within the city limits for $425,000, agreeing to construct the subway if Public Service would

Work underway in 1928 on widening and deepening the bed of the former Morris Canal for new subway to be covered over by Raymond Boulevard.

maintain and operate it. Men and machines tackled the abandoned ditch, digging it deep enough to permit a subway covered by a wide city street. Fill from the project was hauled to Newark Airport during the spring and summer of 1928. From Lock Street north along Branch Brook Park, the deepened canal bed and the tracks placed in it were not covered over.

The street over the old canal bed came first, being opened in late 1932 as Raymond Boulevard in honor of the late mayor. The underground trolley cars began service between Broad Street and Heller Parkway on May 26, 1935. This relieved automobile congestion by diverting surface traffic away from Broad and Market Streets and by enticing motorists from as far away as Caldwell and West Orange to leave their cars at home while they rode the trolley-subway safely and swiftly into the city.

The Pulaski Skyway across the meadows offered similar traffic relief after the opening of the Holland Tunnel in 1927 poured thousands of more automobiles on to the outmoded roads running across the meadows and along Newark's periphery. Drawbridges across the Passaic and Hackensack Rivers on the Lincoln Highway made ground-level travel across the marshland a nightmare of delay.

Engineers built the Pulaski Skyway far above the marshes and rivers. Its completion on November 24, 1932, was hailed as "the outstanding highway engineering achievement in history." The Skyway gave U.S. Route 1 a tie-in with other new highways on the edge of the city, permitting a thirteen-mile ride from Elizabeth to Jersey City without traffic lights. It also offered economic stimulus, particularly to Port Newark and Newark Airport.

Crowd gathered at end of the Pulaski Skyway ramp in November, 1932, to hear the new high level road hailed as "the outstanding highway engineering achievement in history." It cost $6 million a mile.

Pulaski Skyway (named for Casimir Pulaski, Polish hero of the American Revolution) deserved the attention that it got. The three-and-a-half-mile elevated highway rose 200 feet above both the Passaic and Hackensack Rivers, making drawbridges only a memory. Called the longest high level viaduct in the world, the Skyway was also the most expensive highway facility built to that time. It cost $21 million, largely because the twin cantilevered spans over the rivers required 88,461 tons of structural steel—20,000 more tons than the George Washington Bridge.

Motorists who blanched at the cost—nearly $6 million a mile—easily appreciated one benefit. A highway engineer estimated on opening day that the Skyway would save sixty-six million "vehicle minutes" a year. He figured a vehicle minute worth two cents and sixty-six million of them worth $1.3 million. Offsetting that saving were fourteen traffic fatalities in the first year.

Within the city, Newark was altering its skyline to meet 20th century demands.

An augury of change had been the completion in late 1922 of a new $4.5 million city market in the full block at Mulberry and Com-

merce Street. Each floor covered two acres, with the second floor affording parking spaces for 400 automobiles. The new location was not popular initially, since it meant a change in established habits. Many mourned destruction of the quaint old market place over the Morris Canal at the southeastern edge of Military Park. The big new building, with its sparkling white walls and red-tiled floors, quickly overcame objections.

Culture shared in the building boom. The Ancient Arabic Order of the Nobles of the Mystic Shrine, a Masonic order, spent $2.2 million on a huge auditorium and theater on the southern end of Broad Street. Often called the Salaam Temple, the Mosque Theater or just "The Mosque," the auditorium attracted such stage luminaries as Katherine Cornell in its heyday. The building occupied the site of the old home of Dr. William Burnet, Revolutionary War surgeon and adviser to Washington.

Louis Bamberger, head of the growing Market Street department store complex that bore his name, in 1926 gave the city a new $750,000 limestone building to house the Newark Museum. Building of the brass-doored building required the razing of the old frame mansion of former Governor Marcus Ward, the Civil War "Soldier's Friend."

The Museum and its Washington Street neighbor, The Public Library, were enduring tributes to John Cotton Dana, whose enthusiasm and work had built them into cultural facilities acclaimed throughout the country. Dana died in July, 1929, justly cited as "the first citizen of Newark."

The building boom (and the cost of real estate) resulted in the kind of skyscrapers that Walter Pritchard Eaton had feared back in 1917.

The tall look started in earnest in 1923 when the nine-story Newark Athletic Club (later Military Park Hotel) was finished in Park Place. The Newark Lodge of Elks built a massive red brick and limestone home (now the Essex House) across from Lincoln Park in 1924. A year later, the Firemen's Insurance Company completed a ten-story home in Park Place, embellishing it with Corinthian pillars, balustrades and pilasters.

In 1926, the Military Park Building rose twenty-one stories above Park Place, the tallest building in New Jersey at the time. Simultaneously, Kresge Department Store replaced L.S. Plaut's old "Bee Hive" with a ten-story brown brick structure. Next to the Court House, Essex County finished a Hall of Records in 1927 to house its expanding store of governmental activities. Two years later, Newark had to build another monument to growing municipal activity, a Board of Education building near City Hall.

The New Jersey Bell Telephone Company building soared twenty stories in 1928. Topping its buff brick and sandstone home office opposite Washington Park was a soft orange light that glowed each night. Two years later, The American Insurance Company entered the lofty competition by completing what architects hailed as a "masterpiece." This sixteen-story building, next to Newark Library, sought to capture a

Two aging steelworkers pose on framework of N. J. Bell Telephone Company building during construction. Note Newark Library and Sacred Heart Cathedral.

"colonial spirit" in limestone and pale rose brick, topped with Ionic columns and a roof-top cupola.

The high rise race ceased with Newark's tallest buildings completed just as the Depression deepened. The thirty-four story Lefcourt-Newark giant (now the Raymond-Commerce Building) was finished in 1930. It was one story shorter than the National Newark Building, finished in 1931. Almost ignored in this era of roof topping was the twenty-story Federal Trust Building, completed in 1930 on Commerce Street, across from the Lefcourt tower.

Dozens of other new but lesser buildings were raised in a time of apparently endless prosperity. The Mutual Benefit Life Insurance Company deserted downtown Newark for a site on Broad-way, in north Newark, where it built an imposing new home office in 1926. The New Jersey Historical Society followed in 1931, leaving a good downtown address in the belief that the city was growing northward.

The 1920s sped on. Hundreds of thousands of commuters arrived daily from the suburbs to work in the banks, insurance companies and department stores. Bamberger's, the Prudential, Public Service and New Jersey Bell Telephone Company became the favored job centers for young people—and "The Pru" became noted as well as a place where boy met girl and eliminated her from the business world by marrying her. (For many years, the Pru would not employ married women.)

The city had 1,668 factories in 1925, with an

Newark in the 1920s was constantly a state of steel skeletons being filled to form more skyscrapers. On left, Bell Telephone's headquarters at Broad, dwarfs Washington's statue Washington Park. The National Newark and Essex Building, top, opposite page, completed in 1931, won honors city's tallest. Also on top of page is framework of the Military Park Building in 1926, rising above both Public Service and Robert Treat Hotel. bottom of page is the "completed" Newark from the Pennsylvania Railroad bridge. The 34-story Lefcourt-Newark Building and the near neighbor, National Newark, look like twins, but latter is one story taller. The deepening Depression ended the race for the sky

annual payroll of $90 million and Newark continued to boast that no other town manufactured a greater variety of products. More than fifty firms in 1925 had annual productions exceeding $1 million.

Most of the factories were small, employing fewer than thirty. But there were giants among them: Clark Thread Company, Westinghouse, Weston, Balbach's, Baker & Company, J. Wiss, Ward Baking Company, Tiffany, Pittsburgh Plate Glass (making paint in Newark), Benjamin Moore, Murphy Varnish, Mennen, General Electric, Fischer Baking Company, Conmar, and Johnson & Murphy, shoemakers.

Leather, the leading industry since the 1790s, still held top place, followed closely by fine gold jewelry, another commodity with a long tradition in Newark. Weston and Westinghouse kept Newark near the top among cities manufacturing electrical and radio products. One major firm that had sprouted in the radio age was Kolster Radio Corporation; it occupied five buildings in Newark in 1928, employing 3,000. The venerable old Celluloid Corporation was still in town, but merged and expanded through a 1927 merger into the Celanese Corporation. L. E. Waterman, one of the nation's largest makers of fountain pens, came in 1921 to be a leading employer.

Completely out of the industrial picture now was brewing, a victim of prohibition. Newark's beer and ale makers had seldom fallen lower than third place among all manufacturing in the city; in 1915 its 1,800 employees turned out more than $15 million worth of malt liquors. By the time of World War I there were more than 1,400 saloons and scores of restaurants that relied heavily on alcoholic beverages.

Seeing the swift approach of prohibition unless reforms came, brewers worked unsuccessfully to improve saloons. The Anti-Saloon League had its way; the 18th Amendment to the Constitution became law on January 16, 1920. It forbade the manufacture, sale or import of liquor. Officially at least, America was dry.

Brewers tried to stay in business legitimately. Some made an imitation, or "near" beer. Ballantine's made cereal syrup and sold as much as thirty million pounds annually, with a good share of it assuredly going to make home brew.

Scores of speakeasies flourished in Newark, giving "membership" cards such as the above, from an extensive collection at The N. J. Historical Society. Large pictures on these two pages indicate that agents smashing beer barrels and whisky bottles in the Meadows tried vainly to stem the illicit flow.

Krueger's kept its vats shining and bright against a wet day it felt must return. Feigenspan's kept its big "P.O.N." sign shining brightly across the meadows every night, despite the darkness of the brewery below.

Production and consumption of alcoholic beverages went underground. Newark became a center of racketeering and a target area for the

Life Magazine *cartoon in early stages of Prohibition suggested that even the Devil predicted national disobedience.*

effort to enforce the most unpopular law the country has ever endured. Whiskey-laden boats sailed into Newark Bay, and even into Port Newark, to supply hundreds of speakeasies. At the same time, agents at the federal enforcement agency at Broad and West Kinney Streets vainly tried to stem the flow.

Prohibition was not a shining era in Newark or anywhere else in the nation. It was an open secret that gangsters and politicians worked hand in hand, and policemen usually were unable to find speakeasies that anyone who wished could enter merely by securing a "membership card." Racketeers fought one another for control and brought Newark unwanted notoriety on October 23, 1935, when the notorious New York gangster, Dutch Schultz, and three of his henchmen were fatally shot in the Palace Bar.

Newark had legal pleasures, too. In 1922, the city had sixty-three theaters, including two downtown houses that presented major musical shows and such stars as Leslie Howard and George Arliss. Eddie Cantor broke all box office records when he appeared in "Whoopee," and "George White's Scandals" also filled the Shubert Theater. Downtown Newark had five other theaters dedicated to vaudeville, two burlesque stages and eight movie palaces.

Forty-six movie houses were scattered through Newark's well-defined neighborhoods of Vailsburg, Weequahic, Forest Hill, Clinton Hill, Roseville and The Ironbound. People in those sections looked close to home for pleasures. Except for Weequahic, whose rise started in the 1920s with the building of tall apartment houses, all had been flourishing since the 1880s and before. Weequahic rapidly attracted a middle class Jewish population after the apartments were finished.

Newark's reputation as a melting pot persisted despite immigration bans aimed at Southern and Eastern Europeans. By the middle 1920s, two out of three residents were foreign born or children of immigrants, topped by Italians, Russians, Germans, Poles and Irish, in that order. Newark's associated Italian societies proudly dedicated a statue to Christopher Columbus in Washington Park in 1927. In addition, a trickle of Spanish-speaking newcomers had begun, with refugees from Portugal and

Spain settling in the Ironbound during the 1920s. A colony of several hundred Chinese in colorful, mysterious "Chinatown" off Mulberry Street enlivened Newark with such festivities as Chinese New Year's Eve.

It was an exciting time. Newark boosters pointed to the increasing numbers of skyscrapers, the subway, the airport, the mushrooming insurance business and the largest financial center in New Jersey. They boasted that completion of the Passaic Valley trunk sewer in 1924 would end pollution of the Passaic River by carrying sewage from cities between Paterson and Newark out under New York Bay. A year after that, rowers optimistically plied their oars on the river.

Possibly the greatest physical achievement of the 1920s was completion of Wanaque Reservoir in the hills of upper Passaic County. It had none of the immediate impact of towering buildings or an airport wrested from the meadowland muck, but it called for imagination, energy, money and the lives of six men killed during the construction. It assured Newark and seven neighboring communities in the joint venture of a good water supply for at least thirty years.

The first spade was turned on the project in 1920. Ten years later, Wanaque Reservoir backed up slightly more than ninety-four square miles of water. The 100-foot-high main dam cost $1.5 million and was named for Mayor Raymond. When the pipeline that carried water from the Passaic uplands to Newark was opened in February, 1930, the reservoir had cost $26.5 million. About half of it was underwritten by Newark taxpayers.

Population had not increased remarkably, rising only from 414,524 in 1920 to 442,337 in 1930, but educational demands forced the building of three new high schools in the late 1920s and early 1930s. West Side High School, opened in 1926, needed a fifteen-room addition three years later for the expanding population of the Vailsburg-Roseville sections. Arts High, started as a two-year school in 1928, became a four-year institution in 1932. Weequahic's rapid growth prompted the building of a new high school there in 1933. Overall, high school enrollment in the city jumped from 9,000 in 1928 to 15,000 in 1933.

Imagination, money and energy went into the huge Wanaque Reservoir project between 1920 and 1930. Eventually the dam stood 100 feet high, and by completion date, the reservoir cost taxpayers $26.5 million. These pictures were taken during construction.

Simultaneously, there was a demand for higher education. The technical school founded in 1884 had become Newark College of Engineering in 1919, struggling along in its aging High Street buildings. Newark Normal School on Broadway trained teachers on a two-year program (increased to three years in 1928 and to a full four-year, degree-granting course in 1934).

The New Jersey College of Pharmacy, founded in 1892, enjoyed new life when Rutgers University absorbed the Lincoln Avenue school in

1927 and changed its name to Rutgers College of Pharmacy. Meanwhile, five privately owned colleges catering to such special interests as business and law made slow progress toward university status as the 1920s turned into the 1930s. Two of the five, New Jersey Law School and Newark Institute of Arts and Sciences, dated to before World War I.

New Jersey Law School received its first students in 1908 when Richard D. Currier, a New York attorney, started classes in the Prudential Building. The state's first successful law school, New Jersey Law by 1927 had 2,335 students and its graduates filled distinguished legal positions in local and state government.

Liberal arts education came to Newark in 1909 through a New York University program that offered instruction in the Newark Institute of Arts and Sciences. The loosely knit institution, really a series of extension courses, met in the main library and in several public school classrooms.

Mercer Beasley School of Law opened in 1926 to compete for legal undergraduates. A year later, New Jersey Law School started a prelegal department that became Dana College in 1930—named, of course, for the late city librarian. Newark's fifth college level venture, Seth Boyden School of Business, another Currier brainchild, was started in 1929.

A merger began in 1933 when Dana College absorbed both New Jersey Law School and Seth Boyden School of Business and established classes in a former Ballantine Brewery in Rector Street. A year later, Mercer Beasley School of Law and Newark Institute of Arts and Sciences joined forces in a building at Academy Street, taking the name of The University of Newark.

Finally, in October, 1935, Dana College and the University of Newark exchanged vows. Dana College contributed as dowry the converted brewery, where all classes were consolidated. The University of Newark bestowed its name on the marriage. The new university achieved high academic distinction, even as its annual deficits ranged from $20,000 to $40,000.

College problems failed to wring the hearts of most Newarkers. They had troubles of their own. The Depression held America in its grip.

It had begun with a minor business decline in 1927, prompting the layoff of several hundred people in Newark factories. By the late summer of 1929, about 1,200 city families were on relief rolls.

The stock market crash in October, 1929, shocked America. Great fortunes were wiped out overnight, but the agony of depression struck most immediately those who had always labored, day to day, week to week, without ever putting money in the bank, much less in stocks.

More than 7,500 families—about 37,500 persons—were on direct relief in the middle of 1930. The needy stood in long lines hoping to see the Overseer of the Poor in his basement office in City Hall. When the Newark *News* revealed indifference and incompetence in the Overseer's office, he was removed, although he had been appointed "for life." He left behind a desk piled high with unprocessed applications.

In December, 1930, the city decided to create jobs by continuing excavation of the Morris Canal ditch by hand rather than machine, despite an additional cost of $112,500. Five thousand men signed up within three weeks. A month later, 2,245 labored in the ditch at four dollars a day. Careful allocation of jobs gave employment to about 5,000 different persons before the work ended early in March.

Stop-gap jobs did little more than slow the plunge into economic distress. A 1933 report showed that more than 600 factories had closed since 1925 and that payrolls had dropped from a 1925 high of $90 million to a 1933 low of $40 million. Men sold apples in the streets, shoveled snow, ran errands or openly begged. A city-run emergency lodging house for transients attracted 400 men the first night it was opened in an old school on November 27, 1932.

Print by Rowland C. Ellis of the old Ballantine brewery, home of Newark University.

With the skyline of Newark as a backdrop, men worked in a Depression "Shanty Town" in the Meadows. Shacks held their tools or offered shade after labor in the gardens.

A free soup kitchen opened in 1932 served as many as 1,400 men at one meal. Wages plummeted, until by 1933 per capita income in the city was only $429 (compared to $839 in 1929).

Nothing stemmed the slide. State aid started in 1931, followed by federal aid in 1933, but the ranks of those on relief went up and up—to 79,032 in March, 1933; to the high of 94,045 in March, 1935. Thirty-eight thousand Newarkers registered for relief work in July, 1932, hoping for skilled work at twenty-seven dollars a week or unskilled at twenty dollars. By January, 1933, the city had 45,986 registered as unemployed.

The statistics were misleading. Thousands refrained from going on relief until they had used up all savings and exhausted all means of borrowing from relatives or friends. Others considered themselves employed if they eked out enough from odd jobs to keep going.

Hundreds of hardy Newarkers fought the Depression in relief gardens amid the garbage dumps in the meadows. The "squatter farm" project was started in 1932 when the Newark Garden Club sponsored a puppet show in the Shubert Theater to raise funds for seed, tools and fertilizer. Four years later, some 2,000 plots flourished in the meadowland. Nearby, shanties built of packing cases housed tools and offered shade from the noonday sun. Nicknamed "Shanty Town" (or "Hooverville"), the village gardens produced enough vegetables in 1936 for a city official to estimate a saving of $200,000 a year in food relief costs. The average plot that year cost one dollar and sixty-nine cents and yielded about sixty dollars in produce.

Depending on the point of view, the federal Works Progress Administration (WPA) was the saviour, or enslaver, of the unemployed. The WPA financed such projects as the extension of Branch Brook Park into Belleville, a swimming pool in Boylan Street, the planning and building of a new multi-million dollar administration building at Newark Airport and the completion of mile after mile of streets, sewers and sidewalks. Scoffers called the WPA work "boondoggling"; supporters pointed to a creditable list of accomplishments, as well as thousands of able-bodied men relieved of the necessity to beg food and rent.

Prince Street in the Depression days was a place for bargains, ranging from long underwear to vegetables. The scene compares with street markets of earlier days. (See pages 208 and 209, Chapter 20.)

The Depression humbled every level. Engineers were among the first to be laid off. Brilliant and competent men and women gladly took WPA jobs as clerical workers or check booth attendants in the Public Library. Many scholars taught at $14 a week in the WPA emergency junior colleges (Newark had two of the six started in the fall of 1934). Experienced journalists worked on WPA pay to produce in the Newark Library the *Federal Writers Guide to New Jersey,* an enduring reference book.

No group was as hard hit by the Depression as the slowly-rising black population, grown from 16,977 in 1920 to 38,880 in 1930. The rise continued, until in 1940 the figure stood at 45,760, about ten per cent of the total population of 429,760. They had always been hurt by the "last hired, first fired" policy of employers.

At the worst point in the Depression, blacks represented one third of all relief cases although they represented only one-twelfth of the population. Church and private relief agencies offered little help, even to lodging. At one time in 1931, the executive secretary of the Urban League reported that he had 112 black men in his office who claimed they had not eaten for one to twelve days.

The Urban League worked actively to aid black people with only the Social Service Bureau among all other private Newark agencies showing genuine concern for this stratum of Newarkers. When the city opened its lodging house in 1932, it accepted blacks only on a segregated basis. The Depression served to spark many studies of black persons in New Jersey, with emphasis on Newark.

Despite the unhappy days, Newark had a certain vibrancy. The legitimate theaters and vaudeville houses had been hurt by the Depression, but the movie houses survived by offering lowered prices and double features. The major department stores were filled with quality goods at prime prices. A good, full-course meal for one dollar was not unusual.

Things picked up. Just as Prohibition had plunged a segment of Newark into economic gloom, so Repeal in 1933 brought joy. Breweries were allowed to start selling 3.2 beer (3.2 per cent of alcohol) on April 7, 1933, but only Krueger's was prepared to brew. As midnight struck on April 6, crowds jammed the streets in front of Krueger's brewery on High Street.

One minute later, on April 7, Krueger's floodlights suddenly flashed on the freshly painted statue of Gambrinus, the mythical inventor of beer who stood over the Krueger door. The throng cheered, then swept into the brewery office to take away as much beer as their stomachs would carry. It took two days to restore the street corner to normal.

Ballantine's barely survived Prohibition. Control of the old industry passed in June, 1933, to a new company headed by Carl and Otto Badenhausen. Lights flashed on again at Hensler's and the other smaller breweries. Feigenspan's "P.O.N." again had meaning—and continued to shine until Ballantine's absorbed the firm in 1943.

Elsewhere construction on the subway, the airport and Port Newark kept men busy on a combination of private and governmental financing. All transportation construction paled beside the impressive station that the city, Public Service and the Pennsylvania Railroad opened in March, 1935, at a cost of $20 million. Dedication ceremonies on March 2 hailed the builders. The next day, trains rolled on regular timetables.

The limestone and glass walls of Pennsylvania Station gave the dingy east side of town a landmark of beauty. Inside, escalators and stairways carried passengers to the upper level to board trains of the Pennsylvania and Lehigh Valley Railroads or the Hudson & Manhattan Railroad (the "tubes"). On the lower level, beneath the main waiting room, buses and trolleys stopped. City transportation came together in a project that eventually cost $45 million and kept thousands of workers off relief before completion in 1937.

Newark again was busy and gay. It recognized the worth of its library, its museum, its emerging University of Newark. It talked about the renewed hum of industry and the increasing crowds of workers streaming in and out of

Sports were always vital in Newark before 1940. Here a crowd nearly blocks Market Street as it stands outside The Newark News, *waiting patiently for news of the 1926 New York-St. Louis World Series.*

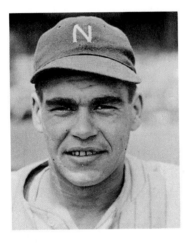

Newark's pride of the 1930s centered on the Wilson Avenue park where championship teams dominated the International League. Many were the heroes, but none was greater than slugger Charlie Keller.

Bam's, the Pru, Public Service and Bell Telephone, the top employers. But whenever two or more men met after the spring of 1932, conversation inevitably turned to the Newark Bears, the pride of Newark.

The city had been in and out of professional baseball leagues since 1883, with indifferent success, and the building of a new ball park in Wilson Avenue in 1926 did nothing to raise the status of the Newark Bears of the International League. Jacob Ruppert, New York brewer and owner of the New York Yankees, supplied both the spark and the cash when he bought the team and the stadium in November, 1931.

Newark won the International League pennant in 1932 by twenty-five games and romped to the 1937 championship by an even greater margin. Players like Red Rolfe, Joe Gordon, Dixie Walker, Spud Chandler and Bob Seeds sent sports writers reaching for superlatives. All but Seeds starred later in the major leagues; he had to be satisfied with the unique feat of hitting seven consecutive home runs in two 1937 games.

But for all its appearance of serenity, Newark was in trouble. Mayor Fiorella LaGuardia of New York declared war on Newark Airport, and the completion of LaGuardia Field in 1940 prompted the airlines to shift their planes across the Hudson. Also, Port Newark languished despite money spent for channel deepening and dock improvements. There was serious talk of abandoning both the airport and the seaport.

On the hill west of the court house, the ugly slums in the Third Ward grew more ramshackle during the Depression as landlords and tenants alike gave them even less care than usual. Traffic downtown worsened amid the slow disappearance of the trolley cars. Rubber-tired trolley buses, capable of running on either gasoline or the trolley wires, appeared in 1935. By the end of 1938 the trolley car was doomed.

As laborers dug up the trolley tracks at the Four Corners, a Newark *News* writer declared poetically:

". . . To many old timers, Broad Street without trolley cars will seem like 'Hamlet' without the Dane."

The old Newark was disappearing. A new Newark must rise to replace it, in spirit as well as in material things. That day was near, yet far away. Newarkers had to look eastward once more, to Germany—and, far to the west, to Japan.

Trolley cars were doomed, and their passing made the streets seem wide again. Looking east from the Court House in the fall of 1941, Market Street was given over entirely to buses and automobiles.

*War came much closer to America in October, 1940, when all men betw[een]
the ages of 21 and 36 registered for the draft (below). Then volunteer d[raft]
boards called them in November. The first group, above, was given [the]
oath in December, 1940, a year before the Pearl Harbor attack.*

Chapter 26

NO TIME TO SLEEP

NEWARKERS WHO READ the *Sunday Call* (or any newspaper) on the morning of December 7, 1941, had reason to feel secure. Japanese diplomats had been regularly visiting Secretary of State Cordell Hull; there seemed no reason for concern from that quarter. The war in German-dominated Europe, while not better, certainly was not worse. The *Call's* advertisements of Monday bargains augured the most prosperous Christmas in years.

Far to the west in Hawaii, the dawn of December 7 was breaking over Pearl Harbor as late morning church services ended in New Jersey. Four young Newarkers, Archie Callahan Jr., Nicholas Runiak and Raymond J. Kerrigan of the U.S. Navy, and Louis Schleifer of the Air Corps, enjoyed the peaceful sleep that their military superiors felt was justified.

Suddenly, a terse short wave radio message at 1:50 P.M., Newark time, told official Washington: AIR RAID, PEARL HARBOR—THIS IS NO DRILL. Minutes later, a frantic an-

286

nouncer interrupted the radio description of
the Giants-Dodgers professional football game
from the Polo Grounds to shout a brief, confused story of a Japanese sneak attack on Pearl
Harbor.

Nipponese dive bombers still raked the installations at Hickam Field and other Hawaiian
bases as the New York football game went on.
In the harbor, Japanese bombs destroyed the
bulk of the United States fleet. Great battleships
burst into flames and sank within minutes. The
Oklahoma, struck by five torpedoes, rolled over
in the shallow water and lay with her keel
pointed skyward. The *Arizona*, the *Vestal* and
other ships were ablaze.

*The slow move toward service began with physical
examinations in the Sussex Avenue Armory.
When the above picture was taken in 1942,
enthusiasm for service was high, and it continued
even at Fort Dix, left, where Newarkers were given
their G.I. uniforms. Below, servicemen could act
like civilians, surrounding a pretty clerk at Newark
Ration Board to get coupons for gasoline.*

287

NEWARK NEWS

Archie Callahan Jr., mess attendant, second class, a nineteen-year-old black Newarker, lay dead in the *Oklahoma's* hull. Raymond Kerrigan, machinist's mate and son of a Newark policeman, perished on the *Vestal*. Nicholas Runiak, 21, seaman, died on the *Arizona*. Pfc. Louis Schleifer, twenty-one years old, stood on the runway at Hickam Field firing his .45-caliber service gun at the enemy until he was killed. Within minutes after the attack, four Newarkers had been sacrificed. (All were honored later, Callahan and Schleifer in neighborhood parks named for them, Kerrigan and Runiak in streets bearing their names).

War had come with apparent suddenness. But, in retrospect, it had long been in the making. The treachery of the Japanese attack and the unprepared state of the Pearl Harbor defenses were the only truly surprising elements.

If there was any cause for surprise, it was that Japan, not Germany, was the first foe. European refugees had been arriving in Newark for several years, fleeing Germany's successive conquests and Hitler's anti-Semitic pogrom. A *Sunday Call* feature in September 1940, told of newly arrived German Jews gathering in the city for the Jewish New Year. Refugee children and their parents, victims of police terror at home, expressed amazement that in Newark the police smiled at them.

Other nationality groups in the city manifested mounting anger at Germany's ruthless advances. Four thousand Poles hailed General Wladyslaw Sikorski, Premier of the Polish Government in Exile, when he visited Newark in April 1941. Lithuanians, Hungarians, Belgians, Hollanders, Greeks, Czechs and others felt growing anguish for relatives in their overrun homelands. The plight of Great Britain and France after the evacuation at Dunkirk in June 1940, was shockingly apparent.

City residents of Italian or German descent generally walked softly. Some Germans fervently supported the German-American Bund and an occasional Italian praised Mussolini, but there was little of the overt feeling that Germans had shown for the Fatherland before World War I. For one thing, the second generation younger people in foreign homes recognized that they were Americans. For another, Hitler's savage

treatment of Jews made even his few supporters reluctant to praise him in public.

Military preparedness had begun long before the Pearl Harbor debacle. Newark men between the ages of twenty-one and thirty-six had lined up on October 16, 1940, to register for the first peace-time draft in America history. A month later, men were selected by Newark's twenty draft boards and early in December of 1940 the first of what would become a continuous flow of trainees left Pennsylvania Station on the way to Fort Dix.

Newark's famed Essex Troop, the 102nd Cavalry Regiment, gathered at armories in Newark, West Orange and Westfield on January 14, 1941, to be sworn into federal service. Ten days later, they entrained for Fort Jackson, South Carolina. Their commanding officer, Colonel Donald W. McGowan, warned them that they were "preparing for war."

Draftees and regulars drilled in a spirit of Never-Never-Land, often using broomsticks for guns and Jeeps for tanks. Essex Troop officers played polo and posed for rotogravure pictures in their high leather riding boots and impeccable uniforms. Enlisted men usually were shown peeling potatoes, as if that was what military service was all about. In the summer of 1941, the possibility of war was not taken seriously by most Americans.

Economically, all trace of the Depression disappeared as the German and Italian armies advanced unchecked through Europe and Africa. Newark factories put up "Men Needed" or "Women Wanted" signs again as they rushed to fill orders for both the Allies abroad and American trainees at home.

The Albert Del Visco Company announced a contract to make 10,000 overcoats and 15,000 jackets for the Army in December, 1940. Whitehead & Hoag made military badges, and Park Crest Neckwear sewed black ties for the Navy. By the spring of 1941, many Newark factories were filling government orders for bedstead card holders, shelter tent poles, waterproof bedding rolls, uniforms, dental supplies, aircraft instruments and plastic cups. The Breeze Corporation announced a $2 million contract for aircraft instruments in May, 1941, raising Newark contracts to major status.

With draftees training at Fort Dix, the Essex Troop preparing in South Carolina and industry busy with military supplies, the city slowly took on a wartime aura. Japan's march through the Far East created shortages of rubber and tin, prompting cities and villages alike to save old tires and tin cans.

Newarkers signed up for Civilian Defense, searching the skies by day and night for possible enemy planes. Radio reports of London's nightly stands against Nazi bombers began to be somewhat understood. More than six months before Pearl Harbor, the city had a sample of what war might bring. The Office of Civil Defense chose Newark for the nation's first city blackout test on Sunday and Monday nights, May 25 and 26. The OCD said the city's harbor, railroads, airport, industry and large residential neighborhoods presented almost every problem to be met in defending a city from aerial bombers.

More than 1,800 male air raid wardens, aided by 1,700 female volunteers, prepared the city for the test. Residents were asked to extinguish all home lights, automobile headlights and store lights when the alarm sounded. Only the Pennsylvania Station, Highways 25 and 29 and the eastern part of Raymond Boulevard were to be illuminated.

Several members of the Senate Military Affairs Committee came to Newark to watch the test. Along with Army personnel, national OCD officials and city leaders, they met on the thirty-fourth floor of the National Newark & Essex Building. Sirens and factory whistles sounded an alert 11:45 P.M. on Sunday. A half hour later, the air-raid alarm wailed across the city.

Newark responded quickly. No automobile headlight could be seen the length of Broad Street. Penn Station's glow and the fringe of lights on the city's eastern edge accentuated the eerie blackness that cloaked the rest of the town. The blackout was a distinct success—and an uneasy reminder that an enemy was in the offing.

Still, it was only make-believe. It took Pearl Harbor to turn the game into war, first against Japan, and then immediately against Germany and Italy as well.

Draft boards stepped up their pace. Unpaid workers studied the records before sending the familiar "Greetings" to chosen draftees, and doctors and dentists examined the selectees without compensation. By war's end, Newark's draft boards had sent 55,852 selectees to service. At least 25,000 other Newarkers enlisted, a total of about 80,000 city men and women in uniform between 1941 and 1945.

Except for the much-altered and expanded Essex Troop (102nd Cavalry Group) Newark had no regiment of its "own," such as the 29th and 78th Divisions of World War I. War cor-

Looking east from the National Newark & Essex Building at midnight on May 25, Newark was bright. Twenty minutes later, only the permitted lights at Penn Station and on border highways could be seen.

This painting of the four hero chaplains, owned by the National Conference of Christians and Jews, was basis for U.S. stamp issued in 1948.

respondent Warren Kennet of the *Newark News* followed the 102nd and did as much as anyone to make New Jersey aware of its troops.

Preparing to embark for Europe, the 102nd Cavalry reached full strength in the summer of 1942 through the addition of draftees and other replacements. It arrived in England in October, 1942—the first American cavalry unit to reach Europe. One squadron (the 117th) was then sent to North Africa as a security force for General Eisenhower and the remainder prepared in England for the inevitable invasion across the English Channel.

Men of the Essex Troop (in the 117th Cavalry) were among those who spearheaded the invasion of Southern France in 1944, and the Troopers who stayed in England (as the 102nd Cavalry) splashed ashore at Omaha Beach in the D-Day attack in June, 1944. General McGowan, who in January, 1941, had warned his men to expect war, commanded the 102nd in the Normandy attack.

Forty per cent of the original Essex Troop won commissions in service. The cavalrymen, riding tanks instead of horses, rolled into France, Belgium, Luxemburg, Germany and Czechoslovakia. More than 300 men of the 102nd and 117th were killed and hundreds more injured before fighting ended.

The casualty lists grew. Day after day, month after month, newspapers carried pictures of men killed and wounded in such little-known places as Salerno, Bastogne, Anzio, Guadalcanal, Iwo Jima, Okinawa and the Coral Sea. Some were the young of Newark's ethnic groups— Germans and Italians as well as Poles, Greeks, Czechs, Russians, Lithuanians and other Europeans. They were Christians and Jews, black and white, sons of old Newark families and sons of first generation Americans.

Newark's major hero, along with the four killed at Pearl Harbor, was the Rev. John P. Washington, one of four Army chaplains aboard the ill-fated troopship *Dorchester* in the North Atlantic. Father Washington grew up in the city's Roseville section and was ordained at St. Patrick's Cathedral in 1935. He served in an Arlington parish before volunteering for service soon after Pearl Harbor.

A German submarine exploded a torpedo in the *Dorchester's* hull on February 3, 1943. As the ship sank, Father Washington and three other chaplains (the Rev. George L. Fox of Vermont, a Methodist; Rev. Clark V. Poling of Schenectady, a Baptist, and Rabbi Alexander Goode of Washington) removed their lifebelts and gave them to soldiers. Locking arms, they prayed together, Protestant, Jew and Catholic, as the *Dorchester* sank.

(Father Washington and the others later were awarded the Distinguished Service Cross. In 1948, a United States postage stamp honored "The Immortal Chaplains.")

World War II tested the mettle of those who stayed at home. These were the mothers and fathers who worked without pay for the rationing boards and draft panels; patrolled the dark streets at night in case of an air raid and generally behaved well in the face of extreme shortages of nearly everything. There were, of course, chiselers and hoarders, and a few out-

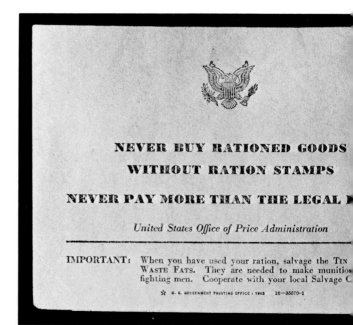

ioning soon became a problem in every home as automobile tires,
...oline, sugar, meat and many other things became scarce. Above, staff
...OPA headquarters sifts applications for fuel coupons. Below, War Ration
...k Four warns against violating regulations.

689995 DD

UNITED STATES OF AMERICA
OFFICE OF PRICE ADMINISTRATION

WAR RATION BOOK FOUR

Helen Dean Dennis
(Print first, middle, and last names)

address *544 Mt. Prospect Ave.*

READ BEFORE SIGNING

...pting this book, I recognize that it remains the property of the United
...Government. I will use it only in the manner and for the purposes
...ed by the Office of Price Administration.

Altered ....
(Signature)

It is a criminal offense to violate rationing regulations.

...n R-145   16—35570-1

right criminals trafficking in counterfeit ration
stamps. But most people had sons in service and
preferred to aid the war effort by complying
with the rules.

Automobile tires were rationed in January,
1942, followed by limitations on gasoline, fuel
oil, sugar, meat and butter. People at first lined
up at the Office of Price Administration (OPA)
for rationing stamps. In June, 1943, the Newark
District of the OPA mailed out four and a half
million ration books, aided by 13,000 volunteer
high school teachers and students who addressed
envelopes, inserted fifty-four tons of ration books
in envelopes and affixed names and addresses.

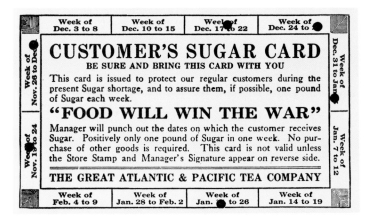

Gasoline rations and a sugar card were reminders of shortages, but nothing told the story better than the sight of a butcher shop window without meat.

Volunteers were everywhere. Two hundred were needed daily to man the OPA; five thousand worked in air raid duties; five hundred people each day checked on scarce apartments or rooms offered for rent and scores of women and teen-agers baby sat with children whose mothers were employed in war work. There were many of the latter. Before war's end, women worked everywhere—in factories, shipyards, railroad yards and elsewhere.

Volunteer agencies gathered food, clothing and money for war victims. Newarkers responded to drives to aid the Finns, British, Poles and others. One of the major operations was the Russian War Relief headquarters at 744 Broad Street, engaged after early 1942 in sending such items as 3,000 field-type kerosene stoves to front-line Russian hospitals and refugee colonies. An appeal in 1944 for fur to be sewn into American sailors' vests collected more than 2,000 fur coats in less than a month.

The pleasantest volunteer service was at the servicemen's centers in the city. Girls from Bamberger's, the Pru, Bell Telephone, Public Service and other businesses talked to and danced with lonely servicemen.

Stage and radio stars entertained at the opening of the Stage Door Canteen in Linden Street on May 20, 1943. Before it closed in August, 1945, the Canteen had been host to 250,000 military visitors. More than 485,000 servicemen used the USO Service Lounge in Penn Station in 1944. That same year, the USO Club in Commerce Street received 240,000. The YMCA entertained 700,000 servicemen between December 7, 1941, and October 30, 1944, while the YM-YWHA sent entertainers out on a regular schedule to fourteen military bases. The Servicemen's Social Center on Green Street and the Irish War Veterans Service Center in Franklin Street were open throughout the war.

Most of the visitors were transients. Newark had a contingent of trainees at Newark College of Engineering, a large detachment at Newark Air Base, a Navy Receiving Barracks at Fulton Street, and after 1944, a military hospital in Weequahic Park. In addition, the United Radio and TV Institute and Casey Jones School of Aeronautics taught military personnel.

Newark industries earnestly fed the war machine. Many factories stepped up to round-the-clock shifts to fill war orders. Westinghouse and Weston supplied delicate instruments of various types; Conmar furnished zippers; C.R. Davis had nearly 500 employees turning out tents, tarpaulins and other canvas goods; Essex Specialty made fuses; National Union Radio, radio parts; J. Wiss & Sons, surgical instruments.

The city's most unusual industrial stories involved the Federal Telephone and Radio Corporation and Federal Shipbuilding and Dry-dock Company. Both sprang from obscurity and achieved major status before peace was declared.

Little Federal Telephone & Radio had been

in Newark since 1931, manufacturing parts and supplies for the International Telephone & Telegraph Corporation. When war closed ITT's European factories in 1939, Federal expanded.

Federal's war work began in 1941 with a few employees in one plant. Within three years, the concern had branched into forty-four different locations scattered throughout Newark—in old factory buildings, former automobile showrooms and warehouses. A network of 30,000 miles of telephone wire was installed to link the various offices and work rooms.

At its peak in 1944, when Federal was the nation's foremost maker of military field telephone equipment, the Newark company employed 11,500 men and women—most of them recruited and trained to work on sophisticated electronics products. In 1943, the company began to erect a spacious new building on the Clifton-Nutley border.

Government contracts for shipbuilding originally had bypassed Newark, since the dilapidated World War I yards of the Submarine Boat Company at Port Newark appeared beyond reclamation. But Federal Shipbuilding and Dry-

Newark's shipbuilding role began in February, 1942, and the Federal facility broke all records for getting into full scale operation.

Boasting that it "never slept," Federal worked night and day to make ships worth $250 million.

dock Company, keeping its Kearny yard operating moderately after World War I, was awarded major contracts as early as 1939. By the summer of 1941 Kearny workers were finishing the light cruiser *Juneau* (which was to explode in the South Pacific in November, 1942, taking the largest toll of lives of any single ship disaster in U.S. Navy history. Many aboard were from Newark and nearby towns).

America had been at war with Japan less than two months when the federal government purchased the Submarine Boat Company yard, estimating that it would cost $12 million to convert it into a modern facility. The first announcement on January 24, 1942, estimated that 10,000 would be employed. Kearny's Federal management was asked to build and operate the Newark yard.

The Navy expressed the hope that ships might slide down the Newark ways within nine months, although admitting that no other major shipbuilding plant had ever been put into full operation so quickly.

Thousands of workers swarmed over the Newark yard, restoring the twenty-eight World War I ways. Fabrication of steel was started in July, the first keel was set in place on August 10, and four more keels were laid on September 5. Two auxiliary vessels were launched on October 10, a full month ahead of the optimistic schedule set in January. Skilled women mechanics and riveters began work in October; eventually Federal hired and trained thousands of women workers.

Peak employment at the Newark yard came in October, 1943, when 19,503 labored on three shifts to make good the boast that the yard "never sleeps." The Newark workers built $250 million worth of warships—seven destroyers, fifty-two destroyer escorts and seventy-eight troop and tank landing ships.

Close by the Federal shipyards, military and civilian personnel at Newark Airport turned in a spectacular record for handling war goods bound for the European Theater.

The government took control of Newark Airport in January, 1942. From then until May, 1945, when shipments began flowing to Japan rather than Europe, The Overseas Air Technical Command's Newark division packaged and

Workers arriving at Federal shipyard on special train give the familiar "V" for victory sign as they head for jobs.

...diers guarding Newark Airport during the war ...phasized the value of the area in sending ...plies overseas. On right, women workers pre-... fighter plane for shipment to European ...ater, and below, landing ships assembled on ...l are trundled to launching way.

shipped slightly less than thirteen million tons of cargo through Port Newark. More than 620,000 different items were handled.

Airplanes, mostly fighters, were flown into Newark Airport for shipment. The OATC reported in 1945 that Newark had shipped 40,026 aircraft, 8,529 gliders and almost 125 million gallons of aviation gasoline—enough to drive the average 1940 automobile around the world at least a hundred thousand times. Also shipped were 26,621 other types of vehicles, small and heavy trailers, huge electrical generators and tanks.

OATC officials praised Newark for its unique juxtaposition of highways, airport, seaport and railroads. Cargo was easily transferred from

The new Prudential building, shown in October, 1942, just before being turned over to the Office of Dependency Benefits.

train or truck to ships at dockside. Military aricraft were flown in, towed to dockside and placed aboard ships within a few hours of arrival. Weyerhauser Steamboat Company was particularly active, at one time having sixty boats that listed Newark as homeport. Several were sunk by German submarines, carrying to their deaths men known in Newark or related to Newarkers.

The federal government gave Newark another unusual assignment in October, 1942. It leased the new twenty-story office building of the Prudential Insurance Company in Washington Street for its Office of Dependency Benefits (ODB), the agency responsible for forwarding allowance and allotment checks to dependents of servicemen. The Prudential had moved only 200 of its own employees into the massive building when the government took over.

ODB hired 10,000 at its peak in 1944, when it handled more than eight million accounts and mailed more than a half billion dollars in checks every month. The volume of its mail equalled that of a city of 100,000, requiring the Newark post office to add special crews.

The government facility hired employees without discrimination. When ODB was at its height, twenty-six per cent of its employees were blacks, working in all departments—as photographers, supervisors, section chiefs, statistical clerks, interviewers and stenographers, as well as messengers and dispatchers. For the first time on a major scale, black people had the chance to prove that they could fill a variety of jobs competently.

As the home front worked and waited, Allied forces ground toward victory in Europe and pushed westward, island by island, toward Japan. The war's end came ever closer.

Victory over Germany came on May 7, followed by the official announcement in a 9 A.M. broadcast by President Harry S. Truman on May 8. Rain fell intermittently during that morning of victory. Small groups gathered near Broad Street to hear President Truman's message on car and store radios. They listened quietly, then burst into wild noise when the President had finished. Confetti showered from office windows and some 25,000 people celebrated in Broad Street before a heavy rain ended the festivities at about noon.

V-E Day was scarcely an unmitigated joy. The war in the Pacific went on. Thousands crowded into all churches during the V-E Day morning, praying for a quick end to all hostilities.

Japan reeled on August 6 when the first atomic bomb shattered Hiroshima. Three days later, a second A-bomb pulverized Nagasaki. By Friday, August 1, Japan admitted defeat but Secretary of State James F. Byrnes informed Emperor Hirohito that the Allies would accept only unconditional surrender.

Japan still held out when Newarkers went to bed on Monday night, August 14. Then, at 1:49 A.M., Newark time, a voice broke into the Japanese government radio programs to say that wires would be cleared for a message of unprecedented importance. Monitoring news men flashed the word: surrender was coming.

Those unable to sleep heard the news flash and began seeping into the darkened streets. By 3 A.M., groups of celebrants were singing and shouting in the streets. The Police Department rushed six busloads of officers to Broad and Market Streets as the crowd built up steadily, closing Broad Street to traffic from Lincoln Park to Central Avenue before 8 A.M.

Japan withheld its announcement, dampening the enthusiasm the next morning. Broad Street was reopened to traffic at 2 P.M., only to be closed again two hours later when official word from Washington said that Japan had surrendered.

Now Newark really went wild. Delirious crowds snake-danced through downtown streets and a roaring, happy throng completely jammed the Four Corners. Big V-Js were scrawled with soap on store windows. Ticker tape filtered through the humid air. Girls kissed every serviceman in sight. Fathers and mothers of service-

men wept with unabashed joy. When the noise and the wildness ran their course, many went to the churches to attend hastily arranged thanksgiving services.

Most residents were in bed long before midnight, leaving behind on the streets tons of confetti and torn newspapers. One man died in a fall and some forty others were injured or overcome by alcohol and had to be treated in city hospitals.

Post-war readjustments were inevitable. The booming shipyard would close. The ODB would prune its payroll sharply and then cease. Second and third shifts in the factories would end. The impressive incomes from both father and mother in war work would be cut back. Newark would have to face its problems—but not on V-J Day. That was a day to cheer.

JAPS ACCEPT TERMS: a newspaper headline proclaimed the news and joyous throngs jammed Broad Street at 4:40 A.M. on August 14—V-J Day.

Chapter 27

DAYS OF DECISION

EVERY AMERICAN CITY faced sweeping changes when World War II ended, but few could see in 1946 how radical the changes would be. Great areas of blight would stab at the public conscience, civil rights leaders would demand redress of century-old wrongs and

industry would join residents in a flight to the suburbs.

Newark was more prepared than most cities. It had a solid history of planning, dating back to 1911 when John Cotton Dana and others recognized that Newark's future could be met

only by detailed self-analysis and a plan of action. In 1944, when few minds elsewhere turned to postwar concerns, Newark had Harland Bartholomew and Associates, aided by a citizens committee, preparing a study of what would face the city when the shooting stopped. Bartholomew had been secretary of the City Plan Commission which had prepared Newark's first plan in 1915.

The planners faced facts in their 1944 report. They saw a city that had been in steady decline, even before the war. By 1939, Newark had lost its employment dominance: in 1909, it had had twenty per cent of all the jobs in New Jersey: by 1939, the figure was only eleven per cent.

From a high of twenty-five per cent of all the state's wages in 1909, Newark had slipped to a mere ten per cent in 1939.

Property values were declining sharply, despite the war boom. Tax records told a melancholy story. The city budget had dropped from $58 million in 1938 to $45 million in 1944, but the tax rate was up from $4.61 to $5.30. The answer was in the exodus of industry—in six years the city had lost $300 million in assessed valuation.

The planning report spared no punches. The City Hospital, it found, was wretchedly inadequate. It had been built for 550 patients and by 1944 often had more than 700. More than $10 million would be needed to repair streets neglected throughout the war. Schools were in run-down condition. Only the rush of war orders kept other industry from fleeing.

More than anything, the planners scored the decaying slums, among the worst in the nation. Thirty-one per cent of all dwelling units in Newark were below "the generally accepted minimum standards of health and decency," the plan said. Thousands of flats were without private toilets, much less bathtubs, and hundreds of them lacked even running water or electricity. Central heating was rare in the slums, and frequent fires caused by defective oil stoves made the poor homeless, stripped of their meager possessions. Not surprisingly, only seventeen per cent of the dwelling units in Newark were occupied by the owners.

Nearly five thousand dwellings were beyond all fitness to live in, the 1944 report said. Nearly all of those were occupied by black families and the sweep of additional black workers into the city to work in war plants worsened the plight of this newest minority group. One half of all black persons lived in "unhealthful and unwholesome quarters," according to the planning report. Anyone who knew the city was aware that owners of slum properties gouged these tenants mercilessly.

Already the suburbs had silently closed their doors to black people. Each day during the war busloads of black workers had rolled westward out of Newark, traveling forty to fifty miles one way to Morris County powder plants. It would have made more sense for them to live

Heart of downtown Newark, three hundred years after its settlement.

299

near their jobs, but suburban communities closed ranks against non-white residents.

Mistreatment of black people was clear by 1946, if politicians and business leaders had cared to acknowledge it. Equally, however, small numbers of earnest volunteers, white and black, for many years had been working together to solve problems of racial tension. This spontaneous desire to seek accord in Newark would serve the city well in years to come.

Blacks were achieving distinction despite the prejudice manifested by most Caucasians. Dedicated social workers were determinedly working to make the cause of blacks known. School teachers were rising, and the children of James Baxter, Newark's first black school principal, were an example. A daughter, Mrs. Grace Baxter Fenderson, served forty-two years as a Newark teacher before retiring in 1948, and his son, Dr. J. LeRoy Baxter, was a member of the New Jersey Assembly from 1927 to 1929.

William M. Ashby, founder of the Urban League in Newark in 1916, continued his relentless struggle to improve the lot of blacks.

William M. Ashby, Urban League founder.

The Rev. William P. Hayes, the Rev. Thomas L. Puryear and Roger M. Yancey, among other Newarkers, worked to improve the life of black families in public housing projects and all were members of the city Housing Commission.

Miss Marie B. Johnson won distinction in 1949 by being one of the first two black women to be admitted to the New Jersey Bar. She thus joined one of New Jersey's most distinguished citizens, Oliver Randolph, who in 1914 became the first black admitted to the Bar. He served as a State Assemblyman in 1922 and 1923 and his distinguished career was capped in 1947 by a tenacious fight to give New Jersey a strong civil rights law.

Oliver Randolph, civil rights leader.

Randolph, son of a Virginia slave who had bought his freedom shortly before the Civil War, was the only black delegate at the Constitutional Convention, called in 1947 to revise the archaic State Constitution. He demanded, and won, a strong anti-discrimination section. It was supported by voters who approved the Constitution in the fall of 1947. That anti-descrimination clause, among other things, ended segregation in state military units—and led directly to the end of discrimination in the national armed forces.

Nothing rankled those seeking equal justice more than the discrimination practiced by the City Hospital staff. City politicians and hospital administrators ignored the self-organized Newark Interracial Council when it began asking in 1936 why the tax-supported hospital had no black doctors on its staff and no black women in its nursing school.

Turning aside rebuffs and discourtesies, the Interracial Council induced the hospital to open its rolls to black physicians in 1946, when Dr. E. Mae McCarroll and Dr. Clarence Jannifer were appointed to the staff. Simultaneously, black women were permitted to enroll in the nursing school.

The 1950 Census showed unmistakable ethnic trends. Newark's total population rose only slightly, from 429,760 in 1940 to 438,776 in 1950. Black residents had increased from 45,760 to 74,965—more than a sixty per cent increase. When newspapers took an occasional glance at misery in the slums, the faces in the pictures invariably were those of blacks.

Economic problems concerned city leaders, both those in City Hall and those at the top of major corporations, more than sociological concerns. The tax rate occupied most thoughts, despite Bartholomew's warning that no problem facing Newark was worse than the increasing housing blight. Yet, for a time, prosperity obscured the decay.

All stores were filled with returned veterans eager for the goods of peace. Industrial employment lasted beyond war's end and Newark ranked tenth among all United States cities in the ratio of the population employed (forty-two per cent). The police and fire departments won widespread praise for their efficiency. Abundant water supplies showed the foresight of many administrations.

Immediately ahead was a spate of building. Anheuser Busch, maker of Budweiser beer, was planning a new $20 million plant southwest of the airport. The Port of New York Authority had started a $2.6 million truck terminal in Wilson Avenue. The new $2.5 million high level Stickle Bridge over the Passaic River was underway. The Housing Authority had applied for a $32 million federal loan to build fifteen postwar low rent projects.

Rutgers University added another reason for optimism late in 1945 by encouraging Newark University to merge into the newly formed State University. The merger was signed in June 1946, and the 2,000 students on the banks of the old Passaic were given the right on July 1 to sing: "On the banks of the Old Raritan, my boys, where Old Rutgers evermore shall stand . . ."

The absorption of Newark University by Rutgers prompted dreams that Newark would become the New Jersey center of higher education and culture. Newark College of Engineering already had 1,600 students (evenly split between day and night classes) and Newark State Teachers College's 500 students recognized that their teaching skills were desperately needed. Adding to the higher educational excitement was Seton Hall's 1946 establishment of an urban division in a seven-story building in Clinton Street.

Demands of returning veterans for housing required immediate attention. The city administration built 400 emergency temporary homes, supervised placement of veterans in converted barracks in Weequahic Park and planned to restrict the newest public housing project, Franklin D. Roosevelt Homes, to veterans. Even with those plans, housing was inadequate.

The situation was particularly grim for the thousands of low income black families clustered on the hill just west of the Essex County Court House. Public housing facilities aided them only slightly. Seven low income projects had been finished just before the war, but by 1946 there were 2,110 white families and only 623 black families in the buildings. Four of the projects housed no black people, despite their desperate need for decent housing at any price.

Post-war mobility hastened the decline of all cities. Jobs were plentiful, money was easy to come by and the GI Bill of Rights gave veterans long term mortgages to encourage home building. New automobiles streamed off the assembly lines and young Newarkers began moving westward, occasionally all the way to California, but more often just over the hill, out of the city to the suburbs of Morris or Monmouth counties.

Before World War II a large proportion of those who worked in Newark still lived in the city. Now they exchanged apartments in town for a heavily mortgaged cottage in the country or near the shore, joining their employers who had fled the city decades before. As the automobile sparked a new wave of moves to the suburbs, rural Southern black families slowly occupied the aging buildings on the hill.

Pre-war difficulties at the airport and seaport had been forgotten in the fever of World War II. When control of both facilities was turned back to the city in 1946, the return of commercial airlines and civilian shippers after peace temporarily kept problems subdued. By October, 1946, when American Airlines transferred twenty-seven flights from LaGuardia Field, Newark's schedule of daily flights rose to 157. Dozens of non-scheduled planes also used the field.

Activity was apparent, but so was trouble. The runways and other parts of the facility needed millions of dollars to be adequate. Residents in the southern end of town complained constantly about the growing noise of planes. Town officials debated the wisdom of retaining the field, some arguing strongly for turning the region to industrial use.

The Port of New York Authority covetously eyed both seaport and airport. In 1946, the Authority offered to spend $50 million on the airport and $26 million on the seaport in return for a long term lease that would give the city $100,000 a year in lieu of taxes. It announced intentions to increase air flights to one thousand daily.

The Authority turned adamant in June 1947, declaring that it could make no more financial concessions. Rumors that the New York-dominated Authority might seek another New Jersey field had been around for months. Finally, on June 9, Mayor Murphy and Commissioners John B. Keenan and Ralph A. Villani agreed in principle to a lease that would give the city an increased share of profits. Transfer of airport and seaport control to the Port of New York Authority came in March 1948.

Port Authority money poured into the region. Taking over a port that had only fourteen

Mayor and Mrs. Ralph A. Villani on their wedding day in 1970. In 1949 Villani became Newark's first Italian-American mayor. His long public career also included service as a municipal judge, three elections to the City Commission, as well as the City Council. Upon retirement in 1973, his wife Marie was appointed as his City Council successor. In 1974, her election as councilwoman-at-large made Mrs. Villani the first woman elected to city-wide office.

useable deep-sea berths and a number of sheds and cargo buildings desperately in need of rehabilitation, the Authority waved its magic checkbook. Revitalization was prompt. The number of workers and the annual payroll (1,537 workers and a $5,379,000 payroll in 1947) moved upward. More shipping companies expressed interest in leases for berths beside the deepened channel.

The rise of Port Newark in less than twenty years of Port Authority management was meteoric. By 1966 about 1,500 vessels were handled annually—a tripling since 1947. About 5,000 workers annually earned more than $25 million—a tripling of jobs and quadrupling of wages. Port Newark by then handled about thirty per cent of all shipping in the New York area. It led the nation in importing foreign automobiles, was the nation's leading importer of frozen meats and was the East Coast's top lumber port. Completion of the parallel Elizabeth channel in 1959 and subsequent work made thirty-seven deep sea berths available. When completed, 8,500 people were employed.

Turning to Newark Airport, the Authority increased the area from 1,400 to 2,300 acres, roughly four times the size of LaGuardia Airport. All three former runways were found

A spokesman for the Civil Aeronautics Administration blandly told the *Star-Ledger* late in June 1951, that people were leaving their windows open in summer and "this makes the noise seem louder." He admitted that poor weather also forced pilots to fly lower—700 feet

National Airlines plane in an Elizabeth street after third major crash.

unsuitable: the Authority abandoned two, rehabilitated the third, and started work in May, 1950, on a $9 million north-south instrument runway with the latest in safety features. Ground was broken in September, 1951, for a handsome $8.5 million terminal.

Statistics told the story. Traffic rose rapidly, topping 100,000 plane departures and landings in 1951, 1,355,000 passengers used Newark Airport and 104 million pounds of freight cargo were lifted off the runways.

Harassed residents in the Weequahic section at the southern end of the runway were not pleased. When about 300 planes used the airport daily during the summer of 1951, noise and vibration moved to ever-higher levels. Weequahic residents called it "aeronautical insomnia," compounded by frightened children, flickering television reception and telephone conversations made unintelligible by the noise of airplanes flying so low that the faces of passengers could be seen from the ground. The City Commission weighed cancelling the Port Authority lease unless the din was curbed.

over Elizabeth and 300 to 400 feet over Weequahic. But, said the CAA official reassuringly, "people living near the airport have nothing to fear from the safety angle."

Closed windows did not shut out the din, any more than CAA words calmed fears. Then, at 3:02 P.M. on Sunday, December 16, a C-46 nonscheduled airliner owned by Miami Airlines started down the runway with fifty-two passengers aboard. Ground observers saw smoke pouring from what they thought was a "burning brake."

The smoking plane lifted off the icy ground and headed south away from Newark's ten degree temperature. At 3:04, the pilot radioed the tower that he was headed back because of a burning engine.

Five minutes later—at 3:09—the plane zoomed low over a heavily populated residential section of Elizabeth, sheared the roof off an abandoned dwelling and ripped through an Elizabethtown Water Company warehouse before landing upside down in a deep, frozen gulley of the Elizabeth River. It burst into flames.

Forty-eight adults, four children and the crew of four had perished in the second worst United States commercial air tragedy to that time. Horror-stricken observers speculated how great the tragedy might have been had the plane crashed a few seconds sooner in residential Elizabeth.

Indignation swelled but planes continued to take off and land. Work continued on the new runway, with assurances to fearful neighbors that this would lessen both noise and the chance of future accidents. Crash investigators sought to soothe airport foes by declaring that this had been a "once-in-a-lifetime" tragedy. It "could never happen again."

As the anger and fear eased, an inbound American Airlines plane roared toward Newark in the mid-afternoon of Tuesday, January 22, 1952, carrying twenty passengers, including former Secretary of War Robert P. Patterson. Fog and rain limited the pilot's visibility to less than three-fourths of a mile. He radioed the Newark tower when he was over Linden, asking guidance from the ground.

It seemed routine enough; there had been many other such landings that afternoon. Even the straying of the plane, first 900 feet to the left of a correct guide pattern and then 900 feet to the right, did not cause alarm. The propeller-driven plane stayed on the radar screen until it was a half-mile south of the Union County Court House in Elizabeth. Suddenly, at 3:45 P.M., it disappeared from the radar.

The plane hedge-hopped over Elizabeth homes, losing ground as it skimmed over Battin High School. As it fell, the craft sheared off the roof and upper structure of a brick building, demolished a two-story garage that had been converted into a home and slammed into a house near the high school. The crash killed all twenty passengers and three crew members. Six other persons died in the flaming buildings.

Now eighty-five were dead. The fact that Battin High School had been just below the plane's path inevitably created nightmares as to how much more deadly the crash might have been.

On the eve of a major two-day investigation slated for February 11, fifty-nine passengers boarded a National Airlines plane bound for Miami. The four-engine plane labored off the Newark runway shortly after midnight. It climbed to 1,500 feet, at which point the pilot radioed that he had lost an engine.

The pilot fought to keep his out-of-control plane away from residential Elizabeth, but at 12:21 A.M., February 11, the stricken craft demolished the top portion of a three-story apartment building occupied by fifty families. Gasoline sprayed the upper part of the building, then burst into flames. Just beyond, the plane crashed into the yard of an orphanage in which nearly a hundred children lay asleep.

Miraculously, the plane broke in two, sparing the lives of the stewardess and thirty-four passengers in the tail section. The other three crew members and twenty-five passengers perished. Four people in the apartment house were killed.

Three disasters had imperiled Elizabeth in fifty-seven days, leaving 117 dead, several houses wrecked, residents terrorized, plus a high school and an orphanage in the paths of falling planes. Closing the airport was inevitable. At 3 A.M., two-and-one-half hours after the third crash, the Port of New York Authority ordered all Newark Airport flights suspended. Airlines shifted planes to New York fields.

There was no intention to close the airport permanently. Work continued on the 7,000-foot instrument runway and on the new terminal. By June a few carefully monitored flights were resumed and in early November the emotional climate was better, particularly with assurances that the new runway would divert traffic from populated areas. Newark Airport reopened fully on November 15, 1952, but its future rested on whether airlines would return. During 1952, traffic plummeted to less that one-sixth of pre-crash levels.

The Port Authority dedicated its new $8.5 million terminal on July 29, 1953. Lieutenant General James H. Doolittle, the nation's foremost aviation ace in World War II, assured the crowd that Newark Airport "is one of the best and safest airports in the world." Conspicuously absent were mayors of adjacent towns.

The airlines returned; Newark Airport was back in business permanently. By 1957, more than 2.5 million passengers went through the

Newark Airport, one of world's busiest, handled 12,000 passengers daily.

terminal. In 1966, about 4.5 million passengers flew in or out of Newark Airport, making it one of the world's busiest terminals.

Port Authority operation of Newark's seaport and airport spurred the local economy considerably, serving partially to mask declining fortunes elsewhere in the city. Many Newarkers sensed that the town was adrift in a sea of governmental corruption, confusion and ineptitude, even as business publicists and city newspapers touted Newark's virtues.

The city unquestionably had great potential. Its transportation system could match that of any city. Industrial diversity continued; Newark ranked high among all cities in the manufacture of beer, leather products, jewelry, foods, electrical goods, instruments and machines. The Prudential and Mutual Benefit insurance companies, plus the state's largest banks, gave the city financial pre-eminence. Newark was far from collapse, but it was seriously ill.

Faced with ever-rising property taxes, several businesses left or threatened to leave for suburban or rural locations. A shudder had swept Newark as early as 1945, for example, when the Prudential warned that it might move out because of New Jersey franchise taxes and Newark's personal tax levies. A compromise by the city, the state and the Prudential averted the showdown, but the uneasiness continued.

Newark's problems centered in the city commission form of government adopted in 1917, under which the mayor was merely a ceremonial figurehead. The commissioners were in essence five separate governments, virtually independent and often willingly or accidentally ignorant of the affairs of other departments. It was difficult to find anyone who could be held responsible for citywide blunders.

The 1949 Commission election shook up the traditional Irish political leadership. Mayor Vincent J. Murphy and Commissioner John A. Brady were defeated. Former Mayor Meyer C. Ellenstein topped all candidates, followed by John B. Keenan, Ralph A. Villani, Leo P. Carlin and Stephen J. Moran. The last two were strong labor leaders, Carlin being president of the Teamsters Union (AFL) and Moran executive secretary of the CIO.

Carlin, who had advocated a changed form of government as early as 1945 when he first ran for the Commission, contended that good government was impossible under a city commission, no matter who was elected. Early in 1953, Ellenstein joined Carlin in advocating reform.

Commenting on such reform, the *Newark News* charged on January 14, 1953, that "no commissioner has any incentive to be economical or industrious." The consequence, the *News* alleged, was a "continually increasing budget, without commensurate service" and a deteriorating, "clique-ridden Board of Education." City leaders had stalled on a new incinerator, failed to build a new City Hospital and had ignored widespread parking problems that threatened to strangle the downtown shopping district.

A reform group calling itself the Newark Citizens Committee on Municipal Government surfaced in the winter of 1953. Banding together representatives of labor, civic groups and business, the Citizens Committee proposed a vote on charter reform for May 12, 1953, when the regular City Commission election would be held. Actually, the ballot question only asked whether a new form *ought* to be studied.

Political scoffers doubted that the committee could get the 28,500 signatures needed to put the question on the ballot. Mrs. Thomas E. Lynn, who resigned as president of the League of Woman Voters to serve on the committee, begged women to solicit signatures. She warned: "It is cold, hard, humiliating work, but that's the price of good government." The signatures were secured on time.

Voters gave smashing approval to the study of a new form of government: *Yes*, 62,687; *No*, 8,168. They also chose five people for a study commission to recommend a new form of government: Alan V. Lowenstein and Raymond Del Tufo, Jr., young lawyers; Mrs. Lynn; John J. Giblin, an AFL official; and James T. Callaghan, a CIO leader.

After twelve weeks, the study commission chose a strong mayor and nine councilmen as the best form of government for Newark. That proposal went before voters in the general election on November 3, 1953. Carlin warmly supported the new form of government; all other incumbent commissioners opposed it. City voters maintained the momentum, approving the proposal, 53,739 to 28,142.

Leo P. Carlin (above), young labor leader and a member of the City Commission, was an early voice in advocating government reform. He campaigned actively, often riding a stagecoach through city streets to advocate change from commission to a strong mayor-council form of government. Under the changed form, voters made Carlin Newark's first elected mayor since 1915.

The new government was chosen on May 11, 1954, with winners to take office on July 1. Open were the posts of mayor, councilmen in five wards (North, East, Central, South and West) and four councilmen-at-large. Carlin upset Franklin and Villani to become Newark's first elected mayor since 1915. Rules of the new government required a candidate to gain more than fifty per cent of the total votes cast. No council hopeful succeeded; a runoff was set for June 15.

That day, voters chose: North Ward, Mario V. Farco; East Ward, Philip E. Gordon; Central Ward, Irvine I. Turner; South Ward, Samuel E. Cooper; West Ward, M. Joseph Gallagher; and councilmen-at-large, Michael A. Bontempo, John A. Brady, James T. Callaghan and Jack I. Waldor.

Turner was the first black ever elected to city leadership. Others of his race had received important appointive posts in the city, but Turner's victory at last placed blacks in the winner's circle, joining members of other once-scorned minorities, the Irish, Italians, Jews and other ethnic groups.

The new administration had a mandate to tackle Newark's mounting problems. Mayor Carlin appointed eighteen heads of Newark's leading industries, businesses, and financial houses to a Greater Newark Development Council, asking them to stir enthusiasm for a "new Newark."

High hopes were chilled in the fall of 1954 by rumors that blew from the northern part of the city, where strong hints were being dropped that the Mutual Benefit Life Insurance Company was about to abandon its Broadway home. The impressive stone palace of the 1920s was outmoded, too expensive to maintain and inadequate for future growth.

Sale of Mutual Benefit's property at 300 Broadway to the Catholic Archdiocese of Newark (for eventual use as Essex Catholic High School) on October 25, 1954, plunged many Newarkers into despair. Mutual Benefit admitted that it had a suburban golf course in mind for a headquarters, but said that Newark was not being ruled out. That appeared to be a way of letting the city down easily. If Mutual Benefit went, an outward rush of firms was easy to imagine.

Newark received one of its finest Christmas presents on December 13, 1954, when Mutual Benefit officials announced that the company would stay, in a towering new home to be built on a four-acre plot opposite Washington Park. The company's announcement prompted self-congratulatory optimism that Newark had come alive as a result of its new form of government.

Newark *was* on the move. Mutual Benefit built not only its $10 million, twenty-story home of white limestone and blue-green glass, but also raised a $1.5 million, six-story office building leased by the Hospital Service Plan of New Jersey (Blue Cross/Blue Shield).

Not to be outdone by Mutual Benefit, the

Mutual Benefit's decision to stay in Newark brought large front page headlines and an editorial cartoon by the News' *nationally-known cartoonist, Bill Crawford. As Crawford saw it, Mutual Benefit stayed because a new broom called "better government" had swept away doubts about Newark's ability to survive. Crawford was one in a series of brilliant* News' *cartoonists, succeeding Lute Pease and preceding Bil (with one "l") Canfield, later a* Star-Ledger *cartoonist.*

The city's resurgence in the 1950s was linked to the Prudential Insurance Company and Mutual Benefit Life Insurance Company. Both had been founded in the city (Mutual in 1845, Prudential in 1873). Mutual's new home stood beside old North Reformed Church; Prudential's was prominent in the downtown skyline.

Prudential Insurance Company laid to rest doubts about its future in Newark. Late in 1955, Prudential released plans for a $20 million, twenty-four story white marble and glass home office, flanked by two seven-story wings. Nearby, it planned a seven-story building for Fidelity Union Trust Company.

Revitalization could be seen everywhere—in the $3 million YM-YWCA opened on Park Place in 1955, the conversion of the aging Center Market on Raymond Boulevard into a modern air-conditioned state government office building, the $6 million Public Service Electric and Gas Company power-distribution center in Plane Street, and the $13 million, seventeen-story Martland Medical Center built beside the old City Hospital. Schools were being built or modernized in a $100 million program. The Port of New York Authority stepped up its spending at Port Newark, topped by a $10 million investment in a modern marine terminal and plans for a second channel to be called Port Elizabeth.

Three years after the new government took office, nearly $250 million in new public and private money had been committed to rebuild downtown Newark. The tremendous building boom of the 1920s was being repeated, with one difference. This time the surge also seemed to carry concern for residential housing.

Thousands of poor families were affected by the quickened pace of public housing. Between 1956 and 1959, two new low-income, high-rise public housing projects were opened, creating 2,762 new apartments. This series of twelve- and thirteen-floor apartment projects was hailed as a wondrous idea in housing the poor. Other buildings were underway to house another 4,500 families, including about 2,500 units for elderly people.

The years sped along. Mayor Carlin won re-election in 1958 but was upset in 1962 by Hugh J. Addonizio, a Newark-born businessman who had been elected to Congress from his Newark home (11th District) in 1948. Addonizio, a Democrat, had been re-elected continuously for seven terms until he resigned in 1962 to win election as mayor.

As the city neared its 300th anniversary in 1966, the impressive pace continued. The *Star-Ledger* occupied a new plant and the *Newark News* pushed work on a five-story addition. First National State, second oldest bank in Newark, started an eighteen-story building at 550 Broad Street. Just up the street, at 570 Broad, a new fourteen-story office building was ready.

Federal and county agencies prepared to consolidate in the city. A new $12.5 million Federal Building was underway to house federal agencies in a sixteen-story tower. Essex County planned a twelve-story structure for county courts, offices and a jail.

Builders began erecting multi-level apartment houses for families with middle incomes. Colonnade Park, just north of the Erie-Lackawanna Railroad station, in 1960 offered 1,230 apartments in a trio of twenty-two story buildings. Weequahic Park Tower rose twenty-one stories and Weequahic Park Plaza went up twenty-four stories, the loftiest residential structure in the city. The two Weequahic buildings housed 450 families.

Four apartment complexes, each fourteen to sixteen stories tall, were opened between 1961 and 1964 to house nearly 650 families in North Newark. Close to City Hall, the twenty-two story Hallmark House, with 440 residential units, coaxed people to live in the heart of the city. Academy Spires, on the former Newark Academy grounds, by 1963 had two twenty-story buildings for 540 families. In total, this middle income housing accommodated nearly 3,500 families.

Housing, public or private, generally meant living tied to elevators. An exception was High Park Gardens, Newark's first middle-income, low-rise garden apartments in the old Third Ward Urban Renewal Area, the city's worst

Columbus Homes, just north of the Lacka-wanna Railroad Station, were typical of high rises built in the 1950s to house the poor. Once hailed as the best in low-cost housing, these badly planned, improperly maintained structures proved to be monumental failures.

RUTGERS UNIVERSITY

Rutgers, the State University, brought enlightenment and hope to Newark in the early 1960s by committing itself to an entirely new complex within walking distance of downtown. It was the first campus in the nation built entirely on urban renewal land.

slum section. Apartments were sold on a cooperative basis to instill pride of ownership.

Confidence that outsiders would want to visit Newark—and stay overnight—was shown in the completion of a fourteen-flight addition to the Robert Treat Hotel, its first expansion in nearly fifty years. Simultaneously, the Holiday Inn opened a 200-unit complex near the Erie-Lackawanna station.

Intense competition for parking spaces was lessened by excavating beneath Military Park to build a three-level underground garage with 1,030 new parking places. Nearby, Prudential funds added 750 more parking spaces and Mutual Benefit built another 660 berths.

Of all the commitments, the most vital might well have been the decisions of Rutgers and Seton Hall Universities and Newark College of Engineering to build new campuses in the city, aided by urban renewal funds to clear blighted areas. Seton Hall chose a new site on Raymond Boulevard, near the Passaic River just off McCarter Highway. Rutgers and Newark Col-

lege of Engineering started work on adjoining campuses on the slope west of Washington Park. State and federal funds were the prime movers for both Rutgers and the engineering college.

When Rutgers came to the city in 1946 to take over Newark University, its main building had been a converted old brewery. Rutgers grew —in a former razor-blade factory, an old YWCA, a brownstone fire house, an erstwhile carriage house and rooms in hotels. By 1965, the 8,600 students at Newark-Rutgers were scattered through twenty-eight makeshift facilities, a "campus" in name only.

Newark College of Engineering at least had a hallowed identity on a two-acre campus on High Street, although its facilities on either side of Central High School were outmoded, at best. Its engineer graduates long had served well in city industries and elsewhere, but as the college sought 20th century eminence, its buildings were reminiscent of 19th century machine shops.

Two high-rise buildings (one five, the other seven, stories tall) began the N.C.E. transformation in the middle 1950s. A decade later, thanks to $7.4 million in state funds, the college built four more new buildings on a campus enlarged from two to twenty acres through an urban renewal plan that razed two hundred substandard dwellings and ramshackle business structures. On dedication day in May 1966, college officials told of two new buildings already underway, four more in the planning stage and an eventual doubling of the campus area to accommodate 12,000 students by 1976.

Rutgers startled the academic world in the early 1960s by announcing that it would create an entirely new campus on a twenty-three-acre urban renewal site. Stretching westward from University Avenue to High Street, the new Rutgers campus was the first in the nation to be built entirely on urban renewal land. The fact that it abutted the Newark College of Engineering campus meant Newark would have a forty-three-acre college/university complex.

The "new" Rutgers had the familiar "tall" look of urban campuses. Everything on the $60 million campus was new, from library to science buildings, to the green grass between the buildings. The exciting new campus had space for 25,000 students.

A thriving seaport, a booming airport, a brisk financial leadership, diversified industry, a bold new concept in urban higher education, housing planned for all economic levels, a modernized government: all of these were

Ample evidence of Newark's colonial heritage remained downtown as the city reached its 300th anniversary in 1966. The tall spire of Trinity Church towered above Military Park, laid out in 1666 for militia training. Broad Street, the widest street in colonial America, was still impressively wide. The city had risen, but it had not strayed from its center at Broad and Market streets.

Hugh J. Addonizio, former congressman, upset Carlin to become mayor in 1962, then won a second term during the tercentennial year of 1966.

actualities as Newark prepared in 1966 to observe its 300th anniversary.

Nevertheless, uneasiness underlay the optimism. Newark was failing to recognize the major challenge facing all northern cities—the influx of rural Southern blacks into heavily populated areas of the North. Compounding the problem was the unmistakeable fact that

Joan C. Hull, head of the education department, and Robert M. Lunny, director, turn back the clock as the New Jersey Historical Society joins the 300th birthday celebration. That year the Society also voted to remain in Newark.

rapidly growing suburban populations were almost completely segregated, sometimes subtly *de facto* but more often blatantly racist.

Blacks surged into Newark and other cities as the 1960s wore on. They had to occupy the worst housing, endure the gouging of slum landlords, take the most menial jobs, face the prospect of being last hired and first fired in an automated society that was eliminating the kind of jobs that always had been economic steppingstones for the downtrodden.

The 1960 Census revealed that the city's 1950 population of 438,776 had dipped to 405,000. White totals were off nearly 100,000, down from 363,487 to 265,000. Concurrently, the non-white population had risen from 74,965 to 138,000 (including about 9,000 Puerto Ricans), about thirty-five per cent of the total. By 1966, the proportion of black residents was at least fifty per cent.

School figures in 1960 showed that the public school enrollment was about two-thirds black. City high schools were sixty per cent non-white. Many elementary schools were all black or nearly so.

The evidences of injustice and evil were blatant enough, if anyone in the city administration had dared to admit this or if the city's drumbeaters—including the newspapers—had taken the trouble to investigate the worsening plight of Newark residents rather than to crow about the building boom.

Owners of abominable housing in the Central Ward extorted exorbitant rents from poor black residents. Black school-children knew that most of their teachers were white. Construction crews building the "new Newark" included extremely few blacks or Hispanics. City Hall employed only a few token blacks and no Hispanics, in a city more than 50 per cent non-white. It was difficult to find a black policeman or fireman. Private businesses, using a variety of excuses, thwarted well-trained people whose color happened to be black.

Newark was a city waiting for an explosion as it reached its 300th anniversary year in 1966. Its leaders ignored the crass discriminations and deepening poverty, preferring to believe that a celebration of 300 years of existence would help insure loyalty to Newark among the poor.

Anniversary plans so occupied Newark that the re-election of Mayor Addonizio went almost unnoticed in 1966. Few among the traditional city leadership considered it significant that a 34-year-old engineer named Kenneth Gibson polled 16,200 votes. Gibson was black, the first ever to seek the office of mayor. He had entered the race only six weeks before the voting.

Newark business and political leaders joined on May 18, 1966, to celebrate the 300th anniversary of the date on which Robert Treat and his Puritan followers first set foot on Newark soil. Up Broad Street moved the traditional parade under banners proclaiming the contributions that many nationalities and many races had made to Newark's history.

After the marching ended and the bands were stilled, an impressive audience filled the beautifully refurbished Symphony Hall (the old Mosque Theater). They welcomed the mayor of Newark-on-Trent, England, and heard speakers extol Newark's past and speculate on its future. That night, the program was repeated in the Robert Treat Hotel. Few discouraging words were heard in this Camelot-for-a-day.

For one day at least, on May 18, 1966, Newark unfurled its flags and marched its bands in tribute to three centuries of life. Yet, as celebrants hailed the slogan, "Pride in Newark," large numbers of Newarkers had never shared in the city's vaunted prosperity.

Most of the information in this chapter is based on the 216-page report submitted to Governor Richard J. Hughes by the Governor's Select Commission ·on Civil Disorder. The committee, appointed two weeks after the disorder, was instructed by Hughes to present a comprehensive, no-holds-barred report. The committee took the Governor at his word. Its analysis, submitted in February 1968, is one of the most comprehensive, nonpartisan documents ever written in New Jersey. Anyone who wishes to comprehend the causes and nature of the Newark riots will do well to read the commission's findings. It is not a pretty story—yet it needed telling in detail. I have relied on that report heavily; much detail in this chapter pertaining to the actual riots is from that well-written, carefully documented study. Other material is from Newark and New York newspapers of the period.

A note from the author

Chapter 28

"THE WHOLE TOWN IS GONE"

Summer's blistering sun faded behind the Orange Mountains on July 12, 1967, closyet another hot, steaming day in the slum-infested Central Ward that stretched westward from the Essex County Court House. Families gathered outside the unbearable confines of the housing projects and the rundown wooden tenement buildings, hoping that the breeze might turn cool. Young men roamed the sidewalks, restless in the summer heat.

The area seethed with resentment and hatred —against the police, against blatant political skullduggery in City Hall and against slumlords and out-of-town storekeepers who gouged the ghetto residents at every turn.

This was 1967, the summer of black discon-tent in every city throughout the nation. The hopes of President Lyndon B. Johnson and the Democratic-controlled Congress to revitalize urban areas and to help poor people had been sidetracked in the massive, costly outpouring of arms and manpower to wage the hopeless war in the jungles of distant Viet Nam.

Black Americans for several years had seen their quest for equality and dignity make major gains under the forceful, dramatic leadership of the Rev. Dr. Martin Luther King, Jr. They had won major voting rights in the South, had desegregated public schools in much of Dixie, had forced southern universities to open their doors to black students and had induced most businesses everywhere at least to ease their

centuries-old practice of discrimination in employment.

Newark's nearly all-white political and business leadership boasted throughout the 1960s that Newark stood alone among major northern cities in an absence of "trouble in the streets." In sharp contrast, Dr. King's assessment of northern cities in the spring of 1967 included an ominous prediction: Newark would be one of ten cities likely to feel the wrath of violence.

Two issues particularly burned throughout Newark's widespread black areas as the summer of 1967 began—an impending prestigious appointment of a secretary to the Board of Education and a proposal to demolish several blocks of Central Ward housing to create a campus for the embryo New Jersey College of Medicine and Dentistry.

The appointment of the Board of Education

secretary was blatant, callous, old-fashioned power politics, cast against a setting of an administration that ignored the fact that nearly seventy per cent of public school students were black. Mayor Addonizio had nominated City Councilman James T. Callaghan, a Democrat whose credentials other than party loyalty were slight. Black leaders proposed City Budget Director Wilbur Parker for the post. He was beyond question a well-qualified professional. Among other things, he was the first black certified public accountant in New Jersey. When Parker's supporters demonstrated vociferously at school board meetings, Addonizio called their actions "out of bounds."

Far more complicated, and potentially far more explosive, was mounting anger over the inept handling of a site for the College of Medicine and Dentistry. When the college decided to leave Jersey City in 1966, trustees politely expressed some interest in the academic atmosphere that was expanding on Newark's western slopes. However, their hearts were really in Madison, twenty miles to the west, where the green acres of the former Dodge family estate seemed cool, bucolic and non-controversial.

City administrators appealed to state political leaders, pointing out that Newark needed the college, not only for the jobs that it would create but equally for the improved health care that likely would result for inner-city residents. Most Newarkers agreed initially that the college would be good for the city's people, black and white, provided that adequate vacant land could be acquired.

College trustees insisted that there was little alternative to a Madison location, claiming Newark could not provide the 150 acres that the trustees considered necessary for a serene campus. Those who knew the Dodge estate were aware that the site could not provide anywhere near the dream of 150 contiguous acres. The ploy seemed transparent: The college would avoid any Newark obligation by demanding exorbitant amounts of land. Newark leaders called the bluff by offering more than 150 acres of urban renewal land in the Central Ward.

College trustees countered, insisting that the first fifty acres must be in a largely built-up area where thousands of impoverished blacks lived. That would be no problem, responded the impetuous Addonizio administration; the city would condemn the land, relocate the people, and the site would belong to the college. Years later, in 1977, Stanley S. Bergen, Jr., second president of the college, looked back on the high-handed action:

"Although it was intended that evacuees be compensated for the value of their land and homes, with relocation costs included, the fact that the community had been neglected in these significant policy decisions—decisions that affected their domiciles and livelihoods—represented a serious breach of trust by both the Mayor and the negotiators representing the State of New Jersey. The community read the actions as a gross lack of sensitivity concerning human rights and control over individual destiny."

It was not a matter of sentimental attachment for home, sweet home, much less "the value of their land and homes." The people who lived in the area were viciously exploited renters caught in the squeeze of absentee slumlords. A *Star-Ledger* reporter on January 22, 1967, termed the section "forty-six acres of rat-infested frame buildings long classified as substandard." He went on:

"There are 1,409 tenement apartment houses in the area, and 1,247 are judged substandard on the basis of no water (much less) hot water, either no flush toilet or a toilet shared by two or more families, no central heating and either no kitchen at all or a kitchen shared by several families."

The writer did not question how city housing officials had let such structures and their landlord owners exist in defiance of every law of fact or decency. He failed to mention that as many as 5,000 people lived in those obviously wretched hovels. Relocating that mass of humanity, according to the politics-ridden Newark Housing Authority, would be "no problem," although thoughts of such relocation had not even been considered before a sprawling college greensward had been proposed.

The existing housing, however wretched, at least was better than the prospect of being homeless in a housing-short city. Newark's least fortunate were being called upon to make the ultimate sacrifice by giving up their hard-won living spaces. An ad hoc Committee Against Negro Removal was quickly formed in the affected area.

Later, as they tried to explain the events of July 1967, many persons in the media and others would clutch at an old cliché—"a long, hot summer"—as if the unpleasant weather was a major factor in the tinderbox of rage in the black areas. They need not have looked beyond *The Star-Ledger* article of January 22, 1967, to know that the Central Ward tinderbox sat on an explosive base. Any stray spark would set it off.

The spark flew at about 9:30 P.M. on July 12, when a black cab driver with a name usually linked with anonymity, John W. Smith, passed a police car on 15th Avenue. Two white patrolmen in the police car stopped Smith, later charging that the driver had veered recklessly past their moving vehicle. Smith protested that the police car had been parked when he passed it. However, Smith's position was complicated by the fact that he was driving while on the revoked list.

A simple summons would not have been surprising and perhaps even in order. Instead, the policemen pulled Smith from his cab and put him in the back seat of the police car (with brutal force, Smith said; with the utmost regard for the prisoner's rights, the police insisted).

Smith was taken to Fourth Precinct headquarters on 17th Avenue in full view of scores of residents of the Hayes housing project. Most of them believed that Smith had been roughly handled. At any rate, it was easy for those who had seen the arrest to believe rumors that the cab driver had been beaten to death. He was not, but he was taken later in the evening to a hospital, suffering from head and rib injuries that definitely were not self-administered. Both policemen were also treated for injuries.

A group of about 200, not large in a city of 400,000 persons, gathered outside the Fourth Precinct station where Smith was booked. They shouted insults and threw stones and bottles but this quite minor hostility was scarcely the stuff of a riot. By 4:30 A.M. on July 13, the city was calm. Police assessed the damage: Property losses of about $2,500, mostly in damaged store windows, and about twenty-five arrests, only twelve of which were for serious crimes (looting or breaking and entering). Five of the arrests were for loitering.

Perhaps wishfully thinking that a long predicted riot had erupted close to metropolitan city rooms and New York TV stations, the media considerably overplayed the happenings of the first night. The TV camera crews and reporters were back late in the afternoon of July 13. Six camera crews were in the area, presumably not to cover $2,500 in property damage much less twenty-five arrests for relatively minor offenses.

Complacent city officials believed that the anticipated violence had come and had been contained. By noon the next day, most were

FIFTY CENTS   JULY 21, 1967

ANATOMY OF A RACE RIOT

TIME

NEWARK
CAB DRIVER
JOHN SMITH

VOL 90 NO. 3

John W. Smith's arrest for a traffic violation put him on TIME's cover for July 21; it was believed the arrest touched off the riots.

writing off the events of the night before as "isolated instances." Many city politicians complained of media overkill. There was little downtown concern that the situation might get out of hand. Secretly, too, there must have been relief among the Addonizio administration at its seeming good luck; the previous night's police actions showed shockingly scant ability or equipment for riot control.

Crowds of black residents took to the streets on the night of July 13, disrupting automobile traffic and posing amiably for the TV crews. Most of the active, noisy crowd was quite young, strangely more jubilant than angry. Governor Richard J. Hughes, who would visit the area the next morning, characterized the throngs as being in "a holiday mood."

The so-called revelry was marred by increasing numbers of looters and the "holiday mood" was increasingly fueled by supplies pillaged from bars and liquor stores. Looters gleefully smashed store windows and stole clothing, food, TV sets, radios, toys or anything else that could be hauled away. Police Director John L. Redden told of lawbreakers who were "literally shopping" in the violated stores. The action had gone far beyond mere mischief.

Nevertheless, Police Director Dominick A. Spina felt at midnight that "perhaps we had won and the violence was over." He based his optimism on apparently successful efforts to contain the disorders to an area in the Fourth Precinct. Police cars containing four or five policemen fanned out through the precinct, dispersing looters. Police Inspector Kenneth C. Melchior felt Newark had returned to "relative quiet," albeit at the expense of looted shopkeepers.

Most encouragingly, there had been no reports of gunfire before midnight, by either police or snipers. City patrolmen controlled area rooftops to prevent possible marksmen from using those vantage points. Mayor Addonizio agreed at midnight that the situation was "pretty well in hand."

State Police monitoring the situation believed the optimism was unwarranted. This entry was written in their official log shortly after midnight on the second night of the disorders:

"Presently, bands of eight to fifteen people traveling on foot and in cars, looting and starting fires .... Four policemen injured, four new areas have broken out in the past 15 minutes .... There is still no organization within the Newark Police Department .... All available transportation in use .... The Fourth Precinct appears to be running its own show .... There are no barricades .... No requests for State Police assistance from Director Spina."

Soon after, "sporadic shooting" was reported by city police although it was far from the sensationalized "battle scene" that some imaginative media and police witnesses were reporting. Then, much as an ebbing forest fire can get strangely and wildly out of control, the disorders leapfrogged out of the "contained area" and exploded far out in the South Ward on Elizabeth Avenue, along Bergen Street, along Clinton Avenue and westward on Springfield Avenue. The "holiday" had become a wild, ugly riot.

Before dawn on July 14, Gov. Richard J. Hughes held a news conference. Mayor Addonizio looked on, definitely in the role of a subordinate, since State Police and National Guard forces had virtually seized control of the city. State Police had been in the riot area since about 3 A.M.; guardsmen reached town at about 4:30. The role of the out-of-town forces will forever be debated. Many, including Newark's police director, believed that the presence of the heavily armed outsiders aggravated grievances on the stricken streets.

THE STAR-LEDGER

Addonizio called Governor Hughes at 2:20 A.M., asking for State Police and National Guard help. State Police began arriving in force between 4:30 and 5:30 A.M. About 3,500 National Guard troops were encamped in City Stadium by 9:30 A.M. Eventually more than 5,000 guardsmen were on the scene.

While orders to mobilize were going out to State Police and National Guard personnel, Colonel David B. Kelly, superintendent of the State Police, proceeded to Newark. He arrived at City Hall at about 3 A.M. There, he said, he found a thoroughly addled mayor:

"I asked him (Mayor Addonizio) what the situation was. He said, 'It is all gone, the whole town is gone.' I asked him where the problem was. He said, 'It is all over.' I asked him if he had any idea of the instigators or troublemakers or what we should look for. He didn't know."

State Police said they were unable to get any clear definition of the riot area or even where disorders were heaviest. The Newark Police Department could not supply city maps. All three units seeking to contain the disorders (Newark and State police and the National Guard) operated on different radio frequencies, making field coordination virtually impossible. Stores selling weapons or liquor had not been ordered closed by city officials.

By noon on Friday, July 14, 137 checkpoints had been established to control traffic into and

National Guardsmen sealed off the riot zone, eventually ringing an area of 14 square miles. Checkpoints, such as this one on Raymond Boulevard, kept traffic out of the region. Guardsmen within the area (below), kept rifles at the ready as they began patrolling the streets.

out of the area. The next day, the riot area was completely sealed off; National Guard forces ringed an area of fourteen square miles.

There forever will be debate on how the State Police and guardsmen affected the disorders. Both of the organizations were nearly all white, a factor certain to spur immediate anger in the black region. The guardsmen especially were very young, completely inexperienced in riot control and most unquestionably were badly frightened. Additionally, the out-of-town law enforcers were heavily and conspicuously armed, creating further animosity. Police Director Spina reflected on the situation:

"It was the feeling of Negro leaders that the augmentation by the State Police and the National Guard created and intensified the unrest."

In assessing the State Police/National Guard influence, it was necessary to recognize that there had been no deaths and very little gunfire before Addonizio's call to the Governor. The first death was reported at 4:10 A.M. on July 14,

nearly thirty-one hours after the arrest of cab driver John W. Smith. The first victim was 16-year-old James Sanders, shot in the back, according to official records, "at or near Sampson's Liquor Store, Springfield and Jones." Another man died from a chest wound before the State Police and guardsmen arrived.

Before the reinforcements reached Newark, only one sniping incident had been noted. As darkness began to settle on the area on July 14, the newcomers, particularly the young and inexperienced guardsmen, began "seeing snipers everywhere" according to Spina. He said:

"I think a lot of the reports of snipers was due to the, I hate to use the word, trigger-happy guardsmen, who were firing at noises and firing indiscriminately at times, it appeared to me, and I was out in the field at all times."

Mayor General James F. Cantwell, National Guard commander, agreed that there was "too much return fire" by guardsmen. He said that to have men on the ground fire up at the building "is the last thing you would do, any

more than if you went deer hunting and let everybody shoot because somebody hears a rustle in the bushes."

Timothy Still, president of the United Community Council, bitterly declared that "the charges of widespread sniping were a lot of malarkey used as justification to shoot people and homes."

Spina told of encountering about 200 guardsmen crouched behind trucks, trees and poles near the Columbus Homes, fearful of impending sniper fire because they had heard a rifle shot. Spina stopped a running guardsman, suspecting that he might have fired the shot. The soldier admitted he had, because a man in a window of the projects had not "ducked back" when so ordered. He added: "I fired a shot across the window to frighten him back inside." Spina countered: "You've just frightened 150 to 200 guardsmen on this street."

Frightening fellow guardsmen normally would have been the least of law enforcement concerns. Far more important were the feelings of many thousands of law-abiding Newark residents, pinned down in their apartments by the wild gunfire. They dared not leave their lodgings, even for food.

Mrs. Eloise Spellman, age forty-one, looked out the window of her apartment in one of the housing projects on July 15. That innocent action made her suspect and touched off a barrage of bullets that sprayed indiscriminately against the side of the entire complex, breaking windows, scarring doors and chipping at the brick walls. One of the bullets pierced Mrs. Spellman's neck, wounding her fatally.

Her son Richard, one of several terrified Spellman children who were crouched in the apartment, recalled: "She looked out the window. When we heard this shot, she screamed . . . and then she fell to the floor . . . there was a lot of blood around her and on her neck." Newark policemen came, this time to help. Outside, the savage, undisciplined shooting continued until one of the policemen draped a white sheet from the window.

Thousands of guardsmen marched constantly, moving from point to point in response to calls for help. Since most of the soldiers were very young and totally inexperienced, the assignment naturally generated anxiety. Snipers were especially feared, as can be seen on the faces of the guardsmen (opposite page) peering upward at the rooftops. Ultimately, investigations and other studies indicated that reports of sniping were greatly exaggerated by law enforcers.

THE STAR-LEDGER

There was looting aplenty, yet as Governor Hughes described it, this facet of the rioting began as something of a "holiday mood," with women and children entering and leaving through shattered shop windows even in broad daylight. Police made many arrests—more than 1,600 of them. Many charged brutality, but Newark police had the double responsibility of keeping order and simultaneously preserving community relationships that might outlast the days and nights of woe.

The nature of the violence changed drastically and suddenly as the newcomers began an apparent retaliation against the region. Now the law enforcers created much of the disorder. They shot at rooftops, windows, doorways and into shops (particularly black-owned shops that displayed "Soul" signs), where "snipers" were fancied to be lurking. Many cases of law officers and guardsmen firing at one another

were reported, with at least prima facie substantiation.

For example, Spina and another witness testified that on Friday night they saw State Police stationed at Bergen Street and Springfield Avenue shooting at a building on Hunterdon Street, supposedly to subdue "snipers." At about 3 A.M. that night, National Guard troops on Hunterdon Street were observed "exchanging fire with the first group." State Police records indirectly corroborated the eye-witness accounts of the gunfire between the law enforcement agencies.

State Police and National Guard gunfire took on the dimensions of a major second front, if use of weapons were the criterion. The two units expended nearly 15,000 rounds of ammunition between them in less than three days of occupation. About 10,500 of the shots were fired by guardsmen. Seldom has so much gunfire been directed at so few verifiable enemies.

The enormous expenditure of ammunition later was largely rationalized because of "sniper fire." However, only a few persons ever were charged as snipers (seven, according to one official report). Two instances of sweeping rooftop surveillance, one by the Newark Police Department and one by the State Police, revealed no snipers.

As the looting and arson eased, the character

of the violence changed. Outraged black residents charged that many innocent persons had been assaulted by police or guardsmen without provocation. Rev. Herbert G. Draesel, an Episcopalian priest, told of police shooting into the Colonnade Bar without warning and then directing their fire at a group on the street, wounding two persons.

Many witnesses told of police brutality, both physical and verbal, levied against black residents who dared leave their homes, even to check on neighborhood stores that they owned. Other witnesses told of state troopers and guardsmen shooting out plate glass windows in black-owned stores. One woman who owned a furniture store in the riot area testified that the store and its contents were ravaged by police fire. The official report to the Governor strongly condemned such actions:

"The damage caused within a few hours early Sunday morning, July 16, to a large number of stores marked with 'Soul' signs to depict non-white ownership and located in a limited area reflects a pattern of police action for which there is no possible justification. Testimony strongly suggests that State Police elements were mainly responsible with some participation by National Guardsmen. These raids resulted in personal suffering and economic damage to innocent small businessmen and property owners who have a stake in law and order and who had not participated in any unlawful act. It embittered the Negro community as a whole at a time when the disorders had begun to ebb."

Police and Guard officials denied indiscriminate use of firearms, although there was agreement even among their officers that some of the gunfire was uncontrolled, deadly and in the somewhat unfortunate allusion by General

Shopowners in the riot area who catered to the black population sought to prevent destruction with "Soul Brother" or "Negro" signs. Some found that police, not rioters, turned against them.

A National Guard tank (above) rumbled north-ward out of town as outside law enforcers began leaving the city on Monday, July 17. City officials said they were glad to see them go. Behind the departed forces, Newarkers began walking their littered streets, surveying the bullet-pocked stores, remembering days of bloodshed and feeling fear for the weeks that lay ahead.

Cantwell, not worthy even of "deer hunters."

The official report called the use of "heavy return fire at suspected sniper locations . . . tragic and costly." It continued: "The heavy fir-ing by police elements against suspected snipers makes it difficult to determine the extensiveness of sniping. There *may have been* some organ-ized sniping activity when the riot had reached its Friday peak." The use of the words "may have been" rather than a full acceptance of sniping was significant.

Twenty-six persons died during the riots, all but two during the State Police/National Guard occupation. Three died from causes other than bullets (a heart attack, a drug over-dose and in a collision between a fire truck and a private automobile). Except for a Newark Police detective and a Newark Fire Department captain shot while answering an alarm, all of these dead were black.

Three women (including Mrs. Spellman) were killed inside their homes by misdirected gunfire. A 73-year-old man was gunned down on the street outside his home. A ten-year-old boy was shot to death while riding in an auto-mobile. None of these could have been mis-taken for an escaping felon, an armed looter or a dangerous sniper, even by the wildest of interpretations. They were the innocent, caught between the looters and the quick-triggered enforcers of the order.

Rioting waned on Sunday. That morning, after grocery store owners were either unwilling or unable to open, emergency food was distributed by the National Guard. It was picked up at a variety of places, including the Jersey City waterfront, and taken to City Hospital for disbursement to points throughout the sealed-off area. The food distributors encountered sniper fire, according to General Cantwell. Civilian volunteers helped distribute the Guard-supplied food as well as groceries and dairy products brought to the city by private donors.

Two persons were killed on Sunday, including 19-year-old James Rutledge. His death was testimony to the carnival of overkill. His body, police records said, was "riddled with bullets and shotgun shells."

The National Guard and the State Police began leaving the city on Monday. Spina was not sorry; he felt that "when we removed the National Guard from the scene there came a feeling among the populace that things were going to be better." General Cantwell, for his part, believed "probably a day earlier we could have started to remove the patrols off the streets."

Mayor Addonizio was glad to see the State Police and National Guard leave. During the occupation of his city he had complained, "I was sort of left out of a lot of things that were going on." He added ruefully: "This is my city and I have to stay here after all the people (State Police and National Guard) pull out."

By Tuesday, most businesses reopened. The "Newark Disorders" were over. More precisely, the bloodshed and violence were finished. City leaders, black and white, had to sort out and to assess the six awesome days and nights of killing, lootings, arson and terror.

There were cold, telling statistics: twenty-six dead, more than 1,500 wounded, at least 1,600 arrested and property damage of $10,251,000. More than one thousand stores and businesses were ruined, including 167 food stores. Newark and New Jersey had been stunned by the ferocity of the conflict and by the evident mishandling by law enforcement agencies.

On August 8, Governor Hughes appointed a distinguished panel of state leaders, black and white, to assess the disorders. Robert D. Lilley,

Newark firemen battled more than 250 fires in five nights, sometimes in the face of gunfire or missles. One fire captain was killed by a gunshot wound while answering an alarm. Damage was great, yet Newark's fire chief believed that most people in the riot zone were not hostile.

president of New Jersey Bell Telephone Company, headed the panel, whose members included two former governors, Alfred E. Driscoll and Robert B. Meyner, and bishops of both the Catholic and Methodist churches. Hughes ordered a "realistic analysis," not a "detailed and meaningless repetition of studies."

He received what he wanted. When the committee's *Report for Action* was released in February 1968, readers found a dispassionate and balanced look at the Newark disorders (as well as smaller simultaneous uprisings in Englewood and Plainfield.)

The hard-hitting, remarkably well-written document spared few from criticism, reserving major sympathy only for the scores of thousands of innocent black families, first victimized in a corrupt city, then ravaged by the tragedy of war in the streets. Neither looters nor snipers, they suffered most, for, like Mayor Addonizio, they also had to stay after the State Police and National Guard had pulled out.

Newark firemen came in for praise, and indeed they acted with admirable professionalism, at times heroically, in the face of extreme testing, including gunfire and assaults. The innocents and the firemen were linked in one telling statement by Fire Chief John P. Caufield as he recounted a tale of 250 fires during the riots:

"Although firemen faced gunfire and missiles of several sorts on various occasions, the people we met were not hostile. It was not directed at us. In some cases, people brought coffee and refreshments while the men were battling fires."

Looters, vandals, arsonists and agitators all received proper scorn in the report to the Governor. Equally, State Police and National Guard actions came in for heavy criticism, particularly for the chaotic, undisciplined use of firearms. The Newark Police Department received low marks for pre-riot mistreatment of blacks and for lack of riot-restraining plans, much less proper equipment. Slum real estate owners, city administrators and the school system all were singled out for harsh criticism.

The commission fully believed reports of outrages committed against black people during the disorders. The report said:

"Although the extent of the excesses cannot be determined by this Commission, they have left a legacy of bitterness, disenchantment and frustration within the Negro community; and they have demonstrated a lack of respect for the rights of Negro citizens, regardless of whether they were involved in unlawful activity."

Mistreatment of black citizens during the disorders was overt and readily documented. The Governor's commission also noted long standing, covert city discrimination against black areas:

"Neighborhoods are dirty because of inadequate street cleaning. A house is gutted by fire and is not torn down. A governmental unit takes over buildings in preparation for urban renewal or highway construction and does not even secure them against trespassers.

"Cars stand abandoned on the streets for months, even when complaints are made. They are stripped of usable parts. Sometimes someone sets fire to them; their hulks stay at the curb. Abandoned buildings and cars reinforce the feeling of the ghetto dwellers that the City does not care about them."

Most disturbing of all was the assessment of the city's political hierarchy:

"There is a widespread belief that Newark's government is corrupt . . . a source close to Newark businessmen said he understood from them (businessmen) that 'everything at City Hall is for sale' . . . . A former state official, a former city official and an incumbent city official all used the same phrase: 'There's a price on everything at City Hall.' "

Naturally there were widespread differences of opinion on the report by the Governor's commission. Two elements created particular dissension: the actions of Newark police in arresting cabdriver John W. Smith and the performance of all law enforcers during the disorders.

Smith, who had been pinpointed as the spark that set off the explosion, went on trial for assaulting the two police officers who had arrested him. Equally, an Essex County grand jury was convened to inquire into the deaths during the disorders.

Smith was found guilty on April 1, 1968, on the assault charges and sentenced to two to three years in prison. Newspapers took care to point out during the trial that the jury of nine men and three women was all white. Smith's lawyers appealed the sentence to the United State Supreme Court, which voted, 8-0, not to hear the case.

The lawyers appealed again, this time through federal courts. Finally, on July 21, 1972, the conviction was reversed in the third United States Circuit Court of Appeals.

Judge Max Rosen ruled that the jury selection did not meet constitutional standards because it excluded a proportionate number of blacks and working class people. During the trial that was clear enough to the press, but it had escaped the notice of the county prosecutor and the judge. Many such cases had been reversed in southern courts; Smith's victory was the first such decision in the north.

Earlier, the grand jury ended its investigation of the riots by proclaiming on April 23, 1968, that there was no cause for indictments in any of the deaths. More than one hundred witnesses testified in eight weeks of hearings.

The grand jury said that "with some exceptions," state and local police and National Guardsmen showed "courage and restraint" in the early stages of the riots. But, "in the later stages of the disturbances, there were examples of poor judgment, excessive use of firearms and a manifestation of vindictiveness that cannot be tolerated in law enforcement personnel."·

Rioters—not those charged with protecting the public—were to blame for the deaths, the grand jury asserted. Still, the jury findings

continued, law enforcers "must so conduct themselves as to deserve the respect of all law-abiding men and women."

Carefully read, the conclusions, although generally more favorable to police and guardsmen, differed little from the report of the Governor's commission.

Newark Police Director Dominick A. Spina told the press that in his opinion the grand jury "did much better job in analyzing the facts relating to the operations of the police, National Guard and the State Police than the Governor's commission." Spina overlooked the fact that he had supplied the commission with some of the most stinging indictments of the out-of-town law enforcers.

Sordid evidence of corruption soon would be read out in open court. Most immediately, Newark somehow had to begin moving from its nadir of despair, doubt and degradation.

The *Newark News* recognized the clear-cut, hardened attitudes that lay behind the uprising in the ghetto: "While Newark knows that sub-standard housing, obsolete schools and unemployment are not exclusive with Newark, it also is not blind to the fact that its Negro relationships have been too often mired in politics."

The failure to appoint Wilbur Parker as secretary to the Board of Education was labeled by the *News* editorial as "political injustice." The *News* rebuked the Housing Authority for not informing residents fully about relocation plans for people affected by the New Jersey College of Medicine and Dentistry.

Still the *News* declared, these and other issues certainly should have been "more susceptible of resolution around a conference table than in bullet-pocked streets." The *News* clearly saw that the task of rebuilding the shattered city must "go far beyond the physical restoration of burned and looted shops."

Newark had reached bottom. If it ever could rebuild, its new foundations would forever rest on the ashes of July 1967.

Carefully stepping over an iron guard rail that had been twisted out of shape during the disorders, a child of the neighborhood must have sensed that Newark was at its worst point in history. For him, and all his neighbors, there had to be a better way than yet shown to deal with poverty, segregation and racism. The city might survive on hope, but not for long.

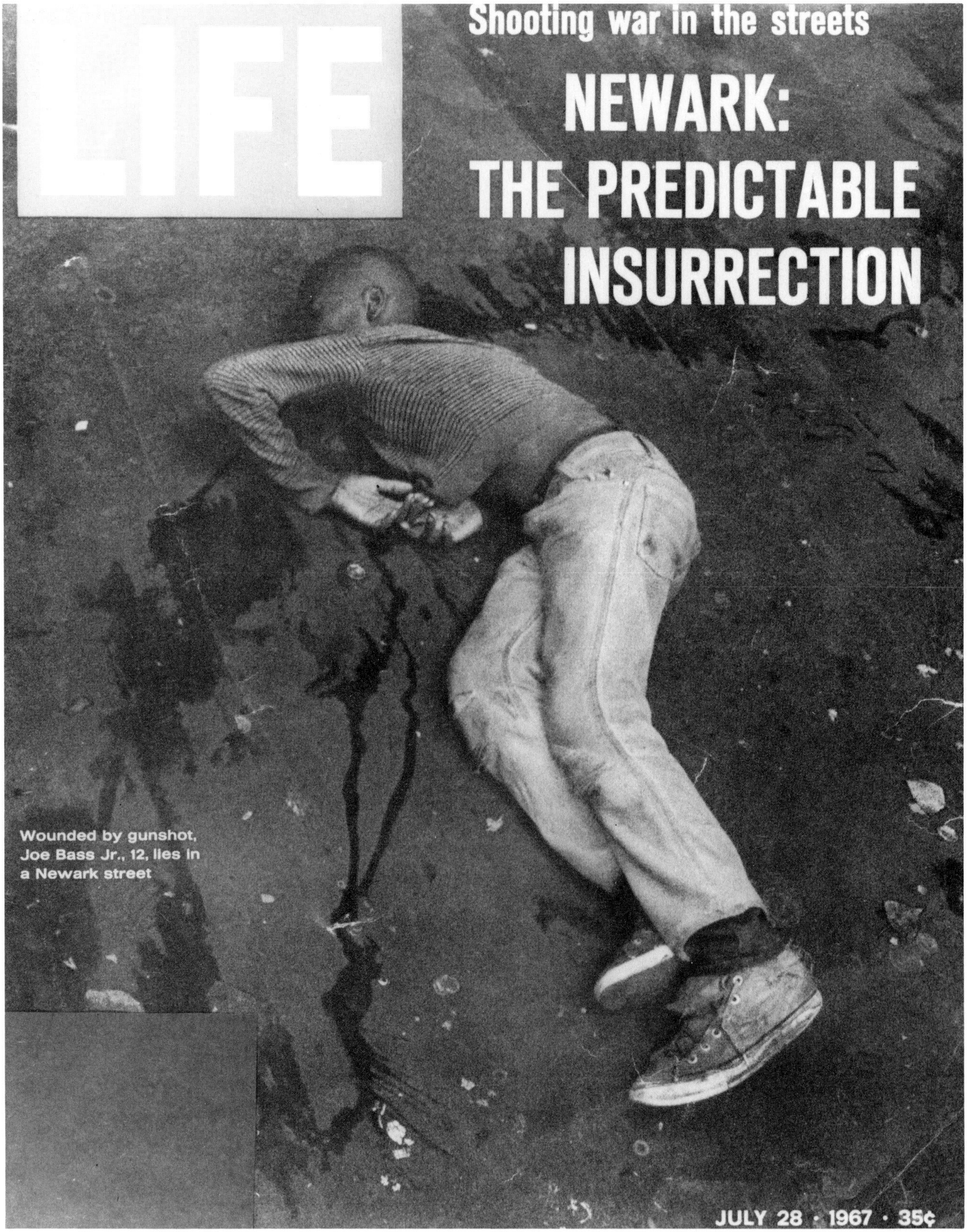
LIFE
Shooting war in the streets
NEWARK:
THE PREDICTABLE
INSURRECTION
Wounded by gunshot,
Joe Bass Jr., 12, lies in
a Newark street
JULY 28 · 1967 · 35¢

NEWARK PUBLIC LIBRARY

Such national headlines as this on the front cover of LIFE on July 28 would haunt the city. Newark now symbolized an urban shame that many observers felt could have been predicted.

Newark in the summer of 1967, where the cruel visibility of ruined neighborhoods was only one evidence of a city so torn by crime and corruption that it was likely "the worst city in America."

Chapter 29

"NEWARK WILL GET THERE FIRST"

Newark did not stand alone in its distress, for violence had erupted in many parts of America in that fateful summer of 1967. Other New Jersey cities, including Plainfield and Englewood, had been shocked by street turbulence at the same time as Newark. Seven days of rioting in Detroit, from July 23 to July 30, killed forty-three persons, injured another 2,000 and left 5,000 homeless in that city's black ghetto.

Yet, when journalists focused on distraught cities, their typewriters and their cameras generally zeroed-in on Newark. Its proximity to the trend-setting New York City media made Newark a convenient target for "learned" discussions on the city as the prototype of disorder and for comedians who found sick humor in the degradation that had been visited upon the area.

The city's most optimistic publicists and

apologists could not explain away the unemployment, the dirt, the crime, the litter, the empty gaping spaces created by "urban renewal," the dissent, and above all, the sickly odor of corruption that pervaded City Hall. Newark, in truth, was probably the worst city in America.

Frightening woes intensified, hastened in large measure by businesses and middle-class residents fleeing outward to suburban and rural fields. In 1968, Donald Malafronte, administrative assistant to Mayor Addonizio and director of the Model Cities program, summed up the despair and the uncertainty when he told an Associated Press reporter: "Wherever American cities are going, Newark will get there first."

(Later, Mayor Kenneth Gibson adopted the pithy Malafronte statement, using it so often that it came to be attributed to him as a rallying cry and as a justifiable plea to keep New Jersey's largest city from total collapse.)

Newark could not be ignored by its neighbors, by its state or by its nation. The Governor's commission on the Newark disorders had warned bluntly in its February 1968 report: "Suburban residents must understand that the future of their communities is inextricably linked to the fate of the city, instead of harboring the illusion that they can maintain invisible walls or continue to walk away."

The commission also forthrightly underscored the even more fundamental issue of segregation that most Americans had been evading for decades: "Equality for the black man was bound sooner or later to land on the doorstep of each of us—and had not the Negro been patient and forebearing, it would have landed there (in Newark) before."

The only way to begin renewal, the commission believed, was "at home, in the way we do business, on our streets, in our shops, our schools, our courts, government offices and wherever members of black and white communities meet."

In that idealistic, simplistic fashion, the healing process began. It began in a powerful evi-

Less than a month after the riots, rebuilding began when this model of "Gateway" was unveiled by Victor Gruen Associates, the architectural firm hired to plan the startling new project. Across the street from venerable Penn Station, the 30-story office building, 10-story motor hotel, a shopping plaza and a three-level parking garage would replace an area of decaying slums. In the lower right can be seen the glass-enclosed bridge designed to link the office building and motor hotel lobbies with the railroad station at track level. Significantly, the $24 million undertaking was underwritten by the Prudential Insurance Company.

GRUEN DESIGN

Groundbreaking was an often-repeated activity for New Community Corporation, founded in January 1968 by Rev. William J. Linder, second from left above. At this ceremony in 1975 he was flanked by George Wheeler, left, representing Mayor Gibson; Willie Wright, president of NCC; and on right, William Blakely, representing Engelhard Industries.

dence of faith by the Prudential Insurance Company. It began with the rise of a remarkable private agency, the New Community Corporation, dedicated to a better life for Newark's underprivileged. It began in frank discussions about the New Jersey College of Medicine and Dentistry, at last out in the open after the sham and deceit that had surrounded early negotiations.

On August 2, a mere twelve days after the riots ended, Prudential amazed the corporate world by announcing it would underwrite for two developers a $24 million project in the rundown area near Penn Station. Dubbed "Gateway," the plan included a thirty-story office building, a ten-story hotel, a shopping plaza and a three-level parking garage. A proposed "skywalk," an enclosed walkway, would link the structures to Penn Station.

The daring Gateway gamble was powerful evidence that the "Pru" would stay, at a time when many other businesses were stepping up plans to flee. Prudential, founded in the city in 1873, had persistently maintained its world headquarters on Broad Street for more than thirty years despite state and national business trends toward decentralization. If the "Pru" had pulled up stakes in 1967, for any reason, Newark might never have recovered.

Gateway received proper recognition in newspapers and journals. Little, if any, attention was paid to a small enterprise founded in January 1968 under the name New Community Corporation (NCC). Its seemingly pretentious goal was "to improve the quality of life of the people of Newark to reflect individual dignity and personal achievement."

Other citizen groups had said essentially the same thing for decades, with no results. New Community Corporation had a major difference. He was the Rev. William Linder, the young pastor at Queen of Angels Church in the riot zone. He had resolved at the height of the disorders that his future would be in Newark—and he knew that the city would rise only if its people could have hope.

Father Linder founded New Community Corporation under the wing of the Mt. Carmel Guild. He insisted that corporate board members must be neighborhood leaders, not downtown business heads. Plans were vague, but two factors dominated: There would be no quest for urban renewal funds and the people who would occupy the proposed NCC housing units would help plan them.

The Engelhard Corporation, a Newark-based company that led the world in platinum production, gave the fledgling group an interest-free loan and the no-cost legal services of Charles Engelhard's personal attorney. On that platinum-tinged base, New Community Corporation grew astonishingly.

(Nineteen years later, in 1987, NCC owned and managed eight housing developments built or renovated at a cost exceeding $88 million low income families' and senior citizens occupied the corporation's 2,265 apartments. NCC also had created 4,000 construction jobs, $29 million in construction wages and $2 million in new taxes for the city. None of the housing had been built with tax abatement—a subsidy usually expected by downtown revivalists. Through the years, too, NCC has expanded into other vitally-needed area services, from health and baby care to a supermarket.)

NCC's efforts were concentrated on the western hill, where the riots had flared. There too, bitterly opposed forces again squared off in 1968 on the controversial issue of the College of Medicine and Dentistry. This time, neighborhood people were included in the discussions along with college, business and city political leaders. Predictably, the first meetings seethed with anger and suspicion:

Only one thing was not debatable. The college would rise in Newark, if it were to rise anywhere at all. Governor Hughes made that clear enough as the talks continued: "If the college is not in Newark, it would be such a burning issue that it might be the death of the college."

Dr. Stanley Bergen, the college's second president, ten years later recalled the acrimony:

"The reaction of many of the faculty, staff, and student body was, 'Why do we need this?' They had been sold the idea of bringing social change and economic improvement to Newark. Instead they found themselves a focal point of controversy, their college held up as a symbol of oppression of poor and minority groups, and the community pitted against them. Suddenly, the medical school was the culprit rather than a struggling institution attempting to find a permanent location while offering the opportunity for vastly improved health services in the process.

"Many faculty members were bewildered by the role that was thrust on them, either by the state or by circumstances; understandably, they felt inadequate to act as agents of social change, preferring to be allowed to pursue the scholarly aspects of their chosen careers as medical and dental educators. Other faculty members took the position, 'I told you so,' and tried to discredit attempts to compromise."

Dr. Robert R. Cadmus, first president of NJCMD, sought accord with neighborhood representatives. These especially included Mrs. Louise Epperson, head of the Committee Against Negro and Puerto Rican Removal and a resident of the affected area; Harry Wheeler, eighth grade teacher in Hawthorne Avenue School and a civil rights leader; and Junius Williams, a Yale Law School student from Virginia, who committed himself on behalf of the Newark Area Planning Association.

College leaders later recalled in a summary of the strife: "This tale, of necessity, was one of contrasts—the rights of people and the wrongs being done to them, the bleakness of the lives of some engaged in the battle and the richness of those apparently sitting in power. There were problems within the College itself . . . the students and College interns felt themselves to be the pawn . . . the faculty was concerned that the College would fold before the issues were settled. Cities, and suburban communities throughout the state, saw their possible opportunity to snare the medical school."

Negotiations dragged on for seven months. At one critical point, Dr. Bergen wrote, "The medical school faculty met and by a majority of only two, voted against disbanding and relinquishing the charter of the school." Two votes —the college lived, if barely.

Then, in February 1968, officials at the federal departments of Housing and Urban Development (HUD) and of Health, Education and Welfare (HEW) ordered serious, public talks. Since the agencies held the money, the contending sides quickly agreed to air the controversy in open meetings.

Five state officials and a total of nine community and college representatives gathered across a twenty-foot-long table, so divergent in philosophies that conciliation seemed impossible. After six meetings, the fourteen persons reached accord in what were called "The Newark Agreements."

College acreage was cut from 167 to 57.9 acres, including the property of city-owned Martland Medical Center, being used temporarily as the college training hospital. The state promised substantial funding to upgrade Martland. (Within three years it committed $10 mil-

No piece of Newark land ever stirred passions more than the blocks of rundown housing to the left, a major cause of the 1967 riots when city officials assigned them to the N.J. College of Medicine and Dentistry. After 1968, when accord was reached and housing was found for displaced persons, the land was cleared (below). The fledgling institution began in the trailer (bottom). The trailer is still used, but the college has grown into many buildings and services that make it a huge, internationally-respected university. Dr. B.F. Rush, chairman of NJUMD's department of surgery, photographed this sequence.

lion, as well as major subsidies for annual operating costs.)

College representatives agreed to expand and improve health care for city residents, not only in the city hospital but in a new hospital that would rise on the medical college campus. Included were ambulance services, narcotic and alcohol rehabilitative programs, and health education.

Provisions were made for admission of minority students. By 1975 the institution claimed the highest percentage of minority students in the nation except for two traditionally black medical colleges.

The contending sides agreed that as many as possible of the 2,600 permanent jobs at the college would be filled by residents within the college's surrounding community. That promise was kept, in the first ten years at least; by 1977, a high percentage of the school's jobs were filled by people who lived in the greater Newark area. (Later, however, some community leaders charged that hospital administrators were guilty of discrimination in their hiring and promotion practices.)

The state agreed to upgrade the recruiting and training of black students for the building trades. It was agreed that at least one-third of all journeyman tradesmen and half of the apprentices were to be hired from the Newark area. Union representatives had to accept that, although they gulped visibly while swallowing the bold challenge to their time-honored, if never admitted, policies of racial exclusion.

Especially difficult was the matter of relocation of the families who would be dispossessed by the new campus. Agreement was not easy; ultimately this had been the central issue of the 1967 disorders. However, by 1972 all families were relocated.

These "Newark Agreements" were a dramatic breakthrough. The last few minutes of the unprecedented sessions became tense as Ralph A. Dungan, chancellor of the State Department of Higher Education and chairman of the "agreements" group, accepted a motion to submit the group's work to a public hearing. A *Newark News* reporter recorded the dramatic moment of decision:

"Loudly and unanimously the audience screamed 'yes' and the last major obstacle to the relocation of the College of Medicine and Dentistry had apparently crumbled.

"As both sides of the negotiating table and representatives of the college scurried about the room, patting everyone on the back and exchanging best wishes, a Princeton University senior, who is doing his senior thesis on the medical school, leaned back in his chair and said aloud: 'It worked! The damn thing worked!' "

The college's own account of the turbulent meetings, published in the spring of 1968, told of the charged atmosphere as the accord was reached: "A jubilant sense of victory rushed about the room on wings, touching everyone. It exploded. Mrs. Epperson threw her arms about Dr. Cadmus and heartily kissed Mrs. Cadmus. Tears were seen on faces. Blacks and whites throughout the room embraced. This was a night to be remembered in the history of Newark."

Just as optimism seeped back to the city, the "odor of corruption" that the Governor's commission had warned against broke into the open. Clear evidence of cynical, persistent official crime was revealed on April 21, 1970, when Mayor Addonizio and fourteen co-defendants were indicted after months of grand jury hearings. The fifteen were charged with operating a pay-off system that had extorted $253,000 from Constrad Incorporated, an engineering firm headed by Paul Rigo of Oldwick. Eventually other charges brought the kickback level to more than $1 million.

Addonizio's co-defendants were well known. They included Anthony ("Tony Boy") Boiardo of Roseland, long identified by the press as an "alleged Mafia figure"; three city councilmen; two former councilmen; two former corporation counsels; a variety of other city officials and bureaucrats; and three contractors. Two of the three indicted councilmen were black. The other thirteen defendants all were white.

Trial was set for June 4, 1970, before a federal court jury in Trenton. That presented considerable inconvenience for Addonizio, who sought a third term in the regular four-year election scheduled for May 12. No less inconvenienced were the three accused councilmen:

Calvin D. West, Irvine Turner and Frank Addonizio, all of whom asked voters to return them to office.

Addonizio recalled for voters city accomplishments during his eight-year administration. As the mayor listed them, they were impressive: a $200 million urban renewal thrust that he called "the largest public housing program in the nation;" a $200 million school reconstruction program and the expanding college/university complex on the western slopes. Such achievements were balanced by the overriding impact of the pending trial.

Addonizio had two main challengers. One was Anthony Imperiale, the tough-talking North Ward "law and order" candidate who had won mixed praise and scorn from visiting journalists during the 1967 disorders as he championed white militancy. The other was Kenneth Gibson, the serious young black city engineer who had been considered merely a "holding" candidate for black forces in 1966 when he surprised the political community by compiling 16,000 votes for mayor.

Gibson placed first on May 12, winning nearly forty-three per cent of the votes and more than doubling Addonizio's total — 37,850 to 18,212. Imperiale finished third. Since Gibson had not polled more than fifty per cent of the votes as required, he and Addonizio faced a runoff on June 16.

The three councilmen under indictment— West, Turner and Addonizio—all were rejected by the voters. Election returns showed that blacks had increased their membership to three on the nine-member council. Most significant for Newark's future was the election of a new-comer to politics, 34-year-old Sharpe James. The director of athletics at Essex County College and past president of the Weequahic Community Council, James was elected as the South Ward councilman.

The United States Supreme Court rejected Addonizio's plea to delay his extortion trial until after the June runoff election. The incumbent mayor had little chance; Gibson won easily, 55,097 to 43,086, thus becoming not only Newark's first black mayor but also the first black mayor of any northeastern city. Significantly, about fifteen per cent of the city's

NEWARK PUBLIC LIBRARY

Kenneth Gibson, in office for only slightly more than one month, was already a symbol of black leadership when NEWSWEEK put him on this 1970 cover to help answer the question: "The Black Mayors: How Are They Doing?"

white population voted for Gibson.

Thousands of Gibson's supporters jammed Broad Street near City Hall in exuberant, but controlled, celebration. Uptown, Addonizio's supporters lost their poise as the returns came in to his headquarters. Vengeful backers of the mayor shouted insults and obscenities at newspaper reporters and overturned television cameras on hand for a "victory celebration." Police were called to quell the near-riot. The mayor, for his part, gracefully conceded defeat and pledged cooperation to Gibson. He said that he was "in one way greatly relieved because he could now spend more time with his family."

That was not to be. United States attorneys vigorously pressed the case against Addonizio. Evidence of official corruption mounted during the six-week trial; the jury returned a guilty verdict against Addonizio. He was freed on bail to await sentencing.

Mayor Gibson and his supporters had little time for jubilation; thousands of abandoned or ruined buildings, evidence of decades of neglect, were visible in nearly every part of the city.

Federal District Court Judge George H. Barlow sentenced Addonizio on September 22, first praising him for his service in World War II, his years in Congress, and his many accomplishments as Newark mayor. Against that, Barlow weighed "crimes of monumental proportions, the enormity of which can scarcely be exaggerated . . . as calculated as they were brazen." He sentenced the disgraced mayor to ten years in a federal penitentiary. Prolonged appeals all the way to the United States Supreme Court failed. Addonizio finally was taken to Atlanta Federal Penitentiary in May 1972. He was paroled in October 1979.

Five of the defendants had been separated from Addonizio's trial. They included three former councilmen, West, Turner and Lee Bernstein; former Newark Corporation Counsel Norman Schiff; and Boiardo. Schiff and Boiardo were separated because of illness, and the councilmen because of legal complications.

None of them ever went to trial.

Jubilation in the Gibson camp faded even before the new mayor took office on July 1. He had inherited a city in a shambles — its administration riddled with dishonesty, its downtown streets shabby, the riot area still a charred, ghostly monument to the horrible nights in July 1967. The city treasury was $65 million in debt, tax levels were high, schools were miserable, and national magazines and urban sociologists seldom missed a chance to debase Newark. If Gibson could merely stabilize this tottering, racially torn city, there would be reason for celebration.

Disillusionment marred much of Gibson's first term, heightened by initial overly optimistic expectations of both whites and blacks. Fred J. Cook, in a far-ranging, perceptive article in the *New York Times Sunday Magazine* of July 25, 1971, recognized that no Newark official could yet escape reminders of the 1967 nights of horror: "Blackened, hollow shells of buildings, some boarded up, some closed off by iron grating, all in ruin."

Yet Cook sensed in Newark a hopeful feeling that good things were possible even if Gibson obviously was hamstrung by an intense clique of Addonizio loyalists among city employees, many of whom openly proclaimed that "Hughie will be back," as well as some who secretly sabotaged operations. The white-dominated city council consistently voted against the new mayor's appointments and policies. Nearly every appointment was questioned, by blacks and whites, for different reasons.

Labor groups, from national teacher organizations to those representing building trades, marched down Broad Street in support of the crippling 11-week teachers' strike in 1971. It weakened school morale and struck a cruel blow at hopes of students and parents.

A prime example of black-white polarization exploded in 1970 when Gibson appointed veteran policeman John L. Redden to be director of police. The council voted unanimously against the appointment. The six white members voted against Redden because they considered him to be "the kind of man no politician could control," especially after he had told the Governor's commission investigating the riots that gambling was rampant in Newark. Black councilmen said "no" mainly because Redden was white.

Gibson told the *New York Times* writer that he felt Redden was "probably the only man in the department I have faith in as being able to do the kind of job that needs to be done. As far as Redden is concerned, I know I'm right." Gibson renominated Redden. Eventually the council accepted the appointment, knowing that it was merely an interim compromise until Gibson felt that he had a proper black nominee.

Cook described the embattled young mayor as "a short, chunky man, broad-shouldered, barrel-chested, with just a wisp of a mustache on his round face. He seems to lack dynamism on the public platform . . . but face to face he exudes a great deal of personal charm . . . though slow to make up his mind, he appears confident and extremely sure of himself once he has arrived at a decision."

Racial tensions in the winter of 1971 were strong factors in a harsh eleven-week teachers' strike that closed about half the city's schools. Buildings that remained open churned with turmoil and doubt. Black parents, whose children were especially hurt by the strike, railed against white teachers who "lived in the suburbs and considered teaching in Newark a 9-to-3 job."

Black-white relationships withered, to the benefit of neither side, much less to the city. Symbolizing the split were two major figures. Anthony Imperiale, a self-appointed guardian of city "law and order," was a virtual folk hero in the mostly white North Ward. His major opponent was a nationally known young poet, Imamu Amiri Baraka, greatly admired in black neighborhoods for his bold espousals of black pride and equal rights.

Imperiale had become a media figure during the riots, when he rallied gun-toting neighbors on patrols of North Ward streets, vowing in vigilante fashion to shoot any rioters who spilled over into that territory. Imperiale made good newspaper copy then and after; even his enemies admitted that. A short, muscular figure, speaking bluntly and in street vernacular, he won considerable media attention. Imperiale denied that he was racist, despite his strong early statements; and as he edged toward ever more lofty political ambitions, he sought increasingly to shed his anti-black image.

Known initially as Le Roi Jones, Baraka was respected in literary circles long before the disorders. Support for Gibson by the short, slender, bearded black poet initially was a boon for the new mayor. Describing an interview with Baraka, Cook called him "more moderate than his slogans suggest . . . . He does not rant but talks quietly, reasonably, as if arguing the undeniable logic of his case." Baraka insisted that he was not a "violent racist."

The two symbols of Newark's racial tensions faced a showdown in Kawaida Towers, a sixteen-story, 210-unit housing project that Baraka and associates in the Temple of Kawaida started in October 1972 on Lincoln Avenue in the North Ward. Imperiale, who had been given his first political power through his election as North Ward councilman in 1968, led white protestors on picket lines at the black-supported site. After the land was cleared and excavated, the matter was referred to the courts, stopping all work. Time and money ran out for Kawaida Towers in June 1976, when the project was abandoned.

The New Jersey Housing Finance Agency had already put about $1 million into planning and site preparation at the Kawaida site and had committed another $5.4 million. In the 1976 settlement, the housing agency received the land, the Kawaida group received $50,000 and all debts were paid. The Lincoln Avenue neighbors were stuck with the unsightly excavation until the Housing Finance Agency agreed

Anthony Imperiale, "law and order" advocate, and Imamu Amiri Baraka, poet and leader in black neighborhoods, confronted one another in a hearing on the controversial Kawaida Towers housing project. Baraka was a Kawaida proponent. Imperiale led the opposition.

Garbage pickup was an overwhelming drain on finance, forerunner of disposal problems throughout the state. This eyesore was on Peshine Avenue, between Madison and Clinton avenues.

in late July to fill in the fourteen-foot-deep excavation.

Newark's most persistent problem was money —to pay policemen, firemen and teachers; to pick up garbage, remove abandoned automobiles and maintain city streets. As Newark's tax rate rose perilously, Gibson appealed for help, first from the state, where he won grudging, if scant, support. He then went directly to Washington. His frank talks in the nation's capital eventually brought large federal grants to Newark and at the same time earned him national urban leadership.

His impassioned pleas were the voice of all American cities. On January 23, 1971, when he told a congressional hearing "that Newark may be the most decayed and financially crippled city in the nation," he added, with an eloquence that echoed in every major city:

"I caution you. Do not misunderstand the implications of urban decay . . . . We are not only talking of saving the 'Newarks' of Amer-

ica. We are talking about saving America itself."

Rising taxes provided another excuse for the exodus of business and middle class residents, black and white. Blue-collar jobs, long recognized as the entry level for those lacking training or with a paucity of educational opportunities, began to disappear. "Urban renewal," in reality "urban demolition," was a mockery.

Newark and all of New Jersey suffered an incalculable loss on August 31, 1972, when the *Newark News* died after nearly ninety years of life and long months of agonizing fatal illness. The paper for decades had wielded great power in the legislative halls at Trenton and was known nationally for accuracy, thoroughness and fairness. It was the closest thing to a state newspaper that New Jersey ever has had. The large staff of *News* reporters was respected, trusted by the public and feared by politicians far beyond the boundaries of Newark and New Jersey.

Many complications weakened the *News*— competition from television, a growing lack of markets for late afternoon papers (as opposed to morning editions) and a lackluster ownership that had let the twentieth century pass it by.

Newark News reporters found little warmth as they led a 175-day strike against the paper's management. Often blamed as the fatal blow to the venerable newspaper, the strike was merely the last ailment to beset the News.

The final blow was a prolonged 175-day strike by reporters, often superficially blamed as the blow that killed the *News*. Actually, the strike was merely the last complication to beset the ailing, if respected, "Old Lady of Market Street" (as the paper often was called by politicians who had felt its sting).

The demise of the *News* stilled what had been long recognized as the strong-voiced conscience of both the city and the state. Newark became the sole domain of *The Star-Ledger*, considered by most critics to be less forceful in its editorial aggressiveness. *The Star-Ledger* broadly expanded its staff, its circulation and its advertising revenues, gradually moving toward the statewide editorial respect that the *News* had commanded for most of its eighty-nine years.

Gibson sought a second term in May 1974, facing Anthony Imperiale. Imperiale had been elected to the State Assembly in 1973, running as an independent and trying always to move away from his once carefully cultivated image as a rough street leader with racist tendencies. Imperiale named a one-time supporter of Baraka to manage his mayoral campaign in black wards and placed his publicity in the hands of a black public-relations agency.

Imperiale's chances seemed bright, particularly since three other candidates had entered the field, making a run-off a distinct possibility. The anticipated bitter campaign between Gibson and Imperiale never materialized, for neither Gibson nor Imperiale took stances considered racist. Surprisingly, there was no runoff; Gibson defeated Imperiale, 42,870 to 34,502.

This time the celebration was muted. Conceding defeat, Imperiale told his supporters and the press that he hoped that this was the last election in which race or ethnic background would play a major role. Gibson and Imperiale met for thirty minutes the day after the election to pledge mutual cooperation. Newark edged closer to maturity.

The healing process took another forward step on July 1, when the City Council, despite a five-to-four white majority, chose Earl Harris as the city's first black council president. That day, too, the council gave unanimous approval to Gibson's appointment of a new police director, black police Lieutenant Hubert Williams.

THE STAR-LEDGE

Henry Martinez, former Newark policeman and son of parents born in Spain, was the first Hispanic elected to any major Newark office. He was elected East Ward councilman in 1974 and was chosen as council president in 1986.

The unanimity was in marked contrast to the seven-month, openly racial battle when Gibson had named police Lieutenant Edward L. Kerr in December 1972 as the city's first black police director. Kerr was not confirmed until July 1973.

Henry Martinez was sworn in on July 1 as the East Ward councilman, the first Hispanic elected to any major office in Newark. Estimates of Spanish-speaking persons in the city ranged from about 50,000 to 70,000, most of them Puerto Ricans. Heavy support for Martinez, a police lieutenant, also had come from a swelling influx of Portuguese to the East Ward —the old "Ironbound," long a traditional area of immigrants and blue-collar workers. The East Ward was in many ways the most solid of any area in the city.

Hispanics chafed under a lack of representation in city affairs. The resentment boiled over on Sunday, September 1, 1974, when

Puerto Ricans and police clashed in a bloody battle at Branch Brook Park. Seeking to break up an illegal dice game involving a few men, Essex County Park policemen were met with jeers and name-calling followed almost immediately by a barrage of rocks and bottles. Vehicles were overturned and two concession stands were set afire.

Newark police in full riot gear, summoned by the park officers, intensified the resentment. As the violence grew, Mayor Gibson arrived. Disregarding the advice of several city leaders that more police be summoned to subdue the crowd forcibly, Gibson walked into the park and mingled in the furious gathering. "I listened to them," he told the press. "They wanted to meet with me. I agreed, but insisted that we all go to City Hall." He then led an impromptu march downtown to his office.

Heated talks that afternoon ended without agreement, then reconvened the following day. Nearly 1,000 persons, mostly very young and very militant, gathered outside City Hall while

Puerto Rican representatives demanded the firing of Police Director Williams, the disbanding of the city's tactical and mounted police forces, the immediate appointment of a Spanish-speaking judge, and the release of nineteen persons arrested during the previous day's disorders.

Gibson agreed to the release of the prisoners but sought time to review the other demands. He could not in reality have acted alone in any of the demands, but his action was interpreted as a refusal by hostile leaders who addressed the crowd. The demonstrators surged up the steps of City Hall, hurling rocks and bottles and breaking front door windows. Police dispersed the crowd, injuring twenty-one persons in the melee.

Rioting spread and accelerated in areas of concentrated Puerto Rican populations, forcing police to close Broad Street in the early evening. Sporadic sniping and looting continued throughout the night. During the melee, city firemen responded to sixty-one calls at the Columbus Homes, a public housing project.

Reporters and cameramen swelled the crowd in city hall when Mayor Gibson met with Puerto Rican representatives to discuss riots that rocked the city after a Labor Day clash in Branch Brook Park.

The Foodtown supermarket near Stone Street was destroyed by fire; bystanders assaulted firemen as they fought the blaze.

Four days of disorder brought two deaths, sixty-eight injuries (including twelve firemen), and seventy-seven arrests. The intensity of the riots did not match the level of the 1967 riots, but once again the city had been served notice that a significant portion of its population deeply resented its policies.

Gustav Heningburg, head of the Greater Newark Urban Coalition and a vital force in Gibson's early years as well as one of the city's most respected and judicious civil rights leaders, declared after the riots: "For all intents and purposes—politically, economically and socially—the Puerto Rican community has been invisible. Until Sunday, nobody had taken them seriously."

The city's image problem grew worse. It was a stock joke among journalists to tell of a New York City television executive (probably apochryphal), who when asked why Newark had been given so little screen exposure, was said to have replied: "Give us a good riot and we'll be over there fast!" Urban critics in academia continued to hold up Newark as the classic horror city. Visiting journalists always relived the 1967 riots, not difficult, because even after a decade fire-blackened ruins remained as grim reminders.

One of the cruelest, if probably deserved, blows at Newark was an article in *Harper's Magazine* for January 1975. The stature of the prestigious magazine, plus the quasi-scientific, pseudo-scholarly nature of the material, heightened the impact. Reduced to its simplest terms, the article analyzed data from the 1970 U.S. Census in twenty-four categories, including crime, health, housing, poverty, public education, "atmosphere" and "amenities." It concluded:

"The city of Newark stands without serious challenge as the worst of all. It ranked among the worst five cities in no fewer than nineteen of the twenty-four categories, and it was dead last in nine of them. Adding one, two, or even three tables couldn't possibly jar Newark from last place, and there is every reason to suppose that more comparisons would simply bury it deeper. Newark is a city that desperately needs help."

Despite such out-of-town scorn, Newark's political and business leadership felt by 1977 that it could look back with pride on the ten years since guns and flames had ravaged the western hill. In a somewhat curious commemoration of the flames of '67, a full-page advertisement in *The Star-Ledger* on July 19, 1977, bore a bold and challenging headline: "A MESSAGE FOR THOSE WHO THINK NEWARK DIED TEN YEARS AGO."

The advertisement showed a panorama of handsome buildings—a new $200 million passenger terminal at Newark Airport, $200 million in construction at the new College of Medicine and Dentistry, $16 million in new Rutgers University structures, $23 million in new county buildings near the courthouse, a new eighteen-story Blue Cross/Blue Shield building downtown, and about one thousand new housing units. None of these, boasted the ad, was here in 1967.

Downtown was not all. The Gibson administration claimed in 1978 that it had produced about 6,500 units of new or renewed housing at a cost of $251 million. Just before Gibson's third term bid in 1978, the mayor announced that another 1,400 such units were underway at a cost of $82.2 million. That spring, HUD Secretary Patricia Harris toured Essex Plaza, the largest rehabilitated apartment complex in Essex County, and termed it "the finest in the nation."

Critics could point out that such impressive change did little to relieve the persistent problem of jobs for minority workers, much less ease significantly the dire shortage of low-income and middle-income housing units. Business-related development most helped suburban commuters who streamed into the city. The college/university complex on the hill, with the exception of Essex Community College, most benefited teaching staffs and students who lived beyond city limits. Essex Community

This ad, reproduced as it appeared in Metro-Newark! *magazine, summarized 10 remarkable years of post-riot growth. The captions, albeit small, told of private and public building in a city whose death was prematurely reported.*

A message for those who think Newark died 10 years ago.

The next time someone tells you that Newark suffered mortal damage from the riots of 1967, show them this. None of the developments pictured here or listed below were in existence ten years ago. All were completed, and nearly all were started, since July, 1967. These tangible steps forward stand as dramatic testimony to our city's spirit and its superior location. They stand also as a promise of a new and great era for the Newark of tomorrow.

Passenger terminal at $500 million Newark International Airport.

$11 million in modernized facilities have been added to St. Michael's Hospital.

$200 million New Jersey College of Medicine and Dentistry covers 47 acres.

$2.3 million Serta Mattress Co. plant in Industrial Meadowlands.

United Hospitals of Newark has added $17 million in new facilities.

18-story Blue Cross-Blue Shield building in downtown Newark.

13-story jail and 14-floor courthouse valued at $23 million are part of Essex County Courthouse complex.

$60 million Gateway Complex includes 30-story office tower, 18-story Western Electric building and 10-story Downtowner Hotel.

Rutgers University has added $16 million in new construction including business administration and law school facilities.

University Court has 270 garden apartment units.

Beth Israel Hospital has constructed over $32 million in new facilities.

$10 million in new construction at N.J. Institute of Technology includes Tiernan Memorial Hall.

$31 million Essex County College accommodates 12,000 students.

206 units for the elderly are in James C. White Manor.

Seton Hall University's $4 million School of Law accommodates 500 students.

To-Sault's townhouse-styled homes comprise 422 units.

Ideal Toy Corporation's 1 million sq. ft. plant in Industrial Meadowlands, valued at over $20 million.

Since 1967, more than 6,000 housing units have been constructed in the city and more than $100 million in industrial-commercial development has taken place.

In addition to the development pictured here, the decade's commercial/industrial construction has included new or expanded facilities for Holiday Inn, J. Wiss & Sons, Vita Food Products, Jersey Millwork, Circle Air Freight, Englehard Industries, Krementz Jewelers and others.

Columbus Hospital added $7 million in new facilities not shown here.

In addition to three housing complexes pictured above, new housing construction included Hill Manor, Brick Towers, High Park Gardens (two sections), Mount Calvary Homes (two sections), Clinton Hill Area Redevelopment Corporation, New Hope Village, Court Street Apartments, St. James Washington Street Apartments, and high-rise housing for the elderly at Kretchmer Homes, Seth Boyden Homes, Stephen Crane Village and Baxter Terrace.

Greater Newark Chamber of Commerce and Newark Redevelopment and Housing Authority

College was committed to Newark in every way.

Newark was still in desperate trouble. The litany of weaknesses had become almost tedious clichés—crime, unemployment, a woeful school system, a towering tax rate made worse by large masses of real estate either non-taxed or given tax abatement. The administration could not deliver basic services without forever teetering on the brink of bankruptcy.

Dr. Ralph J. Caprio, Rutgers University specialist in urban affairs, irked city officials—and his university administration—in March 1978 by predicting that Newark would be bankrupt by 1982. This impending calamity, he wrote, would be a benefit because bankruptcy would force the state to assume the cost of running the city. Bankruptcy would also have, according to Caprio, the salutary effect of focusing on all urban problems in the state.

Gibson immediately responded. He disputed the bankruptcy claim, pointing out that Newark "has a balanced budget, does not use bonds for operating expenses and is not buried beneath a mountain of short-term debt." Rutgers officials defended Caprio's right to express his views, even as they backed away from his pronouncements.

Caprio's pessimism was not without reason. The city desperately needed more income. Many of the amenities—city, county and federal buildings; colleges and universities; parks; the museum and the library—were real liabilities when it came time to balance the city budget. None paid any taxes, yet all required city services at city expense. Every property owner, major businesses and small home owners alike, staggered under the weight of playing host to tax-free entities that constituted about two-thirds of all the city.

One reason for doubting Newark's ability to rise was the abundance of weed-infested, garbage-strewn, vacant land and abandoned, collapsing buildings, nagging reminders of once viable neighborhoods. If all of those destroyed neighborhoods had not been prosperous or handsome, at least they had their own identities and gave order and meaning to people who resided in them. Now many such vanished neighborhoods were city-owned, tax-free legacies of the "bulldoze only" practice of urban renewal travesties.

Especially sad were the large numbers of shuttered small neighborhood stores, shattered homes, and ravaged small apartment buildings. They stood as monuments to a place gone mad, their windows smashed, doors agape or missing, interiors gutted. Derelicts or drug dealers might lurk in such places, threatening danger to anyone who lived nearby. These structures were nearly all city properties, acquired when owners had been permitted to abdicate without either paying back taxes or leaving forwarding addresses.

The most visible, most controversial and most distressing city properties were the huge high-rise public housing projects. Their appalling decline was a triple indictment of neglect by the Newark Housing Authority, of those who had criminally vandalized the structures, and of successive city administrations that had never acted vigorously to protect either the buildings or the tenants.

Three decades before, the towering projects were a pride of Newark. Thirty-seven of the high-rises had been built before the last was completed in 1963. Sociologists reasoned that by piling housing units atop one another they would create open, park-like inner courtyards for resident enjoyment. None of the planners ever expected to live in the projects.

The well-meant concept failed abominably. Corridors were narrow. Elevators often malfunctioned, a disastrous condition in any highrise. Instead of havens for the oppressed, the projects became breeding grounds for crime, often committed against the apartments themselves when tenants or interlopers ripped out plumbing, light fixtures, and other materials for resale.

The 1967 riots had begun outside one of the crowded projects, the Hayes Homes near Springfield Avenue, and had swirled outward from there. National Guard and police bombardments against supposed "snipers" had hastened the blight. Northward, the Columbus Homes project was a monstrous "billboard" that daily advertised both the failure of such public housing and the inability or unwillingness of the city to face up to what was probably its most pressing problem—a paucity of decent low-cost

Columbus Towers in the northern part of the city, heralded as fine public housing when built 25 years before, were a distressing eyesore by 1985. Five of the high-rises were boarded shut, a glaring indictment of everything wrong with public housing.

housing in nearly all wards.

Each day hundreds of thousands of out-of-town people saw the astonishingly ravaged Columbus Homes, visible from Interstate Route 280 or from trains that paused in the former Erie-Lackawanna Railroad station on North Broad Street. No amount of propaganda about progress could overcome the sight of buildings with smashed windows, open to breezes and vandals alike. By 1985, five of the eight Columbus high-rises were boarded shut, squeezing occupants down into the remaining structures.

The high-rise failures were a paradox in a city desperately in need of all kinds of housing —low-cost, moderate and upper level. It was estimated that in 1980 approximately 28,000 people lived in subsidized Newark Housing Authority projects (not all high-rise). Thousands more yearned to get in because of the low rents. About twenty-five per cent of the city's people either lived in public housing or wished they could.

Heralded transportation "improvements" such as the interstate highways of the 1960s and 1970s inflicted additional deep wounds on Newark neighborhoods. Route 78 to the south cut a swath through homes and apartments in the once-proud Weequahic section. Route 280

Critics of federal interstate highways could find Exhibit A in Route 280. It paralleled the tracks of the once-proud Erie-Lackawanna Railroad, cut the northern part of the city off from the southern half and made a mockery of the city's history by edging close to the Plume House built in 1710 and the old House of Prayer church. Similarly, Route 78 in the southern part of the city cut a broad swath through one of the city's finest residential neighborhoods. Interstates were little boon to Newark; they served mainly to accommodate those who had fled or hoped to flee from the city.

sliced asunder good neighborhoods in the northern part of the city. Worse, the interstates served essentially to whisk suburbanites to and from city jobs and college campuses, pushing farther west the outer bounds for those who would flee the city.

Image was much on Gibson's mind in 1978 when he sought an unprecedented third term. Although he did not mention the publication by name, the sting of the 1975 *Harper's Magazine* indictment was evident in Gibson's campaign declaration that "nobody knows which city will be 'best' or 'worst' on the next computer printout."

Gibson said he could seek a third term with pride. Newark, he insisted, had a reduced crime rate, a reduced infant mortality, increased economic development and increased state and federal aid. He declared: "Knowledgeable people no longer 'knock' Newark, and who would take the unknowledgeable seriously?" Newark was not beyond trouble, Gibson agreed, tempering that by saying ambiguously that "all cities are in trouble."

Gibson easily trounced a field of five little-known candidates, capturing seventy per cent of all votes cast. He became the first three-term mayor since Newark changed its form of government from commission to mayor-council.

Post-election hurrahs were muted. Potential deficits dogged the city treasury, leading Gibson to announce late in 1978 that as many as 2,000 city workers, including 200 policemen, must be laid off to reduce the cost of running the city. Police retaliated in a rebellious campaign, featuring pamphlets that warned people to leave the city before dark, to keep their doors locked and "if attacked, scream loud."

Mayor Gibson aggressively sought a fourth term in 1980. Here he campaigned in James Street, a major hope for inner city restoration. David G. Rinsky, left, head of community relations at Prudential and a leader in the James Street Project, introduced the mayor.

That blow at the city's image by those sworn to protect it was nearly matched by a City Council resolution on July 12 that raised Gibson's salary from $32,588 to $52,500 and council salaries from $16,538 to $27,500. The handsome raises did not square with the projected layoffs. Pleas by city officials that they deserved the raises fell on deaf ears. A special referendum in November brought overwhelming public disapproval of the raises and forced their cancellation.

Money problems intensified early in 1980. Although rigid restrictions on spending cut a proposed budget from $246 million to $237 million, Newark's taxes were projected to rise sharply. The budget paring and higher taxes reflected an increasing amount of nontaxable property—buildings and sites claimed by the city from tax delinquents as well as a proliferation of tax-free county, state and federal properties.

Progress seemed agonizingly slow as Gibson sought his fourth term in 1982. He faced his greatest challenge to date, for Council President Earl Harris had decided to run for mayor. Harris, popular, dedicated and experienced, had a public record of commitment to civil rights and social change, dating to the early 1960s when he journeyed to Selma, Alabama, to help start a voter registration drive headed by Dr. Martin Luther King, Jr.

Both Gibson and Harris began their campaigns under a cloud. Late in 1981 newspapers headlined a charge that former Councilman Michael A. Bontempo, eighty years old, director of security at the Newark-owned Pequannock Watershed, had seldom visited the site since he had been given the job in 1974, when he was denied reelection to the council. Records showed that Bontempo lived in Florida and had his checks ($24,255 annually) sent there. His dilatory performance was cast into sharp focus in the spring of 1981 when a group of suburban youths vandalized water pumps, threatening Newark's water supply.

Ironically, Bontempo had been no friend or political ally of either Gibson or Harris. Rather, he had opposed most of Gibson's early efforts. Quite routinely, in the time-honored political practice of rewarding "the faithfuls,"

Bontempo received the Pequannock appointment after not seeking re-election at the polls. Gibson later called it "a perk" (perquisite) for a man who has served the city in public office for forty years.

An Essex County Grand Jury did not sympathize with such largess, however customary. Gibson, Harris and Bontempo were indicted on April 1, 1982, on a wide variety of counts that included conspiracy and misconduct in office. It seemed to be 1970 all over again, with one important difference: Mayor Hugh Addonizio and his co-defendants had been charged with blatant crimes committed to enrich themselves; Gibson and Harris were charged with what most officeholders consider a "crime of the heart"—trying to ease an aged politician through his waning years. That had been as common in Republican-dominated Morris County or Democrat-ruled Hudson as it was in Newark.

The three other candidates in the race gained hope from the woes of Gibson and Harris, but Gibson led all candidates in the vote on May 11. Still, his four opponents, including Harris, gained more than fifty per cent of the votes to force a runoff between Gibson and Harris. The mayor narrowly won his fourth term, 29,284 to 26,594.

Gibson and Harris went on trial on September 11. The case against the Newark officials was diluted when the prosecution rested its case on October 13 by admitting that some of its witnesses may have lied. Five days later, Judge Paul R. Huot dismissed all counts but two, conspiracy and misconduct. The jury found Harris not guilty on both counts and ruled Gibson not guilty of conspiracy. The panel could not reach a unanimous verdict on the misconduct charge against Gibson.

Essex County Prosecutor George L. Schneider asked that all charges against Gibson and Bontempo be dropped. New Jersey Superior Court Judge Nicholas Scalera complied on October 25. Bontempo was free to return to Florida, officially retired. Harris could return to the City Council. Gibson could take up again the compounding problems of his city, assured that Newark was on the threshold of a remarkable rebirth of both prosperity and confidence.

Newark's future is reflected most brightly in the 26-story Public Service Electric & Gas Company building, fronting on an inviting plaza where varied entertainers offer a welcome to the city.

Chapter 30

UP FROM "NOWHERE"

"**W**hat would New York be without the Diors? Newark!"

So read an advertisement that the exclusive Christian Dior fashion house had been contemplating in the early summer of 1982. Its existence was "leaked" to East Ward Councilman Henry Martinez, who led the outraged City Council in demanding an apology, a demand backed by an unlikely ally, *The New York Times.* Seldom given to praising Newark, *The Times* commented on its editorial page that the Dior ad, if run, would place Newark on the list of synonyms for "nowhere."

Dior hastily retreated, first vigorously denying that it ever intended to run the slur, then expressing regrets for an ad that it said it never would use. A Dior executive visited the City Council in September, apologizing in public and sweetening the apology by presenting a one-year scholarship to a senior student at Newark Arts High School.

The potential Dior advertisement was not the worst of slurs that Newark had endured. But the entire incident symbolized the changes stirring within the city. Ten years before, the city administration would have feared even more snickering if it had protested. In 1982 the city was fighting back.

As Gibson began his fourth term, Newark was like a shackled, tattered and beaten giant that had awakened after more than two decades of dreadful nightmares. The awakening was not a roaring, upward leap that broke the bonds of inferiority, but rather an alternating yawning and dozing, a stretching and a slow staggering to an uncertain standing position, always slowed by a desire to sleep again.

Downtown, the city's economic spine grew stronger. The Prudential began Gateway III, an eighteen-story, $64.5 million structure next to its predecessors near Penn Station. Public Service Electric & Gas Company reaffirmed its city ties with a new twenty-six story glass-walled tower. Northward on Broad Street, both Mutual Benefit Life Insurance Company and New Jersey Bell Telephone Company were ready to occupy impressive new structures.

Military Park, training ground for the colonial militia and now the roof of a multi-level parking garage, was to be refurbished with nearly $1 million in city funds. Several buildings near the park were being remodeled, most notably the old Griffith Building on Broad Street, for years the home of a famous organ manufacturer.

Renaissance Newark Corporation, established by business leaders, joined the Newark Economic Development Council in extolling downtown progress. Still, serious doubts persisted among Newark watchers as to whether downtown buildings alone could revive the city. Too many remembered the 1950s and 1960s when a similar rash of building had mesmerized the city into unjustified enthusiasm.

Critics, ranging from urban scholars to neighborhood leaders, argued that the downtown towers mainly benefited suburbanites who used Newark only to earn wages or turn a corporate profit. Cultural and higher-educational institutions, except for Essex County Community College, had decidedly suburban orientations. By night and on weekends, downtown was deserted. A Sunday morning in the commercial district was a time of nearly vacant streets, of uncanny quiet, of old newspapers blowing in the wind.

Transportation facilities most often were cited as the key to Newark's recovery. Gateway's proximity to Penn Station certainly took fullest advantage of the excellent railroad operations.

An elevated passageway linked Gateway buildings with Penn Station's train and bus platforms, protecting commuters from the elements and shielding them from contact with the city.

The location also offered a subtle benefit for timid out-of-towners who worked in the buildings. They would be protected from the elements; they also could avoid contact with the city itself.

Gustav Heningburg, long one of the city's most respected leaders and one of its most articulate critics, questioned at ceremonies opening Gateway III whether new buildings would give long-frustrated Newark residents the work opportunities that they so desperately needed. "The people who live in this city helped to underwrite the subsidies through tax abatements," Heningburg noted. "Employment opportunities must be closely watched."

The main benefit from the burst of building activity would be a dramatic rise in tax receipts. Gateway III alone would generate $1.3 million annually in new tax revenues. That encouraging gain was offset by a complicated tax-abatement agreement intended to encourage private construction. The abatement undoubtedly was necessary, but the fullest tax benefits stood to be long delayed.

The 1967 disorders had ended several generations of dependence on small neighborhood shops and services along most streets in the riot areas. The shops had been modest, struggling little "mom and pop" enterprises for the most part, usually with high prices, but neighborhood people at least did not need an automobile to get a quart of milk or a loaf of bread. Nearly all of the shops were closed soon after the riots.

The disorientation and frustration of people in "non-neighborhoods" was expressed in the summer of 1980 by Carol Whitley, an employee of the Board of Education and chairperson of the Central Ward's Community Advisory Council. Whitley was responding to a proposal to rehabilitate 200 units of housing in the Central Ward, supported with a $5 million underwriting by the Prudential Insurance Company.

Some of the rehabilitated houses would be sold, with federal underwriting; others would be rented, some with and some without federal support. Whitley's group feared the proposal might become "just another subsidized housing project." Explaining that she had grown up in the neighborhood, Whitley expressed concern that current residents would be forced to move out. She looked back to her own days of growing up there: "It was a vital neighborhood and offered many services to the people. I want to see it return to those days."

It was more than nostalgia. Nearly everyone residing in blighted areas feared that housing proposals without community input might lead to units priced far beyond the reach of many area residents. Large block sales of city-owned property to the highest bidder could make redevelopment a quick and cold business, with no regard for those who really wanted to live in the city because it long had been their "neighborhood."

Decent educational opportunity was another city-wide concern. Newark's educational system had been a political football for decades. The Governor's commission report on the 1967 riots severely criticized the schools. Howard J. Ashby, then president of the Board of Education, responded, "There isn't anyone, professional or otherwise, who can say we are doing a good job, because our children just can't read and do arithmetic . . . . We are going to have to call a sharp halt to all of the camouflage."

The Governor's commission concluded bluntly: "The Newark Public School system is in a state of educational crisis. This crisis demands that the State take over the administration of the Newark public schools during the crisis."

Persistent school deterioration led to a May 1982 referendum offering voters the opportunity to change the Board of Education from one appointed entirely by the mayor to one chosen in city-wide voting. In a very low voter turnout, the change was approved; hopes were high that the radical change might be the means of preventing a state takeover.

Fewer than three per cent of eligible voters cared enough in April 1983 to vote for the first education officials elected since 1908. At the same time, that handful of voters rejected a budget requiring the city to provide $50.1 million to the schools, Newark's taxpayers' portion of the $229 million annual budget. The rest was supplied by state or federal allocations.

A firsthand look at the squalid educational conditions was offered in a tour of city schools in November 1983, conducted by Executive Superintendent of Schools Columbus Salley. The tour was part of an effort to whip up support for a $62.6 million capital improvement bond package that would be put before voters on December 6.

Salley's fast-moving group went from Lafayette Street School to Science High School, from Broadway Elementary School to Weequahic High School and finally to Fifteenth Avenue School. Salley could not be accused of seeking out only the worst. Nearly all city schools were

blighted and old; the average age of Newark's ninety schools was seventy-two years. Salley believed it would take at least $500 million to bring city schools up to acceptable standards.

Angry residents protested as new members of the Newark School Board were sworn in on April 10, 1984. Many swarmed near the board table to shout complaints; others were more passive, letting signs express dissatisfaction.

The touring group included a reporter for *The Star-Ledger*. He wrote of badly-leaking roofs, falling plaster and asbestos-covered piping. He saw windows so rusted that they could not be opened. In one school, a locker room could not be used because live steam gushed from an exposed pipe. At Weequahic High School, once one of the nation's foremost academic-oriented public secondary institutions, 2,100 students were crammed into a facility designed for 1,400. It was never so in the days of Weequahic's greatness.

School conditions had been worsening for so long that a jaundiced view permeated even editorial desks. *The Star-Ledger* gave the story modest exposure on page thirty-seven; in most cities the story would have been bannered on page one. In fairness, *The Star-Ledger* supported the bond referendum and gave it good coverage, certainly enough to hope for a solid voter turnout.

The December 6 referendum was the first time in three quarters of a century that Newark voters had a chance to voice an opinion on school construction. An overwhelming majority had not the slightest interest. Only 1.3 per cent of 109,000 eligible voters bothered to record any opinion at the fifteen polling areas. Those voting favored the bond package, 1,047 to 357.

Salley was able to find a bright ray of hope despite the distressing lack of interest: "I'm very pleased that almost 1,500 voters came out to vote 3 to 1 to affirm what we feel is important for Newark education."

Twenty million dollars were allocated for a new high school in the West Ward and $8 million went for rehabilitation of Arts High School, including an addition. Most of the rest was scattered throughout city schools for a wide variety of purposes. However, the board had thoughtfully set aside $12 million to build a new headquarters for itself and its staff.

Citizen disinterest supplied further impetus in the early 1980s to the urging by Governor Kean that the state take over the city's schools and operate them until all students were assured of a quality education, an echo of the nearly forgotten Governor's commission report. Kean cited poor performance on standardized state tests, a high dropout rate and a demon-strably poor educational climate in the city's schools. The proposal met considerable opposition from the educational community and from some parents and school administrators. Opponents charged, among other things, that the move was racially motivated.

Coalition Six, a civic organization in the Central Ward, struck hard at the educational system in a wide-ranging manifesto in April 1985. Declaring that the Newark schools "are worse off than before the riots of 1967," the coalition called for "new and inventive approaches to teaching and learning techniques." It added: "Two generations of young people have been lost .... The Newark public education system is a system that has gone bad."

Who was at fault—politicians, teachers, parents, the city, the state? The coalition did not care: "Regardless of who is to blame, the present education system is in need of complete overhauling."

Some public schools continued to maintain quality in the face of increasing difficulties, but there was general agreement that sweeping changes were needed to lift the quality of city schools. Some middle-class parents moved out, hoping for a better classroom climate. Others sent their children to private schools, mainly Catholic run, in the belief that they offered superior educational advantages.

An especially heart-warming story was the rebirth of St. Benedict's Preparatory School on riot-torn Martin Luther King Boulevard. Founded in 1868, St. Benedict's had served successive generations of sons of German, Irish and Italian immigrants. In the 1960s the school had begun to seek black and Hispanic students. After the riots, enrollment declined and the school was closed in 1972.

St. Benedict's was dead, except for a handful of monks of the Newark Abbey who stayed to help the city. They reopened the school in 1973 with fewer than 100 students. By 1984 St. Benedict's had 370 students, sixty per cent black and fourteen per cent Hispanic. Eighty per cent went on to higher education. St. Benedict's fit that old cliché, "poor but proud," at home in one of the city's most depressed areas.

In October 1984 Robert Brennan of Brielle, a St. Benedict's alumnus and chairman of First

Construction proceeded briskly at St. Benedict's Academy on Martin Luther King Boulevard, thanks to a $5 million grant from Robert Brennan, wealthy financier and St. Benedict's alumnus. The academy had closed its doors briefly after the riots, but a few priests who stayed in place reopened the school as proof that fine education could prosper in the inner city.

Jersey Securities, gave school administrators a check for five million dollars. Although Brennan had graduated from the school in 1962 and had generously supported the school after its reopening, he had never indicated that he would make what was believed to be the largest lump sum donation ever given to an American private secondary school.

Higher education contrasted sharply with the city's public schools. All five campuses prospered. Rutgers and Essex County College served area students well. Seton Hall's law school had grown so prestigious that by 1986 a glut of students forced the school to consider relocating its facility.

The College of Medicine and Dentistry, demonstrating its willingness and capability to improve city health protection as well as its ability to educate doctors and dentists, became a full-fledged university on December 10, 1981. Four years later the University of Medicine and Dentistry added its nationally acclaimed Center for Molecular Medicine.

Most startling was New Jersey Institute of Technology (NJIT). Founded in 1883 with private donations of $4,583 and a city grant of $500, Newark Technical Institute became Newark College of Engineering in 1919 and New Jersey Institute of Technology on January 1, 1975. NJIT's new name designated both its statewide stature and its adaptations to a modern, highly technical society.

Because of its broadened curriculum, its expanding campus and the influx of significant state aid, NJIT properly might better have been named New Jersey *University* of Technology. The proud old institution, long a solid, respected educator of engineers, took a quantum leap forward in 1983, when state voters approved a multi-million-dollar Jobs, Science and Technology bond issue. Much of the money went to NJIT, making "New Jersey Tech" a center for research in toxic wastes, for computer-integrated manufacturing and for "information age" technology. Added dimensions were a new school of architecture and continued growth in its fine undergraduate engineering curriculum.

The old Newark College of Engineering often had been dismissed as "a footnote in higher education" because state legislators were more readily influenced by Rutgers and UMDNJ spokesmen than by the engineering school's pleas for help. NJIT now stood tall among its state neighbors. Rutgers University to the east and the University of Medicine and Dentistry of New Jersey (UMDNJ) to the west.

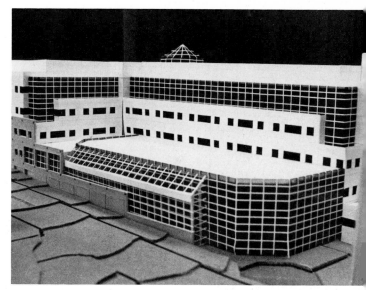

Newark's emergence as one of the nation's foremost urban college-university complexes verges on the incredible. Ground was broken in 1987 for the $27.5 million Information Technologies Building (model shown above) at N.J. Institute of Technology, merely one facet of NJIT's surge to state and national attention. Seton Hall University Law School, left, close to the city's rising glass towers, has expanded rapidly since being founded in Newark in 1951. Below, the University of Medicine and Dentistry of New Jersey is an impressive, vital part of Newark.

On the opposite page, top left, Essex Community College has provided opportunity for thousands of students to begin college educations. Rutgers University, top right, is expanding its substantial campus up the hill from University Avenue.

Southward, Newark International Airport and Port Newark were so massive and so successful that scorners of the city usually forgot that these were major segments of "nowhere." There had been several moves in the state legislature to change the airport name, one such change to honor Woodrow Wilson, the Princeton University president and New Jersey Governor who became a United States President. That easily was turned aside by Newark indignation.

Both the port and the airport were almost insular kingdoms within themselves, run by the Port Authority of New York and New Jersey, which each year paid Newark a modest fee for the privilege of controlling about one-fifth of the city's area. Interstate 78, the New Jersey Turnpike, a myriad of other intersecting major highways, and the old Pennsylvania Railroad embankment cut the airport and port off from Newark, with a semi-moat of dirty marshland adding to the isolation.

Newark Airport in 1987 was the seventh busiest air facility in the world and had taken the metropolitan New York passenger leadership away from Kennedy International Airport. That was in good measure due to the meteoric rise of People Express, the "no-frills" airline, founded in 1980. Nearly thirty million passengers used Newark Airport in 1986.

People Express soared brilliantly, at first. Its appeal to a so-called "backpacker" constituency kept its planes filled with passengers lured by advertised fares as low as $19 to Washington or $49 to Florida. The boom burst in January 1987 when People Express declared bankruptcy. Newark Airport traffic fell twenty-one per cent in the first nine months of 1987, dropping behind not only Kennedy but LaGuardia as well.

Newark Airport surged into first place among New York area airports in 1986, thanks largely to the phenomenal success of People Express, pioneer in "no frills" fares to many destinations. "Backpackers" eagerly bought tickets for Florida, Washington and elsewhere. Early in 1987 People Express declared bankruptcy; passenger traffic through Newark Airport fell 21 per cent in nine months.

355

Freight shippers also streamed to Newark Airport. Seven all-cargo airlines landed and departed from the runways, including United Parcel Service and Federal Express. In 1986, air freight was up to 299,000 tons and still soaring. That year, more than 41,000 tons of air mail (1.2 billion one-ounce letters) cleared the runway.

Cheek-by-jowl with Newark Airport lay Port Newark, one of the most flexible multi-purpose cargo centers in the United States. It was best known as part of the Newark-Elizabeth port complex, the international leader in containerized shipping. Additionally, Port Newark could expedite any import or export, from automobiles to bananas. It handled almost anything with practiced ease, whether it was frozen foods or gypsum; one facility could blend and store 6.5 million gallons of Brazilian orange concentrate. Port Newark's efficiency tended to obscure its greatness.

The usefulness of the airport and port to Newark's economy was diminished by the protracted, stubborn refusal of both the Port Authority and the State of New Jersey to build a direct link between the city and the airport. Various projects had been "studied" for at least three decades, all revolving around Penn Station. All proposals had been given short shrift

Port Newark (above), part of the Newark-Elizabeth complex, could expedite any kind of import or export, from automobiles to orange juice. Immediately to the west lay Newark International Airport (below), a world leader whose ability to handle jet air traffic far exceeded its ability to handle mounting automobile traffic that jammed parking lots.

despite the benefits that would accrue to the city, the state, and the Port Authority. By 1985, the link was at least three decades overdue.

The Port Authority remained convinced that automobiles and buses could best service the airport. It announced in 1986 that another 10,000 parking spaces would be added in the "next few years" to its existing (and usually full) 20,569 berths at Newark Airport. The impact of another 10,000 automobiles on a region already choked by traffic snarls seemed to mean little to the agency.

The Port Authority took sudden interest in Newark in 1983, motivated by the insistence of both Governor Thomas Kean of New Jersey and Governor Mario Cuomo of New York that the body become as aware of the cities that served it as it was in tolls collected on the bridges and tunnels that crossed the Hudson River. Much of that toll money had gone into the World Trade Center. The time had come for the agency to consider similar help for Newark.

Under reordered Port Authority priorities, about $1 billion would be pumped into New Jersey. Newark would be a major beneficiary. A grant of $300 million was assigned for a Newark-based incinerator to handle Essex County garbage. Another $120 million was slated for downtown planning and development. The latter windfall was announced late in June 1983, triggering enthusiastic hopes for the city's revival.

The timing was nearly perfect. Only six months before, Renaissance Newark had commissioned the American City Corporation to develop plans for the Passaic River waterfront north of Penn Station. The first phase of the report centered on a choice twelve-acre triangular plot, near Penn Station and bounded by McCarter Highway, Raymond Boulevard and the river.

The Authority incorporated essentials of the American City Corporation report into its recommendations. Forty million dollars was committed for a multi-story office building plus an underwriting of site preparation and utility improvements for the rest of the section. Plans included an office building, erected with Authority funds; a "world class hotel;" a conven-

tion/exhibition center of 50,000 square feet; parking lots and considerable open space.

The seventeen-story central building would be a legal and communications center, intended to stem the flow of prestigious law firms from the city. Lawyers could buy condominium space, an attractive tax break. The projected $40 million Port Authority contribution would be augmented by a $9.8 million federal grant to construct a 525-car parking garage. When construction actually began in October 1987, close to the Gateway buildings and Penn Station, demands for space necessitated adding three more floors; the cost had risen from $40 million to $43 million.

The condominium tax break was not the sole attraction. Law firms would be linked by fiber optic cable to a teleport that the Port Authority planned to construct on Staten Island, giving firms instant access to advanced world communications via satellites. Seven floors of condominiums were sold before the traditional ground-breaking.

Philip D. Kaltenbacher, chairman of the Port of New York and New Jersey Authority, studying artist's rendition of the landmark Legal and Communications Center designed to provide state-of-the-art backup for lawyers. Scheduled to be 17 stories tall, it was increased to 20 floors to meet the demand for legal space.

357

Mayor Gibson took the wraps off his University Heights proposal on October 3, 1985. It included 1,000 acres, mostly in riot-scarred sections of the city. The imaginative plan was generally well received although opposed by some who felt it offered too little to other neighborhoods.

Riverfront development had exciting potential, as it had in Jersey City and Hoboken. True, there was no close view of New York's skyline, although the truncated towers of Manhattan easily could be seen from the banks of the Passaic. More important, Newark's riverfront was close to Penn Station and the hundreds of trains headed daily for both downtown and uptown New York. As real estate in the "Big Apple" was priced out of the market, it did not take a high-priced consultant to show that middle-priced and high-priced housing could prosper along with offices beside Newark's long-neglected waterway.

Such riverfront housing was part of the broad economic base needed for the city's comeback. The appeal of high-priced living quarters was startlingly demonstrated on June 13, 1986, when 131 residential condominiums went on sale in the old *Newark News* building on Market Street, close to the Gateway Complex. The units ranged in size from 550 square feet to

more than 2,000 square feet and varied in price from $60,000 to $325,000. All were sold within thirty-six hours. A bonus for the city was $350,000 in new tax revenues.

Regardless of how new taxes and high-priced condominiums might be trumpeted, Newark's major problem was how to develop the western and southern parts of the city without bringing traumatic harm to the many thousands of current city residents living close to or beneath poverty levels. Estimates indicated that as many as 100,000 persons—one third of the city's population—might be involved.

Especially disturbing was an area named "University Heights," an irritating eyesore near the ever-broadening higher educational complex. Much of the area had borne the brunt of the 1967 riots; nearly all was either blighted or reaching that stage. In any other city, this would have been prime real estate, bedecked with university-oriented housing and shopping areas.

Failure to transform such depressed areas was often cited by those who charged that the Gibson administration lacked imagination and vision. Finally, in October 1985, the mayor unveiled a University Heights development plan that was nothing if not imaginative and innovative. It encompassed 1,000 acres ranging westward from University Avenue to 12th Street, southward from Route 280 to 15th Avenue.

About half of the 1,000 acres north and west of the university complex was to be "stabilized" by improving what was already there. Higher educational facilities would take up another twenty-five per cent, leaving the rest for housing or retail establishments. A supermarket and supporting mall were proposed for South Orange Avenue near Bergen Street. Another twenty-five-acre retail area was planned for the triangular intersection of South Orange Avenue and Springfield Avenue.

More than seventy-five per cent of the "Heights" land proposed for new housing already was owned by the city or other public agencies, assuring that it would be easy to make attractive plots available for private developers. According to Gibson, the plan would require relocation of fewer than 100 residents—critical in the light of the intense, understandable rage created by the 1967 arbitrary proposal to displace thousands of people for the College of Medicine and Dentistry.

Gibson conceded that the affected area was a "cauldron of controversy." The new plan was offered, he said, "to end those controversies and bring about genuine positive development by setting out a single, unified plan that is responsive to the needs of the existing community, the institutions and the city's taxpayers and which provides a practical, yet significant, development which can be brought to fruition in a short term."

The plan was bold, yet within reach; imaginative yet practical. It stirred both enthusiasm and doubts within the neighborhoods. Central Ward City Councilman George Branch embraced the proposal: "It looks like it will be good for the Central Ward. It will clean up the area and make the ward look better. . . . If the plan provides housing and jobs, I think it's good for the city."

West Ward Councilman Ronald Rice spoke in opposition: "The concepts ignore the needs of 10,000 residents who live in the gray areas outside the project's boundaries." He argued that the proposal was put forth "without city council input or suggestions as to people's needs." Improving the Central Ward, Rice believed, was not feasible "when the community around it is decaying."

Saul Fenster, president of New Jersey Institute of Technology, had a double stake in the future of the plan. Any improvement in the region surrounding all of the higher-education campuses naturally would be cheered. Fenster also was prominent in and later became chairman of Newark Collaboration Group, organized in May 1984 to foster city growth and change.

One more group to herald Newark virtues could have been viewed by cynics as another self-serving, self-appointed business activity. The Collaboration sought to allay such doubts, although its genesis lay in Prudential Insurance Company leadership. There had to be assurance that this group was different, that it had broad representation, and that it was interested in all the city.

The Collaboration met for nearly a year without publicity or fanfare. When in March 1985 it announced its plans and dreams for a Newark comeback, it was buttressed by ten months of candid, if quasi-secret, discussion. The Collaboration sought to cut across a broad swath of the city—businesses, churches, administrators, and perhaps most important and most unusual, a genuine representation of community groups. This was unique; most previous "Better Newark" alliances had either ignored or refused to hear those who most suffered from the ills of the city. County Executive Peter Shapiro characterized the Collaboration as being "more from the bottom up than from the top down."

When the Collaboration finally went public, it had 172 members, a treasury of $200,000 and a director. Deeply-held disillusionments jarred early meetings, as was to be expected if this were indeed a widespread community effort. Central Ward doubts were expressed by an ad hoc Committee for University Heights, which refused to join in the early discussions. It sent the Collaboration a statement that was both comprehensive and eloquent in its direct simplicity:

"We are concerned that affordable housing will not be built in the inner city; that our tax-supported universities share responsibility for upgrading our public school system so that our youth will qualify for the high-tech jobs that will be developed throughout the city, and that minority and area businesses are provided an opportunity to participate in the economic growth that will result from investment in the area termed as 'University Heights.' "

Bluntly put, there was the issue that had plagued Newark (and most major cities) for decades: would minority groups, the most poverty striken, the most abused, the most ignored, have any say in reshaping a Newark of the future? The Collaboration Group, studying its own membership, found that fifty-three per cent of its 280 members were white, by no means a cross section of the city. The Collaboration necessarily had to strengthen black and Hispanic representation if its expressed goals were to be believed. That awareness of under-representation, as much as impressive new downtown buildings, larger campuses or a mighty airport, would determine whether Newark could sustain its rise.

Newark was recovering as winter turned to spring in 1986. Penn Station was a mere ten miles from New York City, where steeply mounting costs induced businesses to look at Newark and its two modern rail lines to Manhattan. Westward, traffic increasingly clogged highways, turning sour the lure of offices in former pastureland. Newark, with huge tracts of available land, looked enticing.

Gibson had ample reason to believe that

Leading candidates for mayor in 1986 were literally in the running. Mayor Gibson (right) was known for his jogging and marathon running. South Ward Councilman Sharpe James often appeared in public in a sweat suit. At a council meeting (left), he discussed icy city streets with Alvin Zach, director of engineering for the city.

voters would return him to office for a fifth term, although he expected South Ward City Councilman Sharpe James to be a formidable opponent in the May 1986 election. James had been part of city government since 1970, riding into the City Council as a Gibson supporter. His voting record had been very supportive of Gibson policies before a slow pulling away in about 1982.

James had taught in Newark at nearly every level. He had been on the faculty of Essex County College since 1968. In 1986, he was professor of education in the division of behavioral sciences. James' City Council colleagues considered him a maverick. He often heaped criticism on councilmen, even as he sought their aid for his own programs. When the council voted new cars for council members, James would not accept his. When the council pushed to raise its own salaries, James voted no.

He cared little for the trappings of office. An avid, practicing athlete, the tall, lean councilman often startled associates by appearing for meetings in tennis shorts or running clothes.

Physical fitness was a Gibson passion as well. Much in the way that he operated his office and his private life, the mayor preferred the lonely life of a long-distance runner. He jogged regularly in the city's parks or along city streets.

Gibson steadily repeated during the campaign that "Newark is no longer a terminal case." He reiterated his achievements: a revitalized downtown, more than 11,000 apartments built or rehabilitated for families and the elderly, greatly improved health care, a sharp decline in infant mortality and a drop in crime. "Newark is heading into a boom period," he told enthusiastic supporters. On the other hand, James replied, unemployment in the city hovered near twelve per cent, twice the state average; public housing was in disrepair, crime was still high.

Election day surprised Gibson. James won easily, getting fifty-five per cent of all votes cast, to forty per cent for Gibson and five per cent for other candidates. Two hours after the polls closed, Gibson went to his election headquarters at the Quality Inn on Park Place and

After his surprise victory over Gibson in 1986, mayor-elect Sharpe James and his family responded happily to the accolades of supporters. One lonely, grieving Gibson supporter summed up the story of defeat.

361

calmly told nearly 700 supporters; "I had written a victory speech but obviously I can't deliver it." He pledged to work closely with James to effect a smooth transition, told his supporters to "go on with the party," and left.

Gibson admirers recalled that sixteen years before, after his first successful election, the fledgling mayor had said: "If I leave Newark a little better than it was when I found it, I will have done what I expected to do." That wish was eclipsed. Gibson had brought stability, trust among business leaders and a rising optimism for Newark's revival. All of those he passed along; anyone who doubted his success did not remember 1970, much less 1967.

Perhaps most significantly, he had proven that a black mayor could be elected in a racially-torn city—and that he could govern effectively. James, in turn, had proved that black voters would turn out a black mayor if they felt he had overstayed his welcome.

The victorious James had no intention of undoing progress. Admirers predicted that he would "come out running" the day after his inauguration on July 1. He advanced the schedule by seven weeks, hitting the deck at full speed the day after his election. "I'm at my best under pressure," James told reporters. "It keeps me going."

Two weeks after the victory and five weeks before inauguration, James announced that Gustav Heningburg would head his transition team. Heningburg called the assignment "one of *déjà vu*." Indeed, he had performed in a similar capacity for Mayor Gibson in 1970. James' choice of a transition leader served notice that the mayor-elect was serious; Heningburg was noted for his keen intelligence and his fierce independence. It was said of him: "Wherever Gus sits is the head of the table."

The business community rallied around James. Prudential Insurance Company provided an acting business administrator, First Fidelity Bank an acting finance director and Riker, Danzig, one of the state's most prestigious law firms, gave extensive legal advice—all without charge. A fifty-five-member independent task force studied the adequacy of services and financial practices in all city departments.

The retiring mayor assisted in the transition, in marked contrast to the turbulent hostility that had greeted Gibson when he literally had to wrest City Hall from the Addonizio machine. Despite the cooperation, Gibson struck an especially crippling blow on the morning of James' inauguration.

As one of his last deeds as mayor, Gibson filled a crucial lone vacancy on the Newark Housing Authority. At one time the city's mayor named all seven housing commissioners, but in 1984 new rules gave the City Council five appointments, with one each to the governor and the mayor. The last-ditch Gibson appointment deprived James of any possible influence on the powerful Housing Authority.

James tried unsuccessfully to block the zero-hour appointment that robbed him of eyes and ears in public housing. He was equally power-

It was "déjà vu" for Gustav Heningburg when James chose him as transition chief. Gibson had asked him to do the same job in 1970. Intelligent, articulate and independent, Gus Heningburg had earned city-wide respect.

Mayor James proved to be a highly energetic mayor. As samples of his visibility, he is shown presenting a Distinguished Citizen Award to Edith Garcia at a salute to unsung heroes of the

Hispanic community; inspecting a deserted building on Mt. Pleasant Avenue with Councilman Ralph T. Grant, Jr.; and enthusiastically unfurling one of the Keep Newark Clean banners to be hung along Broad Street.

less regarding Board of Education policies; the board had been changed by city voters in 1982 from a body named completely by the mayor to one elected by citizens. If Newark's administration could be considered a three-legged stool— housing, education and all other governmental services—James perched precariously on one leg.

The city resounded on inauguration day to James' upbeat, evangelical acceptance speech. Addressing an enthusiastic crowd at Symphony Hall, he warned that City Hall "will function as a business and not as a social or political club." He demanded "a proper dress code, good telephone manners and sound, courteous relations with the public." It really was not too much to ask.

James also sounded another rallying cry—the need for every person to help: "Too many individuals are experiencing an ethical collapse, a spiritual withdrawal, and escaping reality through drugs, alcohol, sex-without-love, making unwanted babies and turning on one another with violence. Without one additional federal dollar we can sweep in front of our

WELCOME HOME
★ ★ ★ HONORABLE ★ ★ ★
MAYOR DAVE SMITH
OF NEWARK, CALIFORNIA
OCT. 20, 1987
NEWARK LOVES YOU!

Mayor Dave Smith of Newark, California, third largest of the 12 Newarks in the United States, "returned home" in October 1987 to be made an honorary citizen of the New Jersey Newark, largest of all its namesakes. All of the other Newarks were named for the town established along the Passaic River in 1666.

Smith visited Newark in response to an invitation from Mayor Sharpe James, who in September had attended a gathering of all Newarks in Smith's town of 37,000 people. At the time, the western city was considering a name change to Newark-By-The-Bay in the hope of "improving its image." The notion was rejected.

Newark, South Dakota, with a population of one, is the smallest of the 12 Newarks. Second largest is Newark, Ohio. On his visit here, Smith said all Newarks were "cousins." He noted that all of the Newarks (except in South Dakota) had similar problems in schools, garbage, pollution and housing.

homes. Without one federal dollar we can clean our vacant lots."

The next day, his wife, Mary Mattison James, came to City Hall with flats of flowers. She planted them around City Hall in symbolic representation of what an individual might do. Inside, the new mayor began tackling immense problems that would not be swept away by a rising tide of hope.

The overwhelming burden of tax inequities was addressed by East Ward Councilman Henry Martinez after he was chosen as Council President on July 1, the first Hispanic to head the council. He told an interviewer:

"The reality is that almost seventy per cent of Newark is tax exempt. . . . These things the mayor must assess with his administration heads—to keep taxes at a reasonable level and to maintain services that people are entitled to. The people will be watching, as they watched Mayor Gibson."

James knew that the watchers would not be as patient as they had been with Gibson. He set out on a sprint, rising at 5:00 A.M. and putting in long days at City Hall. He tried to see everyone, tried to listen, to read his mail, to cut ribbons at the opening of buildings, to talk with school pupils, to see any developer who had a plan for a better Newark, to meet with business and community leaders. If Gibson had been a tortoise, as detractors had insisted, James was off at a hare's pace.

Another human whirlwind hit town less than three weeks after James' inauguration. He was Harry Grant of Englewood Cliffs (nicknamed "Hurricane Harry"), an Iraqi-born builder of homes and a developer of huge malls and office complexes. Grant held Newark and a wide segment of the media enthralled for two months with visions that could not be ignored, even if at times they might be doubted.

First, on July 17, Grant bought at public auction the abandoned, city-owned former Central Railroad of New Jersey station on Broad Street. He paid $1.2 million for about 106,000 square feet of land and office space, a considerable bargain because of the choice center-city location. Grant's purchase put the property back on the tax rolls.

Grant told reporters that he planned to build a bi-level $12 to $13 million shopping mall, featuring restaurants, "exquisite" boutiques, jewelers and other small stores to be occupied by "nationally-known" retailers. He estimated that the 60,000-square-foot mall would create 200 permanent jobs, "seventy-two to eighty per cent" of them reserved for Newark people. "This is soon to be a great town," said Grant.

Three weeks later, on August 14, Grant rose before the mayor and City Council to unveil the portrait of an astonishing giant—a 121-story skyscraper to top all skyscrapers. The steel and glass monolith would rise 1,750 feet, more than 150 feet higher than the world's tallest structure, the Sears Building in Chicago. Dubbed "Grant Tower," the edifice would be tinted green "to pay homage to the Garden State."

Expanding his plans, Grant announced the same day that he would commit $30 million toward building a monorail to link his tower, Penn Station and Newark Airport. The remainder of Grant's estimated cost of $80 million to $100 million would be borne by the Port Authority, the state or some other agency or combination of agencies.

Skeptical councilmen questioned him about financing. Grant responded, "We have the money in the bank right now." He told his audience that he and his staff already had spent more than thirteen months studying Newark's underground utilities and building footings; he saw no possible bar to his skyscraper. Despite a general air of enthusiasm from the council, Councilwoman Marie Villani cautioned the builder: "Newark has been fooled so many times by people who come here with great plans, Mr. Grant. Please do not fool us again."

Eighteen months after Grant's first public announcements, work proceeded very slowly on the mall project; he complained in March 1987 that the council had not yet approved his final plans for restructuring the old railroad station. At the same time, he announced that he had bought the Carteret Savings Bank building on Broad Street as the anchor property for the two-acre "Grant Tower" site that he was acquiring. His breathtaking visions were not yet dimmed, but the intensity definitely was nowhere near hurricane levels.

Mayor James announced in October 1986 that

THE STAR-LEDGER

Harry Grant, nicknamed "Hurricane Harry," startled the City Council in August 1986 by revealing his concept for a 121-story, 1,750-foot tower that he proposed building close to his planned shopping center in the old Jersey Central Railroad terminal.

Taiwanese developers had inquired about investing $500 million in developing the Passaic River waterfront. To show "good faith," they offered to make a $300 million deposit toward a project that would include townhouses, a hotel, a marina and other facilities. A half billion dollars was big money in any language, and even if the Taiwanese proposal never came to fruition, it was, like Grant Tower, a promise that would have been beyond the wildest of Newark dreams five years before.

Considerably more certain was money from the Port Authority of New York and New Jersey. Another payment on the continuing pledge to cities came in November when Governor Kean announced a $15 million industrial park program for the South Ward—$5 million from the state, $1 million from the city and $9 million from the Port Authority. Seven buildings for light manufacturing would occupy the site, creating 2,000 new jobs.

Less encouraging was Port Authority and state "progress" toward some kind of passenger link between the city and Newark Airport. Once again it was being "studied." All that resulted from a $220,000 1987 federally-funded study was "cutting the options" to six—including space-age "people movers" (such as those used in amusement parks), two kinds of "light rail transit" lines and an extension of the PATH service between Penn Station and New York. As 1988 moved along, "options" continued to be offered in lieu of a genuine start on the long-delayed, much-needed link.

Building was booming throughout 1987, with literal emphasis on the "booming" as far as low-cost housing was concerned. Early in May 1987 the Newark Housing Authority signed a $2 million contract to demolish two thirteen-story buildings at the Scudder Homes in the Central Ward. The demolition by explosives would be a boom of monumental proportions, for each unit was longer than a football field and contained two hundred apartments.

Housing Authority officials insisted that never-ending sabotage and tenant neglect had ruined the buildings beyond repair. William Payne, a Housing Authority commissioner, declared: "Simply because people are poor does not mean they should be relegated to deplorable substandard existences." Demolishing high-rises and replacing them with low-rise townhouses, the Authority believed, was the only possible way to move toward a solution of the city's critical and ever-increasing need for affordable, adequate housing. That was sharply disputed.

Councilman Donald Tucker called the demolitions "a waste of time and a travesty" at a time when so many Newarkers needed housing. He termed the Housing Authority plan a "shell game" that would replace thousands of dynamited apartments with only hundreds of townhouses. Often-quoted Gustav Heningburg had "no doubt" that the Authority could level buildings; he had "serious doubts" about its capacity to rebuild.

Housing Authority promises to erect better housing to replace the high-rise projects had a hollow ring in a city where low-income housing shortages had reached a crisis stage. Critics charged that more than 1,500 public housing units would be lost in a city where estimates of homeless persons ranged between 5,000 and 8,000. Opponents of the demolitions charged that a "conspiracy" was under way to force poor residents out of the community, replacing them with newcomers able to pay higher rents in private housing.

Protests were in vain. Following a brief ceremony on May 24 in which Housing Administration officials promised to start townhouse construction in ninety days, demolition experts set off eight hundred dynamite charges planted in one of the buildings. Only four seconds were needed to start the once-proud tower toward its destruction. Within a few weeks, three more of the thirteen-story Scudder Homes succumbed to shattering blasts.

History would judge whether the Housing Authority's program of destruction was folly or wisdom, depending almost entirely on the speed with which the townhouses would be built and the rent levels that would be established. The only certainty was that the Housing Authority had taken a 180-degree turn in its philosophy. More explosives were in the offing.

Downtown, the dramatic transformation of the Gateway-Penn Station area proceeded briskly. Thirteen new stores were opened in Penn Station on April 22, 1987, completing the

Only four seconds after dynamite charges were set off, one of the 13-story buildings in the Scudder Homes projects began to crumble, ending a 25-year belief that low-income housing could best be provided in high-rise towers. Housing Authority members promised to begin replacing the demolished towers with townhouses within 90 days. Strong opposition was raised to the leveling of the Scudder Homes at a time when thousands of homeless Newarkers, typified by the woman to the left, vainly sought affordable accommodations.

first phase of the $33 million refurbishing program. About 180 new jobs had been created in the stores and about $1 million in new rentals was being collected by the New Jersey Transit Authority, managers of the historic station.

Across the street, ground was broken on June 16 for Gateway IV in the Prudential's impressively growing complex. The new facility would include a fifteen-story office tower, a six-story parking garage with 750 spaces, and a continuation of Gateway's aerial walkway. The $32 million main building was opened May 2, 1988, less than a year after groundbreaking.

Two decades had passed since the 1967 riots; it seemed like half a century. Many in the city had not known of the disorders or had chosen to forget those dreadful days and nights. A vigil and march to commemorate the twentieth anniversary of the turbulent times drew only about thirty people on July 12, 1987. Partici-

pants noted sadly that the small turnout possibly indicated that the turmoil was being erased from consciousness.

Ten days later Newark received one of the most startling psychological boosts in its history when Governor Kean announced that the city had been chosen for a $300 million cultural complex to be built in the center of the city. The announcement was a complete surprise. Carl W. Shaver, a New York consultant who recommended the Newark location, said that initially there had been no thought of locating the complex in Newark, "but evidence began to build in favor of making Newark the center." He especially cited the city's fine transportation systems.

The proposed cultural center, second largest in the United States after New York's Lincoln Center, was a shining prospect for any city. Shaver's plan showed the center occupying six

New affordable housing began to transform the area where riots had flamed in 1967. James and Loretta Brown (left) and Charles Cummings discussed homes being built on Boston Street, where they would be neighbors. Cummings, assistant director of Newark Public Library and city historian, believed strongly in Newark's renaissance.

Outsiders come first to sample the Portuguese or Spanish foods, then quickly find that Newark's "Ironbound" is a neighborhood of ethnic diversity and pride. Colonists called the area "Down Neck," deeming it worthless except as grazing ground. Immigrants have streamed into the area since the Irish came early in the 19th century to build the railroads and canals. By the 20th century, the area had been nick-named "The Ironbound" because of the elevated railroad tracks to the west and the factories to the east. The newest group to appreciate the 'Ironbound' are thousands of Portuguese immigrants, who constantly show their pride in the neighborhood.

downtown blocks, running westward from Broad Street to University Avenue between Central Avenue and West Park Street. The proposal would include a 3,000-seat opera house, a 2,500-seat concert hall, an 1,800-seat music theater and two smaller stages, all ranged on either side of a broad plaza replete with fountains, trees and greenery.

Leaders of major downtown firms joined in the concert of pleasure that greeted the contemplated center. Promises were made that corporate heads would enthusiastically help raise matching funds to meet the state's $150 million commitment, although no means of securing the state contribution had yet been planned. Small business people in the affected area reacted with understandable bitterness, for the center threatened hard-earned economic security.

Major concern also was expressed by the Newark Preservation and Landmarks Committee, the only group fighting to retain as much as possible of the city's three centuries of historic vitality. Elizabeth Del Tufo, NPLC president, expressed solid support for the concept and its assignment to Newark. Still, she pointed out in a letter to Governor Kean, the proposed location threatened a significantly historic area of the city. She suggested that the new center might mean doom for the newly-refurbished Symphony Hall on the southern end of Broad Street.

There were also economic worries. The proposed site contained 175 separate properties with an assessed valuation of $14.6 million, plus seventeen parcels owned by Rutgers University, the City of Newark or religious

National attention was focused on Newark in 1988 when Peter W. Rodino, left, dean of the New Jersey delegation in the U.S. Congress, retired and was replaced by Donald M. Payne, the first black congressman in New Jersey history. Rodino, shown here at age 54 (the

same age as Payne when he was elected) was a Newark dividend in the surprise 1948 election of Harry Truman. Payne won easily in 1988 despite a state and national sweep by George Bush. Esteemed during his 40-year career as a civil rights champion, Rodino earned national acclaim in 1974 for his judicious handling of the congressional committee that recommended impeachment proceedings against President Richard M. Nixon. Payne, former teacher and former national Y.M.C.A. president, was Newark's South Ward Councilman for six years before winning election to Congress. The Tenth District, centered in Newark, also includes East Orange, Glen Ridge, Harrison, Hillside, Irvington and South Orange.

Plans for a $200 million Cultural Arts Center close to the heart of downtown Newark stirred city supporters when Gov. Thomas Kean and the designer, consultant Carl W. Shaver, described the project in July 1987 at a press conference. It would include an opera house, concert hall, music theater and smaller facilities, making it second in the nation only to New York's Lincoln Center. Nearly all Newarkers heartily backed the proposal, although serious misgivings were raised by the Newark Preservation and Landmarks Committee, which backed the concept but believed the chosen location might threaten historic sites.

groups. Their tax-free holdings would be engulfed. As for the taxpaying properties, they also would be stricken from the tax rolls.

Governor Kean said he wanted to see the complex finished before the end of his second term in 1990. That undoubtedly was cutting completion time too thin, considering the problems in raising the money, acquiring the property, clearing the site and finishing the buildings.

The plan was imaginative and bold, and could be regarded as the glue that would cement together the reviving city. It would tie the university complex to downtown Military Park and help knit the superb museum and noted library into both the university and the commercial areas. Unfortunately, it would also take at least nine more blocks of valuable property off the tax rolls.

The potential cultural center tax loss was being offset by vigorous housing projects underway as 1987 waned. By December 1, more than 4,500 units, valued at more than $470 million, were either being built or were in various stages of planning. Most spectacular was a pro-

gram in University Heights, destined to add 1,035 units in a project extending over several years and worth more than $250 million. The project would encompass forty-five acres, making it one of the largest housing developments in the state.

K. Hovnanian Corporation of Red Bank, developer of the huge housing project, had been actively engaged for several years throughout the state in building all kinds of housing, specializing in affordable homes. Fifteen per cent of the Hovnanian units would be subsidized to place them within reach of low-income people. Additionally, the Newark-based, minority-owned DH Enterprises, also known as Vogue Housing, had been active with Hovnanian in developing privately owned houses in the city.

Hovnanian's project was named "Society Hill," a designation that would have been greeted with mixed derision and doubt even five years before. The name was calmly accepted in 1987 as proper, for the slope on which the new homes would rise had been prime real estate a century ago, a place where "society" dwelled.

Prices for homes in the development would range from $58,000 to $98,000, about half what they might bring in the suburbs.

Demolition of public housing took a surprising twist in early November when the Newark Housing Authority announced that it had turned the dynamiting of the long-scorned Columbus Homes high-rise buildings over to a private concern. The company would invest $60 million in a package that would level the eight twelve-story buildings and replace them with 573 units of private housing. Proposed prices for the units varied from about $67,500 to about $96,000. The principal figure in the radical replacement of the project towers was former Mayor Kenneth Gibson, whose private firm had joined forces with Mark Smith Corporation of Jersey City.

The redevelopment of the Columbus Homes site would markedly enhance the image of Newark. The high-rise projects had been deteriorating for years, hastened to ruin by a Housing Authority reluctance to invest more money in refurbishing what it considered to be an outmoded, wretched means of housing the city's poor. Nevertheless, there would be 1,500 fewer public housing units—at a time when the city had 8,000 homeless persons and more than 11,000 people on waiting lists for public housing.

Image could not protect the homeless or the miserably housed, proliferating in the midst of a booming national economy that spurned public housing, even as it spawned overnight millionaires. Cities, including Newark, suffered most. If, in the best of political clichés, a "rising tide lifts all boats," Newark's poor didn't even have boats.

Several private non-profit groups tried desperately to build affordable housing, piecing bits and pieces of state or federal aid together with help from foundations or corporations. Included were such groups as the New Community Council and La Casa de Don Pedro.

Private developers were being encouraged to refurbish some of the many city-owned apartment buildings; by late February 1988, about 500 rental units were promised in such buildings.

The coalition of suburban communities that formed to fight the Mt. Laurel II court decision ordering affordable housing in all communities, was permitted to allocate money to Newark (or other cities) to build low-cost housing in cities rather than in their own towns. Such largess helped Newark; it also served to thwart the hopes of young suburban people that they might one day afford to live in the communities where they had grown up.

Mayor James expressed full accord for low-cost housing but he insisted that Newark needed all kinds of housing. In February 1988 he told a *Star-Ledger* reporter:

"I am committed to having an economic mix. Well managed low income housing along with market rate housing works well in Paris, in Baltimore, in other cities I have visited, and can work well in Newark."

Housing aside—and that was a big aside indeed—the city teemed with the sights and sounds of new construction. Almost everywhere downtown in the winter and spring of 1988 there was the roar of jackhammers, the lifting of steel beams, the promise of more and more offices. Planners said space rates could be so attractive that businesses would flock to fill the vacancies.

One such optimist was Time Equities of New York, a commercial real estate firm that in 1986 had bought the old 13-story Gibraltar Building from the Prudential Insurance Company. The Prudential had planned to demolish the castellated structure but Time Equities paid $11 million to back up its belief that office space was a prime necessity in Newark. It would spend another $20 million, Time Equities said, then ask rents of about $15 to $20 per square foot, about half the going rate for comparable space in Manhattan.

Southward from Broad and Market streets, Hartz Mountain Industries had announced a massive $100 million project in the old Waverly Yards. Once the home of the annual 19th century agricultural state fair, the Waverly area had become a giant 20th century railroad yard (Waverly Yards). There long freight trains could be broken up and shunted to other tracks, countless carloads of fruits and vegetables could be unloaded and cargoes from all over the nation could be shipped to other destinations.

The steam engines and diesel locomotives had disappeared. The tract lay open for years. Hartz proposed to turn the cinder-covered acres into industrial warehousing, office buildings and possibly a first-class hotel.

Quite remarkably, since they almost literally had to beg always for funds in the time-honored traditions of private institutions, Newark's cultural facilities were maintaining quality along with national reputations.

Newark Museum's dynamic Samuel C. Miller, rounding out twenty years as the facility's director, was in the last stages of a $7 million expansion program that would double the museum's exhibition space and accelerate its reputation as possibly the finest small city museum in the nation.

Newark Public Library, as good a public library as there is in all of New Jersey, still struggled for funds. Yet in 1987 and 1988, as the library was celebrating its 100th anniversary, library heads undertook not only to maintain exceptional service to the public but also to renovate the building's interior without turning away library users. The renovation could only be a stopgap; Newark Public Library needed at least twice as much space if it were to maintain a hard-won and far-reaching reputation.

The city's two other prime cultural institutions, The New Jersey Historical Society and Symphony Hall, were at a crossroads. Symphony Hall was rescued once again by city business leaders who raised the millions of dollars needed to make the grand old hall fit for the sounds of music. The Historical Society, founded in 1845 and one of the oldest historical societies in the United States, managed to maintain a good public image although the

Elected in 1986 when Sharpe James became Mayor, the City Council shared both credit and responsibility for Newark. Left to right, back row: Anthony R. Carrino, North Ward; George Branch, Central Ward; Marie L. Villani, At Large; Donald Tucker, At Large. Front row, Ralph T. Grant, Jr., At Large; Earl Harris, At Large; Henry Martinez, East Ward, Council President; Donald M. Payne, South Ward; and Ronald L. Rice, West Ward.

Society's warmest supporters recognized that it faced the greatest financial crisis in all its long years.

As winter turned into the spring of 1988, Mayor James, in office nearly two years, had become the most energetic and most articulate spokesman that Newark had enjoyed in recent memory. He could express pride in a city that seemed vigorously on the way out of the impossible morass that Kenneth Gibson had inherited in 1970.

Still, major problems persisted. All of the booming private housing did not obscure the fact that low-income housing needs were growing increasingly acute. All of the prospects for new jobs could not mask the fact that the Newark school system seemed hopelessly unable to provide the education that the majority of the city's boys and girls would need to participate in the economic revival. All of the rapidly increased tax revenues could not erase the fact that nearly seventy per cent of all city property was public land, and therefore not taxable.

That was the bad news. The good news was that Newark was solidly stable, despite its high crime and disease rates, its mass of poor people, and its much-reported incidences of drugs and alcoholism. Viewed properly, such urban problems could be the most challenging tasks facing not only Newark but all the nation in the countdown to the year 2000.

Newark had amenities aplenty—one of the nation's great museums, the esteemed New Jersey Historical Society with its vital collections of New Jerseyana, the nationally respected Newark Public Library, five colleges or universities, a booming airport and a thriving seaport. Church spires pierced the skyline, as they had for more than two centuries. The area near Penn Station glistened, as did the station itself. Restaurants in the Ironbound satisfied faithful out-of-town customers. The Forest Hill section, edged by the cherry trees of Branch Brook Park, was alive and very well.

The uncontrolled, threatening fever of 1967 had been cooled. The muscles of the city had begun to bulge again; and mind and the spirit were reviving. Middle-class families had begun to return, vital if the city were ever to rise above being permanently poor. When all of the new housing was set in place, the appearance of the state's largest city would be improved.

Newark had nearly everything in a physical sense—location, transportation, tradition, and in the fast-moving 1980s an evident desire not only to live but to grow strong. The challenges were clear-cut:

Could an old city, debilitated by corruption and flailed by flaming riots, revive the glory days of old? Could a city with a history of slums, once owned by slumlords rather than the city, rally behind decent living quarters for all people? Could a school system be righted in time to save a new generation from the woeful neglect that young minds had endured for at least three decades?

If all the answers could be yes, Newark would be a shining symbol of city strength, proving that even the worst of cities could be resuscitated. To paraphrase Donald Malafronte and Kenneth Gibson, if American cities could prosper, Newark had the chance to get there first.

NEW JERSEY NEWSPHOTO

High in the sky on one of Newark's ever-increasing downtown towers, this worker symbolizes the real meaning of a "new" Newark—as a place where he can fill a skilled job for which he would not even have been considered 20 years ago.

Newark's revival is certain to depend as much on how well it treats its young as how high it rears its buildings. There is hope, from a tree being planted by a teacher and her students on a public school ground (above) to an extracurricular club meeting at St. Benedict's Academy (upper right). Little children get a decent start in life at Babyland (part of New Community Corporation) and achieve early success in the internationally acclaimed Newark Boys Choir, whose voices have carried these talented youngsters to many parts of the world.

WALTER J. CHOROSZEWSKI

"North Newark," ranging outward from the magnificent spires of Sacred Heart Church, is old and stable. The cathedral's cornerstone was laid in 1899; when finished in 1954, it was the nation's fifth largest cathedral. Forest Hill (upper right) remains an area of handsome, well-kept homes and North Newark's history is as old as the Sydenham House, the city's oldest privately-owned home; its earliest part dates to about 1712. Yet none of these evidences of stability and prosperity surpass the charm of the nearly 3,000 cherry trees in Branch Brook Park, established in 1895 as part of the nation's oldest county park system.

376

Newark's four major cultural facilities have survived, despite city problems and constant quests for funds. Symphony Hall (above) has been refurbished several times since it opened in 1925, and the New Jersey Historical Society (below) has outlasted many fiscal crises since its founding in 1845. Newark Public Library, handicapped always by budgets far too small, still ranks as one of the nation's finest city libraries. Newark Museum, lower left, has successfully carried out a major reconstruction; few, if any, small city museums equal its quality.

NEWARK IN PRINT

The books listed here are the enduring base for a historical study of Newark, yet much of the story is better told in contemporary newspapers and magazines as well as letters and diaries. This is especially true of the turbulent dramatic period of the much discussed riots of 1967 and the resurgence that has been underway in the city since 1980. Fortunately, Nancy Castor of the New Jersey Reference Department has compiled a city bibliography of this period.

The materials below are all secondary sources, with recognition that they only begin to explore Newark's broad history. They have been chosen because they are available in all libraries with good New Jersey collections. Especially notable is the original town minute book from 1666 to 1836, twice reprinted by The New Jersey Historical Society (in 1864 and 1966).

Ashby, William M., *Tales Without Hate.* Newark: Newark Preservation and Landmarks Committee, 1980.

Arend, Geoffrey. *Air World's Great Airports; Newark 1928-1952.* Jamaica, NY: Air Cargo News, 1978.

Atkinson, Joseph. *The History of Newark.* Newark: W.B. Guild, 1878.

Barber, John W., and Howe, Henry. *Historical Collections of the State of New Jersey.* Newark: Benjamin Olds, 1844.

Bebout, John E., and Grele, Ronald J., *Where Cities Meet: The Urbanization of New Jersey.* Princeton: D. Van Nostrand, 1964.

Berg, Samuel. *Harrison Stanford Martland, M.D.: The Story of a Physician, a Hospital, an Era.* New York: Vantage Press, 1978.

Carr, William H., *Three Cents a Week* (History of the Prudential Insurance Company). Englewood Cliffs: Prentice Hall Inc., 1975.

Castor, Nancy. *A Bibliography of Newark, New Jersey, 1966-1986.* Newark: Newark Public Library, 1986.

Conniff, C. G., and Conniff, Richard. *The Energy People,* A History of PSE&G. Newark: Public Service Electric and Gas Company, 1978.

Churchill, Charles W., *The Italians of Newark: A Community Study.* New York: Arno, 1975.

Cummings, Charles, and O'Connor, John. Newark: An American City. Newark: Newark Bicentennial Commission, 1979.

Cunningham, John T., *Clara Maass: A Nurse, A Hospital, A Spirit.* Belleville: Published by the Hospital, 1976.

Cunningham, John T., *Made In New Jersey: The Industrial Story of a State.* New Brunswick: Rutgers University Press, 1954. (Out of print.)

Cunningham, John T., *New Jersey: America's Main Road.* New York: Doubleday, 1966, revised 1976. (Available from Afton Publishing Company, Inc.)

Curvin, Robert. *The Persistent Minority: The Black Political Experience in Newark.* Ann Arbor: University Microfilms, 1975.

Eaton, Walter P., *Newark: A Series of Engravings on Wood by Rudolph Ruzica.* Newark: Carteret Book Club, 1917.

Elger, Norman. *The Newark School Wars: A Socio-Historical Study of the 1970 and 1971 Newark School System Strikes.* Ann Arbor: University Microfilms, 1976.

Essex County Fact Book. Newark: Greater Newark Chamber of Commerce, 1984.

Ford, William F., *The Industrial Interests of Newark, N.J.* New York: Van Arsdale & Company, 1874.

Galishoff, Stuart. *Safeguarding the Public Health, Newark, 1895-1918.* Westport: Greenwood Press, 1975.

Georges, Daniel E., *Arson: The Ecology of Urban Unrest in an American City — Newark, N.J.; A Case Study in Collective Violence.* Ann Arbor: University Microfilms, 1974.

Gordon, Thomas F., *A Gazetteer of the State of New Jersey.* Trenton: Daniel Fenton, 1834.

Hayden, Tom. *Rebellion in Newark.* New York: Random House, 1967.

Hidalgo, Hilda A., *The Puerto Ricans in Newark, N.J.* Newark: Aspira, Inc., 1971.

Hine, C.G., *Woodside, The North of Newark: Its History, Legends and Ghost Stories.* Newark: Hine's Annual, 1909.

Hirsch, Susan E., *Roots of the American Working Class: The Industrialization of Crafts in Newark, 1800-1860.* Philadelphia: University of Pennsylvania Press, 1978.

Historic Newark. Newark: Fidelity Trust Company, 1916.

History of the Newark Female Charitable Society, 1803-1903. Newark: Published by the Society, 1903.

History of the Police Department of Newark. Newark: The Relief Publication Company, 1893.

Holbrook, Albert M. *A Record Worth Preserving; Report and Catalogue of the First Exhibition of Newark Industries, Exclusively.* (Newark Industrial

Exhibition). Newark: Holbrook's Steam Printery, 1882.

Hunt, William S., *Frank Forester, A Tragedy In Exile.* Newark: Carteret Book Club, 1933.

Illustrated History of the Essex Trades Council and Affiliated Unions. Newark: The Essex Trades Council, 1894.

James, Franklin J., Jr., *Race, Housing Value and Housing Abandonment: A Case Study of Newark.* Ann Arbor: University Microfilms, 1980.

Kaplan, Harold. *Urban Renewal Politics: Slum Clearance in Newark.* New York: Columbia University Press, 1963.

Leary, Peter J., *Newark, N.J., Illustrated.* Newark: William A. Baker, 1893.

Linthurst, Randolph, *The Newark Bears* (3 volumes), West Trenton: Author, 1978-81.

Mayer, Ronald A., *The 1937 Newark Bears.* Union City: William H. Wise and Co., 1980.

Newark Fire Department. Newark: Fire Department, 1977.

Newark, The City of Industry. Newark, 1912.

Nichols, Walter S., *The Old Town Church Endowment.* Newark: First Presbyterian Church in Newark, 1916.

Pierson, B.T., *Directory of the City of Newark for 1836-7. With an Historical Sketch.* Newark, 1836. (All Newark city directories, published annually since 1836, are great sources of information.)

Pierson, David L., *Narratives of Newark.* 1917.

Popper, Samuel H., *Newark, N.J. 1870-1910. Chapters in the Evolutions of an American Metropolis.* (Excellent dissertation written for a Ph.D. degree at New York University, 1952.)

Porambo, Ron. *No Cause for Indictment: An Autopsy of Newark.* New York: Holt, Rinehart & Winston, 1971.

Price, Clement Alexander. *The Afro-American Community of Newark, 1917-1947: A Social History.* Ann Arbor: University Microfilms, 1975.

Price, Clement A., "The Beleagured City as Promised Land: Blacks in Newark, 1917-1947." In *Urban New Jersey Since 1870* edited by William C. Wright. Trenton: N.J. Historical Commission, 1975.

Proceedings Commemorative of the Settlement of Newark. Newark: The New Jersey Historical Society, 1866.

Rankin, Edward S., *Indian Trails and City Streets.* Montclair: The Globe Press, 1927.

Records of the Town of Newark, New Jersey, 1666-1836. Newark: The New Jersey Historical Society, 1864. (Reprinted, paperback edition, by the Society in 1966.).

Report for Action. Newark: Governor's Select Commission on Civil Disorders, State of New Jersey, 1968.

Report of the National Advisory Commission on Civil Disorders, Governor Otto Kerner of Illinois, Chairman. New York: Bantam Books, Inc., 1968.

Rice, Arnold S., comp., *Newark: A Chronological and Documentary History, 1966-1970.* Dobbs Ferry: Oceana, 1977.

Rindler, Edward P., *The Migration from the New New Haven Colony to Newark, East New Jersey: A Study of Puritan Values and Behavior, 1630-1720.* Ann Arbor: University Microfilms, 1977.

Rockwood, Charles G., *One Hundred Years, 1804-1904.* (National Newark Banking Company) Newark: Published by the bank, 1904.

Schnall, Kenneth. *A Survey of Ecclesiastical Architecture Built in Newark from 1810-1865.* (Unpublished study written as part of graduate work at Newark State College in 1965.).

Shaw, William H., *History of Essex and Hudson Counties, New Jersey.* Two volumes. Philadelphia: Everts and Peck, 1884.

Siegel, Alan A., *For the Glory of the Union: Myth, Reality and the Media in Civil War New Jersey.* (26th N.J. Volunteer Infantry). Rutherford: Fairleigh Dickinson University Press, 1984.

Stearns, Jonathan F., *Historical Discourses, Relating to the First Presbyterian Church in Newark.* Newark: Daily Advertiser, 1853.

Stellhorn, Paul A., *Depression and Decline: Newark, N.J., 1929-1941.* Ann Arbor: University Microfilms. 1983.

Sternlieb, George, and Burchell, Robert W., *Residential Abandonment: The Tenement Landlord Revisited.* New Brunswick: Center for Urban Policy Research, 1973.

Stone, Mildred F., *Since 1845, A History of the Mutual Benefit Life Insurance Company.* New Brunswick: Rutgers University Press, 1957.

The North Reformed Church, 50th Anniversary, 1906. New York: The Board of Publications of the Reformed Church in America, 1907.

The Old First Presbyterian Church, The Founding Church of Newark, 1666-1966. Newark: Published by the Church, 1966.

Urquhart, Frank John. *A History of the City of Newark, New Jersey* (3 volumes). New York: The Lewis Historical Publishing Company, 1913.

Urquhart, Frank J., *A Short History of Newark,* Newark: Baker Printing Company, 1916.

Ward, Leslie D., *Essex County Court House.* Newark: Essex County Building Commission, 1908.

Winters, Stanley B., *From Riot to Recovery: Newark After Ten Years.* Washington, D.C.: University Press of America, 1979.

Wright, Nathan. *Ready to Riot.* New York: Holt, Rinehart and Winston, 1968.

This completely revised index has been prepared by Karen Diane Gilbert, a librarian in the New Jersey Reference Division of the Newark Public Library.

384